To Dennis

With deep appreciation for all your help with this Guide. This is certainly a better book for your contributions and advice

Bob [illegible]

12-13-02

ROBERT KEATING O'NEILL is Director of the John J. Burns Library and Part Time Faculty, Political Science, at Boston College, Chestnut Hill, Massachusetts. He has been Burns Librarian since 1987. He holds both the PhD in History and the MA in Library Science from the University of Chicago. Previously he was Director of the Indiana Historical Society Library in Indianapolis and Head of Special Collections at Indiana State University, where he was also Associate Professor of Library Science in the College of Arts and Sciences.

His many publications include *Management of Library and Archival Security: From the Outside Looking In* (1998), co-published simultaneously as *Journal of Library Administration*, Volume 25, Number 1, 1998; *Ulster Libraries, Archives, Museums & Ancestral Heritage Centres* (1997); and *English Language Dictionaries, 1604–1900* (1988). He has written numerous articles and reviews.

O'Neill is a past president of the Manuscript Society, 1992–1994, and the Eire Society of Boston, 1995–1997. He continues to serve as a member of the boards of both these organizations. He was also a member of the board of directors of Bookbuilders of Boston. He is a member of the Grolier Club in New York, the Massachusetts Historical Society in Boston, and the Charitable Irish Society in Boston.

He is a Fellow of the Manuscript Society, and received the Society's award of distinction. He chaired two meetings of the Manuscript Society in Ireland, the first in 1991 and the second in 2002. He was honoured by the Irish and American governments for his role in the recovery of stolen Irish artefacts in 1991.

He was a participant in the British Council-sponsored study tour of libraries in Northern Ireland in 1991.

O'Neill is married to the former Helen Ann Parke. The couple have six grown children and live in Holliston, Massachusetts.

To the Irish American Partnership and its President, Joseph F. Leary, Jr, in recognition of their inspirational support of school libraries in Ireland as a bridge between divided communities and as a beacon of hope for the promise and future of young Ireland.

*Education is not the filling of a bucket, but the starting of a fire.*

W.B. Yeats

A VISITORS' GUIDE

# IRISH LIBRARIES

## ARCHIVES, MUSEUMS & GENEALOGICAL CENTRES

Robert K. O'Neill

ULSTER HISTORICAL FOUNDATION
2002

Published 2002
by the Ulster Historical Foundation
12 College Square East, Belfast BT1 6DD
www.ancestryireland.com


ISBN 1-903688-28-0

Printed by ColourBooks
Typeset by December Publications
Design by Dunbar Design

# CONTENTS

# ACKNOWLEDGEMENTS

In compiling this guide, I have had the indispensable help of numerous librarians, archivists and genealogical centre managers, co-ordinators and researchers throughout the island of Ireland. Their names can usually be found as the contact persons in the entry for their respective institutions, but this is not always the case, as a number of people who were very helpful preferred not to have a specific contact person listed or recommended another name. Surveys and follow-up enquiries were no doubt unwelcome intrusions into the already overcrowded schedules of these professionals, yet their generous and gracious gifts of knowledge and time give proof to the adage that if you want a job done well, give it to a busy person. Users of this Guide can be assured that the level of professionalism, courtesy and assistance that they will find in Ireland will be second to none.

A number of individuals in Ireland provided helpful advice and assistance in the compilation of this work. I am particularly grateful to Valerie Adams, Mario Corrigan, Brian Donovan, Conor Kenny, Jack Gamble, Norma Jessop, Aoife McBride, Wesley McCann, Clare McVeigh, Bernard Meehan, Fergus O'Donoghue SJ, Colette O'Flaherty, Siobhan O'Rafferty, Michael Ryan, Evan Salholm, and Brendan Teeling. Professor Kevin Whelan, former Burns Library Visiting Scholar in Irish Studies at Boston College and current Director of the University of Notre Dame's Keough Centre in Dublin, graciously read over the glossary and contributed a number of helpful improvements and clarifications. Ulster Historical Foundation Executive Director Fintan Mullan and UHF Director Dr Brian Trainor encouraged me to undertake this work, and provided support throughout this project. I wish to acknowledge in particular the assistance of Dr Trainor. His enthusiasm, energy and help have been a constant source of inspiration. He not only read the entire manuscript, but also identified those institutions whose resources, especially in the area of genealogy, merited expanded treatment. He personally contacted a number of institutions soliciting additional information, and the results most certainly strengthened this Guide. He also prepared the valuable appendix, *Tithe and Valuation Records for Ireland, c.1823–c.1930*, an expanded version of the appendix he prepared for my Ulster Guide (1997). I am grateful to the Public Record Office of Northern Ireland and to the National Archives, Dublin, for their permission to list, as an appendix to this book, the references to their tithe and valuation holdings for the parishes of Ireland. I wish also to thank Karel Kiely for permission to reprint her article, *Tracing Your Co. Kildare Ancestors*, which offers helpful advice to all interested in tracing their roots anywhere in Ireland. Eamonn Rossi, Karel Kiely and Brian Donovan were especially helpful to me in coming to an understanding of the history and work of IGP. Wendy Dunbar lent her award-winning design talent and expertise to this work, and her contributions made this book a more aesthetically pleasing as well as user-friendly one. G.B. Shaw is credited with the witticism that Americans and their English-speaking neighbours across the Atlantic are two peoples divided by a common language. I cannot express adequately my debt to Brendan O'Brien, the publisher's editorial consultant, who helped me negotiate the difficult linguistic waters that seem to divide the new and the old worlds. Brendan's keen editorial eye and his enviable grasp of Irish history and culture guided me deftly through some murky and sometimes choppy waters, and I am most grateful.

On this side of the Atlantic, Dennis Ahern of The Irish Ancestral Research Association and genealogist extraordinaire read the entire manuscript and offered not only a sharp editorial eye but also his vast knowledge of genealogical resources in Ireland. He gave generously of his time and expertise, and he made a number of important recommendations that were incorporated into this work. This Guide is most certainly better for his contributions. I wish to thank also the Board of TIARA for permission to make reference to TIARA's survey on Irish Heritage Centres. Good friend and Boston College benefactor Anthony John Mourek of Chicago, Illinois, kindly made available his Dublin apartment to me on several occasions during my frequent visits to Ireland to work on this Guide. He also graciously drove me to a number of the libraries and archives that I visited. I shall be forever grateful in particular for his hospitality and friendship during the eventful period between September 11 and September 20, 2001, when I was marooned in Ireland, separated from my family, because of the horrific events of 9/11 in New York City, Washington, DC, and Shanksville, Pennsylvania. I am also grateful to the many friends and strangers in Ireland for their heartfelt expressions of grief and concern. On September 14, 2002, Ireland declared a National Day of Mourning for the victims of September 11, and the image of the extraordinary national outpouring of grief and tributes from the Irish people shall forever remain impressed upon my memory.

That I was able to bring this work to a timely conclusion is due in no small measure to the support of my employer, Boston College. In addition to providing me with leave time to undertake this work, Boston College also provided substantial technical and support services. I am especially grateful to University Librarian Jerome Yavarkovsky and to my Administrative Secretary Margaret McCone for their support and encouragement. Burns Library colleague John Atteberry was always available to read over material and offer valuable suggestions. The Irish American Partnership generously provided a grant to help with the costs associated with an undertaking of this magnitude. For the past decade and a half, the Partnership has been an inspiration and a source of hope to thousands in Ireland who have benefited directly or indirectly from its educational and economic programmes and grants. Joseph F. Leary, Jr, President of the Partnership since its founding in 1987, has championed library services in Ireland, especially at the rural primary school level. In 2000 and 2001 the Partnership provided 15,000 new books to 4,000 students in rural Ireland, with an even more ambitious target set for 2002. To Joe Leary and the Partnership, libraries serve as a bridge between divided communities and as a beacon for the promise and future of young Ireland. Their seminal initiative is inspiring. It is therefore to the Irish American Partnership and to its President, Joe Leary, that this work is dedicated.

No acknowledgement would be complete, however, without recognizing the deep debt I owe to my wife, Helen, whose love, patience and understanding made frequent absences from home and late nights at the computer tolerable. I want also to thank our children – Kathleen, Kevin, Kerry, Daniel, MaryAnn and Timothy – for their support and love, especially during that difficult week following September 11 when I could not be home. Their telephone calls and e-mails were more helpful than they can ever know.

# INTRODUCTION

In 1997 the Ulster Historical Foundation published a book I compiled entitled *Ulster Libraries, Archives, Museums & Ancestral Heritage Centres: A Visitors' Guide*. When time came to update this guide, UHF Executive Director Fintan Mullan asked if I would expand coverage to include the entire island of Ireland. I agreed, somewhat hesitantly, realizing how daunting a task this would be, especially from the other side of the Atlantic. But thanks to the electronic revolution, most especially the Internet, e-mails and the fax machine, plus the extraordinary cooperation of librarians, archivists, curators, and genealogical centre coordinators throughout Ireland, north and south, I was able to complete this project in a little over a year.

As with the Ulster guide, the primary target of this guide is the visitor, chiefly the North American visitor, who may be taking or contemplating a trip to Ireland for the first time. In most instances this visitor will primarily be interested in family history, and this guide is consciously oriented towards the needs of the genealogist. Nevertheless, it is hoped that all researchers, including serious academic researchers, will find it useful. That they do so will be due in no small measure to the incredible support I have received from colleagues in libraries, archives and genealogical centres throughout Ireland and Northern Ireland. These good people have been very generous with their time, contributions and advice, and the extensive information that they have unselfishly made available has made this guide possible.

I started this project by sending a survey form to more than 200 institutions in Ireland and Northern Ireland. The initial response was surprisingly strong, but as I learned from the Ulster guide experience, surveys are just the beginning of the undertaking. Between the summer of 2001 and the spring of 2002 I made five trips to Ireland, visiting many of the institutions represented in this guide. I also sent scores of e-mails and faxes, and made dozens of personal telephone calls. I compiled the entries relying chiefly on the returned survey forms; institutional publications, including historical monographs, brochures, leaflets and pamphlets; institutional websites; and telephone calls. I then e-mailed, mailed or hand-delivered drafts of these entries to the various institutions. The response was gratifying, and I tried to incorporate all the amendments that were provided to me, making some allowances for consistency of format. As a final step, I faxed the amended entry, whenever possible, to the institution to give the appropriate contact person one last opportunity to review the text. In a number of cases, I personally hand-delivered the draft of the entry to the institution. The response to the faxed and hand-delivered entries was especially encouraging and rewarding. Every effort was made to incorporate accurately all amendments into the revised text and to reflect the information as the institution wanted. In those cases where I was not able to get through to the institution by fax, e-mail or regular mail, I telephoned. The final product represents a sincere effort to reflect the information provided to me as accurately and as fully as possible. If I have failed to do so, I apologize and accept full responsibility for any errors or misunderstandings that may appear in this guide.

This is not intended to be a comprehensive guide to libraries, archives and genealogical centres in Ireland. Rather, it is an effort to include those institutions that are likely to be most attractive to and welcoming of visitors, with a focus on local and family history. No doubt some will find institutions that they believe should have been listed here but that are not. Some institutions specifically asked not to be included, some simply did not respond to repeated efforts to solicit their participation, and still others may simply have been overlooked. There are several other very helpful and valuable reference sources that readers may want to consult. I recommend in particular the *Directory of Irish Archives*, 3rd edn, edited by Seamus Helferty and Raymond Refaussé (Dublin: Four Courts Press, 1999). This work includes many of the religious and specialized archives that are not included in this guide, primarily because access for visitors is limited or because holdings fall outside the scope of this guide. The Library Association of Ireland published five editions of its *Directory of Libraries and Information Services in Ireland*, but recently discontinued the printed version in favour of an online version that is not currently available to the public. Copies of the published guides were distributed primarily to libraries and librarians, and were not made widely available to the general public. The RASCAL (Research and Special Collections Available Locally) project, sponsored by the Research Support Libraries Programme (RSLP) and Queen's University Belfast, provides online access to information resources held in local libraries and archives in Northern Ireland. The project has identified over 400 collections in almost 70 institutions, including libraries, museums and archives. The RASCAL Directory is accessible at www.rascal.ac.uk.

In compiling this guide I was struck both by the wealth of resources available in Ireland and by the warm welcome extended to me and to all visitors. Naturally, in doing research, especially family history research, the reader will be drawn in particular to the large repositories in Dublin, such as the National Archives, the National Library of Ireland, the General Register Office and the Valuation Office, or the Public Record Office and the General Register Office in Belfast. But one should not overlook the bounty to be found in the local history collections of city, county and even some branch libraries, which often contain important local resources, including databases for church and civil records, copies of Griffith's Valuation, Ordnance Survey maps, and local newspapers. The entries for the Centre for Dublin and Irish Studies and the Belfast Central Library, for example, reveal an exceptional wealth of materials that visitors too often overlook. Many of the county libraries, such as those of Westmeath and Kildare, also offer rich and varied resources, and competition for microfilm readers may be less intense. Staff are also very knowledgeable and helpful.

Though this publication is aimed primarily at a North American audience, it is published in Belfast; hence, orthography practice follows the UK-English rather than US-English model. Examples include: acknowledgement (acknowledgment), artefact (artifact), catalogue (catalog), centre (center), colour (color), defence (defense), favour (favor), gaol (jail), judgement (judgment), kilometre (kilometer), and labour (labor).

## ENTRY FORMAT

### ARRANGEMENT

Entries are arranged alphabetically by city or town within county. This arrangement, in addition to providing a 32-county organizational structure with which most visitors are familiar, also offers visitors a convenient and easy way to get around to institutions that are grouped together within a relatively small geographical area, especially in the cities of Dublin, Belfast and Cork. To assist visitors who might be uncertain or even confused about geographical location, I have made generous use of '*See*' references. Co. Dublin, in particular, offers some interesting challenges to those unfamiliar with its administrative divisions. In 1994, Co. Dublin was divided into three separate administrative units, called South Dublin, Dún Laoghaire-Rathdown, and Fingal. Nevertheless, all listings here are under the single county of Dublin, subdivided alphabetically by city or town in the following order: Dublin City, Dún Laoghaire, Killiney and

Swords, with *See* references under Dublin City to avoid possible misunderstanding. The entries for Fingal County Libraries, Local Studies Department, and Fingal County Archives are to be found alphabetically among the listings for the City of Dublin within the County of Dublin, as they are both located at the end of O'Connell Street on the near north side of Dublin City. But the headquarters for this library system is located in the town of Swords, the administrative seat of County Fingal, which embraces the area of Co. Dublin north of the River Liffey. Fingal Genealogy is also located in Swords. The City of Belfast presents yet another interesting problem, as it is actually located within two counties, Down and Antrim. But since every entry in this guide for Belfast City is geographically located within the borders of County Antrim, Belfast is listed under County Antrim, with a note to this effect in the heading. While this arrangement may cause some confusion, especially to those accustomed to thinking of Co. Dublin and Dublin City as one, the alternative of listing institutions alphabetically by county, without regard to city or town, would present, I believe, even more confusion in certain counties, especially Antrim and Londonderry (Derry).

Elsewhere, the geographical listings are fairly uncomplicated, but it might be helpful to note that Galway Family History Society West precedes East Galway Family History Society because the former is located in Galway City while the latter is located in the town of Woodford. To make finding institutions even easier, an alphabetically arranged listing by type of institution is provided on pp. xxi–xxix under the following categories:

- Academic Libraries and Archives
- Archives
- Genealogical and Heritage Centres and Services
- Government Organizations and Offices
- Public Libraries
- Special Libraries

While visitors may be familiar and comfortable with the county system, it should be noted that the this system was gradually introduced into Ireland by the Anglo-Normans beginning at the end of the 12th century, but completed in the north only in the seventeenth century with the Flight of the Earls (1607) and the establishment of the Ulster Plantation. Hence, there never was officially a Co. Derry. It was named Londonderry in 1613, and Co. Londonderry is therefore used as the geographical designation. But within County Londonderry, entries are arranged under the city of Derry, as this is both the historic name of the city founded as a monastic site in the 6th century by St Columcille (St Columba) and the name officially adopted by the Derry City Council.

Co. Laois was initially called Queen's County, and Co. Offaly was King's County. '*See*' references are provided for each of these former names, which were changed to their present names following Ireland's independence. Visitors should also be aware that two of the important ports from which many Irish emigrated also underwent name changes with Ireland's independence: Kingstown became Dún Laoghaire and Queenstown became Cobh.

'*See*' references are also used wherever there might be confusion about the official name of an institution. Trinity College Dublin (TCD) is also the University of Dublin, and University College Dublin (UCD) is also the National University of Ireland, Dublin. The Historical Library, Religious Society of Friends, in Dublin, is more popularly known as either The Friends' Historical Library or the Quaker Library. The official name of the institution, as preferred by the institution itself, is the name used as the heading in this guide, with '*See*' references to other names by which the institution might be known.

## TELEPHONE AND FAX NUMBERS

Telephone and fax numbers are given as if you were calling from within Ireland or from within Northern Ireland. The international code is 353 for Ireland and 44 for Northern Ireland. For direct-dialed calls from Canada and the United States, first dial 011, then the country code, the area code (dropping the 0) and the telephone number. Thus, if you were calling the General Register Office in Dublin from the United States, you would dial 011 353 1 635 4000. If you were calling the General Register Office in Belfast, you would dial 011 44 28 9025 2000, again dropping the 0 before the Belfast city code of 028. To call Northern Ireland from within Ireland, dial 048 before the area code; hence, the GRO in Belfast would be: 048 9025 2000. The international code for the UK (44) is not needed. To call Ireland from Northern Ireland, however, the international code for Ireland is needed, preceded by 00; hence, to call the GRO in Dublin from Belfast, you would dial 00 353 1 635 4000, again dropping the 0 from the Dublin city code (01). Remember, there is a five- to eight-hour time difference between the United States and Ireland. When it is noon in Boston, it is 5:00 pm in Ireland.

## E-MAIL ADDRESSES AND WEBSITES

These are perhaps the two areas most subject to change. The information given is as current as the printed format will allow. Indeed, in more than a few cases, changes occurred between the time the information was originally collected and the time the final copy was sent to the institution for editing. Some website addresses were given even though they are currently not accessible. In these cases, it was believed that the sites would be operational by the time this publication appears in print, but there are no guarantees.

## HOURS

Opening hours are also subject to change, and it is wise to contact institutions in advance to be sure that the hours are as indicated. All libraries and archives are closed on Sundays unless otherwise noted. In particular please note that many of the smaller institutions have limited staffing, and vacations and illness may affect announced operating hours.

## ACCESS AND SERVICES

Information here is provided with the visitor chiefly in mind. Access is treated broadly, encompassing not only physical access, i.e. wheelchair-accessible, reader's card required, advance notice, letter of recommendation, etc., but also fax or e-mail services and online access to the institution's OPAC. Services include reference, photocopying, microfilm reader/printer access, Internet access, exhibits, and publications. Fees, if applicable, are provided, but only as a guideline, as they are subject to change. Note: Ireland adopted the euro in January 2002, but Northern Ireland, as part of the United Kingdom, continues to use the pound sterling, and there are no immediate plans to convert to the euro.

## CONTACT

In most instances, the name of the person most likely to be able to help the visitor with his or her question is given. But please keep in mind that personnel change or may be away on holiday or leave. In certain cases, institutions have asked that an individual not be listed as the contact; rather, that a title only be listed, e.g. Archivist. Academic titles, such as Dr, and degrees, such as PhD, for contact persons are not given, as most did not supply them, and I wanted to be consistent. It can be assumed, however, that most of the contact persons, especially in academic settings, have advanced degrees, many of them holding the doctorate. Titles are provided in the case of clerical, military, or police personnel.

## DESCRIPTION

This area is used to provide the visitor with some understanding of the history and place of the institution within a broader context. It is helpful to know, for example, the origin of the name 'Linen Hall Library' or the source of financial support for institutions so that visitors may have a better appreciation of the demands that they may be making on that institution. Many institutions in Ireland, even government-supported ones, are hard pressed to serve their principal clientele due to staff shortages and limited resources. It is important for visitors to understand this and to be patient, polite, courteous and considerate. I am always surprised as a Librarian of a private American academic research library how demanding some enquirers can be, sometimes receiving requests from people with absolutely no ties to the institution demanding that I provide them with answers to a long list of research questions and to do so promptly. Such impolite demands invariably are filed away in the wastebasket, without the courtesy of a reply. Visitors take heed! If you find institutions especially helpful, a note of appreciation is always welcome. For those wishing to express their appreciation to a library or archive in more tangible ways, financial contributions may be sent directly to the institution or channeled through several not-for-profit organizations based in America, such as the Irish-American Partnership, which has made the funding of libraries in Ireland a priority.

## HOLDINGS

This is the most important element of this guide. Despite the devastation wrought by the destruction of the Public Record Office in 1922 during the Civil War, Ireland is still rich in resources. Many of these repositories are well-kept secrets, even among the Irish. A quick perusal of the breadth and depth of holdings to be found in Irish libraries and archives should impress even the most seasoned researcher. The holdings statement, however, is not intended to be comprehensive. Rather, it is meant to highlight the strengths of the institution's collection, with a particular focus on local studies and genealogy. Even in the areas of local history and genealogy, there is a good deal more depth and breadth to the collections than may be indicated by the information provided. I was heavily dependent on the information that institutions made available to me, and, frankly, some were rather modest in describing their holdings. I was often able to collect additional material through personal contacts or from institutional publications, but this could not be done in every case.

## LOCATION

Brief directions are given to each entry's location, often with information on parking or access by public transportation. Public transportation in Ireland is very good, if not always fast. Virtually every entry in this guide can be reached by rail or bus, with perhaps no more than a ten to fifteen-minute walk from the station or depot. Rail service between Dublin and Belfast is especially good, taking only two hours along a scenic route, and upgrades of other rail services are planned. Taxi fares in Ireland and Northern Ireland are quite reasonable, and often the conversation alone is worth the fare. As a concession to this Guide's primary audience, distance is given in miles, not kilometres, even though Ireland has officially adopted the metric system. A kilometre is roughly equal to 0.6 mile. Thus, 100 kilometres is equal to 60 miles.

# THE IRISH GENEALOGICAL PROJECT, THE IRISH FAMILY HISTORY FOUNDATION AND IRISH GENEALOGY LTD

The Irish Genealogical Project was established in 1988 as a joint private/public venture to computerize all the major Irish genealogical resources. The project's goal was to establish a network of 35 genealogical centres, with at least one for each county in Ireland, linked by a central or 'signposting' agency that would refer enquirers to appropriate local centres and provide uniform indexing, servicing and fee schedule guidelines. These centres would create computerized databases of genealogical records to offer a fee-based genealogical research service to those interested in tracing their family roots. Starting in 1990, a Digital VAX system was set up to computerize births, marriages, deaths, Griffith's Valuation, Tithe Applotment Books, graveyard inscriptions, and census records. Some centres subsequently indexed additional types of records, including directories, school rolls, hearth money rolls, and information specific to their locale, such as newspaper indexes. In 1990 this became a cross-border effort, and both the Irish government and the Northern Ireland Office provided financial support for the project for the purposes of creating jobs and promoting tourism.

A number of genealogical centres had been operating successfully before this island-wide project was launched. The Ulster Historical Foundation, for example, was founded in 1956 to promote interest in Ulster history and genealogy. But these centres operated on an *ad hoc* basis, and a more coordinated island-wide project seemed warranted; hence the creation of IGP. However, the project initially failed to fulfil expectations. For a start, the central agency never materialized as planned. To fill this void, the Irish Family History Foundation (IFHF) was established in 1990 by the local centres to set standards for indexing records, genealogical research services, and fees. While IFHF provided an umbrella organization of sorts, facilitating access to websites and establishing recommended fee schedules, it lacked the authority and resources needed to address some of the serious concerns that were surfacing. Furthermore, it did not enjoy the support of all the centres. Participation was voluntary, and several major centres opted to go it alone.

Originally the project was to have been completed by 1993, but this target date proved unrealistic. To begin with, government assistance largely took the form of employment training grants. Young, unemployed people were hired to do the indexing, but they first required training in office and computer skills. At least half their time was spent on non-genealogical-related work, such as gaining marketable skills and looking for employment. This continues to be the case today, and certification of trainees in all skills takes precedence over the indexing of genealogical records. While the governments, with the help of grants from the International Fund for Ireland and the European Union, did initially fund equipment purchases, including the VAX, a photocopier and microfilm reader, they subsequently restricted their funding to training grants, leaving the centres to fall back on their own and/or local resources. Some centres were more successful than others in developing these resources. Several were forced to close, while others were able to offer only partial services.

In 1993 Irish Genealogy Ltd (IGL) was formed to coordinate the activities of the IGP and to oversee its completion. A lack of resources initially limited its effectiveness, but since 1996 adequate funding has enabled IGL to carry out its original mission successfully. IGL is composed of representatives of all the Irish groups interested in the development of genealogy as a business, including IFHF, the Association of Professional Genealogists in Ireland (APGI), the Association of Ulster Genealogists and Record Agents (AUGRA), and government departments, north and south. Although it is intended to be independent of any particular group of stakeholders, it clearly has a mandate to promote tourism. To achieve this end, IGL recognized that it needed to provide tourists and professional genealogists with a network of centres that offers a reliable, comprehensive, computerised database of genealogical records, excellent customer service, and a central referral or 'signposting' agency that will direct customers to one of the IFHF centres or to appropriate professional genealogists. Since 1996 it has made substantial progress towards these goals. All but a few of the heritage centres have now come under IFHF and IGL's umbrella. While these centres continue to maintain absolute autonomy, they recognize the value of acting collectively on many issues. This partnership has resulted in some impressive achievements, some of which are enumerated below. For further information on IGL, contact: Eamonn Rossi, Chief Executive Officer, IGL, 7–9 Merrion Row, Dublin 2; tel. (01) 661 7334; e-mail eamonn.rossi@irishgenealogy.ie. For further information on IFHF, contact: Pat Stafford, Secretary, IFHF, Yola Farmstead, Tagoat, Co. Wexford; tel. (053) 32610; e-mail wexgen@iol.ie.

This Guide makes no effort to evaluate the services offered by individual centres. Readers are advised instead to consult in particular the findings of a survey of Irish Heritage Centres conducted by The Irish Ancestral Research Association, which can be found on its website: http://tiara.ie/results.htm. This survey, as well as surveys or audit reports conducted by *Irish Roots*, by IGL and by the Comptroller and Auditor General of Ireland in the late 1990s, revealed significant inconsistencies in the quality of services offered. These surveys, however, may not accurately reflect the current status of individual centres, and it should be noted that many centres have made a concerted effort to address the failings pointed out in the surveys and/or audits, particularly in the areas of delivery time and customer relations. Improvements in funding and premises have also been made. For example, the 'signposting' service has now been fully developed, with a Central Signposting Index launched on the web at www.irishgenealogy.ie. The Kerry centre will shortly reopen with modern systems and a strong management team. Perhaps most important, the databases themselves have been significantly enhanced, both in terms of the quantity, depth and breadth of the records they contain and in terms of the quality and reliability of these records. Some 16,493,000 records have been indexed in the IFHF centres as of October 2002, and an Accuracy Audit by Eneclann in 2000, using a more statistically reliable sample, found a far lower error rate among centres than that reported two years earlier by the Comptroller and Auditor General. IGL is also replacing the antiquated and cumbersome VAX computer system with a modern server/client IT system with a common software platform. This will secure records onto modern media for posterity.

One last note. Genealogists often complain that they do not have direct access to the databases of these heritage centres: only staff researchers at the various centres are allowed to search the databases. While this may seem frustrating, it should be noted that all centres have signed an agreement with their local bishop/archbishop and his individual parish priests governing the access and use of parish records, which in most cases make up the largest part of any centre's database. This agreement provides for strict controls on the access to and publishing, reproduction and copying of these records to preserve their confidential nature. Some parishes have yet to cooperate with these centres, and no parish priest is required to do so. Making the databases directly accessible to the public is, therefore, not currently an option.

# CLASSIFIED LIST OF INSTITUTIONS

## 1
## ACADEMIC LIBRARIES AND ARCHIVES

DUBLIN CITY UNIVERSITY LIBRARY, Dublin, Co. Dublin

EDGEHILL THEOLOGICAL COLLEGE, Belfast, Co. Antrim

HISTORY AND FAMILY RESEARCH CENTRE – LOCAL STUDIES DEPARTMENT, Newbridge, Co. Kildare

NATIONAL UNIVERSITY OF IRELAND, CORK (UCC) – BOOLE LIBRARY, Cork, Co. Cork

NATIONAL UNIVERSITY OF IRELAND, GALWAY – JAMES HARDIMAN LIBRARY, Galway, Co. Galway

NATIONAL UNIVERSITY OF IRELAND, MAYNOOTH – JOHN PAUL II LIBRARY, Maynooth, Co. Kildare

QUEEN'S UNIVERSITY BELFAST LIBRARY, Belfast, Co. Antrim

QUEEN'S UNIVERSITY BELFAST LIBRARY, ARMAGH CAMPUS, Armagh, Co. Armagh

RUSSELL LIBRARY. *See* ST PATRICK'S COLLEGE, MAYNOOTH, Co. Kildare

ST MARY'S UNIVERSITY COLLEGE LIBRARY, Belfast, Co. Antrim

ST PATRICK'S COLLEGE LIBRARY, Dublin, Co. Dublin

ST PATRICK'S COLLEGE, MAYNOOTH – RUSSELL LIBRARY, Maynooth, Co. Kildare

STRANMILLIS UNIVERSITY COLLEGE LIBRARY, Belfast, Co. Antrim

TRINITY COLLEGE DUBLIN LIBRARY, Dublin, Co. Dublin

UNION THEOLOGICAL COLLEGE – GAMBLE LIBRARY, Belfast, Co. Antrim

UNIVERSITY COLLEGE DUBLIN LIBRARY, Dublin, Co. Dublin

UNIVERSITY OF LIMERICK LIBRARY AND INFORMATION SERVICES, Limerick, Co. Limerick

UNIVERSITY OF ULSTER LIBRARY, BELFAST CAMPUS, Belfast, Co. Antrim

UNIVERSITY OF ULSTER LIBRARY, COLERAINE CAMPUS, Coleraine, Co. Londonderry

UNIVERSITY OF ULSTER LIBRARY, JORDANSTOWN CAMPUS, Newtownabbey, Co. Antrim

UNIVERSITY OF ULSTER LIBRARY, MAGEE CAMPUS, Derry, Co. Londonderry

## 2
## ARCHIVES

BANTRY HOUSE, Bantry, Co. Cork

CARDINAL TOMÁS Ó FIAICH LIBRARY AND ARCHIVE, Armagh, Co. Armagh

CASHEL AND EMLY ARCHDIOCESAN ARCHIVES (Roman Catholic), Thurles, Co. Tipperary

CLARE COUNTY ARCHIVE SERVICE, Ennis, Co. Clare

CORK ARCHIVES INSTITUTE, Cork, Co. Cork

CORK PUBLIC MUSEUM (Músaem Poiblí Chorcaí), Cork, Co. Cork

DIOCESAN ARCHIVE, DROMORE (Roman Catholic), Newry, Co. Down

DIOCESE OF CLONFERT ARCHIVE, Loughrea, Co. Galway

DONEGAL COUNTY ARCHIVES SERVICE, Lifford, Co. Donegal

DOWN & CONNOR DIOCESAN ARCHIVES (Roman Catholic), Belfast, Co. Antrim

DUBLIN CITY ARCHIVES, Dublin, Co. Dublin

FINGAL COUNTY ARCHIVES, Dublin, Co. Dublin

GALWAY CITY LIBRARY – LOCAL HISTORY DEPARTMENT AND ARCHIVES, Galway, Co. Galway

GARDA MUSEUM ARCHIVES, Dublin, Co. Dublin

GRAND LODGE OF FREEMASONS OF IRELAND: LIBRARY, ARCHIVES AND MUSEUM, Dublin, Co. Dublin

GUINNESS ARCHIVE, Dublin, Co. Dublin

IRISH ARCHITECTURAL ARCHIVE, Dublin, Co. Dublin

IRISH FILM ARCHIVE OF THE FILM INSTITUTE OF IRELAND, Dublin, Co. Dublin

IRISH JESUIT ARCHIVES, Dublin, Co. Dublin

IRISH JEWISH MUSEUM, Dublin, Co. Dublin

IRISH THEATRE ARCHIVE, Dublin, Co. Dublin

IRISH TRADITIONAL MUSIC ARCHIVE, Dublin, Co. Dublin

JAMES HARDIMAN LIBRARY. *See* NATIONAL UNIVERSITY OF IRELAND, GALWAY – JAMES HARDIMAN LIBRARY – DEPARTMENT OF SPECIAL COLLECTIONS AND ARCHIVES, Galway, Co. Galway

KERRY LOCAL HISTORY AND ARCHIVES COLLECTION, Kerry County Library, Tralee, Co. Kerry

LIMERICK ARCHIVES, Limerick, Co. Limerick

LOUTH LOCAL AUTHORITIES ARCHIVES SERVICE, Dundalk, Co. Louth

MICHAEL DAVITT MUSEUM, Foxford, Co. Mayo

THE MILITARY ARCHIVES, Dublin, Co. Dublin

NATIONAL ARCHIVES OF IRELAND, Dublin, Co. Dublin

NATIONAL GALLERY OF IRELAND LIBRARY AND ARCHIVE, Dublin, Co. Dublin

NATIONAL PHOTOGRAPHIC ARCHIVE, Dublin, Co. Dublin

NATIONAL UNIVERSITY OF IRELAND, GALWAY – JAMES HARDIMAN LIBRARY – DEPARTMENT OF SPECIAL COLLECTIONS AND ARCHIVES, Galway, Co. Galway

PUBLIC RECORD OFFICE OF NORTHERN IRELAND, Belfast, Co. Antrim

ST PATRICK'S COLLEGE MAYNOOTH ARCHIVES, RUSSELL LIBRARY, Maynooth, Co. Kildare

ULSTER FOLK AND TRANSPORT MUSEUM, Holywood, Co. Down

UNIVERSITY COLLEGE DUBLIN – ARCHIVES DEPARTMENT, University College Dublin, Dublin, Co. Dublin

WATERFORD CITY ARCHIVES, Waterford, Co. Waterford

WATERFORD COUNTY ARCHIVES SERVICE, Dungarvan, Co. Waterford

WICKLOW COUNTY LIBRARY – LOCAL HISTORY COLLECTION AND ARCHIVES, Wicklow County Library Headquarters, Bray, Co. Wicklow

## 3

## GENEALOGICAL AND HERITAGE CENTRES AND SERVICES

ARMAGH ANCESTRY, Armagh City, Co. Armagh

ASSOCIATION OF PROFESSIONAL GENEALOGISTS IN IRELAND, Dublin, Co. Dublin

BRÚ BORÚ HERITAGE CENTRE, Cashel, Co. Tipperary

CARLOW GENEALOGY PROJECT, Carlow Town, Co. Carlow

CLARE HERITAGE AND GENEALOGICAL CENTRE, Corofin, Co. Clare

CORK CITY ANCESTRAL PROJECT, Cork, Co. Cork

CO. CAVAN GENEALOGICAL RESEARCH CENTRE, Cavan, Co. Cavan

CO. DERRY OR LONDONDERRY GENEALOGY CENTRE, Derry, Co. Londonderry

CO. ROSCOMMON HERITAGE AND GENEALOGY COMPANY, Strokestown, Co. Roscommon

CO. SLIGO HERITAGE AND GENEALOGY SOCIETY, Sligo, Co. Sligo

CO. WEXFORD HERITAGE AND GENEALOGY CENTRE, Tagoat, Co. Wexford

DONEGAL ANCESTRY, Ramelton, Co. Donegal

DÚN LAOGHAIRE-RATHDOWN HERITAGE CENTRE, Dún Laoghaire, Co. Dublin

DÚN NA SÍ HERITAGE CENTRE, Moate, Co. Westmeath

EAST CLARE HERITAGE COMPANY, Tuamgraney, Co. Clare

EAST GALWAY FAMILY HISTORY SOCIETY, Woodford, Co. Galway

FINGAL GENEALOGY, Swords Historical Society Co., Swords, Co. Dublin

GALWAY FAMILY HISTORY SOCIETY WEST, Galway, Co. Galway

THE HERITAGE CENTRE, Monaghan, Co. Monaghan

IRISH MIDLANDS ANCESTRY (LAOIS AND OFFALY FAMILY HISTORY RESEARCH CENTRE), Tullamore, Co. Offaly

IRISH WORLD, Coalisland, Co. Tyrone

KILDARE HERITAGE & GENEALOGY COMPANY, Newbridge, Co. Kildare

KILKENNY ARCHAEOLOGICAL SOCIETY, Kilkenny, Co. Kilkenny

KILLARNEY GENEALOGICAL CENTRE, Killarney, Co. Kerry

LAOIS AND OFFALY FAMILY HISTORY RESEARCH CENTRE. *See* IRISH MIDLANDS ANCESTRY, Tullamore, Co. Offaly

LEITRIM GENEALOGY CENTRE, Ballinamore, Co. Leitrim

LIMERICK ANCESTRY, Limerick, Co. Limerick

LONGFORD RESEARCH CENTRE, Longford, Co. Longford

MALLOW HERITAGE CENTRE, Mallow, Co. Cork

MAYO NORTH FAMILY HERITAGE CENTRE, Ballina, Co. Mayo

MEATH HERITAGE AND GENEALOGY CENTRE, Trim, Co. Meath

MEATH–LOUTH FAMILY RESEARCH CENTRE. *See* MEATH HERITAGE AND GENEALOGY CENTRE, Trim, Co. Meath

MONAGHAN ANCESTRY, Monaghan, Co. Monaghan

OFFALY HISTORICAL & ARCHAEOLOGICAL SOCIETY. *See* IRISH MIDLANDS ANCESTRY, Tullamore, Co. Offaly

OFFICE OF THE CHIEF HERALD/GENEALOGICAL OFFICE, Dublin, Co. Dublin

ORDNANCE SURVEY OF NORTHERN IRELAND, Belfast, Co. Antrim

SOUTH MAYO FAMILY RESEARCH CENTRE, Ballinrobe, Co. Mayo

TIPPERARY FAMILY HISTORY RESEARCH, Tipperary, Co. Tipperary

TIPPERARY NORTH FAMILY HISTORY RESEARCH CENTRE, Nenagh, Co. Tipperary

ULSTER HISTORICAL FOUNDATION, Belfast, Co. Antrim

WATERFORD HERITAGE SERVICES, Waterford, Co. Waterford

THE WICKLOW FAMILY HISTORY CENTRE, Wicklow, Co. Wicklow

## 4
## GOVERNMENT ORGANIZATIONS AND OFFICES

OFFICE OF THE CHIEF HERALD/GENEALOGICAL OFFICE, Dublin, Co. Dublin

GENERAL REGISTER OFFICE, Belfast, Co. Antrim

GENERAL REGISTER OFFICE, Dublin, Co. Dublin

NATIONAL ARCHIVES OF IRELAND, Dublin, Co. Dublin

NATIONAL LIBRARY OF IRELAND, Dublin, Co. Dublin

NORTHERN IRELAND ASSEMBLY LIBRARY, Belfast, Co. Antrim

ORDNANCE SURVEY OF NORTHERN IRELAND, Belfast, Co. Antrim

PUBLIC RECORD OFFICE OF NORTHERN IRELAND, Belfast, Co. Antrim

REGISTRY OF DEEDS, Dublin, Co. Dublin

VALUATION OFFICE IRELAND, Dublin, Co. Dublin

## 5
## PUBLIC LIBRARIES

ARMAGH BRANCH LIBRARY, Armagh, Co. Armagh

ATHLONE PUBLIC LIBRARY, Athlone, Co. Westmeath

BAILIEBORO LIBRARY, Bailieboro, Co. Cavan

CASTLEBAR CENTRAL LIBRARY – LOCAL STUDIES DEPARTMENT, Castlebar, Co. Mayo

CAVAN COUNTY LIBRARY, Cavan, Co. Cavan

BALLYMONEY LIBRARY, Ballymoney, Co. Antrim

BANGOR LIBRARY, Bangor, Co Down

BELFAST CENTRAL LIBRARY, Belfast, Co. Antrim

CARLOW CENTRAL LIBRARY, Carlow, Co. Carlow

CENTRAL LIBRARY, Derry, Co. Londonderry

CENTRE FOR DUBLIN AND IRISH STUDIES, Dublin, Co. Dublin

CLARE COUNTY LIBRARY – LOCAL STUDIES CENTRE, Ennis, Co. Clare

CORK CITY LIBRARY, Cork, Co. Cork

CORK COUNTY LIBRARY, Cork, Co. Cork

DONEGAL COUNTY LIBRARY, Letterkenny, Co. Donegal

DUBLIN CITY PUBLIC LIBRARIES, Dublin, Co. Dublin

DUBLIN CITY PUBLIC LIBRARIES – CENTRAL LIBRARY, Dublin, Co. Dublin

DÚN LAOGHAIRE LIBRARY – LOCAL HISTORY DEPARTMENT, Dún Laoghaire, Co. Dublin

ENNISKILLEN LIBRARY, Enniskillen, Co. Fermanagh

FINGAL COUNTY LIBRARIES, Dublin, Co. Dublin

GALWAY CITY LIBRARY, Galway, Co. Galway

GALWAY CITY LIBRARY – LOCAL HISTORY DEPARTMENT AND ARCHIVES

HOLYWOOD BRANCH LIBRARY, Holywood, Co. Down

IRISH ROOM, Coleraine, Co. Londonderry

KERRY LOCAL HISTORY AND ARCHIVES COLLECTION, Tralee, Co. Kerry

KILKENNY COUNTY LIBRARY, Kilkenny, Co. Kilkenny

LAOIS COUNTY LIBRARY – LOCAL STUDIES COLLECTION, Portlaoise, Co. Laois

LEITRIM COUNTY LIBRARY, Ballinamore, Co. Leitrim

LIMERICK CITY PUBLIC LIBRARY, Limerick, Co. Limerick

LIMERICK COUNTY LIBRARY – LOCAL STUDIES COLLECTION, Limerick, Co. Limerick

LONGFORD BRANCH LIBRARY – LOCAL STUDIES, Longford, Co. Longford

LOUTH COUNTY LIBRARY, Dundalk, Co. Louth

MEATH COUNTY LIBRARY, Navan, Co. Meath

MONAGHAN BRANCH LIBRARY, Monaghan, Co. Monaghan

MONAGHAN COUNTY LIBRARY, Clones, Co. Monaghan

M'SKIMIN ROOM, Carrickfergus Library, Carrickfergus, Co. Antrim

NEWCASTLE BRANCH LIBRARY, Newcastle, Co. Down

NEWRY BRANCH LIBRARY, Newry, Co. Down

NEWTOWNARDS BRANCH LIBRARY, Newtownards, Co. Down

NORTH-EASTERN EDUCATION AND LIBRARY BOARD – LIBRARY SERVICES HEADQUARTERS, Ballymena, Co. Antrim

OFFALY COUNTY LIBRARY – LOCAL STUDIES SECTION, Tullamore, Co. Offaly

OMAGH LIBRARY, Omagh, Co. Tyrone

ROSCOMMON COUNTY LIBRARY, Roscommon Town, Co. Roscommon

SEELB LIBRARY HEADQUARTERS – LOCAL STUDIES UNIT, Ballynahinch, Co. Down

SELB IRISH AND LOCAL STUDIES LIBRARY, Armagh, Co. Armagh

SLIGO COUNTY LIBRARY, Sligo, Co. Sligo

TIPPERARY LIBRARIES, Thurles, Co. Tipperary

WATERFORD COUNTY LIBRARY HEADQUARTERS, Lismore, Co. Waterford

WATERFORD MUNICIPAL LIBRARY, Waterford, Co. Waterford

WESTMEATH COUNTY LIBRARY HEADQUARTERS – LOCAL STUDIES COLLECTION, Mullingar, Co. Westmeath

WEXFORD COUNTY LIBRARY, Ardcavan, Co. Wexford

WICKLOW COUNTY LIBRARY – LOCAL HISTORY COLLECTION AND ARCHIVES, Bray, Co. Wicklow

## 6
## SPECIAL LIBRARIES

ARMAGH COUNTY MUSEUM, Armagh, Co. Armagh

ARMAGH OBSERVATORY, Armagh, Co. Armagh

ARMAGH PUBLIC LIBRARY, Armagh, Co. Armagh

AUSTIN CLARKE LIBRARY – POETRY IRELAND/EIGSE EIREANN, Dublin, Co. Dublin

CARDINAL TOMÁS Ó FIAICH LIBRARY AND ARCHIVE, Armagh, Co. Armagh

CENTRAL CATHOLIC LIBRARY, Dublin, Co. Dublin

CENTRE FOR MIGRATION STUDIES, Omagh, Co. Tyrone

CHESTER BEATTY LIBRARY, Dublin, Co. Dublin

CORK PUBLIC MUSEUM (Músaem Poiblí Chorcaí), Cork, Co. Cork

DONEGAL COUNTY MUSEUM, Letterkenny, Co. Donegal

FRANCISCAN LIBRARY, Killiney, Co. Dublin

GPA BOLTON LIBRARY, Cashel, Co. Tipperary

HISTORICAL LIBRARY, RELIGIOUS SOCIETY OF FRIENDS, Dublin, Co. Dublin

HISTORY AND FAMILY RESEARCH CENTRE – LOCAL STUDIES DEPARTMENT, Newbridge, Co. Kildare

THE HONORABLE SOCIETY OF KING'S INNS, Dublin, Co. Dublin

INVEST NORTHERN IRELAND – BUSINESS INFORMATION SERVICES AND EURO INFO CENTRE, Belfast, Co. Antrim

IRISH JEWISH MUSEUM, Dublin, Co. Dublin

IRISH ROOM, Coleraine, Co. Londonderry

THE JESUIT LIBRARY, Dublin, Co. Dublin

LIFFORD OLD COURTHOUSE, Lifford, Co. Donegal

LINEN HALL LIBRARY, Belfast, Co. Antrim

MARSH'S LIBRARY, Dublin, Co. Dublin

MICHAEL DAVITT MUSEUM, Foxford, Co. Mayo

MONAGHAN COUNTY MUSEUM, Monaghan, Co. Monaghan

MUSEUM OF COUNTRY LIFE, Castlebar, Co. Mayo. *See* NATIONAL MUSEUM OF IRELAND, Dublin, Co. Dublin

NATIONAL GALLERY OF IRELAND LIBRARY AND ARCHIVE, Dublin, Co. Dublin

NATIONAL LIBRARY OF IRELAND, Dublin, Co. Dublin

NATIONAL MUSEUM OF ARCHAEOLOGY & HISTORY. *See* NATIONAL MUSEUM OF IRELAND, Dublin, Co. Dublin

NATIONAL MUSEUM OF COUNTRY LIFE. *See* NATIONAL MUSEUM OF IRELAND, Dublin, Co. Dublin

NATIONAL MUSEUM OF DECORATIVE ARTS & HISTORY. *See* NATIONAL MUSEUM OF IRELAND, Dublin, Co. Dublin

NATIONAL MUSEUM OF IRELAND, Dublin, Co. Dublin

NATIONAL MUSEUM OF NATURAL HISTORY. *See* NATIONAL MUSEUM OF IRELAND, Dublin, Co. Dublin

NORTHERN IRELAND ASSEMBLY LIBRARY, Belfast, Co. Antrim

NORTHERN IRELAND HOUSING EXECUTIVE – LIBRARY INFORMATION SERVICES, Belfast, Co. Antrim

REPRESENTATIVE CHURCH BODY LIBRARY, Dublin, Co. Dublin

ROYAL COLLEGE OF PHYSICIANS OF IRELAND, Dublin, Co. Dublin

ROYAL DUBLIN SOCIETY, Dublin, Co. Dublin

ROYAL IRISH ACADEMY, Dublin, Co. Dublin

ROYAL SOCIETY OF ANTIQUARIES OF IRELAND, Dublin, Co. Dublin

SELB IRISH AND LOCAL STUDIES LIBRARY, Armagh, Co. Armagh

ULSTER-AMERICAN FOLK PARK, Omagh, Co. Tyrone

ULSTER FOLK AND TRANSPORT MUSEUM, Holywood, Co. Down

ULSTER MUSEUM LIBRARY, Belfast, Co. Antrim

# COUNTY ANTRIM

INCLUDES BELFAST

## BALLYMONEY LIBRARY

Rodden Foot, Queen Street
BALLYMONEY, CO. ANTRIM, BT53 6JB
Northern Ireland

TELEPHONE: (028) 2766 3589; FAX: (028) 2766 3589
E-mail: olga_mckee@hotmail.com
Website: www.neelb.org.uk

HOURS

M,W,F, 10:00am–5:30pm; Tu,Th, 10:00am–8:00pm; Sat, 10:00am–5:00pm

ACCESS AND SERVICES

Visitors welcome, but borrowing privileges for visitors may be restricted. Consult with Librarian. Disabled access facilities. Fees for photocopying and fax services.

CONTACT

Olga McKee, Team Librarian (Information), Coleraine Group

DESCRIPTION

One of 38 libraries in the NORTH-EASTERN EDUCATION AND LIBRARY BOARD. Ballymoney's special collections offer material of great interest to scholars.

HOLDINGS

Small branch library with a general educational and reading collection. The library houses two special collections, the George Shiels Collection and the Ballymoney Special Collection. The former comprises plays, books, typescripts, cards, correspondence and photographs of the playwright (1886–1949), whose work was often performed at the Abbey Theatre, Dublin. The latter contains titles of local Ballymoney interest, purchased through bequests left to the people of Ballymoney in the 1800s.

LOCATION

Town centre. Parking to the rear of the library building.

## NORTH-EASTERN EDUCATION AND LIBRARY BOARD – LIBRARY SERVICE HEADQUARTERS

Local Studies Service
Demesne Avenue
BALLYMENA, CO. ANTRIM, BT43 7BG
Northern Ireland

TELEPHONE: (028) 2566 4121; FAX: not available to public at present

E-mail: yvonne.hirst@neelb.org.uk
Website: www.neelb.org.uk

HOURS

M,Th,F, 10:00am–8:00pm; Tu,W, 10:00am–5:30pm; Sat, 10:00am–5:00pm

ACCESS AND SERVICES

Visitors welcome, but advance notice preferred. Collection is for reference only. Disabled access facilities. Fees for photocopying, microfilm prints and fax services.

CONTACT

Yvonne Hirst, Local Studies Development Officer

DESCRIPTION

Local Studies Service oversees local study collections at the various libraries within the 38-member library network of the North-Eastern Education and Library Board Library Service, established in 1973. In addition to local collections in most of these libraries, there are a number of important special collections. These include the Langford Lodge Collection, Ballymena; the Hugh Thomson Collection at the IRISH ROOM, Coleraine, Co. Londonderry; the M'SKIMIN ROOM, CARRICKFERGUS; and the George Shiels Collection at BALLYMONEY LIBRARY. It is the goal of the Library Service to collect, record, organize and conserve all appropriate material documenting the life and history of the area it serves.

HOLDINGS

The Local Studies Service, in addition to coordinating local studies collections throughout the NEELB Library Service area, maintains a local studies reference-only collection in Ballymena. This collection includes Griffith's Valuation for Co. Antrim and part of Co. Londonderry; the 1901 Census for Counties Antrim and Londonderry, and Belfast; and Ordnance Survey maps.

*School records:* it is not generally known that PRONI has redistributed considerable parts of its holdings of records of public elementary schools. These are mainly post-1945 school roll books but some earlier roll books and daily report books are included. These records were distributed to Area Library Boards with coverage for their area of responsibility. This means that the collection of records for over 80 schools now held in the library at Ballymena includes records for Draperstown and Magherafelt schools in the southern part of Co. Londonderry and also for schools in Coleraine and District. Samples of these records include: Ballynagashel (Loughguile) roll books 1875–80, 1895–9, 1938–51 10 vols; Cranny (Desertmartin, Co. Londonderry) roll books 1875–8, 1887–90 and 1893–9. For half of the schools, records transferred include pupils' registers dating from *c.*1940.

LOCATION

Town centre.

## BELFAST CENTRAL LIBRARY

Royal Avenue
BELFAST, BT1 1EA
Northern Ireland

TELEPHONE: (028) 9050 9150; FAX: (028) 9033 2819
E-mail: info@libraries.belfast-elb.gov.uk
Website: www.belb.org.uk

HOURS

General Library: M,Th, 9:00am–8:00pm; Tu,W,F, 9:00am–5:30pm; Sat, 9:00am–1:00pm; Newspaper Library: M,Th, 9:00am–7:30pm; Tu,W,F, 9:00am–5:00pm; Sat, 9:00am–12:30pm (Note: Access to Newspaper Library is in Library Street)

ACCESS AND SERVICES

Flagship library of the Belfast Education and Library Board, Belfast Central is open to visitors for reference services but borrowing privileges for non-residents may be restricted. Disabled access facilities. Closed stacks. Photocopying and microform prints available for a fee. Computerized, printed and card catalogues. Linked to the emigration database of the Ulster-American Folk Park. The library offers various leaflets, brochures, and guides to its holdings, including a *Guide to Irish & Local Studies Department*. Other publications of interest are: *Annual Reports: Catalogue of Books and Bound Mss of the Irish Historical, Archaeological and Antiquarian Library of the late Francis Joseph Bigger …* (Belfast, 1930); and *Natural History: A Select List of Fine Books from the Stock of Belfast Central Library*, by Thomas Watson (Belfast, 1988).

CONTACT

Linda Houston, Chief Librarian
Katherine McCloskey, Assistant Chief Librarian
David Jess, Assistant Chief Librarian

DESCRIPTION

The Central Library, opened in 1888, is a major research and reference library. It is part of the Belfast Education and Library Board, which operates another 20 branch libraries throughout the city. In addition to maintaining a strong general collection and several major research collections, the library seeks to provide an up-to-date reference and information service to the general public.

HOLDINGS

The collection includes some 1,000,000 volumes, plus the largest newspaper collection in Northern Ireland. In addition, the library maintains significant collections of periodicals, maps, microforms, music scores, pamphlets, photographs, postcards, music recordings, theatre materials and government documents for Northern Ireland, the Republic of Ireland and the UK. Special collections include the 10,000-volume Natural History Collection; a rare book collection, including incunabula and pre-1701 English printed books; a pamphlet collection, especially of those dealing with the 'Popish Plot'; a Fine Press Collection, including a complete run of Cuala Press, and the Irish Collection. The last of these is the largest in NI, anchored by the 4,000-volume Francis Joseph Bigger Collection. The Bigger Collection is complemented by the Bigger Archive, with 10,000 items of archaeological, historical and biographical interest. This archive also includes a significant body of correspondence with notable local, national and international figures. Bigger (1863–1926), the grandson of United Irishman David Bigger, was a successful lawyer and member of the Gaelic League who assembled an impressive collection of books, pamphlets and bound manuscripts of Irish historical, archaeological and antiquarian interest. Frederic Bigger, the collector's brother, donated the collection in 1927, and a catalogue of 3,000 entries was published in 1930. Other major Irish holdings include some 800 pre-1851 Belfast imprints, an extensive collection of printed maps of Ireland, and several author collections, including books and manuscripts, e.g. Forrest Reid, Amanda McKittrick Ros, Lynn Doyle, and Sam Thompson. Complementing the Irish Collection is the newspaper collection, which contains virtually complete runs of the *Belfast Telegraph*, *Newsletter*, *Irish News* and *Northern Whig*, plus extensive holdings of provincial papers from Ireland, north and south. The library has a newspaper cuttings index covering the 18th and 19th centuries that may provide a short cut to finding information in the papers. The library also houses the deposit collection of UK patents, a superb Music Library, and strong holdings in the humanities, local history, business information, fine arts and literature, and science and technology. The library does not offer genealogical services *per se*, but its holdings in this area are extensive, and staff are willing to assist researchers as far as possible.

LOCATION

City centre, a few blocks north of Belfast City Hall. Public car-parks nearby.

## BUSINESS INFORMATION SERVICES AND EURO INFO CENTRE

*See* INVEST NORTHERN IRELAND, Belfast

## DIOCESAN LIBRARY OF DOWN, DROMORE AND CONNOR

Note: This Church of Ireland library no longer exists. Books were split between the REPRESENTATIVE CHURCH BODY LIBRARY, Dublin, and the ARMAGH PUBLIC LIBRARY, Armagh. Some manuscript material was sent to the PUBLIC RECORD OFFICE OF NORTHERN IRELAND, Belfast

## DOWN & CONNOR DIOCESAN ARCHIVES

73a Somerton Road
BELFAST, BT15 4DJ
Northern Ireland

TELEPHONE: (028) 9077 6185
E-mail: None
Website: None

HOURS

By appointment

ACCESS AND SERVICES

Privately funded archives of the Roman Catholic Diocese of Down & Connor, which includes Belfast. Advance notice required. Apply to Archivist. Photocopying available for a fee.

CONTACT

Diocesan Archivist

DESCRIPTION

Archives for the largest Catholic diocese in Northern Ireland, which historically embraces Belfast, Co. Antrim, most of Co. Down and the Liberties of Coleraine in Co. Londonderry.

HOLDINGS

Houses the official records of the Roman Catholic see of Down & Connor. Of special interest are the correspondence files of various bishops of the diocese dating back to 1803.

LOCATION

In the Fortwilliam section in north-east Belfast, between Antrim Road and the Shore Road.

## EDGEHILL THEOLOGICAL COLLEGE

9 Lennoxvale
BELFAST, BT9 5BY
Northern Ireland

TELEPHONE: (028) 9066 5870; FAX: (028) 9068 7204
E-mail: office.edgehill@netmatters.co.uk
Website: www.qub.ac.uk/ithe/etc.htm

HOURS

Sept.–June: M–F, 9:00am–5:00pm; closed July–Aug.

ACCESS AND SERVICES

Theological library primarily for the faculty and students of this Methodist college. Visitors welcome but restrictions may apply. Photocopying available for a fee.

CONTACT

M. Gallagher, Librarian

DESCRIPTION

Private religious library run by the Methodist Church in Ireland.

HOLDINGS

Library of some 10,000 volumes, with special emphasis on Methodism and theology. Includes some rare material.

LOCATION

The 3.5-acre campus is located about 1.5 miles south of city centre, between Malone Road and Stranmillis Road, near STRANMILLIS UNIVERSITY COLLEGE and QUEEN'S UNIVERSITY BELFAST.

## GAMBLE LIBRARY

*See* **UNION THEOLOGICAL COLLEGE**, Belfast

## GENERAL REGISTER OFFICE

Northern Ireland Statistics and Research Agency
Oxford House
49/55 Chichester Street
BELFAST, BT1 4HL
Northern Ireland

TELEPHONE: (028) 9025 2000; FAX: (028) 9025 2044
E-mail: gro.nisra@dfpni.gov.uk (birth, death and marriage certificate enquiries)
E-mail: groreg.nisra@dfpni.gov.uk (marriage, re-registration and adoptions)
E-mail: grostats.nisra@dfpni.gov.uk (statistical queries)
Website: www.groni.gov.uk

HOURS

M–F, 9:30am–4:00pm; closed public holidays

ACCESS AND SERVICES

Open to the general public, but application forms required. Disabled access facilities. General searches and index searches may be made by any member of the public over 16 years of age. Fees charged for searches and extracts. Current (August 2002) fees: full certified birth, death, marriage and adoption certificates, £9.00; short birth certificate, £9.00; staff search for each five-year period, £4.00; general searches, £19.00; index search, £8.00 (up to six hours or part thereof). The GRO now offers an online certificate ordering service (www.groni.gov.uk). The following public search facilities are available for anyone interested in tracing ancestors:

- Assisted searches. General search of records assisted by members of GRO staff for any period of years and any number of entries. Children cannot be admitted to the search room.
- Index search. Volumes of indexes are available for searching with limited verification of entries by staff. Children cannot be admitted to the search room.

Note: To book the above services please telephone (028) 9025 2000. Appointments should be made up to two weeks in advance, though not compulsory. Access can be gained if the facility is not fully booked.

CONTACT

G.F.C. King, Deputy Registrar General

DESCRIPTION

The GRO is part of the Northern Ireland Statistics and Research Agency and is primarily concerned with the administration of the registration of births, deaths and marriages. The main records held are statutory registers of births, deaths, marriages, still-births and adoptions. The registers themselves are not open to inspection, but the information from them is supplied in the form of certificates. The GRO, formally established in 1922 following partition, stores vital records of Northern Ireland for issue of certified copies to the public. Birth, death and Roman Catholic marriage registrations date from 1864 to present; non-Roman Catholic marriages from 1845 to present; adoptions from 1930 to present; and still-births from 1961 to present.

HOLDINGS

The GRO holds paper indexes for births, 1864 onwards; deaths, 1922 onwards; and marriages, 1922 onwards. It holds computerized indexes for births, 1864 onwards; deaths, 1864 onwards; and marriages, 1845 onwards.

LOCATION

The GRO is situated in the city centre, on the street from the City Hall to the Law Courts and the Waterfront.

## INVEST NORTHERN IRELAND – BUSINESS INFORMATION SERVICES AND EURO INFO CENTRE

LEDU House

Upper Galwally
BELFAST, BT8 6TB
Northern Ireland

TELEPHONE: (028) 9023 9090; FAX: (028) 9049 0490
E-mail: bis@investni.com
Website: www.investni.com

HOURS

By appointment only.

ACCESS AND SERVICES

Visitors welcome but by appointment only. Advance notice and identification required. Disabled access facilities. Library information resources and services are available to any company trading or wishing to trade in Europe, but services are not exclusive to Europe. The entire collection is catalogued online, and printed finding aids are available. Focus is on electronic information services, including CD-ROMs and databases. Invest Northern Ireland has published guides to EU funding in Northern Ireland and to business websites. Charges for photocopying and research.

CONTACT

Librarian

DESCRIPTION

Established in 1989 to provide small businesses with access to a unified European market, Invest Northern Ireland offers entrepreneurs information resources and services through its library division. Invest Northern Ireland maintains a wide variety of resources, including trade directories, environmental rules and regulations, and information on standards to encourage small business development.

HOLDINGS

The library emphasizes access to electronic data, but it does maintain a reference collection of some 5,000 printed books, 200 periodicals, and 200 journals. Strengths of the collection include market information and European legislative sources.

LOCATION

Two miles south-east of Belfast city centre, just off the Saintfield Road.

## LINEN HALL LIBRARY

17 Donegall Square North
BELFAST, BT1 5GD
Northern Ireland

TELEPHONE: (028) 9032 1707; FAX: (028) 9043 8586
E-mail: info@linenhall.com
Website: www.linenhall.com/Home/home.html

HOURS

M–F, 9:30am–5:30pm; Sat, 9:30am–4:00pm

ACCESS AND SERVICES

Independent subscribing research library with some public funding. Open to the public free of charge for reference services. Advance notice for research use advised. Borrowing privileges restricted to members. General stacks and modern Irish interest material are open-access. Otherwise stacks are closed-access. Access to research resources in the Northern Ireland Political Literature Collection requires a written letter of introduction from a university or research institute. Disabled access facilities. Houses the city's largest general lending collection at one location. Photocopying and microform prints available for a fee. Laptops and cameras can be used by arrangement. Membership available immediately. Leaflets for membership and for collections available. Other publications include the annual report and library newsletter. *See also* John Killen, *History of the Linen Hall Library* (Belfast, 1990).

CONTACT

John Gray, Librarian

DESCRIPTION

The Linen Hall Library was founded in 1788 as the Belfast Reading Society and is the oldest library in Belfast. It is also the last surviving subscribing library in Ireland. The library recently opened a spacious and attractive addition to its historic 19th-century headquarters, formerly a warehouse in the linen district.

HOLDINGS

The library houses more than 250,000 volumes, 75,000 pamphlets, plus significant holdings of periodicals, newspapers, manuscripts, maps, microforms, photographs, films and recordings. It maintains a general lending and reference collection, the latter being especially strong in genealogy, heraldry, history and travel. Its great strength, however, is its Irish and local studies collection, with particular strength for Belfast and Counties Antrim and Down. The library seeks to collect in all Irish-interest areas. The Northern Ireland Political Literature Collection, 1968–present, contains some 250,000 items relating to the Troubles, including runs of about 2,000 periodical titles, 11,500 books, 5,000 posters, 55,000 photographs, significant archives, and extensive ephemera. The 'Genealogical Collection' includes some 5,000 volumes, mainly of Ulster interest and Scottish and American connections, plus army, church and educational lists. Other significant collections include the Kennedy Collection of Ulster Poetry, and the Theatre and Performing Arts Collection.

LOCATION

In the heart of city centre, facing the front of Belfast City Hall. New entrance on Fountain Street.

## METHODIST

*see* WESLEY HISTORICAL SOCIETY LIBRARY

## NORTHERN IRELAND ASSEMBLY LIBRARY

Parliament Buildings, Stormont
BELFAST, BT4 3XX
Northern Ireland

TELEPHONE: (028) 9052 1250; FAX: (028) 9052 1922
E-mail: issuedesk.library@niassembly.gov.uk
Website: None

HOURS

M–F, 9:00am–5:00pm (and until half hour after completion of Assembly Sittings if after 4:30pm)

ACCESS AND SERVICES

Usually limited to Members and staff of the Northern Ireland Assembly, and to government personnel. Referrals made to other appropriate sources. Some exceptions may be made. Appointment required. Apply in writing to Librarian, preferably with the sponsorship of an academic institution. Short extracts may be copied. Loans may not be made to visitors. Card catalogue available; a retrospective cataloguing project is under way to transfer card records to machine-readable form.

CONTACT

George Woodman, Reader Services Librarian; e-mail: george.woodman@niassembly.gov.uk

DESCRIPTION

Established in 1921 to serve Members and staff of the Parliament of Northern Ireland, and from 1973 the Northern Ireland Assembly. Also acts as a reference library for government departments.

HOLDINGS

The collection includes some 17,500 books, 70,000 official publications, plus 150 journals, 2,000 microforms, and three photograph albums. In addition to collecting Northern Ireland official publications and legislation, the library focuses on Irish history and Northern Ireland history, government, and politics. The Northern Ireland Collection emphasizes public administration, ethnic/religious conflict, and constitutional law. Collections of special note include a collection of 18th-century and earlier historical and topographical materials, 18th-century journals, acts and other Irish parliamentary material. There is also access to about 45 electronic services, both online and CD-ROM.

LOCATION

Located in the Parliament Buildings, Stormont, east of Belfast city centre. Approach from either Massey Avenue or the Upper Newtownards Road. Limited parking available.

## NORTHERN IRELAND HOUSING EXECUTIVE – LIBRARY INFORMATION SERVICES

The Housing Centre
2 Adelaide Street
BELFAST, BT2 8PB
Northern Ireland

TELEPHONE: (028) 9031 8022; FAX: (028) 9031 8024
E-mail: vivienne.halton@nihe.gov.uk
Website: www.nihe.gov.uk

HOURS

M–Th, 10:00am–5:00pm; F, 10:00am–4:00pm

ACCESS AND SERVICES

Library primarily for use of staff. Visitors welcome to consult for reference purposes, but by appointment only. Advance notice required. Laptops permitted; pencils only. Open stacks. Collection catalogued on computer. Disabled access facilities; free photocopying; free leaflets. Internet access. Restricted city-centre parking.

CONTACT

Vivienne Halton, Library Information Services Manager

DESCRIPTION

The Housing Executive administers a vast network of public housing throughout Northern Ireland. Its library serves the reference and research needs of the staff.

HOLDINGS

The library collection includes some 12,000 volumes and pamphlets, plus some

200 periodical titles gathered to meet staff reference and research needs. Special interests include architecture and planning, construction, landscape design, housing, the public sector, management, finance, and the social sciences, especially sociology. The library also archives Housing Executive publications.

LOCATION

City centre.

## ORDNANCE SURVEY OF NORTHERN IRELAND

Colby House
Stranmillis Court
BELFAST, BT9 5BJ
Northern Ireland

TELEPHONE: (028) 9025 5755; FAX: (028) 9025 5700
E-mail: osni@gov.uk
Website: www.osni.gov.uk

HOURS

M–F, 9:15am–4:30pm; closed public and bank holidays

ACCESS AND SERVICES

For old maps and aerial photographs, tel: (028) 9025 5743 (voice mail); e-mail: oldmaps@osni.gov.uk. Appointment necessary to search for archive maps and aerial photographs. Search fee applies. Copies of maps and aerial photographs are available for purchase. See website for current costs of maps and air photographs.

CONTACT

The Director

DESCRIPTION

OSNI is an Executive Agency with the Department of Culture, Arts & Leisure for Northern Ireland.

HOLDINGS

The archive houses significant holdings of maps and aerial photographs and films: six-inch width series photographs, 1830–1900; six- and 25-inch width series photographs, 1830–1900; six- and 25-inch width series maps, 1900–1950; Irish Grid Maps from 1959 to present; aerial films 1959 to present. The archive also houses many original copies of the earlier county series maps.

LOCATION

Off Stranmillis Road, about 1.5 miles south of city centre, near STRANMILLIS UNIVERSITY COLLEGE.

## PRESBYTERIAN HISTORICAL SOCIETY

Room 218
Church House
Fisherwick Place
BELFAST, BT1 6DW
Northern Ireland

TELEPHONE: (028) 9032 2284; FAX: none
E-mail: none
Website: none

HOURS

M–F, 10:00am–12:30pm; open 1:15–3:30pm on Wednesdays

ACCESS AND SERVICES

Visitors welcome, appointments preferred. Photocopying available for a small fee. Publications include: *A History of Congregations in the Presbyterian Church in Ireland, 1610–1982.*

CONTACT

Alan McMillan, Assistant Secretary

DESCRIPTION

The Presbyterian Historical Society was created in 1906 to promote public awareness of the history of the Presbyterian Churches in Ireland. It is largely supported by the Presbyterian Church of Ireland.

HOLDINGS

The society possesses a library of some 12,000 books and pamphlets. These are mainly concerned with ecclesiastical history and in particular Presbyterian history. The collection includes a large number of congregational histories. A set of *The Witness*, a Presbyterian newspaper, covering the period 1874–1941, is also available for consultation, as are the printed minutes of the General Assembly beginning in 1840.

Manuscript material includes session minutes, baptisms and marriages from individual churches as well as some presbytery minutes. These include session accounts for Armagh Presbyterian Church for 1707–32, session minutes for Aghadowey Presbyterian Church for 1702–61 and baptisms from Cullybackey (Cunningham Memorial) Presbyterian Church covering the period 1726–1815. The *Guide to Church Records* produced by the PUBLIC RECORD OFFICE OF NORTHERN IRELAND (published by ULSTER HISTORICAL FOUNDATION 1994) indicates which congregational records are available at the Presbyterian Historical Society. The society also has a duplicate set of the microfilm copies of Presbyterian church registers held by PRONI covering the vast majority of Presbyterian congregations in Ireland.

Of particular interest is the large amount of biographical data on Presbyterian ministers. This material can be accessed through a card index, while there are also handwritten and printed fasti providing information on clergymen. A small collection of private papers of Presbyterian ministers is available in the Presbyterian Historical Society. These include some of the papers of the most distinguished 19th-century Presbyterian minister, the Reverend Henry Cooke.

LOCATION

City centre, just west of Belfast City Hall, close to the offices of the Ulster Historical Foundation.

## PUBLIC RECORD OFFICE OF NORTHERN IRELAND

66 Balmoral Avenue
BELFAST, BT9 6NY
Northern Ireland

TELEPHONE: (028) 9025 1318; FAX: (028) 9025 5999
E-mail: proni@gov.uk
Website: proni.nics.gov.uk

HOURS

M–W,F, 9:15am–4:45pm; Th, 9:15am–8:45pm (10:00am opening on first Thursday of each month to allow for staff training)

ACCESS AND SERVICES

Publicly funded executive agency within the Department of Culture, Arts & Leisure, open to the general public. Identification required upon first visit arrival. Advance notice not required for individuals but groups must book in advance. Laptops permitted at selected points in the Reading Room. Photocopying and microfilming services are available, which are carried out by staff. The public areas are available to those with a disability. There is no single guide to the records of PRONI but there are exceptionally detailed catalogues, indexes and finding aids to individual collections. Consult with reference staff. Details of the acquisitions can be found in the annual *Deputy Keeper's Reports* up to 1989, indexed under personal names, places and subjects. A summary of more recent acquisitions can be found in the *Annual Report and Accounts*. Though PRONI is the major resource for genealogical information in Northern Ireland, it does not carry out genealogical research of any kind for members of the public. Staff will give guidance to visitors, however. Records generated by government and public bodies are generally not open to the public until 30 years after the date of the last paper. This period of closure may be extended for certain categories of records, e.g. exceptionally sensitive papers, documents containing information supplied in confidence, and documents containing information about individuals, the disclosure of which would cause distress or danger to living persons or their descendants. Publications include: the *Annual/Statutory Report of the Deputy Keeper of Records, Guide to Sources for Women's History, Guide to Educational Records,* plus a variety of handouts on tracing your family tree, local history, and using the records. Publications can be ordered online.

CONTACT

Readers Services Section

DESCRIPTION

PRONI was established in 1923 following Partition and opened in 1924 as the official repository for public records in Northern Ireland, but it also houses the largest collection of private records in Northern Ireland.

HOLDINGS

PRONI has more than 53 shelf kilometres of records. The bulk of its public records deal with Northern Ireland since the early 1920s. The archive also includes older documents from private sources, some dating back to the 14th century, with strong holdings of material from the 1600s. Records fall into three major categories: records of government departments, some going back to the early 19th century; records of courts of law, local authorities and non-departmental public bodies; and records deposited by private individuals, estates, churches, businesses and institutions. Among the series of records held by PRONI are many special collections. Indeed, PRONI is a series of special collections, identified by categories: records of central and local government and public bodies, which include tithe applotment records; valuation maps, plans and surveys; Poor Law records; school records; and Church records (mostly available in a self-service microfilm facility); landed estate records; business records; solicitors' records; records of private individuals; and photographic records. PRONI also holds copies of the 1901 Census for the six counties of Northern Ireland, which are available in the Self-Service Microfilm Room.

PRONI ON THE WEB

Introductions to the major private collections can be read on the PRONI website (www.proni.nics.gov.uk). Most of these were written or compiled by Dr A.P.W. Malcomson, formerly Deputy Keeper of the Records, PRONI. Most relate to landed estates, but there are some introductions to business records, including the shipbuilding firm, Harland and Wolff. A large number of digitized images, mainly of landed magnates and their homes, can also be viewed. Introductions to government departmental and non-departmental records are currently being composed. PRONI also has several useful indexes on its website. A Geographical Index lists counties, parishes, townlands, baronies, electoral divisions, and poor law unions. The Prominent Person Index lists all the occurrences of a name entered into the search field, together with all the reference numbers relevant to that individual. The Presbyterian Church Index gives the name, county, and reference number of all those Presbyterian church records that have been microfilmed by PRONI. The Church of Ireland Index gives the name, county, diocese, and reference number of all those Church of Ireland records that have been microfilmed by PRONI. There are also guides to the different types of records held, along with explanations of each category of record.

LOCATION

Approximately three miles south-west of city centre, between the Lisburn and Malone Roads. The No. 70/71 Malone bus stops within walking distance of PRONI.

## QUEEN'S UNIVERSITY BELFAST LIBRARY

University Road
BELFAST, BT7 1LS
Northern Ireland

TELEPHONE: (028) 9033 5020; FAX: (028) 9032 3340
E-mail: library@qub.ac.uk; or use website for contact
Website: www.qub.ac.uk/lib

HOURS

Main Library: M–F (Oct.–mid-June), 9:00am–10:00pm; Sat, 9:00am – 12:30pm; vacation period, 9:00am–5:00pm. Special Collections: M–F (Oct.–mid-June), 9:00am–9:30pm; vacation, M–F, 9:00am–5:00pm. See below (within this entry) for Seamus Heaney Library

ACCESS AND SERVICES

Publicly funded academic research library open to the general public for reference purposes. Borrowing privileges may be extended to visitors for a fee. Consult with Librarian. Application to use special collections and the departmental libraries, i.e. Agriculture and Food Science Library, Veterinary Science Library, Medical Library, and Science Library (see below), should be made in advance. Identification required. Special access rules apply for each of these units. For Special Collections, application letter should include list of specific collections to be consulted, time of visit, and a letter of reference. Seating in Special Collections is very limited, and advance notice is essential. Laptops are permitted in Special Collections, but battery-operated models are preferred because of limited electrical outlets. Pencils only, and photocopying is done by staff. Consult with Special Collections Librarian for camera use. Most of the library is Disabled access facilities, including Special Collections. The entire book collection is catalogued online, using the LC classification system. Printed manuscripts catalogue.

Queen's departmental libraries are not listed separately in this guide. These are located outside the main library and may be contacted directly as follows: Agricultural and Food Science Library, Agriculture and Food Science Centre, Newforge Lane, Belfast, BT9 5PX, tel. (028) 9025 5227, fax (028) 9025 5400; Altnagelvin Library, Multidisciplinary Education Centre, Altnagelvin Hospital, Derry BT47 1SB, tel. (028) 7134 5171, ext. 3745/(028) 7161 1224; fax (028)

7134 9334; Biomedical Library, University Floor, Tower Block, Belfast City Hospital, Belfast BT9 7AB, tel. (028) 9032 9241, ext. 2797/(028) 9026 3913, fax (028) 9031 5560; Medical Library, Mulhouse Building, Mulhouse Road, Belfast BT12 6DP, tel. (028) 9026 3151; Science Library, Lennoxvale, Belfast, BT9 5EQ, tel. (028) 9033 5441; and Veterinary Science Library, Veterinary Research Laboratories, Stormont, Belfast, BT4 3SD, tel. (028) 9076 0011, ext. 222.

RASCAL (Research and Special Collections Available Locally), hosted by Queen's University Belfast, provides online access to information resources held in local libraries and archives in Northern Ireland. The project has identified over 400 collections in almost 70 institutions, including libraries, museums and archives. The RASCAL Directory is accessible at www.rascal.ac.uk.

CONTACT

Norman J. Russell, Director of Information Services
Mary Kelly, Assistant Librarian for Special Collections; e-mail m.t.kelly@qub.ac.uk; tel. (028) 9027 3607

DESCRIPTION

Queen's College Belfast was established in Ireland by Queen Victoria in 1845, along with colleges in Cork and Galway. In 1908 it was elevated to university rank with its own charter and statutes. Today the university enrols more than 13,000 full- and part-time students. Recently two colleges and a branch campus were added to the university: STRANMILLIS UNIVERSITY COLLEGE, Belfast, ST MARY'S UNIVERSITY COLLEGE, Belfast and the QUEEN'S UNIVERSITY BELFAST, ARMAGH CAMPUS. Within the main library is the new SEAMUS HEANEY LIBRARY, designed as a multidisciplinary study centre for students, providing students not only with study space and computer services but also with easy access to recommended textbooks and course readings. Access to the Heaney Library is restricted to students and staff at Queen's. For more information on the university, see W.T. Moody and J.C. Beckett, *Queen's Belfast* (1959) and B.M. Walker and A. McCreary, *Degrees of Excellence* (1994).

HOLDINGS

The library houses the largest collection in Northern Ireland. The QUB Library alone contains more than 1,000,000 volumes, plus significant holdings of pamphlets, manuscripts, periodicals, newspapers and microforms. The collection is quite diverse, representing the teaching and research interests of the curriculum and faculty, but Irish studies are given special attention. **Special Collections** houses some 50,000 volumes, including some 20 incunabula, manuscript collections, and the archives of the university. Major individual collections include the Hibernica Collection; the Sir Thomas Percy Collection, the 18th-century library of this Church of Ireland Bishop of Dromore; the Edward Bunting manuscript collection; the Thomas Andrews (1813–85) and James Thomson (1822–92) collections of scientific papers; the Somerville and Ross manuscript collection; the Antrim Presbytery Library of Theology; and the Robert Hart (1835–1911) manuscript collection of Far Eastern materials, including diaries and letters. Hart, a native of Lisburn, was Inspector General of Maritime Customs in China from 1868 to 1907.

LOCATION

One mile south of city centre, near Botanic Gardens and the Ulster Museum.

## ST MARY'S UNIVERSITY COLLEGE LIBRARY

191 Falls Road
BELFAST, BT12 6FE
Northern Ireland

TELEPHONE: (028) 9032 7678; FAX: (028) 9033 3719
E-mail: library@stmarys-belfast.ac.uk
Website: www.stmarys-belfast.ac.uk

HOURS

Term: M–Th, 9:00am–9:00pm; F, 9:00am–5:00pm; Sat, 9:00am–1:00pm.
Vacation: M–F, 9:00am–1:00pm, 2:00–5:00pm
Closed: St Patrick's Day, Easter Week, 12–13 July, and Christmas–New Year

ACCESS AND SERVICES

One of two publicly funded university colleges of Queen's University Belfast. Library is open to visiting staff and students from other higher education establishments for reference purposes. Open stacks. Identification is necessary, as is the signing of a visitor's book. Disabled access facilities. The library has a printed guide, photocopying facilities and Internet access.

CONTACT

John Morrissey, Librarian; e-mail: j.morrissey@stmarys-belfast.ac.uk
Felicity Jones, Assistant Librarian; e-mail: f.jones@stmarys-belfast.ac.uk

DESCRIPTION

St Mary's University College was founded in 1900 by the Dominican Sisters to educate young women for the Catholic school system. In 1985 St Mary's amalgamated with St Joseph's, its male counterpart, to form the present St Mary's College. While maintaining its independence, the college has a special relationship with Queen's University, which validates St Mary's degrees. The purpose of the college has expanded with the introduction of a BA degree in Liberal Arts and the education and training of teachers for Irish-medium schools.

HOLDINGS

The collection includes 100,000 items, some 300 direct subscription journals and access to a large range of remote databases. The collection contains a substantial range of non-book materials and teaching and learning resources. Areas of chief curriculum interest include: education; Irish language; religious education and theology; business studies; European studies; human development; philosophy; physical education; design and technology; English; art; history; geography; and science.

LOCATION

One mile west of Belfast city centre, on the Falls Road, close to the Royal Victoria Hospital.

## SEAMUS HEANEY LIBRARY, Belfast

*See* QUEEN'S UNIVERSITY BELFAST LIBRARY

## STRANMILLIS UNIVERSITY COLLEGE LIBRARY

Stranmillis Road
BELFAST, BT9 5DY
Northern Ireland

TELEPHONE: (028) 9038 4310; FAX: (028) 9066 3682
E-mail: library@stran.ac.uk
Website: www.stran.ac.uk

HOURS

Term: M–Th, 9:00am–9:00pm; F, 9:00am–4:30pm; Sat, 9:00am–1:00pm
Vacation: M–Th, 9:00am–5:00pm; F, 9:00am–4:30pm

ACCESS AND SERVICES

One of two publicly funded education colleges in Northern Ireland, recently integrated academically with Queen's University Belfast. Library open to the general public for reference purposes. Visitors welcome, especially out of term, but borrowing privileges may be restricted. Identification required. Open stacks. Access for those with disabilities by arrangement. The library offers photocopying and microform prints, computerized databases, finding aids, and a printed guide.

CONTACT

Wesley McCann, Librarian

DESCRIPTION

Stranmillis was founded in 1922 as a training college for teachers. Today it concentrates on preparing teachers who work with ages three to 13. Its library supports the learning, teaching and research needs of staff and students.

HOLDINGS

The collection includes some 90,000 volumes and 400 journal titles. Areas of chief curriculum interest are: education; English; religious studies; history; art, design and technology; science; geography; physical education; music; and drama. Among special collections of interest are: Ulster collection of books relating to the northern counties of Ireland; a modest collection of 19th-century Irish school books; a microfilm copy of the *Belfast Newsletter*, 1737–1925; and a microfilm copy of the Lawrence Collection of Irish Photographs, 1880–1914 (the original is located at the NATIONAL LIBRARY OF IRELAND, Dublin).

LOCATION

Two miles south of Belfast city centre, on the Stranmillis Road. The campus is spacious and beautifully landscaped. Parking is available by arrangement.

## ULSTER HISTORICAL FOUNDATION

Balmoral Buildings
12 College Square East
BELFAST, BT1 6DD
Northern Ireland

TELEPHONE: (028) 9033 2288; FAX: (028) 9023 9885
E-mail: enquiry@uhf.org.uk
Website: www.ancestryireland.com

HOURS

By appointment. Preliminary enquiry in writing preferred. Normal business hours are: M–F, 9:00am–5:00pm

ACCESS AND SERVICES

Publicly and privately funded, not-for-profit, fee-based genealogical research centre and publisher, open to the public. Research consultancy provided for a fee. Preliminary search assessments to establish whether research is feasible are also carried out for a charge of £20/US$31. For schedule of research fees, contact Executive Director or see website. A full report averages £150–£250. The foundation has undertaken over 10,000 searches for clients throughout the world and each year answers over 3,000 genealogical enquiries. It also publishes a wide range of materials, primarily in the areas of Irish, local, and family history. For a current listing consult the foundation's website.

CONTACT

Fintan Mullan, Executive Director

DESCRIPTION

The Ulster Historical Foundation is the principal genealogical research centre in Ireland, with a concentration on the province of Ulster (six counties of Northern

Ireland, plus Counties Cavan, Donegal and Monaghan in the Republic of Ireland). Founded in 1956 to promote interest in Ulster history and genealogy, it provides a professional and comprehensive research service, publishes books and pamphlets, and organizes annual family history and heritage conferences. It is a member of the Irish Genealogical Project, an island-wide effort to computerize all the major Irish genealogical sources. To this end, it has been at work for years compiling a comprehensive computerized database of genealogical records for Ulster, principally for Counties Antrim and Down, including Belfast. The database is used as a tool, in conjunction with other documentary sources, to provide a comprehensive ancestral research service.

HOLDINGS

The UHF's database contains: pre-1900 church and civil records 1845–1921 for counties Antrim and Down, including Belfast, plus gravestone transcripts for most of Northern Ireland and calendars of flax-growers in Ireland in 1796. The Foundation also houses a collection of some 10,000 family history reports that it has compiled since 1956.

LOCATION

City centre, entrance on Great Victoria Street, two blocks west of Belfast City Hall

## ULSTER MUSEUM LIBRARY

Botanic Gardens
BELFAST, BT9 5AB
Northern Ireland

TELEPHONE: (028) 9038 3000, ext. 240; FAX: (028) 9038 3003
E-mail: brian.kennedy.um@nics.gov.uk
Website: www.ulstermuseum.org.uk/geninf.html

HOURS

Library: by appointment
Museum: M–F, 10:00am–5:00pm; Sat, 1:00–5:00pm; Sun, 2:00–5:00pm; open all year except Christmas and New Year

ACCESS

Collection is designed primarily for use by museum staff, but public is welcome by appointment. Non-circulating collection, but some items may be lent to staff, other libraries and accredited research workers. Consult with Registrar. Publications include: *A Century in Focus: Photography and Photographers in the North of Ireland 1839–1939,* by W.A. Maguire, published by Blackstaff Press in partnership with the Ulster Museum/Museums and Galleries of Northern Ireland (MAGNI) 2000, (a lavishly illustrated volume with photographs from the Ulster Museum's collections; includes a comprehensive list of all known photographers and studios in the north of Ireland; hardback, £20.00 (postage & packing additional)); and *Drawings, Paintings & Sculptures*, a catalogue of the fine-art collections of MAGNI, edited by Eileen Black and published by MAGNI/Ulster Museum and Nicholson & Bass, featuring over 1,500 colour reproductions from the Ulster Museum's fine-art collections, botany, zoology, and history collections, and from the Ulster Folk and Transport Museum and Armagh County Museum (paperback, £24.95; hardback, £35.00; postage & packing per copy, UK £6.50; surface mail to all other places, £10.00).

CONTACT

Brian Kennedy, Head of Curation

DESCRIPTION

The Ulster Museum is the flagship museum in the MAGNI service, which also includes the ULSTER-AMERICAN FOLK PARK, Omagh, Co. Tyrone; the ULSTER FOLK AND TRANSPORT MUSEUM, Cultra, Co. Down; and the ARMAGH COUNTY MUSEUM, Armagh City, Co. Armagh. The Ulster Museum occupies nearly 6,000 square metres of galleries, with large collections in the fields of art, history and the natural sciences.

HOLDINGS

The library contains some 40,000 volumes, with about 200 current periodical subscriptions. There is also a small document archive, and a collection of some 15,000 photographic negatives. Subjects covered include: archaeology, ethnology, art, botany, conservation, design, geology, industrial archaeology, local history, museology, numismatics, photography, zoology, and general reference. Special collections include: Belfast printed books (1700–1850); various manuscript collections relating to local naturalists, e.g. botanist John Templeton (1766–1825), photographer and naturalist Robert J. Welch (1859–1936); and the R.J. Welch Collection of photographic negatives and lantern slides (6,000 items).

LOCATION

Located 1.5 miles south of city centre, just past Queen's University Belfast and the entrance to Botanic Gardens. By bus, take a No. 69 Stranmillis bus, which stops on the Stranmillis Road at the front of the museum. The No. 70/71 Malone bus stops on the University Road, at Queen's University, a few hundred yards north of the Museum.

## UNION THEOLOGICAL COLLEGE – GAMBLE LIBRARY

108 Botanic Avenue
BELFAST, BT7 1JT
Northern Ireland

TELEPHONE: (028) 9020 5093; FAX: (028) 9058 0040
E-mail: librarian@union.ac.uk
Website: www.union.ac.uk/library.htm

### HOURS

Term: M–Th, 9:00am–5:00pm; F, 9:00am–4:30pm; closed one week at Easter, Twelfth Fortnight (July), and a two-week Christmas–New Year period

### ACCESS AND SERVICES

Visitors are welcome; advance notice preferred. Borrowing privileges available to members, who may join for a current fee of £30.00 per year. Card catalogue represents about 65% of the book collection; computer catalogue for books received since 1993. Photocopying available for a fee. The college publishes an annual calendar and a students' handbook.

### CONTACT

Stephen Gregory, Librarian

### DESCRIPTION

Union Theological College was established by the Presbyterian Church in Ireland. The library supports the work of the faculty, students of the college, and ministers.

### HOLDINGS

The library houses more than 50,000 books, with a heavy emphasis on theology and Irish church history. A separate rare book collection features theology and church history. Special collections of note include the Magee College Pamphlets Collection and the Assembly's College Pamphlets Collection. There is also a collection of record books that would be of genealogical interest.

### LOCATION

One mile south of Belfast city centre, immediately behind the main buildings of Queen's University Belfast.

## UNIVERSITY OF ULSTER LIBRARY, BELFAST CAMPUS

Faculty of Art & Design Library
York Street
BELFAST, BT15 1ED
Northern Ireland

TELEPHONE: (028) 9032 8515; FAX: (028) 9026 7278
E-mail: m.khorshidian@ulster.ac.uk
Website: www.ulst.ac.uk/library

HOURS

Term: M–Th, 9:00am–10:00pm; F, 9:00am–6:00pm, Sat, 10:00am–1:00pm
Vacation: M–Th, 9:00am–5:00pm; F, 9:00am–4:30pm

ACCESS AND SERVICES

Visitors welcome but advance notice is preferred and identification required. Borrowing privileges are not extended to visitors on this campus. Disabled access facilities with some restrictions. The entire University of Ulster shares a common catalogue database.

CONTACT

Marion Khorshidian, Campus Library Manager

DESCRIPTION

The Belfast campus originated as a technical college and was established as a University Faculty in 1984, concentrating on art and design mainly at the undergraduate level. It is part of the four-campus University of Ulster system, which also includes Coleraine, Jordanstown (in Newtownabbey), and Magee (in Derry City).

HOLDINGS

The library contains some 60,000 volumes and more than 70,000 slides in support of the campus' curriculum, with strengths in the areas of fine art, design, graphics, fashion, textiles, ceramics, jewellery, metalwork, architecture, film, photography, and print-making. The library regularly sponsors important exhibitions relating to its holdings/interests, e.g. 'The Wood Engravings of Robert Gibbings' (1988), 'Illustrated by Hugh Thomson, 1860–1920' (1989), 'The Dolmen Press, 1951–1987' (1991) and 'Wendy Dunbar: Book Designer' (1994). An illustrated catalogue was produced for each of these exhibitions.

LOCATION

City centre, about one mile north of Belfast City Hall. Royal Avenue becomes York Street just past the Belfast Central Library.

## WESLEY HISTORICAL SOCIETY (Irish branch)

Edgehill College
9 Lennoxvale
BELFAST, BT9 5BY
Northern Ireland

TELEPHONE: 028 91815959
E-mail: robin@roddie.plus.com
Website: None

ACCESS AND SERVICES

The collection is normally open to researchers Monday–Thursday, 9:00am–12:30pm. However, it is advisable to make an appointment with the Archivist. Photocopying facilities available on request.

CONTACT

Rev. Robin P. Roddie, Honorary Archivist

DESCRIPTION

The Irish Branch of the Wesley Historical Society in Belfast administers and maintains a comprehensive and unrivalled collection of works on or relating to Methodism in Ireland. It was founded in 1926 to promote the study of the Methodist Church in Ireland.

HOLDINGS

The collection comprises over 8,000 items and is particularly strong in the works of John and Charles Wesley and Adam Clark. It contains extensive runs of Methodist journals and periodicals, including the *Irish Evangelist* (1859–83), the *Christian Advocate* (1883–1923), the *Irish Christian Advocate* (1923–71) and the *Methodist Newsletter* (1973–). Other series include the Dublin edition of the *Methodist Magazine* (1801–23) and the *Primitive Wesleyan Methodist Magazine* (1823–45) which was unique to Ireland. The collection also includes a range of original and printed manuscript materials. These comprise the archives of the Irish Branch of the Wesley Historical Society from 1926 onwards, original diaries and journals of Irish preachers such as the Reverend Adam Averell (1754–1847), founder of the Irish Primitive Wesleyans in 1818, a complete series of minutes of the Irish Conference from 1752, Methodist church registers, photographs and other ephemera relating to Methodism in Ireland. Of major interest is the biographical information that has been collected on Methodist preachers and ministers in Ireland. Alphabetical name, geographical and keyword card catalogues to the periodicals and journals are available on site for consultation. A shelf list in manuscript detailing archival holdings is also available.

LOCATION

In south Belfast, close to the Malone Road.

## M'SKIMIN ROOM

Carrickfergus Library
2 Joymount Court
CARRICKFERGUS, CO. ANTRIM, BT38 7DQ
Northern Ireland

TELEPHONE: (028) 9336 2261; FAX: (028) 9336 0589
E-mail: jennifer.austin@neelb.org.uk
Website: www.neelb.org.uk

HOURS

M,W,F, 10:00am–8:00pm; Tu,Th, 10:00am–5:30pm; Sat 10:00am–5:00pm

ACCESS AND SERVICES

Visitors welcome. Borrowing privileges available. Disabled access facilities.

CONTACT

Jennifer Austin, Group Librarian, Carrickfergus Group

DESCRIPTION

Special local collection held in the Carrickfergus Library, named after an eighteenth-century historian of Carrickfergus, Samuel M'Skimin. The library is part of the North-Eastern Education and Library Board, which oversees 38 libraries in the north-east region of Northern Ireland.

HOLDINGS

The collection focuses on Carrickfergus and the surrounding area. It houses nearly 1,000 volumes, with a special emphasis on county histories and Irish literature. The collection includes journals, maps, microforms, newspapers, and newspaper cuttings. The library's general collection exceeds 30,000 volumes.

LOCATION

The library is close to the town centre and near Carrickfergus Castle, one of the best-preserved Norman castles in Ireland. Carrickfergus is situated along the coast just north of Belfast.

## THE SOCIETY OF FRIENDS LIBRARY

Meeting House
Railway Street
LISBURN, CO. ANTRIM BT28 1XG
Northern Ireland

TELEPHONE: none
E-mail: none
Website: none

ACCESS AND SERVICES

The library deals with postal enquiries only.

CONTACT

Librarian

DESCRIPTION

The archive of the Religious Society of Friends in Ulster.

HOLDINGS

The Religious Society of Friends, or Quakers as they are commonly known, kept amazingly detailed records, many of which date back to the 17th century. The library in Lisburn holds all the original surviving records of the Ulster Province Meeting and its constituent meetings with the sole exception of the first minute book of the Ulster Province Meeting which is in the HISTORICAL LIBRARY, RELIGIOUS SOCIETY OF FRIENDS in Dublin. These minute books begin in 1674. A large amount of additional documentary source material is also available, including, for the Ulster Province/Quarterly Meeting, copies of marriage certificates (1731–86), a Book of Sufferings (1748–1809), and a register of births and burials (1841–58). Material from the local meetings survives for Antrim, Ballyhagen, Cootehill, Grange (near Charlemont), Lisburn, Lurgan and Richhill. For the Lisburn and Lurgan meetings there are minute books from 1675. Of particular interest from the Ballyhagen meeting is a collection of wills with detailed inventories dating from the late 17th and early 18th centuries. There are also family lists from *c.*1680. Copies of these records are available in the PUBLIC RECORD OFFICE OF NORTHERN IRELAND under T/1062 and MIC/16. A list of the Ulster material, compiled by B.G. Hutton, can be found in the *Guide to Irish Quaker Records, 1654–1860* published by the Irish Manuscripts Commission in 1967.

LOCATION

Lisburn town centre.

## UNIVERSITY OF ULSTER LIBRARY, JORDANSTOWN CAMPUS

Shore Road
NEWTOWNABBEY, CO. ANTRIM, BT37 0QB
Northern Ireland

TELEPHONE: (028) 9036 6964; FAX: (028) 9036 6849
E-mail: m.mccullough@ulst.ac.uk
Website: www.ulst.ac.uk/library

### HOURS

Term: M–F, 9:00am–10:00pm; Sat, 10:00am–5:00pm
Vacation: M–Th, 9:00am–5:00pm; F, 9:00am–4:00pm

### ACCESS AND SERVICES

Visitors welcome but advance notice is preferred. Borrowing privileges and database searching are not usually extended to external visitors. Application for access to special collections preferred. Disabled access facilities. The entire University of Ulster shares a common catalogue database. Fees apply for photocopying and microform print services, with advance notice preferred.

### CONTACT

Mary McCullough, Campus Library Manager

### DESCRIPTION

The Jordanstown campus is part of the four-campus University of Ulster system, which also includes Belfast, Coleraine and Magee (in Derry City). Jordanstown is the largest of the four campus libraries in the University of Ulster system. In 2001/2002 it moved into a new, state-of the-art Learning Resources Centre with over 900 networked reader spaces.

### HOLDINGS

The library houses a collection of 280,000 volumes, plus significant holdings of journals (2,000 titles), microforms, newspapers, pamphlets, and recordings. Its special subject areas are business and management, social services, health sciences, informatics, and engineering. Special collections of note include the Irish Travellers Collection and a collection of radical English-language newspapers and journals on microfilm. The library does not house any genealogical sources of note.

### LOCATION

Seven miles north of Belfast, along the coast.

# COUNTY ARMAGH

## ARMAGH ANCESTRY

33A English Street
ARMAGH, BT61 7BA
Northern Ireland

TELEPHONE: (028) 3752 1802; FAX: (028) 3751 0033
E-mail: ancestry@acdc.btinternet.com
Website: www.armagh.gov.uk/history/ancestry.php3

HOURS

M–F, 9:00am–5:00pm; Sat, by appointment

ACCESS AND SERVICES

Private and publicly funded genealogical service centre open to the public. Visitors welcome but advance notice preferred. Disabled access facilities. No fee for access to library. The centre offers fee-based, professional genealogical research services, and even a genealogical tour planned around the visitor's family history. Fees vary depending on service and time involved. The centre also sells locally produced crafts, family crests, ancestral tree charts, maps, books and material of a genealogical interest.

CONTACT

Feargal O'Donnell, Lead Genealogical Researcher.

DESCRIPTION

Armagh Ancestry, established in 1992, participates in the Irish Genealogical Project (IGP), an effort to create a comprehensive genealogical database for all Ireland from a wide variety of sources, including church and state records, Tithe Applotment Books, Griffith's Valuation, the 1901 Census, and gravestone inscriptions. For a list of other participants in the IGP, see index. Armagh Ancestry offers a genealogical research service for Co. Armagh. Computerization of genealogical records for Co. Armagh has been under way since 1985. Complete records include all the Co. Armagh Catholic registers up to 1900; civil births 1864–1922 and marriages 1845–1922; and some Protestant registers up to 1900. Currently, the centre is inputting civil deaths 1864–1922 and pre-1900 church registers of all denominations. In 1997 the Armagh Records Centre was transferred to Armagh Ancestry. The Records Centre had computerized pre-1900 Catholic parish registers of the Archdiocese of Armagh, covering 60 parishes spread over three counties: most of Armagh, a large part of east and central Tyrone and all of Louth. Armagh Ancestry also offers a PRONI (PUBLIC RECORD OFFICE OF NORTHERN IRELAND) outreach facility.

HOLDINGS

The centre offers a small genealogical library for consultation, with special emphasis on Co. Armagh. Items of special interest include: computerized database of Co. Armagh church and civil records, CD-ROM of Griffith's Valuation, and Tithe Applotment Books.

LOCATION

Armagh Ancestry is located in the city centre, within the St Patrick's Trian Visitor's Complex behind the Tourist Information Centre. Public car-parks nearby.

### ARMAGH BRANCH LIBRARY

Market Street
ARMAGH, BT61 7BU
Northern Ireland

TELEPHONE: (028) 3752 4072; FAX: None
E-mail: selb.hq@selb.org
Website: www.selb.org

HOURS

M,F, 9:30am–6:00pm; Tu,Th, 9:30am–8:00pm; W,Sat, 9:30am–5:00pm

ACCESS AND SERVICES

Visitors welcome, identification required. Borrowing privileges for visitors may be restricted. Consult with Librarian. Disabled access facilities.

CONTACT

A.M. Quinn, Librarian

DESCRIPTION

Small branch library, part of the Southern Education and Library Board network of local libraries, with access to the Board's larger collection through interlibrary loan.

HOLDINGS

General educational and recreational collection, including audiovisual materials, with good reference collection. Access available to the board's larger collection, including SELB IRISH AND LOCAL STUDIES LIBRARY, Armagh.

LOCATION

City centre.

## ARMAGH COUNTY MUSEUM

The Mall East
ARMAGH, BT61 9BE
Northern Ireland

TELEPHONE: (028) 3752 3070; FAX: (028) 3752 2631
E-mail: acm.um@nics.gov.uk
Website: www.magni.org.uk

HOURS

M–F, 10:00am–5:00pm; Sat, 10:00am–1:00pm, 2:00–5:00pm; closed statutory bank holidays

ACCESS AND SERVICES

Publicly funded museum whose library and exhibits are open to the public free of charge. Disabled access facilities; library stacks closed. At least two weeks' advance notification by letter preferred for access to research collections. Laptops permitted; pencils only in library. Photocopying available; free public parking. The library issues leaflets and brochures. Copies of its publication, *Harvest Home: The Last Sheaf, a Selection of the Writings of T.G.F. Paterson Relating to County Armagh* (1975), are still available in the museum shop.

CONTACT

Catherine McCullough, Curator

DESCRIPTION

Armagh County Museum is a branch of the Ulster Museum, Belfast, and part of the Museums and Galleries of Northern Ireland (MAGNI). *See also* ULSTER-AMERICAN FOLK PARK, Omagh, Co. Tyrone; ULSTER FOLK AND TRANSPORT MUSEUM, Cultra, Co. Down; and ULSTER MUSEUM, Belfast, Co. Antrim. A community museum focusing on the County of Armagh, it contains one of the finest county collections in Ireland. The museum is housed in a distinctive classical-revival building, which first opened in 1834 as a school.

HOLDINGS

Museum holdings include art works, archaeological objects, local and natural history specimens, textile, railway, and military artefact collections. Paintings of note include John Luke's *The Old Callan Bridge* and many works by George Russell (Æ). The library houses approximately 10,000 volumes and 48 linear feet of manuscripts, plus a small collection of photographs. The holdings are especially strong in local history, with important collections of maps and prints. Subject areas include: archaeology; history; folk and rural life; fine arts and crafts; natural history; military history; and costume relating to the County of Armagh. Among special collections of note are: the T.G.F. Paterson manuscript collection (300 bound volumes), including working papers with notes on local families and buildings; a collection of Paterson's journal *Armachiana* Vols 1–24, including Paterson's typed notes with indexes; the journals (seven vols) of William Blacker

(1777–1855), including local notes and jottings with an account of the Battle of the Diamond (1795); and manuscripts and illustrated poems of George Russell (Æ) (1867–1935). Of special genealogical interest are the Ordnance Survey maps (1834) for Counties Tyrone and Armagh, a printed copy of Griffith's Valuation for Co. Armagh, and the Paterson Collection.

LOCATION

The museum is situated on the Mall, an urban parkland in the centre of Armagh.

## ARMAGH DIOCESAN ARCHIVES

*See* CARDINAL TÓMAS Ó FIAICH LIBRARY AND ARCHIVE, Armagh

## ARMAGH OBSERVATORY

College Hill
ARMAGH, BT61 9DG
Northern Ireland

TELEPHONE: (028) 3752 2928; FAX: (028) 3752 7174
E-mail: jmf@star.arm.ac.uk
Website: star.arm.ac.uk; climate.arm.ac.uk

HOURS

M–F, 9:00am–5:00pm; closed statutory bank holidays

ACCESS AND SERVICES

Publicly funded, non-circulating library and archives open to researchers by appointment; advance notice to Librarian required. Stacks open except for special collections. Collection catalogued on cards; a printed catalogue for part of the collection is also available. The textbook collection of some 2,000 books is listed in a Microsoft Access database for in-house use. Access to the library is free, but charges may be made for use of library or its services at the discretion of the Librarian. See the Observatory's website for activities and programmes.

CONTACT

John McFarland, Librarian

DESCRIPTION

The Armagh Observatory was founded in 1790 by Archbishop Richard Robinson, Church of Ireland Primate, who also founded the Armagh Public Library. The Observatory continues to function as an important player in astronomical research, and its library and archives, housed in the observatory's original Georgian mansion, seek to maintain a centralized Northern Ireland astronomical collection.

HOLDINGS

The library and archives hold approximately 2,000 books, 5,000 photographs, 200 linear feet of manuscripts, 50 periodical subscriptions, and a very strong collection of some 15,000 journal volumes. In addition to astronomy, the library has strong holdings in mathematics, physics, astrophysics, climate, and climate change. The archives contain documents relating to the administration of the observatory, observations, meteorological records, personal papers, and astronomical drawings. Among special collections of significance are: a collection of historical instruments, the manuscripts of J.L.E. Dreyer, the papers of J.A. Hamilton, the papers of T.R. Robinson, and the T.R. Robinson (1792–1882) Collection of Rare and Antiquarian Books (200 vols). A more detailed list of holdings can be found on the RASCAL (Research And Special Collections Available Locally) website: www.rascal.ac.uk.

LOCATION

The observatory is close to the city centre, and the library is in the main Observatory building. Limited free parking.

## ARMAGH PUBLIC LIBRARY

Abbey Street
ARMAGH, BT61 7DY
Northern Ireland

TELEPHONE: (028) 3752 3142; FAX: (028) 3752 4177
E-mail: ArmROBLib@aol.com
Website: www.armaghrobinsonlibrary.org

HOURS

M–F, 9:30am–1:00pm, 2:00–4:00pm; closed bank holidays

ACCESS AND SERVICES

Private, non-circulating library, open to the public. There is no fee for the casual visitor, but donations are appreciated. There is a £5.00 charge either for use of the library or for a tour, with a flat charge of £25 for tour groups of ten or more. Disabled access facilities available. Advance notice for specific research requests preferred. Fees for photocopying and fax services. Pencils only; laptops and cameras with permission of librarian. No bags allowed. Card catalogue for the book collection; printed catalogue for the manuscript collection. Recently the entire collection was re-catalogued on computer using the local Education and Library Board database. Publications of interest include: James Dean, *Catalogue of Manuscripts in the Public Library of Armagh* (1928), and Colin McKelvie, 'Early English Books in Armagh Public Library: A Short-title Catalogue of Books Printed before 1641', *Irish Booklore* 3: 91–103.

CONTACT

The Very Reverend Dean Cassidy, Keeper

DESCRIPTION

The Armagh Public Library, also known as the Robinson Library, was founded in 1771 by Archbishop Richard Robinson, Church of Ireland Primate, who also founded the Armagh Observatory. It is housed in a late 18th-century classical-revival building.

HOLDINGS

The library houses some 20,000 volumes, including the archbishop's personal collection of early printed books on history, canon and civil law, heraldry, literature, medicine, philosophy, religion, theology, and travel. The Robinson Collection is fully integrated into the library's collection, which has been enhanced over the past two centuries chiefly by other clerical collections. In recent times the library has concentrated on ecclesiastical history, St Patrick and Jonathan Swift. Book highlights include incunabula, Colgan's *Acta Sanctorum Hiberniae* (1645), a Breeches Bible, and a first edition of *Gulliver's Travels*, with marginal emendations in Swift's own hand. The manuscript collection includes medieval and early modern European items, many of an Irish interest, especially concerning lands and tithes records. Other collection highlights include: a fine map collection; a collection of engravings, known as the Rokeby Collection; and Archbishop Marcus Gervais Beresford's collection of Irish artefacts.

LOCATION

The library is located near the city centre, close to the Church of Ireland Cathedral. Ample free parking is available at the cathedral.

## CARDINAL TOMÁS Ó FIAICH LIBRARY AND ARCHIVE

15 Moy Road
ARMAGH, BBT61 7LY
Northern Ireland

TELEPHONE: (028) 3752 2981; FAX: (028) 3751 1944
E-mail: ofiaichlibrary@btinternet.com
Website: None

HOURS

M–F, 9:30am–1:00pm, 2:00–5:00pm; closed statutory bank holidays

ACCESS AND SERVICES

Visitors welcome, but advance notice preferred and identification and references required. Advance notice required for special services. Disabled access facilities. Laptops permitted; pencils only. Fees for photocopying and faxing services.

Access to some collections may be limited to serious researchers. The library hosts an annual series of lectures and seminars relating to Irish history, literature, and Church history. It also offers a full Irish-language service to its readers, and hosts the Armagh Diocesan Historical Society, whose journal, *Seanchas Ard Mhacha* (1954–), is published annually.

CONTACT

Crónán Ó Doibhlin, Librarian

DESCRIPTION

The Ó Fiaich Library, named in memory Cardinal Tomás Ó Fiaich (1923–90), former Archbishop of Armagh and Catholic Primate of All Ireland, is an independent, free, public, non-circulating reference library. It opened in 1999. The library collects and promotes research in the areas that were of special cultural and academic interest to Cardinal Ó Fiaich. The library is in partnership with UNIVERSITY COLLEGE DUBLIN, Department of Archives, the Department of Modern History and the Ó Cleirigh Institute.

HOLDINGS

The library houses a collection of some 20,000 books, 450 periodicals, manuscripts, art and artefacts, maps, microforms, photographs and recordings focusing on Irish history, church history, Irish language and literature, local history, especially the Archdiocese of Armagh, Irish sport, and the Irish overseas. Its principal collections include the personal library and papers of Tomás Ó Fiaich, the archive of the Archdiocese of Armagh (1787–1963), and the Micheline Kerney Walsh Overseas Archive. Of special genealogical interest are the library's reference sources and supplementary information.

LOCATION

The library is visible from the A29, the Dungannon/Moy Road, to the rear of the Catholic Cathedral. The main entrance to the library is on the A29, to the left leaving Armagh City. Parking is available to the right-hand side of the library building.

## ARMAGH RECORDS CENTRE

*See* CARDINAL TÓMAS Ó FIAICH LIBRARY AND ARCHIVE, Armagh

## IRISH AND LOCAL STUDIES LIBRARY

*See* SELB IRISH AND LOCAL STUDIES LIBRARY, Armagh

## QUEEN'S UNIVERSITY BELFAST LIBRARY, ARMAGH CAMPUS

39 Abbey Street
ARMAGH, BT61 7EB
Northern Ireland

TELEPHONE: (028) 3751 0678; FAX: (028) 3751 0679
E-mail: c.haughey@qub.ac.uk
Website: www.qub.ac.uk/arm

HOURS

M–Th, 9:00am–9:00pm; F, 9:00am–7:00pm; Sat, 9:00am–12:30pm
Vacation, M–F, 9:00am–5:00pm

ACCESS AND SERVICES

Visitors welcome, identification required. Borrowing privileges for visitors may be restricted. Consult with librarian. Disabled access facilities.

CONTACT

Colette Haughey, Librarian; e-mail: c.haughey@qub.ac.uk

DESCRIPTION

The library at Armagh provides a service primarily for students studying at the Armagh Campus of Queen's.

HOLDINGS

Library holdings currently consist mainly of recommended textbooks and course readings for the modules and courses that are taught at this campus. Recently, however, the library received the extensive private library of Cardinal Cahal Daly, former Catholic Archbishop of Armagh and Primate of All Ireland. The SELB Irish and Local Studies Library shares accommodations with QUB, Armagh Campus, creating a substantial repository of research materials at one convenient location.

LOCATION

Near city centre, in old City Hospital site.

## ROBINSON LIBRARY

*See* ARMAGH PUBLIC LIBRARY, Armagh

## SELB IRISH AND LOCAL STUDIES LIBRARY

39c Abbey Street
ARMAGH, BT61 7EB
Northern Ireland

TELEPHONE: (028) 3752 8751; FAX: (028) 3752 6879
E-mail: selb.hq@selb.org
Website: www.selb.org

HOURS

To be arranged

ACCESS AND SERVICES

The library shares accommodations with Queen's University Belfast, Armagh Campus, and with the North–South Secretariat, at the old City Hospital site close to the centre of Armagh City. Its entrance is from the main car-park and access to the reading room is via lift or staircase. Visitors welcome. A small section of the stock is on open access in the reading room and the remainder is held on the floor below. Individual study carrels can be hired for specified periods. Photocopying facilities available. A separate room houses the microforms collection and microform readers. Publications include brochures and the pamphlet *Irish Railway Literature: A Select List of Publications.*

CONTACT

Mary T. McVeigh, Irish Studies Librarian

DESCRIPTION

The library was established by the Southern Education and Library Board in the late 1970s, and its policy has been to collect material on all aspects of Irish life and learning from earliest times to the present, but with particular emphasis on the area covered by the SELB, i.e. Co. Armagh, South Down and East Tyrone.

HOLDINGS

The library houses more than 20,000 volumes, 350 journal titles, 3,000 maps, 3,800 microforms, 50 newspapers, 1,500 pamphlets, and 2,500 photographs. It also houses a small collection of manuscripts. Among its special collections are pamphlet collections on 18th- and early 19th-century political and economic history, and the Francis Crossle Manuscript Collection on the Newry area, including some 200 notebooks compiled by Dr Crossle containing histories of families in the Newry area.

LOCATION

Near city centre, in old City Hospital site, with entrance from the main car-park. Take lift or stairs to reading room.

# COUNTY CARLOW

## CARLOW CENTRAL LIBRARY

Tullow Street
CARLOW TOWN, CO. CARLOW
Ireland

TELEPHONE: (0503) 70094; FAX: (0503) 40548
E-mail: library@carlowcoco.ie
Website: www.carlow.ie

HOURS

M–F, 9:45am–5:30pm; Sat, 9:45am–1:00pm; open 6:30–8:30pm on Tu,Th

ACCESS AND SERVICES

Visitors welcome. Membership required for borrowing privileges. Identification required for application. Photocopying services available for a modest fee. Free Internet access.

CONTACT

Thomas King, County Librarian; e-mail: library@carlowcoco.ie

DESCRIPTION

Carlow County Library operates branches in Carlow, Muine Bheag (Bagenalstown) and Tullow.

HOLDINGS

The Local Studies Collection is housed in the Carlow branch. This collection includes the Jackson, Bruen, and Tyndall Collections, and the Baggot Papers, Burton Papers and Vigors Papers. It also includes an extensive newspaper collection on microfilm and/or hard copy. Newspapers held include: *Nationalist and Leinster Times*, Sept. 1883–1998 (microfilm), 1981 to present (hard copy); *Carlow People*, 1997 to present (hard copy); *Carlow Sentinel*, 1832–1920 (microfilm); *Carlow Morning Post*, 1818–Nov. 1822, 1828–Jan. 1835 (microfilm); *Carlow Post*, 1853–1878 (microfilm); *Carlow Independent*, 1879–June 1882 (microfilm); *Leinster Independent*, 26 Dec. 1834 – 18 Apr. 1840 (microfilm); *Leinster Reformer*, 1840–41 (hard copy); *Carlow Standard*, 2 Jan.–19 Apr. 1832 (microfilm); *Carlow Vindicator*, 1892 (microfilm); *Carlow Weekly News*, 27 Mar. 1858 – 24 Oct. 1863 (microfilm); *Finn's Leinster Journal*, 1767–1806 (microfilm); *Leinster Journal*, 1807–12 (microfilm); *Irish Times*, 1965–Mar. 2002 (microfilm), May 2002 to present (hard copy). Map holdings include: Down Survey Barony & Civil Parish Maps with Terriers of Co. Carlow 1654; Ordnance Survey six-inch maps for Co. Carlow 1840 and 1879; Ordnance Survey Large-Scale (5ft) Town Maps: Carlow, Muine Bheag, Tullow, Leighlinbridge 1873; Archaeological Survey Maps with index volume of Co. Carlow (Office of Public Works) 1986. Other sources, especially of genealogical interest, include: Tithe Applotment Books for Co. Carlow (*c.*1830); Griffith's Valuation of Co. Carlow and valuation maps, 1853; Carlow Poor Law Union Minute Books 1845–1923; Census of Population for Co. Carlow, 1901 (complete records); Census of Population for Co. Carlow, 1911 (complete records); folklore – Carlow Schools Folklore Manuscripts on microfilm 1937–8; and directories, including a range of Thom's and other local directories.

LOCATION

Town centre

## CARLOW GENEALOGY PROJECT

Old School
College Street
CARLOW TOWN, CO. CARLOW
Ireland

TELEPHONE: (0503) 30850; FAX: (0503) 30850
E-mail: carlowgenealogy@iolfree.ie
Website: www.irishroots.net/carlow.htm

HOURS

M–Th, 9:00am–1:00pm, 2:00–5:00pm; F, 9:00am–1:00pm, 2:00–3:30pm

ACCESS AND SERVICES

Visitors are welcome, but current premises are temporary. Enquiries by mail, e-mail, telephone and fax preferred. The project is currently offering a fee-based, partial research service to the public. Catholic Church records are the only source that can be searched at present. Civil records are expected to be available in early 2003. The 1901 Census and Griffith's Valuation are expected to be available in late 2003. Initial enquiries are acknowledged within one or two weeks. Clients are informed of research results within one or two months.

CONTACT

Mary Moore, Project Coordinator

DESCRIPTION

A member of the Irish Family History Foundation, Carlow Research Centre offers computerized searching of vital records for those interested in tracing their roots in Co. Carlow. Common Carlow surnames include: Byrne, Doyle, Farrell, Kavanagh, Kinsella, Lawler/Lalor, McDonald/McDonnell, Murphy, Nolan, Walsh. Main towns and villages in Co. Carlow include: Ardattin, Bagenalstown, Ballinabranagh, Ballinkillen, Ballon, Ballymurphy, Borris, Carlow, Clonegal, Clonmore, Fennagh, Garryhill, Graiguecullen, Grange, Hacketstown, Kildavin, Leighlinbridge, Myshall, Nurney, Old Leighlin, Rathoe, St Mullins, Tinryland, and Tullow.

HOLDINGS

Currently only Catholic records from Co. Carlow are indexed. Civil records are being indexed and computerized.

LOCATION

Town centre.

# COUNTY CAVAN

## BAILIEBORO LIBRARY

Market Square
BAILIEBORO, CO. CAVAN
Ireland

TELEPHONE: (042) 966 5779; FAX: None
E-mail: Bailieborolibrary@Hotmail.com; cavancountylibrary@eircom.net
Website: None. See county library website: www.iol.ie/~libcounc/cavan.htm

HOURS

M,W,F,Sat, 10:30am–5:15pm; Tu,Th, 1:30–8:30pm

ACCESS AND SERVICES

Visitors welcome. Advance notice preferred and identification required. Disabled access facilities. No borrowing privileges for non-members. Photocopier available. Free Internet access for members. Approximately 20% of collection catalogued by computer, the remainder on cards.

CONTACT
Fiona Burke, Senior Library Assistant

DESCRIPTION

Former market house converted to a library in 1992. The system is operated by Cavan County Council Library Services.

HOLDINGS

The library houses a book stock of some 9,000 volumes, with a good local history collection, including a copy of Griffith's Valuation for most of Co. Cavan.

LOCATION

Town centre.

## CAVAN COUNTY LIBRARY

Farnham Street
CAVAN, CO. CAVAN
Ireland

TELEPHONE: (049) 433 1799; FAX: (049) 433 1384
E-mail: cavancountylibrary@eircom.net
Website: www.iol.ie/~libcounc/cavan.htm

HOURS

M,Th, 11:00am–1:00pm, 2:00–5:00pm, 6:00–8:30pm; Tu,W, 11:00am–5:00pm; F, 11:00am–1:00pm, 2:00–5:00pm

## ACCESS AND SERVICES

Visitors welcome. Advance notice preferred and identification required. Disabled access facilities. Photocopiers, microform readers/printers, and Internet services available.

## CONTACT

Josephine Brady, County Librarian

## DESCRIPTION

The library is the central library in the county's 12-library system. Of these, only the Cavan Library and the Bailieboro Library operate at least five days per week. The system is operated by Cavan County Council Library Services.

## HOLDINGS

The library houses a strong local history collection, approaching 4,000 volumes, including many 18th- and 19th-century books on Cavan Town and Co. Cavan; maps, including the 1835 Ordnance Survey for Co. Cavan, the Cavan–Leitrim Railway, and the South-Western Section of Farnham Estate; important holdings of social and genealogical concern, including Cavan Assizes, 1807–51, which record individuals charged with crimes and the verdicts rendered; 18th- and 19th-century legal documents, such as leases, rentals and wills for Co. Cavan, account and fee books, and inspectors' reports from Bailieboro Model School, 1860s–1900s; Minute Books for the Board of Guardians (1839–1921) and the Rural District Council (1899–1925); diaries, including the diary of Randal McCollum, Presbyterian minister, Shercock, Co. Cavan, describing social conditions in Cavan 1861–71; photographs and postcards; and the correspondence and papers of various local personages. There is an extensive microfilm and photocopy collection of materials relating to Co. Cavan, especially rich in family history sources, newspaper holdings and directories. Genealogical sources also include the 1821, 1901 and 1911 Censuses, Griffith's Valuation, and Tithe Applotment Books.

## LOCATION

Town centre. Nearby car-parks and limited on-street parking.

## CO. CAVAN GENEALOGICAL RESEARCH CENTRE

Cana House
Farnham Street
CAVAN, CO. CAVAN
Ireland

TELEPHONE: (049) 436 1094; FAX: (049) 433 1494
E-mail: canahous@iol.ie
Website: cavangenealogy.com (registered but not operational at present)

### HOURS

M–F, 9:00am–5:00pm; closed Christmas and Easter holidays, and public holidays

### ACCESS AND SERVICES

Visitors welcome. Disabled access facilities, with a ground-floor reception area and ramped entrance. No admission fee, but fees are charged for genealogical searches. There is a 35 euro registration fee for a full search of the database and the centre also offers a single record search for 20 euro. Otherwise, prices are as per the Family History Foundation's price list. The centre offers for sale various parish histories and other books relating to Co. Cavan and all the publications of *Cumann Seanchais Bhreifne* (Breifne Historical Society). There is a small gift shop, which includes the work of artists and craftspeople from the region.

### CONTACT

Mary Sullivan, Manager
Concepta McGovern, Senior Researcher

### DESCRIPTION

The centre is a publicly and privately funded genealogical research facility. It is a member of the Irish Genealogical Project, an island-wide effort to computerize all the major Irish genealogical sources. It is also the Irish Family History Foundation's designated genealogical research centre for Co. Cavan.

### HOLDINGS

The centre has been building a database of all genealogical sources that are known to exist for Co. Cavan; to date its database holds over 700,000 records. These include: baptisms; marriages; burials; 1821, 1901 and 1911 Census records; pre- and post-famine land records; gravestone inscriptions; occupational and commercial directories covering the towns dating from 1824; and numerous other genealogical records. The earliest Church records held at the centre date from 1701 and most Roman Catholic parish registers have been indexed to 1920. The centre has a small reference library, which includes books, journals, manuscripts and maps.

LOCATION

Cana House dates back to around 1810 and is located at the back of St Felim's Boys' School on Farnham Street. It is a five-minute walk from the town's main street, and the centre is signed at the gateway entrance, which it shares with the school.

# COUNTY CLARE

## CLARE HERITAGE AND GENEALOGICAL RESEARCH CENTRE

Church Street
COROFIN, CO. CLARE
Ireland

TELEPHONE: (065) 683 7955; FAX: (065) 683 7540
E-mail: clareheritage@eircom.net
Website: www.clareroots.com

HOURS

M–F, 9:00am–5:30pm

ACCESS AND SERVICES

Clare Heritage is a not-for-profit, fee-based genealogical research centre offering a professional service to persons wishing to trace their Clare ancestry. A fee of 135 euro (or equivalent) covers a preliminary report and administrative costs and includes an initial search of the source material that the centre holds, e.g. parish registers, land records, Census returns, civil records. A fee of 315 euro (or equivalent) may be required to complete a full search and covers all expenses and time expended by the centre. The fee will not exceed 315 euro (or equivalent) without prior consultation and advice as to the probability of positive results. Application can be made online with a credit card.

CONTACT

Antoinette O'Brien, Coordinator

DESCRIPTION

The Clare Heritage and Genealogical Research Centre was founded in 1982 by the late Dr Ignatius (Naoise) Cleary. It is a member of the Irish Family History Foundation, the coordinating body for a network of government-approved genealogical research centres in the Republic of Ireland and Northern Ireland that have computerized tens of millions of Irish ancestral records of different types. The Clare Centre now holds data on just over 500,000 people who were born in Co. Clare during the 19th century and into the middle of the 20th century. Common surnames in Co. Clare include: McMahon, McNamara, O'Brien, Moloney, Ryan, Kelly, McInerney, O'Connor, Keane, O'Halloran, Hogan, Burke, Murphy, Lynch, and Walsh. The main towns and villages include: Ennis, Kilrush, Kilkee, Miltown Malbay, Ennistymon, Ballyvaughan, Corofin, Sixmilebridge, Newmarket-On-Fergus, Killaloe, Tulla, Scariff, Feakle, Quin, Kilfenora, Lisdoonvarna, Liscannor, Broadford, Kildysart, Mullagh, and Quilty.

HOLDINGS

The centre has indexed all available Roman Catholic Parish Registers (pre-1900 baptismal and marriage records) for the 47 Clare parishes. The age and condition of these records vary from parish to parish; some records date back to 1802. Because civil recording of births, marriages and deaths does not begin until 1864, parish records remain the main source of genealogical data in Ireland. Also available are: all available Church of Ireland records; Tithe Applotment Land Records (1820s); Griffith's Valuation (1855); 1901 Census; civil records – marriages and deaths (1864–1995) and births (1900–50); New South Wales Archives 1848–69 (6,000 assisted emigrants entries, R. Reid); *Clare Journal* newspaper (1779–1900); birth, marriage and death notices; and tombstone inscriptions from approximately 80 Clare graveyards. Access is also available to: 19th-century workhouse records; reports on some convict trials; many Clare wills; Ordnance Survey maps showing parish and townland boundaries; and a reference library which includes publications and lists on landed gentry, Irish surnames, histories of Co. Clare and its parishes, and various family histories.

LOCATION

The centre is in the village of Corofin, eight miles north of Ennis.

## CLARE COUNTY ARCHIVES SERVICE

Clare County Council
New Road
ENNIS, CO. CLARE
Ireland

TELEPHONE: (065) 682 1616; FAX: None
E-mail: jhayes@clarecoco.ie
Website: www.clarelibrary.ie/eolas/library/local-studies/clarearchives.htm

HOURS

By arrangement through CLARE COUNTY LIBRARY – LOCAL STUDIES CENTRE

ACCESS AND SERVICES

Visitors welcome. Material can be requested and will be made available to researchers through the Local Studies Centre. One day's notice will be required for production of material. As material is processed and listed it will be made available for public inspection.

CONTACT

Jacqui Hayes, Archivist; e-mail: jhayes@clarecoco.ie
Tel: (065) 684 6414

DESCRIPTION

The Archives Service provides for the preservation of, and access by the public to, the archives of Clare County Council, Ennis Urban District Council, Kilrush Urban District Council and Kilkee Town Commissioners, all dating from 1899. It seeks to collect archives relating to community, church, sporting and social organizations as well as material relating to individuals or families of relevance to Co. Clare, with the aim of documenting as many aspects of the county's history and development as possible for this and future generations.

HOLDINGS

Board of Guardian minute books for the Poor Law Unions of Corofin 1850–1924, Ennis 1849–1922, Ennistymon 1839–1924, Kilrush 1842–1923 and Scarriff 1921–2 and Rural District Council Minute Books 1899–1923 for Corofin, Ennis and Ennistymon.

LOCATION

Access through Local Studies Centre. See below for directions.

## CLARE COUNTY LIBRARY – LOCAL STUDIES CENTRE

The Manse, Harmony Row
ENNIS, CO. CLARE
Ireland

TELEPHONE: (065) 684 6271; FAX: (065) 684 2462
E-mail: peter.beirne@clarelibrary.ie
Website: www.clarelibrary.ie/eolas/library/local-studies/locstudi1.htm

HOURS

M, 9:30am–1:00pm, 2:00–5:30pm; Tu–F, 9:30am–1:00pm, 2:00–5:00pm; Sat, 10:00am–2:00pm

ACCESS AND SERVICES

Visitors welcome. No disabled access facilities. Fees for photocopying and microfilm prints. The entire collection is catalogued online.

CONTACT

Peter Beirne, Local Studies Librarian

DESCRIPTION

The Local Studies Centre is housed in the Clare County Library and focuses on material of Irish interest in all subject areas, with special attention to Co. Clare. There is a separate archives department, CLARE COUNTY ARCHIVES SERVICE, Clare County Council, New Road, Ennis, Co. Clare.

HOLDINGS

The Irish Collection houses books (some 8,000) and periodicals relating to Ireland. Journals of specific relevance to Clare include *The North Munster Antiquarian Journal*, *Dal gCais*, *The Other Clare*, *Molua*, *The Clare Association Yearbook*, and *Sliabh Aughty*. Local parish and sporting magazines are also collected. A separate Clare Collection (some 2,000 titles) contains newspapers, photographs, manuscripts, microfilm and maps relating specifically to Co. Clare. The following local newspapers are available: Dunboyne Collection of newspaper clippings, 1824–73; *Ennis Chronicle and Clare Advertiser*, 1828–31; *Clare*

*Freeman and Ennis Gazette*, Feb. 1853–Jan 1884; *Clare Journal & Ennis Advertiser*, 1828–1917; *Limerick Reporter*, 1845–52; *Celtic Times*, 1887; *Clare Champion*, 1903–present; *Clare People*, 1977–80; *County Express*, 1979–present; *Ennis Express*, 1979–82; *Sunday Tribune*, 1983–7; *Irish Times*, 1859–70; 1916–22; 1987–present; *Saturday Record*, Jul. 1898–Sept. 1936; and *The Clare Independent & Tipperary Catholic Times*, 1877–85. The photographic collection contains approximately 4,000 prints of Clare scenes. The Lawrence Collection (1870–1914) is the largest in the archive. Other collections include the Westropp Collection (1900), the McNamara Collection (1910), Irish Tourist Association Survey (1943), and the Bluett (1940s–1960s) and O'Neill (1950s) Collections. Among the special collections are: Schools Folklore Scheme; Twigge Mss; Ordnance Survey Field Name Books; Petworth House Archive (Clare material); *Clare Journal*, 1828–1916; Dorothea Lange Contact Prints; *Clare Champion*, 1903–present; and some estate papers on microfilm. Of special genealogical interest are Griffith's Valuation, Census 1901/1911; Tithe Applotment Books; a first, second and third edition of Ordnance Survey six-inch maps (complete for Co. Clare), and voters' lists. See also holdings of CLARE COUNTY ARCHIVES SERVICE. See website for a more detailed listing of holdings.

Clare County Library has a very active publications programme. In collaboration with the Government training agency FÁS it has issued a dozen titles since 1995. These are still available in print and include:

| Title of Book | Unit Price |
|---|---|
| *Folklore of Clare* | 19.00 euro |
| *Archaeology of the Burren* | 25.30 euro |
| *The Clare Anthology* | 25.30 euro |
| *The Stranger's Gaze* | 25.30 euro |
| *A Handbook to Lisdoonvarna* | 12.60 euro |
| *The Antiquities of County Clare* | 31.70 euro |
| *Kilrush Union Minute Books* | 140.00 euro |
| *Sable Wings Over the Land* | 19.00 euro |
| *County Clare: A History and Topography* | 10.10 euro |
| *Two Months at Kilkee* | 15.15 euro |
| *Poverty Before the Famine* | 19.00 euro |

Available from CLASP Press, Library Headquarters, Mill Road, Ennis, Co. Clare

LOCATION

Turn left at the end of Abbey Street. Located on the left, beside De Valera Library.

## EAST CLARE HERITAGE COMPANY

TUAMGRANEY, CO. CLARE
Ireland

TELEPHONE: (061) 921 615; FAX: None
E-mail: eastclareheritage@eircom.net
Website: www.eastclareheritage.com

HOURS

June–Sept. (open daily); enquiries by mail accepted throughout the year

ACCESS AND SERVICES

East Clare Heritage Company is a totally voluntary and community-based company with charitable status formed in 1989. In 1991 it opened a heritage centre in a 10th-century church at Tuamgraney. The centre offers a fee-based genealogical research service for persons interested in tracing their East Clare family roots. The company charges a fee of 75 euro for a preliminary search of its records. In most cases this is all that will be charged. Enquirers will be notified of any additional costs. Advice is freely given on the availability of records and the possibility of positive results. Applications are available through the company's website. The company publishes local histories and newsletters that include genealogical material. Some of the families covered to date in its publications are the Woods, Reades, Tandys, Logans, Bourchiers, Allens, Tiernans, Huleatts, and Bloxams of Mountshannon; the Reids, Ringroses, Walnutts and Davises of Scariff; the O'Gradys, Bradys, Drews, Parkers and Crottys of Tuamgraney; and the Goonanes of Whitegate. The company has also set up an O'Grady website at www.gradyhistory.com. The company provides boat trips and guided tours to the famous monastic site of Holy Island on Lough Derg.

CONTACT

Gerard Madden, Secretary

DESCRIPTION

East Clare Heritage Company provides a comprehensive family research facility for East Clare and encourages the publication of family history in its annual journal *Sliabh Aughty*. This journal also contains a brief history and the gravestone inscriptions of an East Clare graveyard. To date most of the graveyards are indexed. The tenth edition of this publication is now being published and all ten editions will be available in disk form soon. The company is headquartered in a church built around 950AD, which is claimed to be the oldest church in continuous use in Ireland, England, Scotland and Wales. This proud tradition is being maintained, and service is held here on the last Sunday of each month throughout the year. The church is built on the site of an earlier monastery founded by St Cronin in the 7th century. The Vikings raided the monastery in 886 and again in 949. Cormac Uí Cillín, the Abbot of Tuamgraney, rebuilt the church and erected a round tower prior to his death in 964. Although no trace of the round tower remains, it has the distinction of being the earliest for which there is a written record. Brian Boru, High King of Ireland (1002–1014), repaired the round tower and re-edified and enlarged the church. The building operates as a visitor centre during the summer months. It also houses a folk museum. Dr Edward McLysaght, Ireland's foremost family historian, is interred in the grounds of the church. Tuamgraney is also the hometown of the novelist Edna O'Brien.

## HOLDINGS

In addition to gravestone inscriptions noted above, the company has access to all the standard genealogical reference sources for East Clare, including: Griffith's Valuation; Tithe Applotment Books; Church and civil records; the 1901 Census; Ordnance Survey maps; school registers; and numerous deeds and other legal documents. It also has a number of family histories and continues to compile information on families with East Clare connections.

## LOCATION

Tuamgraney is near the western edge of Lough Derg in Co. Clare. It is about a 40-minute drive from Shannon Airport.

# COUNTY CORK

## BANTRY HOUSE

BANTRY, CO. CORK
Ireland

TELEPHONE: (027) 50047
E-mail: None
Website: www.bantryhouse.ie/home.htm

HOURS

Mar.–Oct.: Sun–Sat, 9:00am–6:30pm

ACCESS

Bantry House is open to the public for an admission charge. Fee schedule: house, gardens and the Armada Exhibition Centre, 9.50 euro per person (accompanied children up to 14 years of age who are not part of a school group are admitted free); students and seniors, 8.00 euro; groups of 20 or more, 6.00 euro; admission to the garden and Armada Exhibition Centre only, 4.00 euro. Admission to the house and grounds is free to residents. Its archive has been deposited at the Boole Library, UNIVERSITY COLLEGE CORK.

CONTACT

For Bantry House: Egerton Shelswell-White, owner
For archives: Carol Quinn, Archivist, University College Cork; e-mail: c.quinn@ucc.ie

DESCRIPTION

Bantry House has been in the White family since 1739, and was the seat of the four Earls of Bantry (1816–91). The house contains furniture, paintings and other *objets d'art* collected for the most part by the 2nd Earl of Bantry, who was also responsible for laying out the formal gardens.

HOLDINGS

This archive contains the formal records of the legal, financial and general administration of Bantry House and estate, and also the more personal records relating to the lives and personalities of the White family who have lived in Bantry House for over 200 years. These documents contain much invaluable social information about the White family and the circles in which they moved, as well as records relating to the tenants who occupied and worked the estate. For further details, see the website for UCC Archives. Please note that this collection is not yet fully processed and is, therefore, not currently accessible. Consult with UCC Archives on current status.

LOCATION

Bantry House is in Bantry Town and overlooks Bantry Bay, 60 miles south-west of Cork City.

## CORK ARCHIVES INSTITUTE

Christ Church
South Main Street
CORK CITY, CO. CORK
Ireland

TELEPHONE: (021) 427 7809; FAX: (021) 427 4668
E-mail: cai@indigo.ie
Website: www.corkcorp.ie/facilities/facilities_archive.html

HOURS

Tu–F, 10:00am–1:00pm, 2:30–5:00pm

ACCESS AND SERVICES

By appointment only, with at least one week's notice if possible. The application form for permission to read records is available in PDF format on the institute's website. Photocopying service available. The institute is unable to undertake genealogical research on behalf of the public.

CONTACT

Brian McGee, Archivist

DESCRIPTION

Cork Archives Institute is the official repository for the local authority records of Cork City and County and is co-funded by Cork City Council, Cork County Council, and University College Cork. The institute acquires, preserves and makes available local archives including those from local private sources such as societies, businesses, families, and individuals. Contents are related mainly to the history of Cork and consist of records, manuscripts, plans and drawings, and some photographs that have been identified as worthy of permanent preservation because of their historical or evidential value.

HOLDINGS

Cork Archives Institute holds one of the finest collections of local archives in Ireland. Collections include the archives of current and former local authorities such as Cork City Council, Cork County Council, town government for Youghal 1609–1965, Poor Law Unions for most of Co. Cork, Rural District Councils and Urban District Councils.

As well as complete sets of minute books of Boards of Guardians for most of the Poor Law Unions in the county 1839–1924 (except Fermoy and Schull) the archive has the most complete collection of workhouse admission registers in the Republic of Ireland. Some of these archives also include pupils' registers for the workhouse 'national' school (in the case of Cork) and books recording deaths and births in workhouses.

*Cork Poor Law Union:*
Workhouse 'Indoor Relief' or admission registers 1840–1920 with indexes from 1853.

Record of death books 1853–1931.

Pupil registers (male) for workhouse national school 1873–1904.

*Kinsale Poor Law Union:* indoor registers 1841–1917; admission and discharge books 1845–1925; pauper discharge books 1855–1884; death record book 1842–1899; register of patients in Fever Hospital 1849–1850.

*Midleton Poor Law Union:* indoor registers 1841–1923; birth register 1844–1930.

*Youghal Poor Law Union:* indoor register 1848–1851; Poor Rate books 1852–1900.

For Youghal there are also town rate books 1833 and voters registers for parts of the county from 1858.

*School records:* there are holdings for Crosshaven and Templebreedy (1880–1972) national schools and a massive collection of *c.*120 vols for Cork District Model School including registers and roll books 1865–1988.

Business records include those of Beamish & Crawford Brewery, Cork Distillers, Cork Butter Market, Cork Gas Company, R&H Hall corn merchants, Sunbeam & Wolsey textile manufactures, Cork Steam Ship Company, Ogilvie & Moore provisioners, and Hickey & Byrne printers. Personal papers include those of politicians, soldiers, civic leaders and literary figures such as Richard Dowden, Mayor of Cork; Liam de Roiste, TD; Seamus Fitzgerald, politician; Liam Ó Buachalla, cultural activist; Geraldine Cummins, author and playwright; and Siobhán Lankford, soldier. A wide variety of landed estate papers are held, such as: Colthurst family, Blarney; Newenham family, South Cork; Courtenay family, Midleton and the Earls of Bandon. The Ryan-Purcell collection is of particular interest because as well as being a land owner, he acted as agent for a number of estates in North Cork. Also held are records of some trade unions, clubs, societies, religious organizations, and schools, including those of Cork Workers' Council, Cork Typographical Union, Cork Presbyterian Congregation, Cork Grafton Club, the Sick Poor Society, Cork Theatre and Cork District Model School.

LOCATION

City centre, next to the Lucey Park.

## CORK CITY ANCESTRAL PROJECT

c/o Cork County Library
Farranlea Road
CORK CITY, CO. CORK
Ireland

TELEPHONE: (021) 434 6435; FAX: None
E-mail: corkancestry@ireland.com
Website: www.irishroots.net/Cork.htm

HOURS

To be announced

ACCESS AND SERVICES

This project is still in development. Only indexing of records is being done at present. However, enquiries may be telephoned or posted to the above number/address. On completion of its indexing project, the centre will offer a fee-based genealogical research service to persons interested in tracing their family roots in Cork City.

CONTACT

Karen O'Riordan

DESCRIPTION

The centre is a member of the Irish Genealogical Project (IGP), an effort to create a comprehensive genealogical database for all Ireland from a wide variety of sources, including church and state records, vital records, Tithe Applotment Books, Griffith's Valuation, the 1901 Census, and gravestone inscriptions.

HOLDINGS

Currently indexing church records for Cork City.

LOCATION

In Cork County Library, near County Hall.

## CORK CITY LIBRARY

Headquarters (Central Library)
57–61 Grand Parade
CORK CITY, CO. CORK
Ireland

TELEPHONE: (021) 427 7110; FAX: (021) 427 5684
E-mail: citylibrary@corkcity.ie
Website: www.corkcitylibrary.ie

HOURS

Tu–Sat, 10:00am–1:00pm, 2:00–5:30pm

ACCESS AND SERVICES

Visitors welcome, but borrowing privileges may be restricted. Membership available for a fee. No membership is required to use the reference or information facilities of the library. These services are provided free of charge except for photocopying charges. Photocopying, fax, and public Internet workstations available. Exhibitions are a regular feature in the Central Library and at all branch libraries. Cork City Library hosts a number of national exhibitions and also exhibitions that involve local organizations and groups.

CONTACT

Hanna O'Sullivan, City Librarian
Tina Healy, Assistant Librarian, Reference Library
Kieran Burke, Assistant Librarian, Local Studies Department
Kitty Buckley, Assistant Librarian, Music Library

DESCRIPTION

Cork City Library is one of the services provided by Cork Corporation. The main objective of the library service is to act as an informational, educational, recreational and cultural centre for the people of Cork. The following public departments are situated at the Central Library on the Grand Parade: adult lending library, children's library, reference department, local history department, and a music library. The library administers five full-time branch libraries and one part-time mobile library service. Three of the branch libraries are on the north side of the city in Hollyhill, Mayfield and at Cathedral Cross; two branches are on the south side in Douglas and Ballyphehane. Plans are being developed to upgrade the Central Library.

HOLDINGS

The reference library houses 30,000 books, including directories, encyclopaedias, government publications, yearbooks and dictionaries, Irish-interest material, journals, periodicals, and Sunday and daily newspapers. Access to the newspaper and journal collection is enhanced by an index, created and added to on a daily basis by library staff, and by online information from databases and the Internet and CD-ROMs. The local studies department or Cork Collection contains some 5,500 books on the history, geography, antiquities, archaeology, folklore and culture of Cork, city and county. The collection also contains microfilm, a comprehensive local newspaper archive, journals, periodicals, manuscripts, maps and photographs. The music library has a stock of 20,000 records, tapes and compact discs in addition to 2,500 scores and 3,000 books. The collection caters for all musical tastes including classical, jazz, light opera, folk, choral, military band music, rock and popular. Audio art tapes, including plays, poetry, prose, and talking books, are available. Free membership of the music library is available for registered visually-impaired citizens. Listening facilities are available in the library. The lending library contains 45,000 adult books and 14,000 children's books.

LOCATION

City centre.

## CORK COUNTY LIBRARY

Farranlea Road,
CORK CITY, CO. CORK
Ireland

TELEPHONE: (021) 454 6499; FAX: (021) 434 3254
E-mail: corkcountylibrary@eircom.net
Website:
www.corkcoco.com/cccmm/services/library/cntyhll/Countyhall_library.htm

HOURS

Reference/Local Studies Department: M–F, 9:00am–1:00pm, 2:00–5:30pm
Lending Department: M–F, 9:00am–5:30pm

ACCESS AND SERVICES

Visitors welcome, but those wishing to avail of microfilm viewers should make appointment. Photocopying (subject to copyright regulations), advice and guidance on research are available; telephone enquiries welcome, but staffing levels limit ability to engage in correspondence on queries. Public Internet workstation available.

CONTACT

Kieran Wyse
Niamh Cronin

DESCRIPTION

Farranlea Road is the headquarters of Cork County Library, which provides a public library service throughout the county via a network of 27 branches and five mobile libraries.

HOLDINGS

Large collection of printed books in Local Studies Collection and Irish Studies Collection. Microfilm holdings include 1901 Census returns (Cork City and County), Tithe Applotment Books (Cork), and 19th- and 20th-century Cork newspapers. Other holdings include Griffith's Valuation (Cork City and County).

LOCATION

Near County Hall, two miles west of city centre.

**CORK PUBLIC MUSEUM (Músaem Poiblí Chorcaí)**

Fitzgerald Park
CORK CITY, CO. CORK
Ireland

TELEPHONE: (021) 427 0679; FAX: (021) 427 0931
E-mail: museum@corkcity.ie
Website: www.corkcity.ie/facilities/facilities_museum.html

HOURS

M–F, 11:00am–1:00pm, 2:15–5:00pm (–6.00pm June–Aug.); Sun, 3:00–5:00pm; closed bank holiday weekends

ACCESS AND SERVICES

Visitors welcome. Admission free. The museum offers exhibits and programmes to the public. Exhibit themes include: prehistory Cork; and Cork crafts, including Cork glassware and Youghal needlepoint lace. The museum also houses an important archives collection anchored by the Michael Collins Collection. A project to create a computer database of the museum's collections has been completed and to date over 24,000 objects have been inputted. Work to create a database of digital images of the museum's collections is under way. The museum now holds a large archive covering the 1916–21 War of Independence period, with particular emphasis on Co. Cork native Michael Collins and on Thomas MacCurtain and Terence MacSwiney, first and second Republican Lord Mayors of Cork respectively (both died in office – MacSwiney by hunger strike in Brixton Prison; MacCurtain murdered by police).

CONTACT

Curator

DESCRIPTION

Cork Public Museum has been preserving and exhibiting the region's cultural heritage since 1945. Recently it expanded its exhibition and storage areas. It is funded by Cork City Council.

HOLDINGS

The museum houses artefacts and archival material that document the history, archaeology and industrial life of Cork City and the surrounding area. Of special interest is the museum's Collection of the Correspondence of Michael Collins, donated in July 2000 by Mr Peter Barry, former TD and Minister for Foreign Affairs. The correspondence between Michael Collins and Kitty Kiernan forms the largest body of the collection. The collection also contains letters from Harry Boland, another leading figure in the fight for independence, a friend of Collins and unsuccessful suitor of Kitty. There are a small number of letters to Collins from various individuals, from Collins to Cumann na mBan and to Kiernan from other individuals.

LOCATION

Fitzgerald Park, off Western Road, along the River Lee.

## NATIONAL UNIVERSITY OF IRELAND, CORK (UCC) – BOOLE LIBRARY

University College Cork
College Road
CORK CITY, CO. CORK
Ireland

TELEPHONE: (021) 490 2281; FAX: (021) 427 3428
E-mail: library@ucc.ie
Website: booleweb.ucc.ie/user/services/external.htm

HOURS

Reading (1st term): M–Th, 8.30am–9:45pm; F, 8:30am–8:45pm; Sat, 10:00am–12:45pm
Reading (2nd & 3rd terms): M–Th, 8:30am–10:15pm; F, 8:30am–9:15pm; Sat (2nd term), 10:00am–5:45pm; Sat (3rd term), 10:00am–9:45pm; Sun (Mar.–May) 10:00am–5:45pm
Summer Vacation (July–mid-Sept.), Lending: M–F, 9:15am–4:15pm; Reading: M–F, 8:30am–4:15pm; Sat, 10:00am–12:45pm

ACCESS AND SERVICES

Visitors admitted at the discretion of the Librarian. Annual membership fee for borrowing privileges. Disabled access facilities. Photocopying and microform prints available for a fee. Leaflets and booklets describing services available. Consult website for special regulations governing external users and use fees. For access to SPECIAL COLLECTIONS AND ARCHIVES see separate entry below. The Medical Library, located at Cork University Hospital, is jointly funded by UCC and the Southern Health Board. Staff and students of UCC, and healthcare professionals working in the University Hospital, St Finbarr's Hospital, and Erinville Hospital, may consult in, and borrow from, the Medical Library. Other healthcare professionals may apply to the Librarian for consultation or borrowing facilities as external readers, on payment of the appropriate fee. One fee covers both the Boole Library and the Medical Library. Consult Subject Librarian Rosarii Buttimer (ext. 1276).

CONTACT

Information Desk; e-mail: informationdesk@ucc.ie or by telephone: (021) 490 2794
Margot Conrick, Head of Information Services; ext. 2926; e-mail: margot@ucc.ie

DESCRIPTION

The Boole Library is the main library for University College Cork, part of the National University of Ireland system that also includes campuses in Dublin, Galway, Limerick, and Maynooth. Its first purpose is to serve the university by 'supporting study, teaching and research as efficiently as possible'. The Boole Library brings together in one large centre many sources of information not readily available elsewhere in Munster. They include books, periodicals, audiovisual materials, a European Community Documentation Centre, online searching, and inter-library loans, together with the professional expertise to interpret the collections to its users.

HOLDINGS

Subjects of concentration include: humanities, law, medicine (CUH), medicine (UCC), official publications, European Documentation Centre, science, and social sciences. The library houses a collection of 600,000 books, 4,000 periodicals (including national and foreign newspapers), a European Documentation Centre which receives most of the basic documents of the European Communities and those of some international organizations, all Irish Government publications, a representative collection of British official publications, tapes, LPs, compact discs, videos, and slides. SPECIAL COLLECTIONS AND ARCHIVES are treated separately immediately below.

LOCATION

The university is located one mile west of city centre. Follow signs to the library.

## NATIONAL UNIVERSITY OF IRELAND, CORK (UCC) – SPECIAL COLLECTIONS AND ARCHIVES

Boole Library
University College Cork
CORK CITY, CO. CORK
Ireland

(Spec. Coll.) TELEPHONE: (021) 490 2282; FAX: (021) 427 3428; (Archives) TELEPHONE: (021) 490 3180; FAX: (021) 427 3428
E-mail: (Spec. Coll.) specialcollections@ucc.ie; (Archives) h.davis@ucc.ie
Website: booleweb.ucc.ie/search/subject/speccol/speccol.htm

HOURS

Special Collections: Term: M–F, 9:00am–8:15pm; Out of Term: 9:30am–4:45pm; July–Sept.: 9.30am–4.15pm
Archives: By appointment only.

ACCESS AND SERVICES

Visitors are welcome but advance notice and identification are required. Wheelchair-accessible. Pencils only; laptop facilities available. Photocopying and microfilm printing facilities are available by arrangement with Special Collections Librarian and are subject to copyright and other restrictions. All material is for consultation only and may not be removed from the library. Printed and electronic guides are available, viz. *Special Collections Boole Library University College Cork: an Introduction*; *Primary Sources for Medieval Studies in the Boole Library Special Collections*; *Sources for Seventeenth to Nineteenth Centuries Historical Studies in the Boole Library Special Collections*. The library's website gives detailed descriptions of holdings.

CONTACT

Helen Davis, Special Collections Librarian; e-mail: h.davis@ucc.ie
Carol Quinn, Archivist; e-mail: c.quinn@ucc.ie

DESCRIPTION

Special Collections of the Boole Library consist of primary source materials in a variety of formats (book, manuscript, map, newspaper, microform, electronic) which support research and teaching in the humanities and social sciences, spanning all periods from classical and early Christian to modern, with a particular emphasis on Ireland (especially Munster) and the Irish diaspora. Private libraries donated by individuals are sometimes maintained as discrete units by special arrangement. Since 1997 this category includes archival collections relating primarily, but not exclusively, to Munster families and businesses.

HOLDINGS

Special Collections holdings include archives, books, manuscripts, facsimiles of manuscripts, maps, microforms, newspapers, pamphlets, journals, theses, photographs and recordings. These collections are divided into three main categories: Manuscripts, Printed Books and Archives Service.

**Manuscripts**: Highlights from the Manuscript Collections include: Gaelic manuscripts, divided into two main series: (1) the 'Torna Collection' containing manuscripts which belonged to Professor Tadhg Ó Donnchadha, Professor of Irish at University College Cork (1916–44), and catalogued by Professor Padraigh de Brun of the Dublin Institute for Advanced Studies, Clár Lámhscribhinni Gaeilge Cholaiste Ollscoile Chorcai: Cnuasach Thorna (Ref. Coll 017 DEBR). Torna MSS are identified numerically with 'T' prefix. (2) 'Other Gaelic Manuscript Collections' consists of over 200 manuscripts purchased by or donated to the library. Seventy-seven of these belonged to Professor James E.H. Murphy, Professor of Irish at Trinity College Dublin (1896–1919). A catalogue of this collection has been compiled by Dr Breandan Ó Conchuir, Department of Modern Irish at University College Cork and published by the Dublin Institute for Advanced Studies (1991), Clár Lámhscribhinni Gaeilge Cholaiste Ollscoile Chorcai: Cnuasach Ui Mhurchu (Ref. Coll 017 OCON). Most of the remainder belonged to Canon Power, Lecturer in and later Professor of Archaeology at University College Cork (1915–32). The catalogue of these and the other Gaelic MSS in the collection has been prepared by Dr Breandan Ó Conchuir, and is currently in press. There is a list available at the enquiry desk in the research room. Non-Gaelic manuscripts are grouped as 'manuscripts in English and/or bilingual'. These include the papers of various eminent professors (including George Boole, Tadhg Ó Donnchadha (Torna), Daniel Corkery, Cormac Ó Cuilleanain) and reflect part of the intellectual history of the college; they constitute a large portion of this collection. Archival descriptive lists of the Boole and Corkery papers are available at the enquiry desk. Access to other items in the collections is gained through the list at the enquiry desk in the research room. Please note that Torna's papers are entirely independent of the Torna Collection of Manuscripts. Also included in this category are documents belonging to and relating to individuals or enterprises, e.g. William O'Brien; Kinsale Manorial Records. An archival finding list is available for the William O'Brien papers; otherwise access is through the list at the enquiry desk in the research room.

The Manuscript Collection also includes several manuscript estate maps, music scores, and minor Middle Eastern and Far Eastern Manuscripts. In addition, there are 'manuscripts on microfilm', which include a large collection of manuscripts of Gaelic and historical interest, such as the Gaelic Manuscripts in the Royal Irish Academy, the Folklore Collections at University College Dublin, manuscripts in the National Archives, Public Records Offices in London and Belfast, and other institutions in Ireland and abroad. List of holdings is available at the enquiry desk. Of special genealogical interest are microfilm copies of Petty's Parish Maps for most of Munster, the originals of which are in the National Library; the 1901 Census returns for most of Munster; and all published censuses up to and including 1911. Holdings of manuscripts in facsimile are quite extensive. Among these are: the Books of Kells, Durrow, and Lindisfarne; those published by the Irish Manuscripts Commission and the Royal Irish Academy; the Domesday Book; the Utrecht Psalter; and several Books of Hours. Early English Manuscripts in Facsimile series are also available, as are modern manuscript facsimiles, including the works of John Milton and James Joyce, and the letters of Paul Valéry.

**Printed Books:** Major printed book collections include: Pre-1850 Books – some 13,000 books and pamphlets published before 1850; St Fin Barre's Cathedral Library, which consists of some 3,000 books and pamphlets, mostly pre-1850, of theological, political and general interest; the Torna Collection of books and journals belonging to the late Prof. Tadhg Ó Donnchadha, which forms the nucleus of a research collection for Celtic studies; Munster Printing – a collection of books, pamphlets and ephemera printed in Munster irrespective of date. Special collections of individual donors include the Arnold Bax Collection of Memorabilia. Bax (1883–1953) was Master of the King's Musick (1941–53). This collection consists of his own compositions, a portion of his library, some of his letters and some personal effects. Other collections include the Corkery Collection, containing a portion of the library of Daniel Corkery (1878–1964), whose papers are also available in Special Collections; the de Courcy Ireland Collection containing a wide range of books, periodicals and ephemera dealing with maritime history and travel, acquired from Dr John de Courcy Ireland (1911–); and the Friedlander Collection, named in memory of Elizabeth Friedlander (1903–84), German artist and designer who lived in Kinsale, Co Cork, and designed covers for Penguin books, the Nonesuch Press and many other prestigious publishing houses during her long life. Within this collection are Penguin and other publishers' books on a wide variety of subjects, including book design, layout, calligraphy and the arts, and printing in general. Her books and some of her papers were donated to University College Cork by Mr Gerald Goldberg. There is no catalogue available at present. Another collection of importance is the Ó Riordain Collection consisting of the annotated collection of the poet and essayist Sean Ó Riordain (1916–77), which reflects the poet's interests in worldwide literature.

**Archives Service**: Major collections include: Attic Press/Róisín Conroy Collection generated and collected by Róisín Conroy as co-founder and publisher of Attic Press and as an activist in the Irish Women's Movement; family papers belonging to the Grehan family, a descriptive list for which is at present in preparation; Estate Collections – Bantry House Collection (unprocessed); Seward Estate, Youghal, Co. Cork; Ryan of Inch Family Papers; Political Papers – Thomas MacDonagh Collection, Neville Keery Papers (unprocessed); Literary Papers – John Montague Papers (unprocessed); Correspondence of Frank O'Connor and Sean O'Faolain; Nancy McCarthy papers (unprocessed). Other collections include the Peters Photographic Collection (Second World War). Please note that access to unprocessed collections is not permitted.

LOCATION

Special Collections and Archives are located in the basement of the Boole Library. A new facility is being planned.

## MALLOW HERITAGE CENTRE

27/28 Bank Place
MALLOW, CO. CORK
Ireland

TELEPHONE: (022) 50302; FAX: (022) 20276
E-mail: mallowhc@eircom.net
Website: www.irishroots.net/Cork.htm

HOURS

M–F, 10:30am–1:00pm, 2:00–4:00pm

ACCESS AND SERVICES

The Mallow Centre is a fee-based organization that offers genealogical research services to those interested in tracing their roots in Co. Cork, especially East and North Cork. Enquiries are welcome. An application form can be found on the centre's website. An initial search fee of 63.50 euro (or equivalent) per family must accompany the application. A delay of four weeks can be expected for a reply to an initial enquiry. Chief surnames in rural Co. Cork include: McCarthy, O'Callaghan, McAuliffe, Fitzgerald, Sullivan, Murphy, Walsh, O'Connor, and O'Connell.

CONTACT

Martina Aherne

DESCRIPTION

Mallow Heritage Centre is the designated heritage centre for the Diocese of Cloyne. It is a member of the Family History Foundation, the coordinating body for a network of government-approved genealogical research centres in the Republic of Ireland and in Northern Ireland that have computerized tens of millions of Irish ancestral records of different types. It is also a member of the Irish Genealogical Project (IGP).

HOLDINGS

The centre holds baptismal and marriage records of 46 parishes out of the 120 parishes within the County of Cork, totalling 1,000,000 entries on its database, the third largest record database in Ireland. Main records include: Roman Catholic baptismal and marriage records, a few dating from 1757; and Church of Ireland records for the North Cork area only, the earliest dating from 1730. A variety of the main genealogical sources are currently being computerized and tombstones from several cemeteries have been transcribed.

LOCATION

Mallow is located on the main Cork–Limerick Road, half an hour's drive north of Cork City. The Heritage Centre is next to the Hibernian Hotel, just west of the town centre.

# COUNTY DONEGAL

*for* COUNTY DERRY
*see under* COUNTY LONDONDERRY

## DONEGAL ARCHAEOLOGICAL SURVEY

*See* DONEGAL COUNTY MUSEUM, Letterkenny

## DONEGAL COUNTY LIBRARY

Central Library and Arts Centre
Oliver Plunkett Road
LETTERKENNY, CO. DONEGAL
Ireland

TELEPHONE: (074) 24950; FAX: (074) 24950
E-mail: dglcolib@iol.ie
Website: www.donegal.ie/library

HOURS

M,W,F, 10:30am–5:30pm; Tu,Th, 10:30am–8:00pm; Sat 10:30am–1:00pm

ACCESS AND SERVICES

Visitors welcome, with access to borrowing privileges. Disabled access facilities. Photocopying, print-outs from the Internet and microfilm reader are available for a modest fee. The library offers free public access to the Internet in the Central Library and seven other service points, with a total of some 50 PCs available to the public. The County Library is currently developing a WebOPAC facility, and it is expected that the catalogue, with all the library's holdings including local material, will be available online (via www.donegal.ie/library) before the end of 2002.

CONTACT

Liam Ronayne, County Librarian; tel. (074) 21968; fax (074) 21740
Donna Quinn, Assistant Librarian, Central Library; tel. (074) 24950; fax (074) 24950

DESCRIPTION

This is the main library of the county's 17-member library network, with library administration located at Rosemount, close to the Central Library in Letterkenny.

HOLDINGS

The library houses more than 40,000 volumes, with access to the system's some 400,000 volumes, including significant holdings of early printed books (some 300 pre-1851 volumes). Local authors collections include: Patrick MacGill, Peadar O'Donnell, Seumas MacManus and John Kells Ingram. These collections consist mostly of printed editions of their works, plus a small amount of original papers and illustrative matter. The Collection of Personal Papers includes: Cathal Ó Searcaigh's personal archive – manuscripts of his poetry and other writings, original editions of his published work in monograph and journal form, videos and tapes of his broadcast work, and other relevant papers and materials that are currently being deposited with Donegal County Library. Cathal Ó Searcaigh's own library of poetry and other literature will be housed in his house in Mín a'Leagha, Gort a'Choirce, and will be catalogued by Donegal County Library, and maintained by Donegal County Library *in situ*.

The County Library's Archives Collection includes: Grand Jury Presentments from the 1790s; Board of Guardian records; almost complete sets of minute books and some admission registers and outdoor relief registers for seven of the eight Poor Law Unions which covered Co. Donegal; minutes of Donegal County Council, its committees, and Managers' Orders; minutes of the county's ten Rural District Councils, 1899–1925; minutes and other papers of a number of harbour commissioners in the county, and for the Londonderry & Lough Swilly Railway Company. There is also a small collection of private records, including: some estate papers; records relating to local voluntary bodies; and school records. The library continues to develop its collection of photographs and prints relating to the county, which includes prints from the late 18th and 19th centuries, mainly of Donegal scenes and persons; postcards; topographic paintings; photographs taken by the Library Council staff, purchased from professional photographers, or donated to the library. The map collection includes an almost complete set of the 1837 six-inch Ordnance Survey maps backed with linen and kept in leather boxes; full sets of other OS maps of the county in various scales, and non-OS maps. Since 1987 the library has been collecting ephemera relating to the county, publicity material and programmes for local events, exhibition catalogues, posters, annual reports of local organizations, local election material and material relating to Donegal constituencies in Dáil, Presidential, and European elections, and other relevant material.

LOCATION

Housed within a recent (1995) three-storey building on the corner of Lower Main Street and Oliver Plunkett Road, in the town centre.

## DONEGAL COUNTY MUSEUM

High Road
LETTERKENNY, CO. DONEGAL
Ireland

TELEPHONE: (074) 24613; FAX: (074) 26522
E-mail: jmccarthy@donegalcoco.ie
Website: www.donegal.ie

HOURS

M–F, 10:00am–4:30pm; Sat, 1:00–4:30pm; closed for lunch, 12:30–1:00pm

ACCESS AND SERVICES

Visitors welcome, but advance notice of at least two weeks is required if a researcher desires to view a particular artefact or group of artefacts. Access will also depend on availability of staff. Identification required. Disabled access facilities. Fax and photocopying services available. The museum contains two exhibition galleries: one for temporary exhibitions, the other for a permanent exhibition telling the story of Donegal from the Stone Age to the 20th century. Collections are catalogued manually and on computer.

CONTACT

Curator or Research Assistant

DESCRIPTION

Donegal County Museum was first opened to the public in 1987, and housed in what was once the Warden's house of the Letterkenny Workhouse, built in 1843. Several renovations and an extension to the museum were carried out between 1990 and 2000. The role of the museum is to collect, record, preserve, communicate and display for the use and enjoyment of the widest community possible the material evidence and associated information of the history of Donegal.

HOLDINGS

The museum develops and cares for a comprehensive collection of over 8,000 original artefacts relating to the County of Donegal in the areas of archaeology, geology, natural history, social and political history, and folklife. It also houses the archives of the Donegal Archaeological Survey, consisting of maps, plans, drawings, and files relating to the Survey. The Survey was published in book form and contains a description of the field antiquities of Co. Donegal from the Mesolithic period to the 17th century.

LOCATION

Signposted in Letterkenny, a five-minute walk from bus station or town centre.

## DONEGAL COUNTY ARCHIVES SERVICE

Donegal County Council
Three Rivers Centre
LIFFORD, CO. DONEGAL
Ireland

TELEPHONE: (074) 72490; FAX: (074) 41367
E-mail: nbrennan@donegalcoco.ie
Website: www.donegal.ie/dcc/arts/archive.htm

HOURS

M–F, 9:00am–12:30pm, 1:15–4:30pm

ACCESS AND SERVICES

Public access to the Archives Service is by advance appointment only, by arrangement with the Archivist. The service offers a research room, occasional exhibitions, lectures, and Heritage Week (1–7 Sept.) events.

CONTACT

Niamh Brennan, Archivist; e-mail: nbrennan@donegalcoco.ie

DESCRIPTION

Donegal County Archives holds the archives of Donegal County Council, its predecessor bodies and private historical collections of local interest. The priorities of the service include the cataloguing and conservation of archival materials to make them accessible to the public, and the general development of the Archives Service.

HOLDINGS

Donegal County Council has some of the finest surviving local archives in Ireland, including one of the nation's best county collections of records of Boards of Guardians of the Poor Law Unions in the county. The principal function of the Board of Guardians was to supervise and run workhouses where the destitute were accommodated. Workhouses in Donegal were in Letterkenny, Ballyshannon, Stranorlar, Dunfanaghy, Carndonagh (run by the Inishowen Board), Donegal, Glenties and Milford.

There are almost complete sets of minute books *c.*1840–*c.*1923 for all Poor Law Unions in the county except Donegal (where minutes only survive for the years 1914–23). A considerable number of 'indoor relief' or workhouse admission registers also survive and these give very detailed information about destitute persons entering or leaving the workhouse. The coverage is:

| | |
|---|---|
| Dunfanaghy Poor Law Union | 1891–1915 |
| Glenties | 1851–1922 (with gaps) |
| Inishowen | 1844–59, 1899–1911 |
| Letterkenny | 1864–78 |

There are also some outdoor relief registers for Letterkenny 1855–99 and Milford 1847–99 and minute books for the dispensaries at Killygordon and Stranorlar 1852–99.

Records of administration for landed estates include some rentals and maps for the Murray Stewart estate, Killybegs and other areas in South West Donegal 1749–1880, as well as maps for the Cochrane of Redcastle and Harvey of Ballyliffin estates, both in Inishowen *c.*1860–1900 and one Harvey rental *c.*1900 including lands at Inch.

Pupils' registers and roll books for public elementary or 'national' schools are being collected. Registers *c.*1900–*c.*1960 are available for over a dozen schools including schools at Dunfanaghy, Lifford and Ray.

The archive holds very rare court records (19 vols) for local petty sessions mainly at Ballyshannon 1828–55. These include:

- Registry of Criminal Proceedings at Ballyshannon Petty Sessions

  1828–48; 1849–51; 1851–3

  Details include date; informant's name and address; name and residence of person charged; offence (e.g. 'waylaying and assault', 'entering his orchard and stealing apples'; 'stealing three bricks'); witnesses sworn; and determination (e.g. 'fined', 'committed to gaol').

- Registry of Civil Proceedings at Ballyshannon Petty Sessions

  1828–48; 1848–50; 1851–6

  Details include date; complainant's name and address; defendant's name and address; complaint (e.g. 'non payment of county cess', 'having a quantity of flax on the public road', 'wilfully driving your mare into his grazing land',) witnesses sworn; adjudication (e.g. 'dismissed', 'no appearance', 'postponed', 'settled', 'fined').

- Registry of Summons issued from Ballyshannon Petty Sessions

  1828–33; 1831–9; 1833–7; 1844–8; 1848–50

  Details include name and address of complainant; name of person summoned; date; offence (e.g. 'assault and forcibly carrying away turf', 'house breaking'); and decision (e.g. 'dismissed', 'no jurisdiction', 'conviction', 'fined').

LOCATION
First floor, Three Rivers Centre, Lifford.

## LIFFORD OLD COURTHOUSE

The Diamond
LIFFORD, CO. DONEGAL
Ireland

TELEPHONE: (074) 41733; FAX: (074) 41228
E-mail: seatofpower@eircom.net
Website: www.infowing.ie/seatofpower

HOURS

M–F, 9:00am–4:30pm; Sun, 12:30–4:30pm

ACCESS AND SERVICES

Formerly called 'Seat of Power Visitor Centre', the Centre's full name is now '"Lifford Old Courthouse", Donegal's Amazing 18th Century Court, Jail &

Asylum'. Visitors welcome; there is an admission fee for the exhibits. Current (2002) fees: adult, 4.45 euro; children, 2.20 euro; students and seniors, 3.15 euro; family, 11.45 euro. Advance notice required for large groups. Late openings can be arranged in advance. Historic Courthouse Restaurant open all day below the courtroom adjoining the cells. Free brochures available. Access to archives by appointment.

CONTACT

Gillian Graham, Manager

DESCRIPTION

The old courthouse was built in 1746 by Dublin architect Michael Priestly and functioned as a courthouse until 1938. It was restored and reopened as a Heritage Centre in 1994. It traces the history of Lifford, especially its struggle for 'seat of power' status in Donegal, and the history of the O'Donnell dynasty, using audiovisual aids and displays. In addition, there are audiovisual displays of famous trials held in the courtroom and of the prisoners and inmates held in the original underground cells and lunatic asylum. Lifford was also the administrative centre for the Plantation. The building is believed to have been built on the foundation of Lifford Castle, a 16th- and 17th-century O'Donnell stronghold.

HOLDINGS

The courthouse houses the Rupert Coughlan Collection of documents, manuscripts and charts on the O'Donnell family and chieftains; and historic local artefacts, letters, and photographs relating to the Old Courthouse and Gaol. The building houses the Lifford branch of the Co. Donegal Library Service.

LOCATION

Located in the Diamond, Lifford, Co. Donegal, one mile west of Strabane, Co. Tyrone, and 14 miles from Derry City.

## DONEGAL ANCESTRY

The Quay
RAMELTON, CO. DONEGAL
Ireland

TELEPHONE: (074) 51266; FAX: (074) 51702
E-mail: donances@indigo.ie
Website: indigo.ie/~donances

HOURS

Genealogy Centre: M–Th, 9:30am–4:30pm; F, 9:30am–3:30pm; other times by appointment only
Heritage Centre: M–Sat, 10:00am–5:30pm; Sun, 2:00–5:30pm

## ACCESS AND SERVICES

Visitors are welcome to the centre. Donegal Ancestry offers a fee-based genealogical research service and a consultation service for anyone wishing to discuss a family history query with the centre's trained researchers. A consultation fee applies, and an appointment is not necessary. Computerization of church records is ongoing. Types of research report include: location searches, searches of specific sources, preliminary report (this involves an initial search, a full assessment of all relevant sources, and advice on the feasibility of conducting further research), staged report (to facilitate customers who want to spread the cost of research over time), and full report. The last of these is an exclusive and individually designed full family history report that will explain the sources available for research, the administrative geography, the family names, the local history and maps, transcripts or copies of the records uncovered (when appropriate, certificates may also be included). Research fees: a preliminary report costs a minimum of 76 euro (or equivalent). Follow-on research fees may vary with time involved and length of report; a full costing is prepared for all research and furnished to customers before any research is undertaken. Enquiries are dealt with in rotation, and, due to the large volume of work currently on hand, it could take up to 12 weeks for new research to be undertaken. Every effort is made to facilitate customers where possible.

## CONTACT

Joan Patton, Manager
Susan McCaffrey and Kathleen Gallagher, Researchers

## DESCRIPTION

Donegal Ancestry is the Irish Family History Foundation's designated genealogical research centre for Co. Donegal. The centre provides a fee-based family history research service using computerized and non-computerized records and covers the geographic area of Co. Donegal. Principal towns and villages in Co. Donegal include: Ballyshannon, Donegal, Bundoran, Ballybofey, Lifford, Raphoe, Letterkenny, Dunfanaghy, Buncrana, Cardonagh, Greencastle, and Moville.

## HOLDINGS

Sources available to Donegal Ancestry for consultation include: pre-1900 parish registers; civil birth, marriage, and death records; Griffith's Valuation; Tithe Applotment Books; 1901 Census returns; graveyard inscriptions; Hearth Money Rolls; Passenger List Extracts; 1630 Muster Rolls; estate records; school roll books; Poll of Electors Extracts mid-1700s; Ordnance Survey Memoirs; and other miscellaneous sources.

## LOCATION

Ramelton is seven miles north of Letterkenny (the largest commercial centre in Co. Donegal). The main road from Letterkenny leads directly onto the Mall in Ramelton; turn right at the bottom of the hill and follow the road to the left, which runs parallel to the Leannan River, and you will see the restored adjoining warehouses on the quayside. The genealogy centre is located in one of the two buildings; the adjoining building has a heritage exhibition that outlines the path of Ramelton's development from its origins at the time of the Plantation of Ulster in the 17th century up to the present. Guided tours are available. Note: Ramelton sometimes appears as Rathmelton (the historic spelling), especially on maps and road signs, but it is pronounced locally as Ramelton.

# COUNTY DOWN

## SEELB LIBRARY HEADQUARTERS – LOCAL STUDIES UNIT

Windmill Hill
BALLYNAHINCH, CO. DOWN, BT24 8DH
Northern Ireland

TELEPHONE: (028) 9756 6400 ext. 235/236/237; FAX: (028) 9756 5072
E-mail: ref@bhinchlibhq.demon.co.uk
Website: www.seelb.org.uk

HOURS

M–F, 9:00am–5:00pm

ACCESS AND SERVICES

Visitors welcome, but due to space restrictions please make an appointment before your visit to ensure that all the relevant material can be made available. Disabled access facilities. Local Studies can send out Ordnance Survey maps, street directories and old newspapers in bound volumes to be consulted at any of the South Eastern Education and Library Board's 26 libraries. Some of the member libraries (Downpatrick, Dairy Farm, Lisburn, and Bangor) also have microfilm reader/printers to which microfilm copies can be sent. Most books from the Local Studies Collection can be borrowed through the local branch library, but rare works of local or special interest are only made available for consultation in Ballynahinch. The Library Service does not do genealogical searches but is happy to assist and advise users seeking genealogical information.

CONTACT

Deirdre Armstrong, Local Studies Librarian
Malcolm Buchanan, Senior Information Librarian

DESCRIPTION

Local Studies is located at the Library Headquarters of the South Eastern Education and Library Board in Ballynahinch, Co. Down.

HOLDINGS

The Local Studies Collection contains books, maps, newspapers, and illustrations on the history, topography, industry, transport, literature, and culture of Co. Down and South Antrim, the area served by the SEELB Library Service. Local Studies also collects information and cultural materials on the rest of Ulster and the whole island of Ireland. Of special importance is its indexing of local newspapers project. Since 1973 staff in the Local Studies Section have been preparing an index from the local newspapers in Down and South Antrim and other newspapers such as the *Belfast Telegraph* and *Irish Times*. The index currently contains more than 250,000 entries and is available as an online database. Specific newspaper indexes are available for purchase. These include *County Down Spectator* (1904–64), £1.50; *Down Recorder* (1836–86), £5.00; *Mourne Observer* (1949–80), £2.00; *Newtownards Chronicle* (1871–1900), £3.00; *Newtownards Chronicle* (1901–39), £5.00; *Northern Herald* (1833–6), £1.50;

*Northern Star* (1792–7), £3.50. These papers are held on file on microfilm. For a nominal fee, photocopies of newspaper articles can be supplied. Payments can be made by International Reply Coupon or by sterling cheque. Visitors also have free access to the ULSTER-AMERICAN FOLK PARK's (Omagh, Co. Tyrone) Emigration Database.

LOCATION

Town centre, at the eastern end of Windmill Street near the intersection of Crossgar Road, and situtated on a historic 1798 battle site.

**BANGOR LIBRARY**

80 Hamilton Road
BANGOR, CO. DOWN, BT20 4LH
Northern Ireland

TELEPHONE: (028) 9127 0591; FAX: (028) 9146 2744
E-mail: jgreid_@hotmail.com
Website: www.seelb.org.uk

HOURS

M–W, 10:00am–8:00pm; F, 10:00am–5:00pm; Sat, 10:00am–1:00pm, 2:00–5:00pm

ACCESS AND SERVICES

Visitors welcome, but identification required to join and have borrowing privileges. Borrowing privileges for visitors may be restricted. Consult with Librarian. Disabled access facilities. Photography by arrangement with Branch Library Manager. Fees for photocopying, microform prints, fax services and Internet access. In late 2001 the library opened a centre of excellence allowing access to 20 PCs, including adaptive technology.

CONTACT

Stephen Hanson, Branch Library Manager
Julie Reid, Senior Library Assistant; e-mail: jgreid_@hotmail.com

DESCRIPTION

Established in 1910 with financial assistance from the Carnegie Trust, Bangor is a busy branch library serving the needs of some 18,000 registered clients in this historic community, site of one of Ireland's great early monastic establishments.

HOLDINGS

The library houses a general educational and recreational collection of some 37,000 volumes, with access to the 341,000 volumes held by the combined libraries of the South Eastern Education and Library Board, headquartered in

Ballynahinch. In addition to its print collection, the library offers a local studies database, which gives access to over 3,500 journal and newspaper articles indexed online. Of genealogical interest is the library's printed copy of Griffith's Valuation and a 3,000-volume reference collection. Available on microfilm is the *County Down Spectator* from 1904 to the present.

LOCATION

Hamilton Road runs between High Street and Upper Main Street in Bangor town centre.

## HOLYWOOD BRANCH LIBRARY

Sullivan Building
86–88 High Street
HOLYWOOD, CO. DOWN, BT18 9AE
Northern Ireland

TELEPHONE: (028) 9042 4232; FAX: (028) 9042 4194
E-mail: hwoodlib@hotmail.com
Website: www.seelb.org.uk

HOURS

M,Tu,Th, 10:00am–8:00pm; W,F,Sat, 10:00am–5:00pm

ACCESS AND SERVICES

Visitors welcome. Borrowing privileges for visitors may be restricted. Disabled access facilities. Fees for photocopying and fax services. Free access to Internet and e-mail for library members. Charges will apply for Internet use for non-members.

CONTACT

Josephine Quinn, Branch Library Manager

DESCRIPTION

Attractive, inviting facility housed in a renovated 1862 building. Part of the South Eastern Education and Library Board, headquartered in Ballynahinch.

HOLDINGS

The library houses a general educational and recreational collection of some 25,000 books, with access to the combined resources of the regional Library Board. It houses a small but good local studies collection, with some standard genealogical reference sources for the local area, including Griffith's Valuation. Ordnance Survey maps of the area may be requested from the central Local Studies Collection.

LOCATION

Town centre.

## ULSTER FOLK AND TRANSPORT MUSEUM

Cultra
HOLYWOOD, CO. DOWN, BT18 0EU
Northern Ireland

TELEPHONE: (028) 9042 8428; FAX: (028) 9042 8728
E-mail: uftm@nidex.com
Website: www.nidex.com/uftm/index.htm

HOURS

Museum: (Mar.–June) M–F, 10:00am–5:00pm, Sat, 10:00am–6:00pm, Sun, 11:00am–6:00pm; (July–Sept.) M–F, 10:00am–6:00pm, Sat, 10:00am–6:00pm, Sun, 11:00am–6:00pm; (Oct.–Feb.) M–F, 10:00am–4:00pm, Sat, 10:00am–5:00pm, Sun, 11:00am–5:00pm; closed for a few days at Christmas

ACCESS AND SERVICES

Museum is open to general public. Separate admission charges to Folk Museum and Transport Museum (adult, £4; child, £2.50, with reduced rates for seniors, students, families, groups, etc.; children under five are free). Mostly Disabled access facilities. The museum publishes a wide range of material, including the journal *Ulster Folklife*, exhibition catalogues, educational study packs and worksheets for schools. For access to library and archives, please make appointment. The library offers reference assistance, photocopying, microfilm reader/printer, photographic reproductions, and database searching.

CONTACT

Roger Dixon, Librarian

DESCRIPTION

The museum occupies 177 acres just east of Belfast in northern Co. Down. It is devoted to preserving the ways things were in the north of Ireland, especially around the turn of the twentieth century. While your primary purpose in visiting the museum may be to do research in its library and archives, it would be worthwhile to take time to explore the Folk Museum's exhibits and reconstructed farms, houses, workshops, mills, schools, churches, and other facilities that take you back in time. The Transport Museum also offers an array of distractions, from old railway engines and cars to the modern De Lorean automobile, which was manufactured in Belfast. The museum is part of the Museums and Galleries of Northern Ireland (MAGNI) service, which also includes the ULSTER-AMERICAN FOLK PARK, Omagh, Co. Tyrone; the ULSTER MUSEUM, Belfast, Co. Antrim; and its branch, the ARMAGH COUNTY MUSEUM, Armagh City, Co, Armagh.

HOLDINGS

Library and archive collections support the various interests of the museum, especially folk life, social history and transport. The book collection, which exceeds 25,000 volumes, and an extensive range of periodicals are available for reference purposes only. The archive boasts an extensive collection of photographs from the late 19th century to the present. The largest collection of photographs is the 70,000-item archive of Harland and Wolff Ltd, which records the shipping activity of the company from 1895 to the mid-1980s. Harland and Wolff built the *Titanic*, and the museum's archive houses what is probably the world's largest and most important collection of photographic negatives and ship plans relating to this ill-fated liner and other famous ships built by the yard. The museum also houses Ireland's largest collection of Lloyd's shipping and yacht registers along with an extensive collection of sound recordings documenting stories, language, music, customs, beliefs, and traditions, including the BBC (NI) archive and the tape-recorded survey of Hiberno-English. The most important recent addition is the Living Linen archive, which has recorded the knowledge and experience of people associated with the industry. The museum also maintains an Ulster Dialect Archive, and has compiled an Ulster Dictionary onto a computer database.

LOCATION

About ten miles east of Belfast on the A2 Belfast/Bangor Road, 2.5 miles outside Holywood.

## NEWCASTLE BRANCH LIBRARY

141/143 Main Street
NEWCASTLE, CO. DOWN, BT33 0AE
Northern Ireland

TELEPHONE: (028) 4372 2710; FAX: (028) 4372 6518
E-mail: ncastlib@hotmail.com; info@seelb.org.uk
Website: www.seelb.org.uk

HOURS

M–W, 10:00am–8:00pm; F, 10:00am–5:00pm; Sat, 10:00am–1:00pm, 2:00–5:00pm

ACCESS AND SERVICES

Visitors welcome, but identification required. Borrowing privileges for visitors may be restricted. Consult with Librarian. Disabled access facilities. Photocopying and fax services available.

CONTACT

Corwyn Rogers, Branch Library Manager

DESCRIPTION

Small branch library, part of the South Eastern Education and Library Board system, headquartered in Ballynahinch.

HOLDINGS

Houses a collection of more than 10,000 volumes, with access to the system's larger collection, including its LOCAL STUDIES UNIT in Ballynahinch. Modest local studies collection focusing on Newcastle and South Co. Down.

LOCATION

Located beside the Shimna Bridge on the main street in this popular seaside resort town.

## DIOCESAN ARCHIVE, DROMORE (Roman Catholic)

44 Armagh Road
NEWRY, CO. DOWN, BT35 6PN
Northern Ireland

TELEPHONE: (028) 3026 2444; FAX: (028) 3026 0496
E-mail: bishopofdromore@btinternet.com
Website: www.dromore.org (in development)

HOURS

By appointment only

ACCESS AND SERVICES

Enquiries welcome, but advance notice required. Researchers are asked to know exactly what they are looking for, as the archive is not fully processed.

CONTACT

Most Rev. John McAreavey

DESCRIPTION

Small Roman Catholic diocesan archives. The diocese of Dromore is part of the Archdiocese of Armagh and includes portions of Counties Down, Armagh and Antrim.

HOLDINGS

The archive comprises the written materials handed down by diocesan bishops from approximately 1850. The volume of material is very uneven. The archive is in the process of being reorganized following its removal from the bishop's house while the house was being refurbished.

LOCATION

Bishop's House, Newry.

## NEWRY BRANCH LIBRARY

79 Hill Street
NEWRY, CO. DOWN, BT34 1DG
Northern Ireland

TELEPHONE: (028) 306 4683/ 4077; FAX: (028) 3025 1739
E-mail: selb.hq@selb.org
Website: www.selb.org

HOURS

M,F, 9:30am–6:00pm; Tu,Th, 9:30am–8:00pm; W,Sat, 9:30am–5:00pm

ACCESS AND SERVICES

Visitors welcome, but identification required. Borrowing privileges for visitors may be restricted. Consult with Librarian. Disabled access facilities. Photocopying, fax and Internet services available.

CONTACT

Christina Sloan, Branch Librarian

DESCRIPTION

Branch library of the Southern Education and Library Board system.

HOLDINGS

Houses a general educational and recreational collection of more than 40,000 volumes, with access to the system's larger collection. Strong reference collection, including local history of Newry and surrounding areas.

LOCATION

City centre.

## NEWTOWNARDS BRANCH LIBRARY

Queen's Hall, Regent Street
NEWTOWNARDS, CO. DOWN, BT23 4AB
Northern Ireland

TELEPHONE: (028) 9081 4732; FAX: (028) 9081 0265
E-mail: info@seelb.org.uk
Website: www.seelb.org.uk

HOURS

M–W,F, 10:00am–8:00pm; Sat, 10:00am–1:00pm, 2:00–5:00pm

ACCESS AND SERVICES

Visitors welcome, but identification required. Borrowing privileges for visitors may be restricted. Consult with Librarian. Disabled access facilities. Photocopying and fax services available.

CONTACT

Joan Thompson, Branch Librarian

DESCRIPTION

Branch library of the South Eastern Education and Library Board system.

HOLDINGS

Houses a collection of more than 20,000 volumes, with access to the system's larger collection. Modest local studies collection focusing on Newtownards and North Co. Down.

LOCATION

Town centre.

# COUNTY DUBLIN

## BLACKROCK LIBRARY, Michael Smurfit Graduate School of Business

*See* UNIVERSITY COLLEGE DUBLIN LIBRARY, Dublin

## ASSOCIATION OF PROFESSIONAL GENEALOGISTS IN IRELAND

Steven C. ffeary-Smyrl, Hon. Secretary
30 Harlech Crescent
CLONSKEAGH, DUBLIN 14
Ireland

TELEPHONE: Not for publication; FAX: Not for publication
E-mail: apgi@dublin.com
Website: indigo.ie/~apgi

ACCESS AND SERVICES

By appointment. See below for information on brochure.

CONTACT

Steven C. ffeary-Smyrl, Honorary Secretary

DESCRIPTION

APGI is an association of individual professional genealogical researchers who subscribe to a strict code of practice. APGI acts as a regulating body to maintain high standards among its members and to protect the interests of clients. Members act as advisers in the National Library's Genealogy Advisory Service. There are currently 22 members, all of whom are accredited by an independent board of assessors. Some offer special areas of interest, e.g. 'research within Ulster only'. A brochure listing members and their addresses with telephone numbers, e-mail addresses and websites, where applicable, is available through the Hon. Secretary or through the website. Fees apply for research undertaken at the request of clients.

## AUSTIN CLARKE LIBRARY – POETRY IRELAND/ÉIGSE ÉIREANN

Upper Yard, Dublin Castle
DUBLIN 2
Ireland

TELEPHONE: (01) 671 4632; FAX: (01) 671 4634
E-mail: poetry@iol.ie
Website: www.poetryireland.ie

HOURS

M–F, 2:00–5:00pm; other times by arrangement

ACCESS AND SERVICES

Visitors welcome. Advance notice preferred; identification required. No fees; laptops permitted; disabled access facilities with advance notice.

CONTACT

Joseph Woods, Director

DESCRIPTION

Library sponsored by Poetry Ireland, a not-for-profit organization founded to promote and support poets and poetry in Ireland.

HOLDINGS

Special collections include: Austin Clarke collection of 6,000 volumes of poetry, prose, criticism and drama; John Jordan Collection of 2,000 volumes of poetry, prose, criticism and fiction.

LOCATION

The library is located on the grounds of Dublin Castle, off Dame Street, next to City Hall and diagonally across from Christchurch Cathedral. There is also an entrance off Ship Street if you are approaching the library from St Patrick's or Christchurch Cathedrals. It is a ten-minute walk up Dame Street from Trinity College. The library is on bus routes 50, 51B, 54A, 56A, 77, 77A, and 123.

## CENTRAL CATHOLIC LIBRARY

74 Merrion Square
DUBLIN 2
Ireland

TELEPHONE: (01) 676 1264; FAX: (01) 678 7618
E-mail: None
Website: None

HOURS

M–F, 11:00am–6:30pm; Sat., 11:00am–5:00pm

ACCESS AND SERVICES

Visitors and enquiries welcome, but advance notice preferred. Membership fees apply: general public, 20 euro per year; students and seniors, 10 euro. No disabled access facilities. Inter-library loan programme serves entire nation. Open and closed collections; closed collection accessible only on request. Sheaf and card catalogues available. Printed catalogue of older books available. Photocopying (excludes early printed books) available for a fee at the discretion of the Librarian. Staff does the photocopying. Laptops and photography permitted with approval of Librarian. A series of four lectures is held each spring and autumn. Copies of library brochures available on request. Borrowing privileges limited to members. Library regularly holds book sales.

CONTACT

Teresa Whitington, Librarian

DESCRIPTION

The library is a voluntary subscription library founded by Fr Stephen Brown, SJ in 1922 to provide reading matter and reference services on church and religious affairs. It is entirely self-funded, relying on membership fees, donations and bequests.

HOLDINGS

The collection totals more than 100,000 volumes dealing with all branches of human knowledge with which religion is concerned. It also includes journals and pamphlets. Though its focus is Catholica, the library's holdings vary widely and include an important reference collection. Closed collections include: the Art Library – a small archive dealing with the work of the Academy of Christian Art, a collection on European art, including Celtic art, and a non-European art collection donated by Sir John Galvin, a member of the board of the Chester Beatty Library; the Irish Room – journals, books on Irish history and nineteenth-century Irish fiction; the Leo Room – sociology, politics and international affairs; the Carnegie Collection – philosophy, religion and sociology (many dealing with non-Catholic and non-Christian traditions); the Periodicals Collection; and some 1,200 older printed books (1541–1850), mostly of a Catholic interest. Among the reference books are several standard works on genealogy.

LOCATION

Nearly half-way along the south side of Merrion Square from the Upper Merrion Street end. The south side is the side running from Upper Merrion Street to Upper Mount Street and the Pepper Canister Church (St Stephen's). No. 7 bus stops about five minutes' walk from the library. From the north side of the city, the No. 13 bus stops near the library. The library is a 10-minute walk from Pearse DART Station.

## CENTRAL LIBRARY

*See under* DUBLIN CITY PUBLIC LIBRARIES, Dublin

## CENTRE FOR DUBLIN AND IRISH STUDIES

Pearse Street Library
138–146 Pearse Street
DUBLIN 2
Ireland

TELEPHONE: (01) 664 4800; FAX: (01) 676 1628 (temporary – see ACCESS AND SERVICES)
E-mail: dublinstudies@dublincity.ie
Website: www.iol.ie/dublincitylibrary/ga.htm

ACCESS AND SERVICES

Currently closed to the public while undergoing extensive renovations. When construction is completed in late 2002, visitors will be welcome. The library is intended for serious students and researchers as well as the general public. Readers wishing to use the library's collections are advised that no ticket or appointment is necessary, though the library is considering introducing a reference ticket that will be issued on the spot.

CONTACT

Máire Kennedy, Divisional Librarian

DESCRIPTION

The Centre for Dublin and Irish Studies houses the special collections of the City's public library system, most especially the valuable collection of books on early Dublin contained in the library of Sir John T. Gilbert, the Dix Collection, the Yeats Collection, the Swift Collection, and the Dublin and Irish Collections. It also houses one of the strongest genealogical collections in Ireland.

HOLDINGS

**The Dublin Collection.** The Dublin Collection comprises a number of special collections relating to Dublin and Dubliners. New material is acquired as it becomes available, including second-hand and antiquarian books, newspapers, periodicals, photographs, maps, prints, drawings, theatre programmes, playbills, posters, ballad sheets, audiovisual materials, and ephemera, as resources allow. The collection includes the following special collections.

- *The Gilbert Library*, the most extensive of the special collections, is made up of the manuscripts, books and other printed materials collected by Sir John T. Gilbert (1829–98), historian and archivist. The collection reflects Gilbert's interest in the social, political and cultural history of Ireland, particularly of Dublin. Notable features of the library include early Dublin newspapers, fine Dublin bookbindings of the 18th century, Dublin almanacs and directories. Of special interest are the manuscripts of the municipal records of the city of Dublin and records of the Dublin guilds. A printed catalogue of the Gilbert Library compiled by Douglas Hyde and D.J. O'Donoghue is available. John T. Gilbert's many original historical works and his edited volumes are prominent in the library. He is perhaps best known for his three-volume *History of the City of Dublin*. He compiled and edited the *Calendar of Ancient Records of the Corporation of Dublin*, the first seven volumes of which were published in his lifetime. His widow (the novelist Rosa Mulholland) continued the work, and 19 volumes of the *Calendar* were published from 1889 to 1944. The *Calendar* comprises a record of the monuments in the possession of Dublin City Council and is an extremely valuable source for the history of the city.

- *The Dix Collection.* The gift of Irish bibliographer E.R. McClintock Dix, this collection contains some 300 Dublin and Irish imprints, mainly from the 17th and 18th centuries, and a number of 18th-century fine bindings.
- *The Yeats Collection.* This consists mainly of first editions of Yeats works, including those from the Dun Emer Press founded by Lilly and Lolly Yeats.
- *The Swift Collection.* Consisting of books, manuscripts, periodicals and ephemera, this contains an extensive collection of rare and valuable items, and is growing annually.
- *The Directories Collection.* This is one of the most heavily used collections, and includes an almost complete set of Dublin directories from 1751 to the present. Specific holdings include: *Watson's Almanack* 1729–1837; *Wilson's Dublin Directories* 1751–3; 1761–1837; *Pettigrew & Oulton's Dublin Directories* 1834–47; *Thom's Irish Almanac and Official Directories* 1844–present. The early directories, from 1751 to 1833, are in surname order only, and from 1834 street listings are available as well as the name sequence. *Pigott's Directory of Ireland* 1822–4 on microfiche is the earliest directory in the collection to cover all of Ireland, followed by *Slater's Directory of Ireland* published in the years 1846, 1856, 1870, 1881 and 1894. The 1894 edition has a very useful general directory of private residents of Ireland.
- *The Newspaper Collection.* The newspaper collection covers a range of titles published from the 1700s to the present. The early Dublin newspapers, including rare and some unique items dating from 1700–50, form an important part of the collection. Current and recent issues of the newspapers are not available for viewing for a period of six months, as all newspapers are sent out for binding. (Daily newspapers are available for reading in in the Business Information Centre, DUBLIN CITY PUBLIC LIBRARIES – CENTRAL LIBRARY, Ilac Centre, Dublin 1.)

**The Family History Collection**. The library has a strong collection of source materials for family history. These include: Griffith's Valuation 1847–64, held on microfiche and covering 32 counties; Tithe Applotment Books 1823–38, held on microfilm and covering 32 counties; Ordnance Survey first edition six-inch maps; Ordnance Survey Letters, held in typescript copies and arranged by county; and Census Returns of 1901 and 1911. The 1901 and 1911 returns have been microfilmed and the library holds a full set for Dublin City and County. Church of Ireland Registers of Dublin parishes from the REPRESENTATIVE CHURCH BODY LIBRARY, Dublin, have been microfilmed and purchased for the library. Many date from the 17th to the end of the 19th century. Selected Dublin parish registers were published in book form and are held in the library: St John's, Dublin 1619–99 baptisms, marriages, burials; St Michan's, Dublin 1636–85 baptisms, marriages, burials; St Catherine's, Dublin 1636–1715 baptisms, marriages, burials; Monkstown, Co. Dublin 1669–1786 baptisms, burials; St Nicholas Without 1694–1739 baptisms, marriages, burials; St Andrew's, St Anne's, St Audoen's, St Bride's 1632–1800 marriages; St Marie's, St Luke's, St Catherine's, St Werburgh's 1627–1800 marriages; St Patrick's 1677–1800 baptisms, marriages, burials; Register of the Parish of St Thomas, Dublin 1750–1791, edited by Raymond Refaussé, Representative Church Body Library, 1994. Also available are: Registers of the French Conformed Churches of St Patrick and St Mary, Dublin (1893); and a set of Huguenot records relating to Ireland on microfiche. There are a number of publications that may be of special interest to genealogists. These include: Shipping Indexes of persons who left Ireland for America during the nineteenth century; The Famine Immigrants 1846–51, covering those arriving at the port of New York during the great Famine; Memorials of the Dead, a series of volumes compiled by Richard Flatman, and another series by Brian Cantwell listing gravestone inscriptions in cemeteries in Dublin, Wicklow and Wexford – they are not published but are available in bound typescripts; and First World War Memorial Records, published in 1923 in eight volumes listing the Irish soldiers who died in the First World War. The names are in alphabetical order. Other helpful standard reference sources include: *Who's Who* (1897–1998 is available on CD-ROM) *Burke's* and *Lodge's Peerages*; biographical dictionaries; Indexes to Wills (published indexes to wills, compiled before the destruction of the Public Record Office); King's Inns Admission Papers; *Alumni Dublinensis*, containing a list of students of Trinity College Dublin from 1593 to 1860; Civil Survey for Dublin and other counties, 17th century; and Palmer's *Index to The Times 1790–1905* on CD-ROM.

**The Irish Collection**. The Irish Collection is made up of about 90,000 items: books and other materials relating to Ireland, by Irish authors, or in the Irish language. A comprehensive collection of material of Irish interest published outside Ireland is also available, as well as a considerable amount of material of genealogical interest. This general collection gives a national context to the Dublin special collections.

LOCATION

The library is situated on Pearse Street. Take the DART to Pearse Station and walk two blocks eastwards along Pearse Street. No. 3 bus from O'Connell Street to Ringsend stops across the street.

## CHESTER BEATTY LIBRARY

Dublin Castle
DUBLIN 2
Ireland

TELEPHONE: (01) 407 0750; FAX: (01) 407 0760
E-mail: info@cbl.ie
Website: www.cbl.ie

HOURS

Exhibition hours: (May–Sept.) M–F, 10:00am–5:00pm; (Oct.–Apr.) Tu–F, 10:00am–5:00pm; (All Year) Sat, 11:00am–5:00pm, Sun, 1:00–5:00pm. Reading Room Reference Hours (with reader's ticket): M, by appointment only; Tu–F: 10:00am–5:00pm. Access to Mss Collections by appointment only, M–F, 10:00am–12:45pm, 2:15–4:45pm

ACCESS AND SERVICES

Visitors welcome and exhibition visitors need no appointment or reader's ticket. Reference library readers must apply for a reader's ticket. No admission fees to the library or the galleries. Disabled access facilities. No photography in the galleries or of the collections. Photocopying done only by order through the Reference Librarian. Laptops permitted; pencils only; gloves may be required for use in Reading Room. The gift and bookshop offer library publications, including catalogues of artefacts, a guidebook and a CD-ROM. Free brochures are available in five languages. The Chester Beatty Library is a 'must-see' even if you have no plans to use its rich collections. The exhibitions alone are worth a visit. Chester Beatty Library was named 'European Museum of the Year 2002'.

CONTACT

For reference questions, contact Celine Ward, Reference Librarian;
e-mail: reference@cbl.ie
For Mss research, write to Director or Specialist Curator.
See website for details: www.cbl.ie.

DESCRIPTION

The library was formed by the American-born mining engineer and philanthropist Chester Beatty (1875–1968), who moved his priceless collections of art works, manuscripts and illustrated printed books to Dublin in 1950. The library was originally built on Shrewsbury Road in Ballsbridge, Dublin 4, and relocated to its current premises in 1999. Beatty bequeathed his library to a trust for the benefit of the public. It is now supported by the Government of Ireland. The library boasts a state-of-the-art exhibition gallery in a modern addition to the renovated and redesigned 18th-century Clock Tower Building in the grounds of Dublin Castle. Facilities include a restaurant, gift and book shop, audiovisual presentations, roof garden, wheelchair access and baby-changing facilities.

HOLDINGS

The library houses one of the world's finest collections of manuscripts, prints, icons, paintings, early printed books and *objets d'art*, with special strengths in the areas of the Middle East and Asia. Items from the collection date back to 2700BC. Among the highlights of the collection are: Egyptian papyrus texts, exceptional early Biblical papyri, illuminated copies of the Koran (Qur'an), the Bible, and European medieval and renaissance manuscripts.

LOCATION

The library is located in the garden behind the main buildings of Dublin Castle, off Dame Street, next to City Hall and diagonally across from Christchurch Cathedral. There is also an entrance off Ship Street if you are approaching the library from St Patrick's or Christchurch Cathedrals. It is a 10-minute walk up Dame Street from Trinity College. The library is on bus routes 50, 51B, 54A, 56A, 77, 77A, and 123.

## DUBLIN CITY ARCHIVES

(*see also* IRISH THEATRE ARCHIVE, Dublin)

City Assembly House
58 South William Street
DUBLIN 2
Ireland

TELEPHONE: (01) 677 5877; FAX: (01) 677 5954
E-mail: cityarchives@dublincity.ie
Website: www.dublincity.ie/dublin/archives2.html

HOURS

By appointment with the Dublin City Archivist

ACCESS AND SERVICES

Visitors welcome, but by appointment only. Identification and advance notice required. Not Disabled access facilities. Laptops permitted; pencils only. Photocopying and microform prints available for a fee. There are a number of publications specifically relating to the holdings of the archives. These include: Sir John T. and Lady Gilbert (eds), *Calendar of Ancient Records of Dublin*, in 19 vols (Dublin, 1889–1944); Mary Clark, *The Book of Maps of the Dublin City Surveyors* (Dublin, 1983); Niall McCullough, *A Vision of the City: Dublin and the Wide Streets Commissioners* (Dublin, 1991); Philomena Connolly and Geoffrey Martin, *The Dublin Guild Merchant Roll* (Dublin, 1992); Mary Clark and Raymond Refasussé, *Directory of Historic Dublin Guilds* (Dublin, 1993); Mary Clark and Gráinne Doran, *Serving the City: The Dublin City Managers and Town Clerks* (Dublin, 1996); Colm Lennon and James Murray, *The Dublin City Franchise Roll* (Dublin, 1988); and Jane Ohlmeyer and Éamonn Ó Ciardha, *The Irish Statute Staple Books* (Dublin, 1998).

CONTACT

Mary Clark, City Archivist

DESCRIPTION

Dublin City Archives houses the historic records of the municipal government of Dublin from the 12th century to the present. On 1 January 2002 Dublin Corporation changed its name to Dublin City Council.

HOLDINGS

The Dublin City Archives contains a wealth of published and unpublished records, including City Council and committee minutes, account books, correspondence, reports, court records, charity petitions, title deeds, maps and plans, photographs and drawings, all of which document the development of Dublin over eight centuries. Among the principal civic collections are: royal charters of the city of Dublin, 1171–1727; medieval cartularies, including two important bound manuscripts, one written on vellum, the White Book of Dublin (also known as the *Liber Albus*) and the Chain Book of Dublin; Dublin City Assembly Rolls, 1447–1841; Board of Dublin Aldermen, 1567–1841; journals of sheriffs and commons, 1746–1841; Tholsell Court of Dublin, 16th–18th centuries; Dublin city treasurer's accounts, 1540–1841; Freedom records, 1468–1918; City surveyor's maps, 1695–1928; minutes and reports of Dublin City Council, 1841 onwards; photographic collection, including Liffey Bridges and North Strand bombing; records of Dublin Corporation committees and departments, 1840–1970; and electoral registers, 1937 onwards. Other collections of importance include: Records of some trade and religious guilds to 1841; Wide Streets Commission, 1757–1849; Paving Board, 1774–1840; charitable committees, including Mansion House Relief Fund, 1880; Rathmines and Rathgar Township, 1847–1930; Pembroke Township, 1863–1930; Civic Institute of Ireland, 1918–60.

LOCATION

South William Street is located two blocks west of Grafton Street, near the Powerscourt and St Stephen's Green shopping centres. The nearest DART stations are Tara Street and Pearse.

## DUBLIN CITY PUBLIC LIBRARIES

Library Headquarters
Cumberland House
Fenian Street
DUBLIN 2
Ireland

TELEPHONE: (01) 664 4800; FAX: (01) 676 1628
E-mail: dubcilib@iol.ie
Website: www.iol.ie/dublincitylibrary

HOURS

See separate listings for DUBLIN CITY PUBLIC LIBRARIES – CENTRAL LIBRARY, CENTRE FOR DUBLIN AND IRISH STUDIES, and DUBLIN CITY ARCHIVES. Call or visit website for hours of branch libraries listed below. Library Headquarters is not open to the public.

CONTACT

Deirdre Ellis-King, Dublin City Librarian
Margaret Hayes, Deputy City Librarian

DESCRIPTION

The Headquarters Library is responsible for the overall administration of library services in a network of 31 libraries and service points. These include: Ballyfermot Library, tel. (01) 626 9324/5; Ballymun Library, tel. (01) 842 1890; Cabra Library, tel. (01) 869 1414; Central Library, tel. (01) 873 4333; Charleville Mall Library, tel. (01) 874 9619; Coolock Library, tel. (01) 847 7781; Dolphin's Barn Library, tel. (01) 454 0681; Donaghmede Library, tel. (01) 848 2833; Drumcondra Library, tel. (01) 837 7206; Finglas Library, tel. (01) 834 4906; Inchicore Library, tel. (01) 453 3793; Kevin Street Library, tel. (01) 475 3794; Marino Library, tel. (01) 833 6297; Pembroke Library, tel. (01) 668 9575; Phibsboro Library, tel. (01) 830 4341; Raheny Library, tel. (01) 831 5521; Rathmines Library, tel. (01) 497 3539; Ringsend Library, tel. (01) 668 0063; Terenure Library, tel. (01) 490 7035; Walkinstown Library, tel. (01) 455 8159; Children's & Schools, tel. (01) 475 8791; Community & Youth Information Centre, tel. (01) 878 6844; Mobile Libraries, tel. (01) 869 1415; Civic Museum, tel. (01) 679 4260; and City Archives, tel. (01) 677 5877.

HOLDINGS

See separate listings for Central Library, Centre for Dublin and Irish Studies, and Dublin City Archives.

LOCATION

City centre

## DUBLIN CITY PUBLIC LIBRARIES – CENTRAL LIBRARY

Ilac Centre
Henry Street
DUBLIN 1
Ireland

TELEPHONE: (01) 873 4333; FAX: (01) 872 1451
E-mail: dubcilib@iol.ie
Website: www.iol.ie/dublincitylibrary

HOURS

M–Th, 10:00am–8:00pm; F,Sat, 10:00am–5:00pm

ACCESS AND SERVICES

The Central Library is open to the public. For those wishing to borrow material from the library, full membership is available on production of identification and proof of residency. Visitors are welcome to use all other facilities but will need to provide personal ID when using some services.

CONTACT

Michael Molloy, Divisional Librarian

DESCRIPTION

Located within a shopping centre in Dublin's city centre, the Central Library is the largest in a network of 31 libraries and service points administered by the DUBLIN CITY PUBLIC LIBRARIES.

HOLDINGS

The Central Library offers a wide range of services in addition to its extensive collection of adult and junior material for loan. These include: Internet access, photocopying, computerized catalogue, newspapers, periodicals, exhibitions, lectures, and tours. The Central Library also offers a Business Information Centre, Open Learning Centre, and specialist Music Library.

- The **Business Information Centre** is a reference service and a key information source for those starting a business or doing research. It holds sample business plans, journals and newspapers, company information, market research and financial markets information, and national and international statistics. It also offers reference books, national and international directories, journals, databases, newspaper cuttings, and an extensive collection of company reports.
- The **Open Learning Centre** offers a wide range of self-learning opportunities in language and computers. Courses in audio and video are available in approximately 80 different languages. Courses are available in basic computer skills, wordprocessing, spreadsheets, databases, and use of the Internet. All courses must be booked in advance and a certificate is awarded to students who complete 50 hours of study using the learning facilities. The centre also facilitates conversation exchange in Italian, Spanish, French, German, Irish, Japanese and Russian.
- The **Music Library** is a valuable resource for anyone with an interest in music. The library offers a lending and reference service, including music CDs, cassettes and videos for loan. It also stocks literature on all aspects of music, sheet music including vocal scores, songbooks, tutor books, and orchestral sets. In addition the library provides listening facilities for leisure or study purposes, and a wide range of music periodicals. A number of computer databases have been produced including a tracks index, a sheet music index and databases of music and choral societies in Dublin City.

LOCATION

The Central Library is in the Ilac Shopping Centre, between Henry Street and Parnell Street, in city centre. By bus, take any bus to the city centre; by train, take the DART to Tara Street or Connolly Station.

## DUBLIN CITY UNIVERSITY LIBRARY

Dublin City University
DUBLIN 9
Ireland

TELEPHONE: (01) 700 5212; FAX: (01) 700 5602
E-mail: infodesk@dcu.ie
Website: www.dcu.ie/~library

HOURS

Term: M–Th, 8:30am–10:00pm; F, 8:30am–9:00pm; Sat, 9:30am–5:00pm
Inter-semester and summer: consult library website for current hours for these periods

ACCESS AND SERVICES

Visitors are welcome, but must apply for a non-graduate external membership to gain access to collections and services. An annual fee is charged. Accessible to persons with a disability. All locally-held material can be found by using the library catalogue (OPAC), available via the Internet. The library also provides access, via the library web page, to an extensive collection of online information resources including full-text journals and newspapers. Reciprocal arrangements with other university libraries are in place and visiting facilities can be arranged. Users can also avail of photocopying/printing/scanning facilities, read microforms, watch videos and access the Internet. DCU shares an integrated OPAC with Mater Dei Institute of Education (Clonliffe Road, Dublin 3; tel. (01) 874 1680; fax (01) 836 8920) and ST PATRICK'S COLLEGE, the first system in Ireland to provide full web search facilities in both English and Irish. The catalogues of the three libraries complement each other and provide a single search point for over 350,000 book titles. DCU is also a member of ALCID (Academic Libraries Co-operating in Dublin), which gives students and faculty access to the libraries of: Mater Dei; NUI Galway; NUI Maynooth; Royal College of Surgeons in Ireland; Royal Irish Academy; St Patrick's, Drumcondra; Trinity College Dublin; University College Cork; University College Dublin; and University of Limerick.

CONTACT

Paul Sheehan, Director of Library Services; tel. (01) 700 5211;
e-mail: paul.sheehan@dcu.ie
Ellen Breen, Sub-Librarian, Information & Public Services; tel. (01) 700 5210;
e-mail: ellen.breen@dcu.ie

DESCRIPTION

Dublin City University was established in 1980 to respond to the challenges being set for higher education by rapidly diversifying industrial and business sectors in Ireland and in the European Union. The university currently enrols more than 9,000 students. In 2000, it opened its new state-of-the-art library building, designed to facilitate all forms of research and learning. The university includes St Patrick's College, Drumcondra; and Mater Dei Institute of Education, each with separate libraries, but linked by the same library management system. See separate listing for ST PATRICK'S COLLEGE.

HOLDINGS

The library's collection contains approximately 180,000 volumes and 800 print subscriptions, and mirrors the academic programmes offered by DCU. These include: business; education; computing and mathematical sciences; engineering and design; humanities; applied language and intercultural studies; communications; and science and health, including nursing and sport.

LOCATION

The university is located on an 85-acre campus in the northern suburbs of Dublin, near Glasnevin cemetery and the Botanic Gardens. It is served by buses no. 11, 11A, 13, 13A, 19A, and 60.

## DUBLIN COUNTY ARCHIVES

*See* FINGAL COUNTY ARCHIVES, Dublin

## DUBLIN UNIVERSITY

*See* TRINITY COLLEGE DUBLIN, Dublin

## DÚN LAOGHAIRE LIBRARY

*See* DÚN LAOGHAIRE LIBRARY – LOCAL HISTORY DEPARTMENT, Dún Laoghaire, Co. Dublin

## DÚN LAOGHAIRE-RATHDOWN HERITAGE SOCIETY

*See under* DÚN LAOGHAIRE, Co. Dublin

## FINGAL COUNTY ARCHIVES

11 Parnell Square
DUBLIN 1
Ireland

TELEPHONE: (01) 872 7968; FAX: (01) 878 6919
E-mail: fincolib@iol.ie
Website: www.iol.ie/~fincolib/archives.htm

HOURS

M–F, 10:00am–1:00pm, 2:00–4:30pm

ACCESS AND SERVICES

Visitors welcome. Research facilities are provided free of charge. Advance appointment required. In order to facilitate researchers, appointments outside normal hours may be arranged if sufficient notice is given. Archives are for reference purposes only; materials are not available for loan. Access to the storage area is not permitted. Depending on the age and condition of the material, photocopying services may be provided. Please note: some records may have to be withdrawn for conservation treatment and may not always be available for consultation.

CONTACT

Patricia McCarthy, Archivist

DESCRIPTION

Under the terms of the 1993 Local Government Act, Dublin County Council was replaced by the three new Councils of Fingal, South Dublin, and Dún Laoghaire-Rathdown. The archives of Dublin County Council were transferred to Fingal County Archives, which is now located within the headquarters of Fingal County Libraries. All material relating to the former Dublin County Council and its predecessor bodies including Boards of Guardians and Grand Juries is housed here.

HOLDINGS

Fingal County Archives contains a small number of manuscript Grand Jury Minute Books and a more extensive collection of printed Presentment Books for the period 1818 until 1898, when most of the Juries' functions were transferred to the newly established County Councils. Fingal County Archives also contains material for the Boards of Guardians and Rural District Councils of Balrothery, Dublin North, Dublin South and Rathdown, and the Rural District Council of Celbridge. The Dublin County Council records constitute the largest body of material in the archives. Dublin County Council was established under the 1898 Local Government Act. In the early years of its existence its main functions were the maintenance of roads and mental hospitals and the raising of rates. In 1930 the Council took over the functions of the Boards of Guardians and Rural District Councils and as the century progressed the Council's functions expanded to include the provision of roads, planning, libraries, community and environmental services. Fingal County Archives contains a large number of collections dealing with the establishment and provision of these services. It also contains a small number of collections of private individuals and organizations that have a connection with the County of Dublin.

LOCATION

Dublin city centre, at the north end of O'Connell Street.

## FINGAL COUNTY LIBRARIES

Local Studies Department
11 Parnell Square
DUBLIN 1
Ireland.

TELEPHONE: (01) 878 6910; FAX: (01) 878 6919
E-mail: fincolib@iol.ie
Website: www.iol.ie/~fincolib/localhs.htm

HOURS

By appointment

ACCESS AND SERVICES

Visitors welcome. Photocopying and microfilm print services available for a modest fee. Local Studies produces publications and exhibits to promote the collection. In addition to postcards of the area, Local Studies has published several books, including: *Fingal Past and Present*; *Discovering Fingal: A Photographic Tour*, Vol. 1, 1997; and *Discovering Fingal: A Photographic Tour*, Vol. 2, 2002.

CONTACT

Jeremy Black, Local Studies Librarian

DESCRIPTION

Part of the Fingal County Libraries system, headquartered at County Hall Main Street, Swords, Co. Dublin, tel. (01) 890 5524; fax (01) 890 5599, under the sponsorship of Fingal County Council. The Council was established on 1 January 1994 following the dissolution of Dublin County Council and the Corporation of Dún Laoghaire and their replacement with three new administrative counties, South Dublin, Dún Laoghaire-Rathdown and Fingal.

HOLDINGS

A comprehensive collection of material relating to the Fingal area has been assembled since 1994 and is currently housed at Parnell Square. Items contained in the collection include: antiquarian and new books covering standard reference texts, history, topography, ecclesiastical, transport, maritime, postal and many more; periodicals, including older standard research titles and those with specific local history interest; prints, focusing on sketches of the archaeological and architectural views of Fingal; photographs, including copies of the relevant Fingal subjects taken from the primary collections of the National Library of Ireland, with some private photographic material also available; postcards (800 items capturing scenes of Fingal from the early part of the 20th century); pictures (watercolour, oil and ink drawings by local artists and some original paintings); maps (Ordnance Survey, townland, Down Survey and contemporary development items); videos (copies of videos produced within the Fingal area by various groups); newspapers (bound editions of the *Fingal Independent* since 1994); and ephemera (material including pamphlets, letters, coins, posters, postal items, memorabilia and curiosities make up a growing portion of the collection).

LOCATION

Dublin city centre, at the north end of O'Connell Street.

## FINGAL GENEALOGY

*See under* SWORDS, Co. Dublin

## FRANCISCAN LIBRARY

*See under* KILLINEY, Co. Dublin

## THE FRIENDS' HISTORICAL LIBRARY

*See* HISTORICAL LIBRARY, RELIGIOUS SOCIETY OF FRIENDS, Dublin

## GARDA MUSEUM/ARCHIVES

Record Tower
Dublin Castle
DUBLIN 2
Ireland

TELEPHONE: (01) 671 9597; FAX: (01) 666 9992
E-mail: hds1@eircom.net
Website: www.garda.ie (link to historical society)

HOURS

M–F, 9:00am–5:00pm; Sat and Sun by appointment

ACCESS AND SERVICES

Visitors welcome but advance notice preferred, especially to use archives or library. No admission charge. Disabled access facilities, but only to ground floor. Pencils only when using original material. Laptops and photography permitted. Printed finding aids available.

CONTACT

Inspector John P. Duffy, Archivist; personal e-mail: hds1@eircom.net

DESCRIPTION

An Garda Síochána Museum/Archives collects and preserves archival material and artefacts relating not only to An Garda Síochána, but also to the Irish Constabulary, the Royal Irish Constabulary and the Dublin Metropolitan Police. It serves both as a support service within the Police Force, with a primary responsibility to provide a records management service, and as an outreach resource for the general public.

HOLDINGS

The Historical Library houses a collection of police-related publications, including monthly Garda publications from 1922 to the present. The book collection numbers approximately 1,000 catalogued bound volumes. The Archives contain photographs, sound recordings and documents outlining the history and development of policing in Ireland in the 19th and 20th centuries. The sound recordings are of retired RIC/DMP and Garda members. In addition to documenting policing in Ireland, the collection seeks to document the impact of Irish policing on the English-speaking world and the British colonies. Of special interest is the large genealogical collection on policing from 1822 to 1922. The archives also contain the Dublin Metropolitan Police Personnel Register from 1836 to the 1970s.

LOCATION

The Museum/Archives is located at the Record Tower of Dublin Castle, off Dame Street, next to City Hall and diagonally across from Christchurch Cathedral. There is also an entrance off Ship Street if you are approaching the Museum/Archives from St Patrick's or Christchurch Cathedrals.

## GENEALOGICAL OFFICE

*See* OFFICE OF THE CHIEF HERALD/GENEALOGICAL OFFICE

## GENERAL REGISTER OFFICE

Joyce House
8–11 Lombard Street East
DUBLIN 2
Ireland

TELEPHONE: (01) 635 4000; FAX: (01) 635 4527
E-mail: Tom_Joyce@health.irlgov.ie
Website: www.groireland.ie

HOURS

M–F, 9:30am–12:30pm, 2:15–4:30pm

ACCESS AND SERVICES

Visitors welcome in research room on a first-come, first-served basis. For 1.90 euro, researchers can do a five-year search of a given type of index book: birth, marriage or death, or for 15.24 euro they can gain access to all index volumes for up to six successive hours. The index books contain references to microfilm records of the actual register entries, copies of which are then available from the research room staff at a cost of 1.90 euro each. Copies may not always be available on the day ordered. Details of the type and extent of records held by the GRO can be found on the research page of its website. A birth certificate contains the date and place of birth, forename, father's name, place of residence and occupation, mother's name and maiden surname, name and address of person who registered the birth. A death certificate contains the name and address of the deceased person, date and place of death, marital status, occupation, age at last birthday, cause of death, name and address of person who registered the death. A pre-1957 marriage certificate contains the date and place of marriage, both spouses' age, name and marital status, occupation and pre-marriage address, their fathers' names and occupations. A post-1957 marriage certificate contains the date and place of marriage, both spouses' age, name, marital status, occupation, and pre-marriage address, their parents' names and the couple's future intended place of residence. Requests for certificates should be made in writing, including as many details as possible of the event(s) in question. Credit cards not currently accepted, but check website as plans are in the offing to introduce credit card payments. Cheques (international money orders or personal) in US dollars or pounds sterling are acceptable, at appropriate exchange rate for the euro, and should be made payable to General Register Office. Cash should be sent by registered post. There is ordinarily a five- to six-week backlog, though requests may be processed more expeditiously for good cause. Please note: The GRO does not provide research assistance. Contact the ASSOCIATION OF PROFESSIONAL GENEALOGISTS IN IRELAND, Dublin.

CONTACT

Tom Joyce; e-mail: Tom_Joyce@health.irlgov.ie

DESCRIPTION

The GRO is solely concerned with the administration of the civil registration system in Ireland. It will provide photocopies or certified copies of entries in its Birth, Death, or Marriage Registers on receipt of a postal application accompanied by appropriate fee. See website for fee schedule. The records and index are in a manual format, arranged chronologically, so specific details, especially dates, are needed for a search. Other details, such as location of the event, parents' names, mother's maiden name, are helpful.

HOLDINGS

Index books for birth, death and marriage records after 1864. Microfilm records of the actual register entries. Note: prior to 1864, the only source for registration of baptisms, marriages and burials, except for non-Catholic marriages, which have been civilly registered since 1845, is parish registers. To use these resources effectively, it is necessary therefore to know the religious affiliation and often even the place of baptism, marriage or burial of the ancestor. Catholic parish registers are still held by the parish priest, but most up to 1880 are available on microfilm in the National Library of Ireland. Access may require the written permission of the parish priest. Church of Ireland parish registers up to 1870 are public records. Most are still held in the local parishes, while some are held at the NATIONAL LIBRARY OF IRELAND, Dublin, or the REPRESENTATIVE CHURCH BODY LIBRARY, Dublin, or the PUBLIC RECORD OFFICE OF NORTHERN IRELAND, Belfast, Co. Antrim. Presbyterian Church records are arranged by congregation and enquiries should be directed to the Presbyterian Historical Society, Belfast.

LOCATION

Lombard Street East runs off Pearse Street, near Pearse DART Station, a few blocks north and east of Trinity College.

## GILBERT LIBRARY

*See* CENTRE FOR DUBLIN AND IRISH STUDIES, Dublin

## GRAND LODGE OF FREEMASONS OF IRELAND: LIBRARY, ARCHIVES AND MUSEUM

Freemasons' Hall
17 Molesworth Street
DUBLIN 2
Ireland

TELEPHONE: (01) 676 1337; FAX: (01) 662 5101
E-mail: library@freemason.ie
Website: None

HOURS

By appointment only

ACCESS AND SERVICES

Visitors welcome, but by appointment only; advance notice and identification required. No disabled access facilities. Laptops permitted; pencils only. No access charges to library, but fees are charged for postal and e-mail queries. Printed finding aids available; approximately half the 12,000-volume book collection catalogued on cards. Descriptive lists available for some correspondence files and minute books. General readers may consult all published works, while only members may borrow books. See HOLDINGS for further restrictions. Access to archival material is also limited. Records prior to 1900 are available to the general public, but the Grand Secretary's permission is required for access to post-1900 material. Records of current lodges and other Masonic bodies deposited with the Archives may only be consulted with the permission of the bodies concerned. Photocopying available but with severe restrictions. Microfilm reader/printers available.

CONTACT

Barry Lyons, Librarian

DESCRIPTION

The Library, Archives and Museum of the Grand Lodge of Ireland serves as the repository for the history of Irish Freemasonry in Ireland and abroad. Started in the 1730s, the purpose of the library/archives is to collect, preserve and exhibit items and information relating to the development of the Masonic Order. The collection is funded by the Grand Lodge, and acquisitions come primarily as gifts from members and the public.

HOLDINGS

The collection houses approximately 12,000 volumes. The Chetwode Crawley Library contains books printed between 1527 and 1851, and these volumes can neither be lent nor photocopied. Books printed since 1851 form the modern section, and members may borrow recently published books or older books from this section that are available in duplicate. The library contains books on all Grand Lodges, organized geographically. The archives, consisting of some 800 boxes of material, house the records of the Governing Bodies of the Order, as well as representative collections from Lodges and Chapters. Membership registers date from 1760, and the correspondence files date from the 1820s. The latter include some 100,000 pieces from the Secretaries of Irish Lodges from around the world to the Grand Secretary. Pre-1900 records of schools and other charities supported by the Masons are available for research, but with restrictions.

LOCATION

The Grand Lodge is located in central Dublin, opposite Buswell's Hotel, near Kildare Street, close to the National Library and the National Museum.

## GUINNESS ARCHIVE

Guinness Storehouse
St James's Gate
DUBLIN 8
Ireland

TELEPHONE: (01) 471 4557; FAX: (01) 408 4737
E-mail: eibhlin.roche@diageo.com
Website: None

HOURS

M–Th, 9:30am–1:00pm, 2:00–5:00pm; F, 9:30am–1:00pm, 2:00–4:30pm

ACCESS AND SERVICES

Visitors welcome at no charge, but by appointment only; advance notice preferred. Disabled access facilities. Laptops permitted; pencils only. Photocopying is available for a fee. The archive service is very recent and the collections are largely uncatalogued.

CONTACT

Eibhlin Roche, Guinness Archivist

DESCRIPTION

The archive is the only corporate archive in Ireland fully open to the public. It serves as an information resource for Guinness Ireland as well as for the researching public. The archive supports the Guinness Museum as a whole in providing artefacts for exhibit.

HOLDINGS

The collection includes books and journals relating to brewing and brewery history; maps, plans, photographs, film, brewing ledgers relating to the Guinness company history; records from all brewery departments; artefacts and Guinness memorabilia. Major collections include: Correspondence with Lord Iveagh; Brewery Memoranda, 1802–25, 1869–97; Board Orders, 1909–15; Head Brewers' Desk Diaries, 1881–1993; Brewery Annual Reports; Hains & Shands Reports on Overseas Trade, 1906–25; Brewery Guide Books, 1888–1955; Guinness posters, bottles, dripmats, and labels; Minute Books of the Brewers' Guild of Dublin, Minute Books of the Coopers' Guild of Dublin, and Minute Books from Robert Perry & Sons Ltd. Of special genealogical interest are employee ledgers and personnel files.

LOCATION

The archive is located in the Guinness Storehouse – the Guinness Visitors' Experience at the Guinness Brewery.

## HISTORICAL LIBRARY, RELIGIOUS SOCIETY OF FRIENDS

Swanbrook House
Bloomfield Avenue
DUBLIN 4
Ireland

TELEPHONE: (01) 668 7157; FAX: None
E-mail: None
Website: www.ipag.com/quakers

HOURS

Thursdays only, 10:30am–1:00pm

ACCESS AND SERVICES

Visitors welcome, and no prior appointment required. Though the library is open only for a short while on Thursdays, exceptions are sometimes made to allow researchers access to materials on Thursday afternoons, staffing permitting. The library is staffed entirely by volunteers. Photocopying and microfilm equipment are available. There is a fee for postal queries. The library maintains card indexes to its holdings including separate indexes for its photographic archive and its museum collection. These indexes have been recently computerized and are available on CD-ROM. The library offers recent publications for sale.

CONTACT

Mary Shackleton, Honorary Curator

DESCRIPTION

The library is supported by the Religious Society of Friends, the Quakers, who arrived in Ireland in the 17th century.

HOLDINGS

The Quakers have kept excellent records ever since their arrival in Ireland, and Swanbrook is therefore an especially rich repository of information for Irish social, political, religious, and genealogical studies. The collections include books, pamphlets, photographs, recordings, and museum pieces, such as examples of Quaker embroidery and bonnets. Records generally reflect the concerns of Quakers through the centuries, and subject interests include famine relief, the anti-slavery campaign, care of the mentally ill, education, temperance, peace, prison reform, refugees, and commercial interests. Of special interest to genealogists, each meeting kept minutes, and from these minutes were transcribed registers of births, marriages, and deaths that are available in the library. Microfilm copies of these registers are available at the NATIONAL LIBRARY OF IRELAND, Dublin and the NATIONAL ARCHIVES OF IRELAND, Dublin. The library also houses tapes of Quaker lectures and addresses, and tapes of reminiscences by elderly Irish Quakers.

LOCATION

The library is located in the Ballsbridge area of Dublin, on the south side of the Liffey, about two miles south-east of St Stephen's Green.

## THE HONORABLE SOCIETY OF KING'S INNS

Henrietta Street
DUBLIN 1
Ireland

TELEPHONE: (01) 878 2119; FAX: (01) 874 4846
E-mail: library@kingsinns.ie
Website: www.kingsinns.ie

HOURS

By appointment only

ACCESS AND SERVICES

Visitors welcome, but by appointment only; advance notice, references and identification required. No disabled access facilities. Laptops permitted; pencils only. Charges for genealogical and other research undertaken vary by category of user. Registered members of the society (Category A) are exempted from search fees but do pay reduced photocopying and facsimile charges and normal postage charges. Academics (Category B) may be charged a search fee depending on length of time involved in the search, and pay a slightly higher charge for photocopying and facsimile services and normal charges for postage. All others who have been granted permission to use the library facilities (Category C) are required to pay a minimum fee of 14.00 euro per search plus normal charges for photocopying, facsimiles and postage. Photocopying done by staff at 12c per page surcharge for all users. Consult library staff for fee schedule. Publications of interest and available at the library include: *King's Inns Portraits*, catalogued by Wanda Ryan-Smolin at 13.00 euro; and several free leaflets, including *Library Guide*; *How to Find Irish Cases …*; accession lists; and *The Honorable Society of King's Inns* by Daire Hogan.

CONTACT

Jonathan Armstrong, Librarian

DESCRIPTION

The library was founded in 1787. The society itself dates from 1541. King's Inns trains students wishing to become barristers (lawyers), and the focus of its collection is on the law, with history, literature, classics, biography, typography, science, and natural history also well represented.

HOLDINGS

In addition to its book collection, the library houses architectural records, art and artefacts, manuscripts, maps, microforms, newspapers, and pamphlets. Of special interest are the holdings of: British Parliamentary Papers; Irish Appeals to the House of Lords; the Pamphlet Collection; the Papers of John Patrick Prendergast, Irish language manuscripts, and rentals under the Encumbered Estates Act of 1849. Of special genealogical interest are the King's Inns Admission Papers 1607–1867 (abstracts published by Irish Manuscripts Commission), plus a printed copy of Griffith's Valuation and a collection of Ordnance Survey maps.

LOCATION

Henrietta Street is off Bolton Street, almost directly opposite Bolton Street College, on the north side of the Liffey, west of Parnell Square. King's Inns can also be approached via Constitution Hill, opposite Broadstone Bus Garage.

## IRISH ARCHITECTURAL ARCHIVE

73 Merrion Square
DUBLIN 2
Ireland

TELEPHONE: (01) 676 3430; FAX: (01) 661 6309
E-mail: info@iarc.ie
Website: www.iarc.ie

HOURS

Tu–F, 10:00am–1:00pm, 2:30–5:00pm; closed month of August

ACCESS AND SERVICES

Visitors and enquiries welcome. No reader's ticket or appointment necessary. No disabled access facilities. Laptops permitted; pencils only. Photocopying available for a fee of 25c to 50c; photographic prints, 20 euro to 140 euro, depending on size and nature of the print required. Card catalogue available. *See* D. Griffin and S. Lincoln, *Drawings from the Irish Architectural Archive* (Dublin, 1993).

CONTACT

Colum O'Riordan, Archive Administrator
David Griffin, Archive Director

DESCRIPTION

The Irish Architectural Archive is a charitable company established in 1976 to collect, preserve and make available the records of Ireland's architectural heritage. The archive is a non-confrontational body, which does not involve itself in any way in matters of planning or conservation controversy. The archive also pursues an active publications policy and outreach programme, including exhibitions to bring the riches of its collections to as wide an audience as possible.

HOLDINGS

The Irish Architectural Archive collects, preserves and makes available records of every type relating to the architecture of Ireland. The holdings date from the 1690s to the 1990s and comprise in excess of 100,000 architectural drawings, 300,000 photographs, 12,000 items of printed matter, and several dozen architectural models. The collections include information, primary or secondary, on every notable Irish architect, on every important Irish building period or style, and on most significant holdings in the 32 counties of Ireland. Major collections include: Ashlin & Coleman, Boyd Barrett Murphy O'Connor Collection, Burgage Collection, Rudolf Maximillian Butler Collection, Charleville Forest Collection, Cullen & Co. Collection, C.P. Curran Collection, Dublin Artisans Dwellings Co. Collection, Emo Court Collection, Desmond FitzGerald Collection, Charles Geoghan Collection, Guinness Drawings Collection, Alan Hope Collection, Brendan Jeffers Collection, Alfred Jones Biographical Index, McCurdy & Mitchell Collection, Raymond McGrath Collection, Munden & Purcell Collection, Donal O'Neill Flanagan Collection, Patterson Kempster Shortall Collection, Anthony Reddy Associates Collection, Fred Rogerson Collection, RIAI Murray Collection, Royal (Collins) Barracks Collection, Royal Institute of the Architects of Ireland Archives, Robinson Keefe & Devane Collection, Scott Tallon Walker Collection, Michael Scott Collection, Sibthorpe Collection, Stephenson Gibney Collection, Townley Hall Collection, Tyndall Hogan Hurley Collection, and the Workhouse Collection.

The archive's photograph collection is one of the largest in Ireland. Aside from ongoing photographic survey work carried out by the archive, photographic collections include Automobile Association Photographs, BKS Aerial Photographs, Buildings of Ireland Photographs, Alec R. Day ARPS Collection, J.V. Downes Slide Collection, Kieran Clendining Collection, Green Studio Collection, Thomas Gunn Collection, and the Westropp Albums.

LOCATION

Halfway along the south side of Merrion Square, which is the side running from Upper Merrion Street to Upper Mount Street and the Pepper Canister Church (St Stephen's). No. 7 bus stops about five minutes' walk from the archive. From the north side of the city, the No. 13 bus stops near the archive. The archive is a ten-minute walk from Pearse DART Station.

## IRISH FILM ARCHIVE OF THE FILM INSTITUTE OF IRELAND

6 Eustace Street
DUBLIN 2
Ireland

TELEPHONE: (01) 679 5744; FAX: (01) 677 8755
E-mail: *See* CONTACT
Website: www.fii.ie

HOURS

Film and tape viewing: M–F, 10:00am–1:00pm, 2:00–6:00pm; Tiernan MacBride Library: M–F, 2:00–5:30pm (Wednesdays open until 7:00pm). Appointment necessary for paper archive, film and tape viewing but not for access to library. Booking should be made with Irish Film Archive staff by phone at least 48 hours in advance. Archive staff must be informed of cancellations at least 24 hours in advance of appointment.

ACCESS AND SERVICES

Visitors and enquiries welcome. See above. Information relating to film, tape, stills, posters and library holdings is held on computer database. Limited access to these databases is available via website. Archive staff facilitate public enquiries relating to the content of any aspect of the collections. Access to the collections may be restricted due to donor stipulations or to preservation concerns. The Tiernan MacBride Library is accessible for reference purposes only, but all materials may be photocopied. Use and access charges apply, except for access to the Paper Archive Collection. Currently, charges are as follows: film, 15 euro per hour; tape, 6.50 euro per hour. There is a daily tape rate of 20 euro per visit per day, 75 euro per week. Access charges to the Tiernan MacBride Library are: students, 1.50 euro per hour per visit or 15.00 euro per annual membership; general public, 2 euro per visit or 20 euro per annual membership.

CONTACT

Kasandra O'Connell, Head of Archive; e-mail: koconnell@ifc.ie
Sunniva O'Flynn, Archive Curator; e-mail: soflynn@ifc.ie
Emma Keogh, Librarian; e-mail: ekeogh@ifc.ie
Eugene Finn, Film Archivist; e-mail: efinn@ifc.ie

DESCRIPTION

The Irish Film Archive, which includes the Tiernan MacBride Library, is a part of the Film Institute of Ireland, and is funded by the Arts Council of Ireland and by user charges. It acquires, preserves and provides access to the national audiovisual heritage. The archive holds collections of film and videotape made in and about Ireland and documents relating to the history of film in Ireland.

HOLDINGS

The film collection now numbers more than 15,000 cans, reflecting the history of professional and amateur production in Ireland from 1897 to the present. Much of the collection has been transferred to videotape for reference purposes, totalling over 1,000 VHS tapes of Irish material. The paper collection of the Film Archive includes stills, posters and document collections relating to Irish cinema. Still and poster collections include: 1,193 stills, 453 posters, 288 transparences, and 21 video prints. The Tiernan MacBride Library subscribes to a wide range of film journals, and readers have access to film-related CD-ROMs. The library also holds a valuable collection of material relating to all elements of Irish cinema. Files of clippings on Irish film production are maintained and updated on a daily basis. Collections of special note include: Lord Killanin Collection, Pat Murphy

Collection, Tiernan MacBride Collection, and Gael Linn Collection. The Tiernan MacBride Collection is the most comprehensive collection of film-related publications in Ireland. It contains approximately 1,800 books covering all aspects of national and international cinema.

LOCATION

The IFA is located in the Temple Bar area of Dublin, off Dame Street, opposite Dublin Castle, a few blocks west of Trinity College.

## IRISH JESUIT ARCHIVES

35 Lower Leeson Street
DUBLIN 2
Ireland

TELEPHONE: (01) 676 1248; FAX: (01) 676 2984
E-mail: archives@s-j.ie
Website: www.jesuit.ie/irl/history.htm

HOURS

By appointment only

ACCESS AND SERVICES

Advance notice required. Disabled access facilities; laptops permitted; pencils only. No photocopier, microfilm/fiche reader/printer or other electronic aids available, and none may be brought in. Printed finding aids are available.

CONTACT

Fergus O'Donoghue, SJ, Province Archivist

DESCRIPTION

The Irish Jesuit Archives is the official repository for the records of the Irish Jesuits from the 16th to the 20th centuries. It is part of the central administration of the Irish Jesuit Province, though located some distance from the Provincialate. The major part of the holdings represents the concerns of central administration, but there are extensive holdings of the papers of individual Jesuits.

HOLDINGS

The archives house the Irish Jesuit papers relating to work in Ireland, Australia, Hong Kong and Zambia. Earliest papers date back to 1577. In addition, the archives include the MacErlean transcripts of Irish Jesuit material in European archives from 1527 to 1774. The collection includes 800 photographs.

LOCATION

The IJA is located close to the city centre, a five-minute walk from the south-east corner of St Stephen's Green. Entrance by 35 or 36 Lower Leeson Street.

## IRISH JEWISH MUSEUM

3/4 Walworth Road
SOUTH CIRCULAR ROAD, DUBLIN 8
Ireland

TELEPHONE: Museum Office: (01) 453 1797; FAX: None
Curator: TELEPHONE: (01) 490 1857; FAX: (01) 490 1857
E-mail: None
Website: None maintained by the museum itself; several sites reference the museum.

### HOURS

May–Sept: Sun,Tu,Th, 11:00am–3:30pm
Oct–Apr.: Sunday only, 10:30am–2:30pm

### ACCESS AND SERVICES

Visitors welcome. No admission charge. Access to manuscripts and photographs requires permission of Curator. The museum features exhibitions that document the Jewish experience in Ireland over the past century and a half, most especially the communities of Belfast, Cork, Derry, Dublin, Limerick, and Waterford. A feature of particular interest is a kitchen depicting a typical Sabbath/Festival meal setting in a Jewish home at the turn of the 20th century. Adult and school tours are available by request. Call (01) 490 1857 for further information.

### CONTACT

Curator

### DESCRIPTION

The museum seeks to document the religious, historical and cultural life of the Jewish people in Ireland. Though the collection focuses on the past 150 years, Jews have been in Ireland since 1492. The museum is located in a former synagogue, which consisted of two adjoining terraced houses. The original synagogue, with all its fittings, can be viewed upstairs. The home of Rabbi Herzog, first Chief Rabbi of Ireland and father of Dr Chaim Herzog (1918–97), the Irish-born first President of Israel, is nearby. The fictional boyhood home of Leopold Bloom, the hero of Joyce's *Ulysses,* is also close by, at 52 Upper Clanbrassil Street. There are some 1,400 Jews living in Ireland today; 1,200 in the south, 200 in the north.

### HOLDINGS

The Jewish Museum contains a substantial collection of memorabilia relating to Ireland's Jewish communities, whose commercial and social life is documented in photographs, paintings, and other displays. The museum also contains a collection of material on Judaism in general.

LOCATION

The museum is based in Portobello, off Victoria Street, just south of the city centre, an area that once had a sizeable Jewish population. Buses include: 16, 19, and 122 to Victoria Street, South Circular Road and 14, 15, 65, and 83 to Lennox Street, off South Richmond Street.

## IRISH THEATRE ARCHIVE

City Assembly House
58 South William Street
DUBLIN 2
Ireland

TELEPHONE: (01) 677 5877; FAX: (01) 677 5954
E-mail: cityarchives@dublincity.ie
Website: www.dublincity.ie

HOURS

By appointment only with the Honorary Archivist of Theatre Archive

ACCESS AND SERVICES

Visitors welcome but by appointment only. Advance notice and identification required. No disabled access facilities. Laptops permitted; pencils only. Photocopying and microfilm prints available for a fee. No borrowing privileges permitted. Publication: *Prompts: Bulletin of the Irish Theatre Archive.*

CONTACT

Mary Clark, Honorary Archivist

DESCRIPTION

The Irish Theatre Archive is operated by Dublin City Council under the auspices of DUBLIN CITY ARCHIVES. Its mission is to collect and preserve materials relating to the history of theatre in Ireland.

HOLDINGS

The archive houses an impressive array of materials relating to theatre in Ireland. Types of material include: programmes; posters; photographs; press cuttings; prompt-books; costume and stage designs relating to theatre, amateur groups and theatre clubs; together with plays in typescript and manuscript. Theatre collections include: An Damer; Cork Theatre Company; Dublin Masque Theatre Guild; Dublin Theatre Festival; Gaiety Theatre, Dublin; Irish Theatre Company; Olympia Theatre, Dublin; Rough Magic Theatre Company; Brendan Smith Academy; and Theatre Royal, Dublin. Collections of actors, costumiers and designers include: P.J. Bourke, Eddie Cooke, Ursula Doyle, Donald Finlay, James N. Healy, Eddie Johnston; Nora Lever; Micheál Mac Liammóir, Dennis Noble,

Jimmy O'Dea, Shelah Richards, and Cecil Sheridan.

LOCATION

South William Street is located two blocks west of Grafton Street, near the Powerscourt and St Stephen's Green shopping centres.

## IRISH TRADITIONAL MUSIC ARCHIVE

63 Merrion Square
DUBLIN 2
Ireland

TELEPHONE: (01) 661 9699; FAX: (01) 662 4585
E-mail: Not for publication
Website: www.itma.ie

HOURS

M–F, 10am–1:00pm, 2:00–5:00pm; closed Christmas through New Year and bank holidays

ACCESS AND SERVICES

Visitors welcome. Advance notice preferred; identification and references required; no access charge. No disabled access facilities. Book collection is fully catalogued on computer and most of the extensive collection of sound recordings is catalogued on computer and indexed; non-circulating collection. The archive offers listening, viewing and reading facilities; photocopying and faxing are available for a fee; laptops permitted.

CONTACT

Róisín Ní Bhriain, Secretary.

DESCRIPTION

The archive was established in 1987 as a multimedia reference and resource centre for the collection, preservation and promotion of traditional song, music and dance of Ireland. Dedicated to the promotion of public education in Irish traditional music, it is a public, not-for-profit institution supported by the Arts Council of Ireland, the Arts Council of Northern Ireland and private donations. It boasts the largest collection in existence of the materials of Irish traditional music.

HOLDINGS

The archive collects comprehensively and broadly all materials, including sound recordings, books, photographs, and videos, for the appreciation and study of Irish traditional music. Its collections extend beyond Ireland to include areas of Irish settlement abroad, especially in Britain and North America. The archive also includes a representative collection of traditional music of other countries. The collection includes some 8,000 volumes of books, 750 films, 130 journals, 10 linear feet of manuscripts, 1,200 pamphlets, 5,500 photographs, 18,000 recordings, and 6,400 pieces of sheet music.

LOCATION

Halfway along the south side of Merrion Square, which is the side running from Upper Merrion Street to Upper Mount Street and the Pepper Canister Church (St Stephen's). No. 7 bus stops about five minutes' walk away from the archive. From the north side of the city, the No. 13 bus stops near the archive. The archive is a 10-minute walk from Pearse DART Station.

## THE JESUIT LIBRARY

Milltown Park
Sandford Road
DUBLIN 6
Ireland

TELEPHONE: (01) 269 8411; FAX: (01) 260 0371
E-mail: jeslib@eircom.net
Website: www.milltown-institute.ie

HOURS

By appointment only

ACCESS AND SERVICES

Visitors welcome, but by appointment. Advance notice is therefore required, as are references. The services of the library are leased on an annual basis to the Milltown Institute of Theology and Philosophy, a third-level college located in the same building. See website above. Books may be borrowed by members of the Jesuit order and by registered students and staff of the Institute of Theology and Philosophy. Photocopying services available. Approximately 90% of the collection is catalogued, either on computer or on cards. The catalogue is not yet available through the Internet, however, and there is no printed catalogue. OPAC (Online Public Access Catalogue) is available in the library.

CONTACT

Patricia Quigley, Librarian

DESCRIPTION

The Jesuit Library, Milltown Park, is the Library of the Irish Province of the Society of Jesus. It is a private library specializing in theology (including scripture and spirituality) and philosophy.

HOLDINGS

The library houses a collection of some 150,000 bound volumes, which mainly cover theology, church history, philosophy, the human sciences, scripture, and Irish material. It is strongest in theology, scripture, patristic studies, spirituality, and medieval and modern European philosophy. It receives more than 170 current periodicals, the areas covered being principally theology, church history, scripture, spirituality, and philosophy. The library also contains a collection of rare and Irish books, curated by Fr Brendan Woods, SJ. Access to the Irish collection is strictly closed.

LOCATION

Milltown Park is located in Milltown, south-west of Donnybrook, about two miles south-east of St Stephen's Green through Ranelagh. From city centre or Lower Baggot Street, take buses 11, 44, 44a, and 48a.

## MACBRIDE LIBRARY (TIERNAN MACBRIDE LIBRARY)

*See* IRISH FILM ARCHIVE OF THE FILM INSTITUTE OF IRELAND, Dublin

## MARSH'S LIBRARY

St Patrick's Close
DUBLIN 8
Ireland

TELEPHONE: (01) 454 3511; FAX: (01) 454 3511
E-mail: keeper@marshlibrary.ie
Website: www.marshlibrary.ie

HOURS

M,W–F, 10:00am–1:00pm; Sat, 10:30am–1:00pm

ACCESS AND SERVICES

Visitors welcome. Admission fees: general public, 2.50 euro; students and seniors, 1.25 euro; children, free. Researchers admitted free but are required to make application in advance to the Keeper of the library. See website for details. No disabled access facilities but special arrangements can be made for researchers; laptops permitted; pencils only. Marsh's Library offers an impressive exhibits programme, and catalogues for these exhibits are available for purchase, if still in print. See website for listing. To commemorate its 300th anniversary, the library produced an exhibit and accompanying illustrated catalogue entitled *This Golden Fleece: Marsh's Library, 1701–2001: A Tercentenary Exhibition*, compiled by Muriel McCarthy and Caroline Sherwood-Smith (Dublin, 2001). See also *All Graduates and Gentlemen: Marsh's Library*, by Muriel McCarthy (Dublin, 1980). For the full library catalogue see the website.

CONTACT

Muriel McCarthy, Keeper of the Library

DESCRIPTION

Marsh's Library was founded in 1701 by Narcissus Marsh, Archbishop of Dublin and a deeply religious and scholarly man. The first public library in Ireland, it contains some 25,000 volumes, largely reflecting its founder's sophisticated interest in the full spectrum of 17th-century knowledge. The library remains virtually the same as it was 300 years ago, and it is one of the cultural treasures of Ireland, used by luminaries from Jonathan Swift to James Joyce. It is cited in *Ulysses*. Some modern physical additions have been made to the library, including a conservation bindery and seminar room, but without altering its appearance. Visitors to Marsh's can step back three centuries in time.

HOLDINGS

The library was built on four major acquisitions. The first was the 10,000-volume personal library of Bishop Stillingfleet, covering a variety of subjects, including theology, science, mathematics, history, medicine, lexicography, and witchcraft. The Stillingfleet Collection occupies the first gallery. The second acquisition was the library of a French Huguenot medical doctor, Elias Bouhéreau, whose interests included Protestantism, theology, and medicine. The third collection was the library of Archbishop Marsh himself. Marsh was particularly interested in science, mathematics, and music, but he was also interested in oriental languages and rabbinical and medieval writers. He collected books in Hebrew, Arabic, Turkish, and Russian. The fourth major collection was bequeathed to the library in 1745 by Bishop Stearne, whose collecting interests closely paralleled those of Stillingfleet, Marsh, and Bouhéreau. Exhibits at Marsh's have drawn heavily on the collection's rich holdings, especially in the areas of Bibles, music, medicine, natural science, botany, religious controversy, orientalia, and travel. The library also houses early manuscripts and printed books in the Irish language.

LOCATION

Marsh's is discreetly tucked away behind St Patrick's Cathedral. Entry is through a stone archway in St Patrick's Close. It is near the National Archives, within easy walking distance (10–15 minutes) of St Stephen's Green.

## MATER DEI INSTITUTE OF EDUCATION LIBRARY

*See* DUBLIN CITY UNIVERSITY LIBRARY

## THE MILITARY ARCHIVES

Cathal Brugha Barracks
RATHMINES, DUBLIN 6
Ireland

TELEPHONE: (01) 804 6457; FAX: (01) 497 4027
E-mail: None
Website: None

HOURS

Tu–Th, 10:00am–4:00pm; closed public and Defence Force holidays and a period over Christmas and New Year

ACCESS AND SERVICES

By appointment only. Identification and advance notice required. References required for academic researchers. Access limited to five persons at any one time; hence, appointment well in advance by letter or phone is mandatory. No disabled access facilities. Laptops permitted; pencils only. No photography. Free brochures and leaflets available.

CONTACT

Officer in Charge/Military Archivist

DESCRIPTION

The Military Archives is the place of deposit for the records of the Department of Defence, the Defence Forces, and the Army Pensions Board. The function of the archive is to collect, preserve, and make available material relating to the history of the development of the Irish Defence Forces from the formation of the Irish Volunteers in November 1913 to the present day, inclusive of overseas service with the United Nations since 1958.

HOLDINGS

The archive houses approximately 20,000 linear shelf feet of archival material, including Department files, military documents, records and some related photographs/films. Major collections include The Bureau of Military History (1913–21), which includes 1,773 witness statements, 334 sets of contemporaneous documents, photographs (including actions sites of the Easter Rising 1916), press cuttings and voice recordings; Collins Papers 1919–21; liaison documents (British Evacuation and Truce); Civil War operations and intelligence reports; internment camps and some prison records 1922–4; captured documents (IRA) 1922–4; the Army Crisis 1924; Military Mission to the United States 1926–7; Volunteer Force files; Emergency Defence Plans 1939–46; Military Intelligence and Directorate of Operation files 1939–46; Office of the Controller of Censorship files; internment camp records and Department of Defence files for the 1939–46 period; as well as Air Corps and Naval Service material and records. Other collections of special interest include bound volumes of *An tÓglach* (1918–33) and *An Cosantóir* (1940 to present), plus other military periodicals and newspapers; the National Army Census 1922; records and history of units that served overseas on United Nations Peacekeeping Missions; and 800 personal papers collections.

LOCATION

Located at Cathal Brugha Barracks, Rathmines, Dublin, adjacent to Portobello Bridge, approximately three miles from the city centre on the south side of the Liffey. Take bus 14A or 15 from city centre.

## MILLTOWN PARK LIBRARY

*See* THE JESUIT LIBRARY, Dublin

## NATIONAL ARCHIVES OF IRELAND

Bishop Street
DUBLIN 8
Ireland

TELEPHONE: (01) 407 2300; FAX: (01) 407 2333
E-mail: mail@nationalarchives.ie
Website: www.nationalarchives.ie

HOURS

M–F: 10:00am–5:00pm; closed 17 Mar., Good Friday, Easter Monday, 25 Dec.–2 Jan., and bank holidays

ACCESS AND SERVICES

Visitors welcome; disabled access facilities; identification and reader's ticket required (the reader's ticket can be applied for on the day of the first visit); no access charge; laptops permitted; pencils only; photocopies and microform print-outs available for a modest fee. There are 20 microform readers in Bishop Street, including five reader–printers, available on a first-come, first-served basis. The NAI publishes *Reports of the Director* and *Reports of the National Archives Advisory Council.* Also available are helpful leaflets, including *Reading Room Information* (1 Nov. 1999) and *Sources for Family History and Genealogy* (1 Nov. 1999). For up-to-date research guides and information consult website; especially helpful for genealogical researchers.

CONTACT

Archivist, Reference Desk

DESCRIPTION

The National Archives was formally established in 1988 with the amalgamation of the Public Record Office of Ireland and the State Paper Office. It is a government agency, open free of charge to the public.

HOLDINGS

The NAI is the official depository for the records of the Irish government. All government departments and state agencies are required to deposit their papers with the National Archives, although the Minister for Arts, Heritage, Gaeltacht and the Islands may approve places other than the National Archives as places of deposit for specified Departmental records. Exceptions include MILITARY ARCHIVES (Dublin, see separate entry) and the Geological Survey records, located at Beggar's Bush, Haddington Road, Dublin 4. In addition to government records, the archives include some private and business collections. Types of record include architectural records, manuscripts, maps, microforms and photographs. The archives of the following government departments and state agencies are held at the Bishop Street location: Agriculture, Food and Rural Development; Arts, Heritage, Gaeltacht and the Islands; Education and Science (part of); Enterprise, Trade and Employment; the Environment and Local Government; Finance; Foreign Affairs; Health and Children; Justice, Equality and Law Reform; the Marine and Natural Resources; Public Enterprise; Social, Community and Family Affairs; Tourism, Sport and Recreation. Also at Bishop Street are the Offices of the Attorney General; the Comptroller and Auditor General; Public Works; and the Secretary to the President. In addition, the records of the following government agencies are to be found at Bishop Street: Fair Trade Commission, Government Information Services, Labour Court, Ordnance Survey (part), Patents Office, Registry of Friendly Societies, and the Valuation Office and Boundary Survey.

The following archives at Bishop Street, formerly held at the Public Record Office at the Four Courts, are among the most consulted records: Census 1901; Census 1911; Cholera Papers (Board of Health); Customs and Excise; Famine Relief Commission; National School applications, registers and files; Valuation Office and Boundary Survey; archives salvaged in 1922 (part) (note: the Four Courts was badly damaged and many public records destroyed in 1922 during the Irish Civil War); Chancery pleadings; Church of Ireland parish registers; Ferguson manuscripts; Genealogical abstracts (Betham, Crosslé, Groves, Grove-White and Thrift); Irish Record Commission; O'Brien set of Encumbered/ Landed Estates Court Rentals; will books and grant books.

Bishop Street also houses archives acquired from private sources (M, D, T, 975–999, 1000– series, etc.); and trade union archives.

Archives formerly held in the State Paper Office in Dublin Castle and now at Bishop Street include: Rebellion Papers; State of the Country papers; Official Papers; Outrage papers; Convict Reference Files; Privy Council Office; Chief Crown Solicitor's Office; Dáil Éireann Records, Government and Cabinet Minutes; and the Office of the Governor General. (Note: most of the archives of the General Prisons Board, formerly in the State Paper Office, are not currently available for immediate inspection, but the Board's correspondence registers, letter books, minute books and other Board volumes are available.)

The following archives are available only in microform at Bishop Street: Tithe Applotment Books; Griffith's Valuation; Census 1821–51 (fragments); Books of Survey and Distribution; Lodge's Records of the Rolls; and the shipping agreements and crew lists, pre-1922.

Note: some archives remain at the Four Courts, and may eventually be transferred to Bishop Street. These include: court records; wills, 1900–78; administration papers, 1900–78; Schedules of Assets (Principal Registry), 1922–78; archives salvaged in 1922 (part); Companies Registration Office; National School salary books; Office of Public Works (part); prison registers; Quit Rent Office (part); Royal Hospital Kilmainham; shipping agreements and crew lists, post-1922; business records; Board of Guardians records; and hospital records. Requests for these records require advance notice (at least one day), and they are made available at Bishop Street. It is advisable to telephone several days in advance to check on exact position of archives to be consulted, as the above location list is subject to change.

Some records are stored in a warehouse and may require up to an eight-week delay before they can be retrieved. These include: General Prisons Board (part); Ordnance Survey (part); Quit Rent Office (part); and the Taxing Master of the High Court.

### LOCATION

Bishop Street is located a few blocks west of St Stephen's Green and south of Dublin Castle, backing up to St Patrick's Cathedral. The National Archives is on the west end of Bishop Street, at the corner of Bride Street.

## NATIONAL GALLERY OF IRELAND LIBRARY AND ARCHIVE

Merrion Square West
DUBLIN 2
Ireland

TELEPHONE: (01) 663 3546; FAX: (01) 661 5372
E-mail: alydon@ngi.ie
Website: www.nationalgallery.ie

### HOURS

M–F, 10:00am–5:00pm; closed Christmas, Easter and bank holidays.

### ACCESS AND SERVICES

Visitors welcome, but by appointment only. Advance notice and identification required. References required of research students. Applications can be made by phone or in writing. No borrowing privileges for external readers. Wheelchair accessible. Laptops permitted. The number of external readers is limited to ten at any one time, and charges apply for readers from profit-making organizations at a rate of 130 euro per year. Access is through the main gallery. Books are catalogued on computer. Photocopying available for a fee, with restrictions for age and condition of book and for copyright.

CONTACT

Andrea Lydon, Librarian

DESCRIPTION

The National Gallery is Ireland's major museum of art. The library is located in two rooms (the Reading Room and the Stacks) in the gallery basement.

HOLDINGS

The library houses a collection of some 30,000 volumes and includes exhibition catalogues from galleries and museums worldwide. It maintains research-level collections on European Art from the Middle Ages to the 1950s and on Irish Art from the Middle Ages to the present. It maintains study-level holdings in the areas of general art, museum studies, education in art, architecture, Irish history, conservation, and the decorative arts. The library also contains the gallery's archive, consisting of the gallery minute books, and documents relating to its history and foundation. In addition, the archives include the papers of various individuals connected with the gallery, including some Irish artists.

LOCATION

The National Gallery is at the north end of Merrion Square West, near Clare Street, next to the Parliament Buildings. The library is located near the main entrance, one flight down. There is also an entrance on Clare Street to the new Millennium Wing of the National Gallery.

## NATIONAL LIBRARY OF IRELAND

Kildare Street
DUBLIN 2
Ireland

TELEPHONE: (01) 603 0200; FAX: (01) 676 6690
E-mail: info@nli.ie
Website: www.nli.ie

HOURS

Main Reading Room: M–W, 10:00am–9:00pm; Th–F, 10:00am–5:00pm; Sat, 10:00–1:00pm
Manuscripts Reading Room: M–W, 10:00am–8:30pm; Th,F, 10:00am–4:30pm; Sat, 10:00–12:30pm; closed Christmas, Easter and public holidays

ACCESS AND SERVICES

Visitors welcome. Identification required. Students must have a letter from academic supervisor. Advance notice for group visits required. Non-circulating collection. Certain collections or part collections are held off-site and a 24-hour call-up applies. Disabled access facilities. Laptops permitted; pencils only. Photocopying available for a fee, with restrictions for age and condition of material and for copyright. The library hosts a regular programme of exhibitions, based on materials in its collection. The library website carries information on the exhibitions programme. Published histories of the library include: Noel Kissane (ed.), *Treasures from the National Library of Ireland* (Drogheda, 1994); Noel Kissane, *The National Library of Ireland* (Dublin, 1984), Vol. 42 of Irish Heritage Series; Patrick Henchy, *The National Library of Ireland, 1941–1976* (Dublin, 1986), and Gerard Long, 'The Foundation of the National Library of Ireland, 1836–1877', in *Long Room*, No. 36 (1991): 41–58. A full listing of the library's publications can be found on its website. The entire library collection is catalogued, about half online. There is a printed catalogue of manuscripts entitled *Manuscript Sources for the History of Irish Civilisation*, which, with its three-volume supplement, lists manuscript material catalogued prior to 1976. Manuscripts catalogued since 1990 can be found on the online catalogue and a card catalogue covers the period 1976–90. There are special lists of various photographic and other collections. The newspaper collection is listed in the NEWSPLAN database which can be consulted via the library's website.

CONTACT

Brendan O Donoghue, Director and Chief Herald
Dónall Ó Luanaigh, Keeper (Collections)
Brian McKenna, Keeper (Systems)
Fergus Gillespie, Keeper (Genealogical Office) and Deputy Chief Herald
Noel Kissane, Keeper (Manuscripts)
Aongus Ó hAonghusa, Keeper (Administration)

DESCRIPTION

The National Library is Ireland's major public research library, established 'to collect, preserve and make accessible materials on or relating to Ireland, whether published in Ireland or abroad, and a supporting reference collection'. To this end it seeks to build a comprehensive collection documenting the history, culture and life of Ireland. The library's current collection of some 6,000,000 items constitutes probably the most outstanding collection of Irish documentary material in the world. In 1943 the library took responsibility on behalf of the State for matters relating to heraldry in Ireland. The OFFICE OF THE CHIEF HERALD OF IRELAND (Dublin), formerly the Office of the Ulster King of Arms, has functioned as part of the library since that date. Since 1998, the library's photographic collections have been housed in purpose-built premises – the NATIONAL PHOTOGRAPHIC ARCHIVE – in Dublin's Temple Bar.

HOLDINGS

The library houses a collection of some 1,000,000 printed books, including pamphlets; approximately 17,000 linear feet of manuscripts; some 150,000 maps, in either print or manuscript form; about 2,500 current periodical titles; around 10,000 reels of microforms; 300 current newspaper titles, plus complete files of many non-current titles; about 300,000 photographs, which are held in the library's National Photographic Archive; and some 90,000 prints and drawings, including significant holdings of architectural records. Library collections concentrate on Irish history and society, including the Irish Diaspora. Major collections are described in detail on the library's website. These include the Lawrence Collection, a collection of some 40,000 photographic plates documenting Ireland from the last decade of the nineteenth century to the First World War; numerous literary manuscript collections, including the William Butler Yeats Collection, the James Joyce Collection, the George Bernard Shaw Collection, the Patrick Kavanagh Collection, and, most recently, the Sheehy Skeffington Papers and the Brian Friel Collection. The library continues to add to these outstanding collections. For example, in 2001 Michael and Gráinne Yeats added a major addition of some 100 notebooks, 130 files of loose papers, and some 3,000 pages of automatic writing by W.B. Yeats and George Yeats to the family's earlier gifts of Yeats material to the National Library. Also in 2001 the library purchased the manuscript draft of the 'Circe' episode of James Joyce's *Ulysses* for IR£1,384,953. In May 2002 the National Library made an even more stunning Joyce acquisition. It purchased for 12.6 million euro a very large collection of previously unknown Joyce manuscripts, notebooks and workbooks from Mr and Mrs Alexis Léon. These acquisitions, combined with existing holdings, give the NLI the foremost Joyce collection of manuscripts in the world.

The library's history holdings are second to none, and include the papers of a number of family estates dating back as far as the 16th century. Among the more notable of these landed estate archives are: Castletown (Co. Laois), Clements (Counties Leitrim and Donegal), Clonbrock (Co. Galway), Coolattin (Co. Wicklow), De Vesci (Co. Laois), Doneraile (Co. Cork), Headfort (Co. Meath), Inchiquin (Co. Clare), Lismore (Co. Waterford), Monteagle (Co. Limerick), O'Hara (Co. Sligo), Ormond (Counties Tipperary and Kilkenny), Powerscourt (Co. Wicklow), Prior-Wandesforde (Co. Kilkenny), Sarsfield (Co. Cork), and Wicklow (Co. Wicklow). Estate archives contain the records of the administration of estates by landlords and their agents, and generally include leases, rentals, accounts, correspondence, and maps.

Of special genealogical interest, the library holds microfilm copies of almost all Catholic parish registers from their respective start dates to 1880, microform copies of Griffith's Valuation and the Tithe Applotment Books. The list of parish registers on microfilm can be consulted on the library's website. (It is in PDF format and therefore requires a copy of Adobe Acrobat Reader.) The library does not provide copies of, or transcriptions from, registers. Original registers are generally in the custody of the parish priest. Also of interest to genealogists are the library's holdings of newspapers, trade and social directories, and the many works of family and local history in the printed books collection. In the Department of Manuscripts, the records of the former landed estates (including rentals and mapped surveys) are valuable genealogical resources. The archives of the Office of the Ulster King of Arms, including a large collection of Irish heraldic and genealogical material, are held as a distinct collection – the

Genealogical Office or GO Manuscripts – within the library. Other relevant material in the library's collections includes the annual printed Army Lists, Royal Irish Constabulary publications, the 1796 Spinning Wheel Premium Entitlement List (on microfiche), and various other records of trades and professions.

The library's Genealogy Service is designed to assist those who wish to research their family history in Ireland and is freely available to all visitors to the library. The service is operated by professional genealogists and experienced library staff who will advise on research methodology and sources. Free brochures, especially for the novice genealogist, are available. These include *Getting Started*, *Parish Registers in the National Library of Ireland* and *Valuation Records*.

LOCATION

The library is located in Dublin city centre, adjacent to Leinster House (the seat of the Irish Parliament) and to the National Museum of Ireland, close to Trinity College Dublin.

## NATIONAL MUSEUM OF IRELAND

National Museum of Archaeology & History, Kildare Street, DUBLIN 2
National Museum of Decorative Arts & History, Collins Barracks, Benburb Street, DUBLIN 7
National Museum of Country Life, Turlough Park, CASTLEBAR, CO. MAYO
National Museum of Natural History, Merrion Street, DUBLIN 2

TELEPHONE: (01) 677 7444; FAX: (01) 677 7450
E-mail: marketing@museum.ie
Website: www.museum.ie

HOURS

Archive: by appointment only
Museum: Tu–Sat, 10:00am–5:00pm; Sun, 2:00–5:00pm; closed Good Friday and Christmas Day

ACCESS AND SERVICES

Visitors welcome. Admission free. Access to archives by appointment only – contact Librarian. Forty-minute guided tours are available daily for a fee of 1.50 euro per adult; children under 16 free. School tours are free, but must be pre-booked – contact Education Department at (01) 677 7444, ext. 453. A range of rooms and spaces are available for hire, including museum reception, AV theatre and meeting room. For details contact the marketing department at (01) 677 7444.

CONTACT

The Librarian

DESCRIPTION

The National Museum houses the nation's artefacts dating back to 7000BC. The museum is based in four sites, as listed and described below.

NATIONAL MUSEUM OF ARCHAEOLOGY & HISTORY

Opened in 1890 on Kildare Street in Dublin, this museum contains artefacts dating from 7,000BC to the 20th century. *The Treasury* displays outstanding examples of Celtic and medieval art such as the famous Ardagh Chalice, the Tara Brooch and the Derrynaflan Hoard. Other permanent exhibitions include: *Ór – Ireland's Gold*; *Prehistoric Ireland*; *Viking Age Ireland*; *Medieval Ireland, 1150–1550*; *The Road to Independence*; and *Ancient Egypt*.

NATIONAL MUSEUM OF DECORATIVE ARTS & HISTORY

Opened in 1997, Collins Barracks joins the other two already famous Dublin buildings in the possession of the museum. On display are fine examples of silver, ceramics, glassware, folklife, clothing, jewellery, coins and medals. New permanent exhibitions include *Airgead – A Thousand Years of Irish Coins & Currency* and *Eileen Gray 1876–1976*, which looks at the life and work of this leading Irish-born architect and designer. Collins Barracks, incidentally, is the oldest continuously occupied barracks in the world.

NATIONAL MUSEUM OF COUNTRY LIFE

Set in the spectacular grounds of Turlough Park in Castlebar, Co. Mayo, this recently opened branch of the museum is home to the national folklife collection. Visitors to the site will also see the restored Turlough Park House and adjourning courtyards built in 1865. The exhibition represents the traditions of rural life throughout Ireland and encourages visitors to remember a vanished world, made real again through the vivid detail of domestic furniture and utensils, hunting, fishing, and agricultural implements, objects relating to games and pastimes, religion and education, dress and footwear.

NATIONAL MUSEUM OF NATURAL HISTORY

The Natural History Museum opened in 1857 as the museum of the Royal Dublin Society. It had developed as a cabinet-style zoological museum with animals from all over the world. The history of collecting extends over two centuries and has resulted in a rich variety of animals, many of which are now endangered or extinct. Exhibitions in this museum have changed little in style for over a century, adding to the charm and rarity of this national treasure.

HOLDINGS

The archives house the documentation, including correspondence, related to the museum's administrative, archaeological and historical work. Included among these collections are papers of some naturalists and archaeologists associated with the museum.

LOCATION

The **National Museum of Archaeology & History** is located on Kildare Street, opposite the NATIONAL LIBRARY OF IRELAND. The **National Museum of Decorative Arts & History** is located at Collins Barracks, Benburb Street, Dublin 7, tel. (01) 677 7444; FAX: (01) 677 7828, one mile west of the city centre along the north quays. The **National Museum Of Natural History** is located on Merrion Square, Dublin 2, parallel to Kildare Street, and the **National Museum of Country Life** is located in Turlough Park, Castlebar, Co. Mayo.

## NATIONAL PHOTOGRAPHIC ARCHIVE

Meeting House Square
Temple Bar
DUBLIN 2
Ireland

TELEPHONE: (01) 603 0230; FAX: (01) 677 7451
Email: photoarchive@nli.ie
Website: www.nli.ie

HOURS

Exhibitions and Reading Room: M–F, 10:00am–5:00pm. Exhibitions: Sat, 10:00am–2:00pm (summer only)

ACCESS AND SERVICES

Visitors welcome. The archive, which is part of the National Library of Ireland, hosts a regular programme of exhibitions, mainly based on materials in the collections held there. Reprographic services are available for a fee, subject to copyright and other possible restrictions. Some 8,000 images from the collection have been digitized and can be viewed on the National Library of Ireland website via the Catalogue of Photographs. *Into the Light, An Illustrated Guide to the Photographic Collections of the National Library of Ireland* by Sarah Rouse was published in 1998. A selection of images from the collection feature in *Ex Camera 1869–1960*, by Dr Noel Kissane.

CONTACT

Gráinne Mac Lochlainn, Assistant Keeper

DESCRIPTION

The National Photographic Archive houses the photographic collections of the National Library of Ireland. Opened in 1998, the archive building incorporates a substantial environmentally controlled storage area, together with darkrooms and a conservation area. A reading room, an exhibition area and a small retail space combine to enhance access to the collections in the care of the archive.

HOLDINGS

There are some 300,000 photographs, the vast majority of which are Irish, in the various collections held by the National Photographic Archive. While most of the collections are historical, there is also some contemporary material. Subject matter ranges from topographical views to studio portraits, and from political events to early tourist photographs. The archive maintains an active collecting policy. The largest collections are those created by the postcard and portrait studios that were in operation in many towns and cities of Ireland at the turn of the 20th century. These include the Lawrence, Poole, Eason, and Valentine collections. The Clonbrock collection of some 3,500 glass-plate negatives from 1860–1930 provides an important record of life on a landed estate. The Keogh collection, comprising 330 glass-plate negatives, includes important images of the key political figures and events in Dublin during the period 1915–30. Other collections include the Wynne collection (Co. Mayo 1867–1960), the Morgan collection (aerial photographs of Ireland during the mid-1950s), the Wiltshire collection (Dublin 1951–70) and the O'Dea collection (Irish railways 1937–66).

LOCATION

The National Photographic Archive is located in Meeting House Square in the Temple Bar area of Dublin, close to the Irish Film Centre and the Gallery of Photography.

## NATIONAL UNIVERSITY OF IRELAND, DUBLIN

*See* **UNIVERSITY COLLEGE DUBLIN**, Dublin

Note: UCD is part of the National University of Ireland system, but it petitioned the Irish government successfully to keep its familiar name, i.e. UCD, so its full title is now University College Dublin, National University of Ireland.

## OFFICE OF THE CHIEF HERALD/GENEALOGICAL OFFICE

2–3 Kildare Street
DUBLIN 2
Ireland

TELEPHONE: (01) 603 0230; FAX: (01) 662 1061
E-mail: herald@nli.ie
Website: www.nli.ie

HOURS

Heraldic Museum: M–W, 10:00am–8:30pm; Th,F, 10:00am–4:30pm; Sat, 10:00am–12:30pm. To consult manuscripts see opening hours of the NATIONAL LIBRARY OF IRELAND Manuscripts Reading Room.

ACCESS AND SERVICES

Visitors to the Heraldic Museum are welcome. In order to consult manuscripts, it is necessary to obtain a National Library of Ireland manuscript reader's ticket. The main manuscript series are listed in a printed catalogue of manuscripts entitled *Manuscript Sources for the History of Irish Civilisation*, and its three-volume supplement. The manuscripts are known as the GO (Genealogical Office) series. A summary catalogue of the holdings of the office appears in *A Guide to the Genealogical Office* published by the Irish Manuscript Commission in 1998.

CONTACT

Brendan O Donoghue, Chief Herald
Fergus Gillespie, Deputy Chief Herald

DESCRIPTION

Founded as the Office of the Ulster King of Arms in 1552, the Office of the Chief Herald is the oldest office of State in Ireland. The Chief Herald is the Heraldic Authority for Ireland, responsible for the regulation of heraldic matters and the granting and confirming of coats of arms. The office has been a department of the National Library of Ireland since 1943 and, since 1995, the post of Chief Herald has been held by the Director of the National Library of Ireland.

HOLDINGS

Documents deriving from the functions of the office include the Registers of the Chief Herald, armorials and ordinaries of arms, funeral entries, lords' entries and records of knights dubbed. Roger O'Ferrall's *Linea Antiqua* is the most important source for ancient genealogies of Gaelic families and also contains exemplifications of arms. Other collections may be considered equally important to the researcher and certain information from now-lost sources previously held in the Public Record Office of Ireland is of particular value. For example, the genealogical and historical information contained in the abstracts from the plea rolls of Henry III to Henry VI are a most important source for Norman genealogy. Extracts from the pipe rolls from Henry III to Edward III contain similar information. For a later period (1536–1810) tabulated pedigrees contained in the abstracts of wills proved at the prerogative court of the Archbishop of Armagh can be consulted. Other collections that, while not pedigrees, have been acquired as sources of genealogical information include Ecclesiastical Visitations, a list of high sheriffs of counties, a roll of freemen of the City of Dublin, lists of freeholders, and a list of gentlemen attainted by King James. The Office of the Chief Herald does not undertake genealogical research or searches in the records of the office on behalf of members of the public. A list of researchers who have indicated a willingness to carry out research on a professional fee-paying basis is available from the office. The National Library's Genealogy Service is freely available to all visitors who need advice on carrying out their own family history research in Ireland (*see* NATIONAL LIBRARY OF IRELAND).

LOCATION

The Office of Chief Herald is located in Dublin city centre, near the National Library of Ireland and Leinster House (the seat of the Irish Parliament) and Trinity College Dublin.

## ORDNANCE SURVEY OF IRELAND

Note: Archives transferred to NATIONAL ARCHIVES OF IRELAND, Dublin

## PEARSE STREET LIBRARY

*See* CENTRE FOR DUBLIN AND IRISH STUDIES, Dublin

## POETRY IRELAND/ÉIGSE ÉIREANN

*See* AUSTIN CLARKE LIBRARY, Dublin

## THE QUAKER LIBRARY

*See* HISTORICAL LIBRARY, RELIGIOUS SOCIETY OF FRIENDS, Dublin

## REGISTRY OF DEEDS

Henrietta Street
DUBLIN 1
Ireland

TELEPHONE: (01) 670 7500; FAX: (01) 804 8406
E-mail: david.hickey@landregistry.ie
Website: www.irlgov.ie/landreg

HOURS

M–F, 10:00am–4:30pm

ACCESS AND SERVICES

Visitors welcome. The registry provides a variety of services for the public, including the registration of deeds, search facilities (negative searches/common searches), copy facilities, and genealogical services. Fees for service: search by members of the public in respect of each name, for each county, for each period of ten years or part thereof, 1.25 euro; certified copy of memorial, 12 euro; plain copy of microfilm of a memorial, 60c per page; providing any service for which no other fee is prescribed, 6 euro; common search per name, per county, for each period of ten years or part thereof, 6 euro; negative search per name, per county, for each period of ten years or part thereof, 12 euro; general search, without limitation, each day by each member of the public against all indexes prior to 1970, 6 euro.

CONTACT

Dave Hickey; e-mail: david.hickey@landregistry.ie

DESCRIPTION

The Registry of Deeds provides a system of voluntary registration of deeds and conveyances affecting land. The system is based on a grantors' index, e.g. person(s) who dispose of an interest in a property. In the case of property disposed after death, it is the executor of the deceased that is the grantor and it is the executor's name that will appear in the names index and not the name of the deceased person. A deed and memorial (synopsis of deed) is required for registration in the Registry of Deeds. Once registered, the deed is returned to the lodging party and the memorial is retained by the Registry of Deeds.

HOLDINGS

Documents retained in the Registry of Deeds include: memorials (1708 to present, microfilmed 1930 to present), transcripts (1708–1960 with some gaps), abstracts (1833–1969), names index or index of grantors, and lands index (1708–1946). A **memorial** is the synopsis of an original deed, with information on the names of all parties to the deed, location of the property and details of the type of transaction. A **transcript** is the handwritten/typed copy of the memorial. An **abstract** is the summary of the memorial, containing the name of the grantor, grantee, description of property and type of deed. The **names index** is the index of names of the persons who disposed of an interest in the property. The **lands index** is an index of all transactions compiled in order of the names of the townland/street (in city) affected.

LOCATION

The registry is located at King's Inns, on Henrietta Street, just off Bolton Street, almost directly opposite Bolton Street College, on the north side of the Liffey, west of Parnell Square. The registry can also be approached via Constitution Hill, opposite Broadstone Bus Garage.

See also Land Registry Offices:

- Chancery Street, Dublin 7, tel. (01) 670 7500 (Counties Meath, Westmeath, Cavan, Louth, Monaghan, Donegal, Leitrim, Longford)
- Irish Life Centre, Lower Abbey Street, Dublin 1, tel. (01) 670 7500 (Counties Kildare and Wicklow)
- Nassau Building, Setanta Centre, Nassau Street, Dublin, 2, tel. (01) 670 7500

(Counties Dublin, Galway, Mayo, Sligo, Clare, Roscommon)

- Cork Road, Waterford, tel. (051) 30300 (Counties Cork, Kerry, Limerick, Waterford, Tipperary, Laois, Offaly, Carlow, Kilkenny and Wexford).

## REPRESENTATIVE CHURCH BODY LIBRARY

Braemor Park
CHURCHTOWN, DUBLIN 14
Ireland

TELEPHONE: (01) 492 3979; FAX: (01) 492 4770
E-mail: library@ireland.anglican.org
Website: www.ireland.anglican.org

HOURS

M–F, 9:30am–1:00pm; 2:00–5:00pm

ACCESS AND SERVICES

Visitors welcome, but advance notice preferred. No disabled access facilities. Laptops permitted; pencils only. Fees for photocopying. Of special genealogical and historical interest are the publications of the library, including a series of parish registers. These include registers edited by Raymond Refaussé for the Parish of St Thomas, Dublin, 1750–1791, and for the Church of St Thomas, Lisnagarvey, Co. Antrim, 1637–46; by Colin Thomas for the Cathedral Church of St Columb, Derry, 1703–32 and 1732–75; by Susan Hood for the Holy Trinity Church, Cork, 1643–68; by James Mills for the Parish of St John the Evangelist, Dublin, 1619–99, the oldest extant parish registers in Ireland; and by Suzanne Pegley for the Parish of Leixlip, Co. Kildare, 1667–1778, the library's most recent publication. Also of interest: *A Library on the Move: Twenty-Five Years of the Representative Church Body Library in Churchtown*, edited by Raymond Refaussé (1995); *A Handlist of Church of Ireland Parish Registers in the Representative Church Body Library* (1996); and *A Handlist of Church of Ireland Vestry Minute Books in the Representative Church Body Library* (1996).

CONTACT

Raymond Refaussé, Librarian and Archivist

DESCRIPTION

The library was founded in 1931 and has been developed as the theological and reference library of the Church of Ireland and as the Church's principal repository for its archives and manuscripts. It seeks to collect any printed, archival and manuscript material that is produced by or related to the Church of Ireland. The library is owned and funded by the Church of Ireland and is managed by the Library and Archives Committee of the Representative Church Body, which is the perpetual trustee for the real and movable property of the Church of Ireland.

HOLDINGS

The library houses some 40,000 volumes, focusing on theology and history, plus architectural records, archives and manuscripts, microforms, pamphlets, photographs, and recordings. Major archival collections include: Church of Ireland archives chiefly for the Republic of Ireland, representing more than 700 parishes, mainly in Counties Carlow, Clare, Cork, Dublin, Galway, Kerry, Kildare, Kilkenny, Mayo, Meath, Westmeath, and Wicklow; the records of 17 dioceses; and the records of 15 cathedrals, especially Christ Church and St Patrick's in Dublin, St Canice's in Kilkenny, and St Brigid's in Kildare. The archives also house medieval and early modern manuscripts, the records of the General Synod and the Representative Church Body from 1870 to the present, and the records of societies and organizations related to the Church of Ireland, including schools, educational societies, missionary organizations, and clerical groups from the 18th to the 20th centuries. In addition, the collection includes miscellaneous ecclesiastical manuscripts, such as the papers of bishops, clergy and laity, correspondence, diaries, research notes and writings, scrapbooks, photographs, transcripts of non-extant Church of Ireland records from the 17th to the 20th centuries. Also of interest are: the microfilms of church records in other custodies from the 17th to the 20th centuries; photographs of Church buildings, clergy, laity and church plate; and an oral history collection. *See also* the NATIONAL ARCHIVES, Dublin, and the PUBLIC RECORD OFFICE OF NORTHERN IRELAND, Belfast, for additional parish registers. Some original parish records are still in the custody of local clergy.

LOCATION

The library is adjacent to the Church of Ireland Theological College in Churchtown in the southern suburbs of Dublin. Take bus No. 14 from D'Olier Street (city centre) to Mount Carmel Hospital (Braemor Park). The library is opposite No. 33 Braemor Park.

## ROYAL COLLEGE OF PHYSICIANS OF IRELAND

6 Kildare Street
DUBLIN 2
Ireland

TELEPHONE: (01) 661 6677; FAX: (01) 676 3989
E-mail: robertmills@rcpi.ie
Website: www.rcpi.ie

HOURS

M–F, 9:30am–1:00pm, 2:00–5:00pm

ACCESS AND SERVICES

Visitors welcome, but identification required and advance notice preferred. The library is not actually open to the public, but it is willing to assist genuine

researchers in medical history or genealogy. At present there is no charge for these research services but this policy is currently under review. No disabled access facilities. Laptops permitted; pencils only. There are no fees for a modest amount of photocopies, but there are fees for microform prints, e-mail, fax and scanning services. Advance notice for special service requests advisable. The library offers free college brochures and a copy of an article about the library, and a history of the college is available for purchase.

CONTACT

Robert Mills, Librarian; e-mail: robertmills@rcpi.ie

DESCRIPTION

The college was founded in 1654, and the library dates from 1713.

HOLDINGS

The library houses a collection of some 30,000 volumes of printed books, plus significant holdings of manuscripts, pamphlets, photographs and some 400 journal titles, though only about 15 are current. The library also holds architectural records relating to the RCPI building, and a collection of portraits and sculpture that adorn the building. The collection focuses on medicine from earliest times to the 19th century, medical history, and medicine in Ireland. Major collections include medical textbooks from the 15th century to the early 20th century, the 5,000-item Kirkpatrick Collection on Irish Medical History, the 600-volume Churchill Collection on the history of obstetrics and gynaecology, and the Travers Collection of fine books on medicine, history, science, and theology. Of special interest to genealogists are the Kirkpatrick Archive, a collection of biographical records (10,000 names) of Irish doctors from earliest times to the 1950s, the college registers from 1692 to the present, and medical directories and registers published from the 1840s to the present.

LOCATION

The college is located in the city centre, next door to the National Library of Ireland, and a short walk from Trinity College.

## ROYAL DUBLIN SOCIETY

Ballsbridge
DUBLIN 4
Ireland

TELEPHONE: (01) 668 0866; FAX: (01) 660 4014
E-mail: library@rds.ie
Website: www.rds.ie

HOURS

Reading Area and Issue Desk: Tu,F, 10:00am–5:00pm; W,Th, 10:00am–7:00pm; Sat, 11:00am–5:00pm; Reading Area only (Issue Desk not in operation): M, 10:00am–5:00pm; closed on public holidays and bank holidays and the last week in December

ACCESS AND SERVICES

The library is primarily a facility for members of the society. Membership is open to all, subject to normal application and election procedures. An annual fee structure applies, with local, regional, and overseas rates. Bona fide researchers should furnish a written application from the relevant faculty of their educational institution or from their organization. A charge applies subject to the nature of the research or assistance required. A computer catalogue is used for the general collection. A card catalogue exists for the scientific publications. A photocopying service operates through the library desk. Laptops permitted.

CONTACT

Mary Kelleher, Librarian; tel. (01) 240 7288; e-mail: mary.kelleher@rds.ie
Gerard Whelan, Assistant Librarian/Library Administrator; tel. (01) 240 7256; e-mail: ger.whelan@rds.ie

DESCRIPTION

The Dublin Society was founded in 1731 (it became 'Royal' in 1820) for the improvement of Husbandry (Agriculture), Manufactures, and other Useful Arts and Sciences. One of the newly formed society's first acts was to establish a library. This became one of the most significant collections in Ireland, going on to form the nucleus of the NATIONAL LIBRARY OF IRELAND collection when that body was established in 1877. The society retained many of its scientific collections of books and journals, which it continued to collect. The science collection developed through a publication exchange programme with many institutions and like-minded societies across the world. Selected publications of some North American institutions can be found in the holdings. In the 19th century, Dublin was to some degree regarded as the second city of the British Empire and the society's holdings reflect a diversity of learned enquiry of that age.

HOLDINGS

The general library contains over 100,000 volumes including over 4,000 relating to Ireland, many of them old and rare. There are 6,000 works and pamphlets on all branches of agricultural science including some 1,500 items of equestrian interest. These works form one of the most important collections on agriculture in the country. Of special research interest, the library contains the records of the Royal Dublin Society. These are in manuscript form from its foundation, and in printed annual volumes since 1764. The diverse activities and interests it pursued are recorded, through the minutes of its meetings and a diversity of publications. The society acted as an intermediary for distributing funds that were awarded as premiums, provided by the Irish parliament prior to the Act of Union (1800) and afterwards from the British parliament. It was through the society's many

endeavours that leading institutions of the state came into being, including the National Museum, the National Museum of Natural History, the Botanic Gardens, the National Veterinary College, the National Library and the National College of Art and Design.

LOCATION

The library is located in the main body of the RDS complex, with access through the members' entrance. The RDS is situated in Ballsbridge, approximately 2 miles south-east of Dublin city centre, on the Merrion Road. Travel by public transportation on any of the following: No. 7, 7A, 45, 46, 63, and 84 bus routes. Two DART (rail) stations (Lansdowne Road and Sandymount) are within a ten- to 15-minute walk of the RDS.

## ROYAL IRISH ACADEMY

19 Dawson Street
DUBLIN 2
Ireland

TELEPHONE: (0) 676 2570, (01) 676 4222; FAX: (01) 676 2346
E-mail: library@ria.ie
Website: www.ria.ie

HOURS

M–F, 10:00am–5:30pm; closed public holidays and other bank holidays, Tuesday after Easter, and the last week of December. Also, library closes to readers for three weeks in May–June for cleaning and checking of stock.

ACCESS AND SERVICES

Visitors welcome, but registration required. Registration forms are available online at www.ria.ie/library/open.html or telephone, fax, write, or e-mail request for a form. Completed forms accompanied by a letter of introduction from an academy member or the faculty of a university together with valid ID, student's card or passport should be presented to the library. Reader's ticket issued for initial period of one year on payment of 12 euro. Holders of a valid ALCID (Academic Libraries Cooperating in Dublin) card may gain automatic access to the academic library and are not required to pay a fee. Laptops permitted; pencils only. Gloves issued with use of vellum manuscripts. The library offers an ongoing exhibitions programme and participates in the academy's celebrated publications and lecture programmes. Access to exhibitions is free of charge. The entire collection is catalogued: 80% card catalogue; 20% online. The online catalogues are accessible on the Academy website. The library is currently managing a retrospective cataloguing project which aims to have all the catalogue records for printed works in the collections available on the academy website by 2005. A published *Catalogue of Irish Manuscripts in the Royal Irish Academy* (28 fasc. 1926–70) is available for purchase from the Dublin Institute of Advanced Studies.

CONTACT

Siobhán O'Rafferty, Librarian; e-mail: s.orafferty@ria.ie
Bernadette Cunningham, Deputy Librarian; e-mail: b.cunningham@ria.ie

DESCRIPTION

The Royal Irish Academy was founded in 1785 as a society for 'promoting the study of science, polite literature and antiquities'. Anchored by its celebrated library, the academy promotes the sciences and the humanities through publications, lectures, conferences and cooperative programmes with other institutions. Currently, for example, it is working with the Department of Foreign Affairs on the multi-volume publication of a major series of historical documents charting the development of Irish diplomacy and foreign policy since 1919. The Academy also sponsors research on the *Irish Historic Towns Atlas*, the *Dictionary of Celtic Latin from Medieval Sources*, the *Dictionary of Irish Biography* and *Foclóir na Nua Ghaeilge.*

HOLDINGS

The library houses an extraordinary manuscript and book collection, plus important holdings of artefacts, drawings, journals (approximately 6,000 titles), maps, pamphlets (50,000), photographs, antiquarian drawings, portraits and recordings. Its collection of over 2,000 manuscripts includes many of the oldest and most treasured original documents of Irish cultural history. These include the *Cathach*, or Psalter of St Columba, the oldest surviving Irish manuscript, written in Latin *c.*560–630AD; the Stowe Missal, the oldest extant mass book of the early Irish Church, *c.*792–803AD; the Book of the Dun Cow, the oldest extant manuscript in the Irish language, before 1106AD; and the Annals of the Four Masters, written between 1632 and 1636 in Irish, chronicling Irish history from earliest times to 1616. The library houses the largest collection of Irish language manuscripts anywhere, plus important medieval and early modern manuscripts in Latin, French and English. It contains important modern manuscript material. Of special genealogical interest are the records of the 19th-century Ordnance Survey and the papers of De La Ponce, Marquess MacSwiney and H.A.S. Upton. The library also houses the papers of individual members, including those of its founder, Lord Charlemont; and drawings of Irish antiquities. The Printed Book Collection of more than 100,000 volumes includes the 30,000-item Charles Haliday Pamphlet Collection, the library of composer and poet Thomas Moore, the Celtic Studies library of Osborn Bergin, the Rev. Richard Kirwan collection of early scientific works, a collection of early Irish imprints, and an Irish and international journal collection.

LOCATION

The RIA is nestled between St Ann's Church and Mansion House, the Lord Mayor's residence, on Dawson Street, one block west of the National Library of Ireland, close to the north side of St Stephen's Green.

## ROYAL SOCIETY OF ANTIQUARIES OF IRELAND

63 Merrion Square
DUBLIN 2
Ireland

TELEPHONE: (01) 676 1749; FAX: (01) 676 1749
E-mail: rsai@gofree.indigo.ie
Website: None

HOURS

M–F, 2:00–5:00pm; closed August, 23 Dec.–1 Jan. incl., Holy Thursday–Tuesday after Easter incl., and bank holidays.

ACCESS AND SERVICES

Visitors welcome, but advance notice required. Staff happy to answer queries by post, fax or e-mail. No disabled access facilities. Laptops permitted; pencils only. Fee schedule applies: 4 euro per afternoon for non-members. Special permission from council to view Du Noyer sketches. Photocopies cost 25–35c per sheet, post extra. The society publishes the *Journal of the Royal Society of Antiquaries of Ireland*, free to members, otherwise 33 euro annually.

CONTACT

Nicole Arnould, Librarian

DESCRIPTION

The society was founded in 1849 'to preserve, examine and illustrate all Ancient Monuments and Memorials of the Arts, Manners and Customs of the past, as connected with the Antiquities, Language, Literature and History of Ireland'. To this end, it sponsors lectures, talks and excursions and publishes a journal. It also maintains a research library, open free to members and to the public for a modest fee.

HOLDINGS

The library houses a collection of books and manuscripts focused primarily on pre-1800 Irish history. It also has a fine photographic collection, including a photographic survey done by members around 1870 to 1910, and a collection of glass slides made during a survey of the poor areas of Dublin in 1913, called 'Darkest Dublin'. Other important collections are: Sketches by Georges Du Noyer, and manuscript notes by Elrington Ball for his *History of County Dublin*. Journal articles and photographic collection of some genealogical interest.

LOCATION

Merrion Square is located midway between Lower Baggot Street and Lower Mount Street, opposite Leinster House, seat of the Dáil (Irish parliament), bordered on the west by Upper Merrion Street and on the east by Fitzwilliam Street East. The society is located nearer the Upper Merrion Street end, close to Leinster House.

## ST PATRICK'S COLLEGE LIBRARY

St Patrick's College, Drumcondra
DUBLIN 9
Ireland

TELEPHONE: (01) 884 2170
E-mail: info.library@spd.ie
Website: www.spd.dcu.ie/library

### HOURS

Term: M–Th, 10:00am–10:00pm; F, 10:00am–5:30pm; Sat, 10:00am–1:00pm
Out of Term: M–F, 10:00am–1:00pm, 2:00–5:00pm

### ACCESS AND SERVICES

Members of the public wishing to read in the library may do so on application at the issue desk. Borrowing privileges are not available. General enquiries should be made to the Library Information Desk. St Patrick's College shares an integrated OPAC with DUBLIN CITY UNIVERSITY and The Mater Dei Institute of Education, the first system in Ireland to provide full web search facilities in both English and Irish. The catalogues of the three libraries complement each other and provide a single search point for over 350,000 book titles. Photocopy cards of various values are on sale in both the library and the resource centre and may be used in both places. A reader–printer is available for reading and copying microfilm and microfiche. All special collections are non-circulating and may be consulted only in the library. Some collections, e.g. Belvedere House Library, may be visited only by arrangement with the Librarian.

### CONTACT

Evan J. Salholm, Librarian; e-mail: evan.salholm@spd.dcu.ie

### DESCRIPTION

St Patrick's College was founded in 1875. In 1883 it was officially recognized as a denominational teacher training college, and in that year moved from No. 2 Drumcondra Road to historic Belvedere House (*c.*1640) on its present campus. From its beginnings until 1999, the college was administered by the Vincentian community, a Catholic religious order. It is now administered by a lay president, Dr Pauric Travers. While St Patrick's College maintains an independent and separate identity, it has been a college of Dublin City University since 1993, and all its courses are accredited by the university. The Catholic identity of the college is fostered through religious worship and campus ministry, and all student teachers complete a course in religious education. Current enrolment is approximately 1,700 students.

### HOLDINGS

The college library now contains over 150,000 books and 550 journals as well as microfiche, microfilm and other materials. The collection is a balanced one for a humanities college, with particular strengths in Celtic and Irish languages and literature and in Irish history. Special collections include: Belvedere House Library, the old Vincentian community library, which includes collections of publications by former students and faculty members; Dolmen Press and Three Candles Press collections; collection of pre-1880 publications; rare children's books, including Irish, e.g. Patricia Lynch; Padraic Colum Collection of printed material; Collection of Gaelic League, including letters written to Henry Morris, a member of the League and a graduate of the college; collection of Irish school textbooks; and a collection of P.W. Joyce (in development). Note: several of these special collections are currently uncatalogued.

LOCATION

St Patrick's College of Education, Drumcondra, is located on the N1, two miles north of the centre of Dublin City, and nine miles south of Dublin Airport. The area is well serviced by public transport. Frequent buses from the city include 3, 11, 16, and 41. Drumcondra Station, on the North-West Suburban Rail service (Maynooth Line) is within walking distance of the college. The college has good parking facilities.

## TIERNAN MACBRIDE LIBRARY

*See* **IRISH FILM ARCHIVE OF THE FILM INSTITUTE OF IRELAND**, Dublin

## TRINITY COLLEGE DUBLIN LIBRARY

College Street
DUBLIN 2
Ireland

TELEPHONE: (01) 677 2941; FAX: (01) 671 9003
E-mail: Consult library staff directory through website for specific departments
Website: www.tcd.ie/Library

HOURS

**Old Library**: Visitor areas (including Book of Kells exhibition): M–Sat, 9:30am–5:00pm; Sun (Oct.–May), 12:00 noon–4:30pm; Sun (June–Sept.), 9:30am–4:30pm; Sunday opening hours apply on bank holidays with the exception of those falling in May–August, when weekday hours apply. Hours for the Department of Manuscripts and for the Department of Early Printed Books: Manuscripts: M–F, 10:00am–5:00pm, Sat, 10:00am–1:00pm; Early Printed Books: M–F, 10:00am–10:00pm (June–Sept. closes at 5:00pm); Sat, 10:00am–12:45pm

Other libraries: **Berkeley Library** (Arts & Sciences and Music); **Lecky Library** (Letters, Business, Economics, and Social Sciences); **Hamilton Library** (Science, Engineering, Systems, and Health Sciences), and **Ussher Library** (including the

Conservation Centre and Map Library): M–F, 9:00am–10:00pm; Sat, 9:30am–4:00pm (during term); Sat, 9:30am–1:00pm (out of term). During term, the Lecky and Hamilton Libraries alternate Saturday hours. Also, there is the **Map Library** and the **Music Library** (scheduled to be housed in the new Ussher Library in 2002), the **John Stearne Medical Library** (at St James's Hospital), and the **Occupational Therapy Library** (at the School of Occupational Therapy in Dún Laoghaire). Consult the website for hours and access requirements.

ACCESS AND SERVICES

For research, access is restricted to students, faculty, and alumni of Dublin University (TCD), and to academic staff and doctoral students whose libraries participate in the ALCID scheme (Academic Libraries Co-operating in Dublin). Others should apply in writing to the Librarian specifying the nature of their research and the special collections that they wish to consult. For tours of the exhibits in the three public areas of the Old Library, i.e. the Colonnades, the Treasury and the Long Room, the public is welcome, but a fee is charged. These are the areas that attract large numbers of tourists, principally to see the library's well-designed exhibitions in the Colonnades; its world-famous collection of medieval manuscripts, notably the Book of Kells and the Book of Durrow, in the Treasury; and the magnificent Long Room, which houses many of the library's oldest printed books plus the oldest surviving harp from Ireland, probably from the 15th century. The Old Library also houses the University's Department of Manuscripts in the west pavilion and the Department of Early Printed Books and Special Collections in the east pavilion. Access to these departments is by appointment only. The library shop is a popular attraction, offering a good range of books plus a wide assortment of gift items related to Trinity College and the Book of Kells. The library's online catalogue indexes more than two-thirds of its holdings, including all books received since 1963, all periodicals, and many special collections.

CONTACT

Eileen McGlade, Keeper of Readers' Services

DESCRIPTION

Trinity College was founded in 1591, and has the largest research library in Ireland. Every year around half a million visitors view a selection of the library's great treasures, most notably the Book of Kells, the brilliantly decorated Latin text of the Four Gospels and preliminaries executed around 800 AD and widely considered the greatest Irish art treasure from the Middle Ages. Trinity is Ireland's most historic seat of learning, and the early 18th-century Old Library is worth a visit for its architectural splendour.

HOLDINGS

The library houses more than 4.25 million volumes, 30,000 current periodicals, and significant holdings of maps, music and manuscripts. It is a legal deposit library for Irish and British publications, retaining this privilege to the present day. Its manuscript holdings date from earliest times to the present; they include one of the world's most celebrated collections of medieval manuscripts. Its modern literary holdings include one of the world's premier collections of Samuel Beckett material. Note: separate, more detailed listings are provided below for the MANUSCRIPTS DEPARTMENT and the DEPARTMENT OF EARLY PRINTED BOOKS.

LOCATION

Trinity College is located in the city centre, entrance opposite the Bank of Ireland building, formerly the home of the pre-1801 Irish parliament.

## TRINITY COLLEGE DUBLIN LIBRARY – DEPARTMENT OF EARLY PRINTED BOOKS

College Street
DUBLIN 2
Ireland

TELEPHONE: (01) 608 1172; FAX: (01) 671 9003
E-mail: charles.benson@tcd.ie
Website: www.tcd.ie/Library

HOURS

M–F, 10:00am–10:00pm (June–Sept. closes at 5:00pm); Sat, 10:00am–12:45pm

ACCESS AND SERVICES

See above for general guidelines for library use at TRINITY COLLEGE DUBLIN LIBRARY. The department's holdings may be read only in the Early Printed Books Reading Room, which is reserved for readers using this material. Special guidelines are in force for handling material in the Reading Room, which includes the use of pencils only. Books from other reading rooms may only be transferred with special permission. There is a printed catalogue to the collection, known as the *Catalogus librorum impressorum qui in Bibliotheca Collegii Sacrosanctae et Individuae Trinitatis ... juxta Dublin, adservantur.* Dublinii: E Typographeo Academico, 1864–87. Nine volumes (Vol. 9 = supplement). It is available on microfiche, and is the main working catalogue of the collection containing the holdings of pre-1850 books. There is also the Guardbook Catalogue of Accessions 1873–1963. Material catalogued since 1963 is available online and contains a high level of detail, such as entries for printers and publishers, illustrators, papermakers, binders and provenance. Finally, there is the *Catalogus librorum in Bibliothecae Collegii Sanctae et Individuae Trinitatis Reginae Elizabethae juxta Dublin.* Dublinii: typis et impensis Johannis Hyde (*c.*1715?).

CONTACT

Charles Benson, Keeper of Early Printed Books; e-mail: charles.benson@tcd.ie

HOLDINGS

The department houses some 300,000 pre-1900 volumes, plus some modern collections. The early library collection reflected the academic interests of the university in theology and religious controversy, classical literature, law, mathematics and natural philosophy. Among the early collections of note acquired by the library were those of Archbishop James Ussher (10,000 vols) in 1662, the Butler family (1,400 vols) in the late 18th century, and the Fergal family (20,000 vols) in 1802. In 1801 the library became a legal deposit library for United Kingdom publications. Until the late 19th century, accessioning policies were very conservative, cataloguing only those items judged to be of academic merit or suitable religious tenor. A consistent and active purchasing programme for antiquarian materials did not begin until the 1960s, but made up for many of the earlier deficiencies in the collection. While the department maintains a good representation of very early printing from all over Continental Europe, the focus is on imprints from North-West Europe, with considerable strengths in works printed in France and the Low Countries from the 16th to the 18th centuries, and, above all, in Irish and English works. Political history is another area of strength, especially the Netherlands, 1580–1780; the English Civil War; the Fronde; England 1680–90 and the 1720s; England and Ireland, 1780–1820, where the printed works are enhanced by the Nicholas Robinson collection of caricatures; French Revolution, 1789–1800 (about 12,000 items); Ireland and England in the 19th century, where the collections are being enhanced by the acquisition of English newspapers (2,000 volumes) 1800–*c.*1940 from the National Library on long-term deposit.

One of the library's great strengths is in English-language drama from 1660 to the present. Holdings of authors educated at TCD, such as Congreve, Farquhar and Goldsmith, are particularly good. French drama holdings are good but uneven, with particular strength in the 17th century. There are minor collections of Dutch, German and Spanish drama. Poetry in English is strong, especially for the period 1710–40, including much Swiftiana. Popular verse is represented in the J.D. White Ballads (900 items *c.*1860–90). Eighteenth- and 19th-century English fiction, once an area of weakness, has been strengthened by recent purchases. There is some 17th- and 18th-century French fiction. Classical literature is present in quantity from the incunabula period on.

Not surprisingly, theology and religious controversy are among the strongest areas in the collection, with an especially strong collection of Bibles. There are about 1,200 Reformation tracts printed before 1545. Coverage of Anglican theology is excellent for the entire period and that of Roman Catholic theology is surprisingly good up to the end of the 17th century, reasonable for the 18th century, and now improving for the 19th century. There is some Quaker and Presbyterian material.

The department also boasts significant holdings of pre-1830 maps, including most of the major atlases, the oldest being an edition of Ptolemy's *Cosmographia* of 1490. Ortelius, Mercator and Blaeu are well represented. In addition there are some 2,000 sheet maps printed before 1790. Ordnance Survey maps from the 1830s to the present can be found in the Map Library. There is a good collection of early mathematical books, including Euclid's *Opus elementorum* 1482, plus good holdings in geology, physics, chemistry, medicine, botany, engineering, and architecture. There is a small amount of 17th-century music and a fair collection of Handel's operas. The bulk of the early music, however, dates from the 1760s to the 1820s and came from Townley Hall in Co. Louth. There are about 1,600 items from this period, including recent purchases. Other early music collections are those of Ebenezer Prout (3,500 items) and the Strollers, an amateur *Singverin* (1,900 items). There is also music from the College Choral Society and College Chapel. Irish and English law is held in considerable quantity from the earliest editions, and more recently editions of French customary law and *mémoires* are being collected.

For the post-1901 holdings there is a collection of recruiting posters issued in Ireland during the First World War, the Samuels Collection of subversive ephemera taken up by the Royal Irish Constabulary (1914–21), the Cuala Press Archives, the personal library of James Stephens, and Irish nationalist and radical newspapers, 1901–30.

LOCATION

The Early Printed Books Reading Room is in the East Pavilion of the Old Library building with access from the Entrance Hall of the Berkeley Library.

## TRINITY COLLEGE DUBLIN LIBRARY – MANUSCRIPTS DEPARTMENT

College Street
DUBLIN 2
Ireland

TELEPHONE: (01) 698 1189; FAX: (01) 671 9003
E-mail: mscripts@tcd.ie
Website: www.tcd.ie/Library

HOURS

M–F, 10:00am–5:00pm; Sat, 10:00am–1:00pm

ACCESS AND SERVICES

See above for general guidelines for library use at TRINITY COLLEGE DUBLIN LIBRARY. Manuscript readers should first obtain a reader's ticket from the Berkeley Library and permission to consult the manuscripts should be applied for in advance to the Keeper of Manuscripts. The department offers photography and microfilming services. Guides include T.K. Abbott, *Catalogue of the Manuscripts in the Library of Trinity College, Dublin* (Dublin and London, 1900), a general catalogue of accessions to 1900, continued after that date in typescript form. An introductory leaflet is available throughout the library. Sectional language catalogues have appeared in print, including T.K. Abbott and E.J. Gwynn, *Catalogue of the Irish Manuscripts in the Library of Trinity College, Dublin*

(Dublin, 1921) and Marvin L. Colker, *A Descriptive Catalogue of the Mediaeval and Renaissance Latin Manuscripts in the Library of Trinity College Dublin* (Scholar Press for Trinity College Library Dublin, 1991). Peter Fox (ed.), *Treasures of the Library, Trinity College Dublin* (Dublin, 1986) discusses some of the library's major holdings.

CONTACT

The Keeper of Manuscripts

HOLDINGS

Major collections include: corpus of medieval manuscripts, largely from the collection of James Ussher (d. 1656), but also including the library's greatest treasures: the Book of Kells (*c.*800), Book of Durrow (*c.*675), Book of Armagh (807), Book of Dimma (8th century), Book of Mulling (8th century), Matthew Paris's life of St Alban (13th century), and the Fagel Missal (15th century). Also of great significance are: college muniments, 16th–20th century; Roman inquisitorial records, 16th–20th century; depositions of 1641; 1798 rebellion papers; and the archives of the Royal Zoological Society of Ireland, 1836–*c.*1953. Family and private paper collections include: William King (1650–1729), Archbishop of Dublin; Thomas Parnell (1679–1718), poet; Earls of Donoughmore, 16th–20th century; Wynne family of Hazlewood, Co. Sligo and Glendalough, Co. Wicklow, 18th–20th century; Elvery family of Carrickmines and Foxrock, Co. Dublin, 19th–20th century; Sir William Rowan Hamilton (1805–65), mathematician and astronomer; Michael Davitt (1846–1906), author and politician; John Dillon (1851–1927), politician; Robert Erskine Childers (1870–1922), author and politician; Liam de Roiste (1882–1959); politician and author; John Millington Synge (1871–1909), poet and dramatist; Susan Mitchell (1866–1926), poet and editor; Thomas Bodkin (1887–1961), art historian and gallery director; Thomas MacGreevy (1893–1967), poet and gallery director; Denis Johnston (1901–84), playwright and journalist; Frank Gallagher (1898–1962), journalist; Joseph Campbell (1879–1944), poet; James Stephens (1880–1950), author; Máirtin Ó Cadhain (1906–70), writer in Irish; George MacBeth (1932–93), poet and novelist; John Banville (born 1945), novelist; Samuel Beckett (1906–89), author; Herbert Butler (1900–91), essayist; Gerald Barry (born 1952), composer; John B. Keane (1928–2002), author.

LOCATION

The Manuscripts Room is located in the Old Library with entry via the Library Shop and the Long Room.

## UNIVERSITY COLLEGE DUBLIN – ARCHIVES DEPARTMENT

Library Building
University College Dublin
Belfield
DUBLIN 4
Ireland

TELEPHONE: (01) 716 7547; FAX: (01) 716 1146
E-mail: seamus.helferty@ucd.ie
Website: www.ucd.ie/~archives

HOURS

M–Th, 10:00am–1:00pm; 2:00–5:00pm. Schedule may vary due to staff leave, so it is advisable to check in advance.

ACCESS AND SERVICES

Visitors welcome, but by appointment only. Advance notice required. Disabled access facilities. Laptops permitted; pencils only. Collections are not available unless catalogued. Fees for photocopying, microform print and digital imaging services. The Department's website gives the best current indication of holdings, and is updated regularly. There is a 66-page, published *Guide to the Archives Department University College Dublin* (1985), compiled by Alisa C. Holland and Seamus Helferty, that is very detailed but dated.

CONTACT

Seamus Helferty, Principal Archivist

DESCRIPTION

The University Archives mainly houses the deposited private collections of papers of public figures, such as politicians and public servants; and the official papers of the university and its predecessors. Though it occupies space in the library, the Archives Department is independent of the library.

HOLDINGS

The collections overwhelmingly date from the Independence period (1921–present) and relate to the political, cultural and economic development of modern Ireland. Major collections include papers of Frank Aiken, Todd Andrews, Kevin Barry, Ernest Blythe, Colonel Dan Bryan, Michael Collins, the Cumann na nGaedheal and Fine Gael parties, the Fianna Fáil party, Desmond FitzGerald, Michael Hayes, T.M. Healy, Sighle Humphreys, Hugh Kennedy, Tom Kettle, Sean MacEntee, Sean Mac Eoin, Patrick McGilligan, Eoin MacNeill, Mary MacSwiney, Terence MacSwiney, Richard Mulcahy, Donnchadh Ó Briain, Daniel O'Connell, Kathleen O'Connell, Cearbhall Ó Dálaigh, Diarmuid Ó hEigeartaigh, Ernie O'Malley, The O'Rahilly, Desmond Ryan, Dr James Ryan, Moss Twomey and Eamon de Valera.

Other collections include the records of predecessor institutions of the university, including the Catholic University of Ireland, 1854–1911; the Royal College of

Science for Ireland, 1867–1926; the Museum of Irish Industry, 1846–7; Albert Agricultural College, 1838–1926; and the Royal Veterinary College of Ireland, 1900–60. The Franciscan 'A' Manuscript Collection, formerly housed in the FRANCISCAN LIBRARY, Killiney, Co. Dublin and still the property of the Franciscans, includes the Martyrology of Tallaght (fragment of the Book of Leinster), the Annals of the Four Masters, the Psalter of St Caimin and the Liber Hymnoroum. Family and estate paper collections dating from the 17th century include the Bryan family (Dublin); Caulfeild (Tyrone); de Clifford (Down); Delacherois (Down); Fitzpatrick (Laois); Hart-Synnot (Dublin); Herbert (Kerry); Hutchinson and Synge Hutchinson (Dublin and Wicklow); Potter (Down); Rice of Mountrice (Kildare); Upton (Westmeath and Louth); and Wandesford (Kilkenny). The archives also include the trade union archives and labour-related paper collections deposited through the Irish Labour History Society. These include archives of actors, bakers, coopers, municipal employees, plasterers, shoe and leather workers, and woodworkers' trade unions.

LOCATION

The Archives Department is located in the Library Building on the main University Campus in Belfield, on the south-east side of Dublin, accessible by bus from city centre. See directions below for UCD LIBRARY.

## UNIVERSITY COLLEGE DUBLIN LIBRARY

University College Dublin
National University of Ireland
Belfield
DUBLIN 4
Ireland

TELEPHONE: (01) 716 7694; FAX: (01) 283 7667
E-mail: Library@ucd.ie
Website: www.ucd.ie/library/index.html

ACCESS AND SERVICES

Visitors having genuine scholarly needs that can be met without detriment to the students and staff of the college are welcome. A fee may be required. Readers must show, on request, a valid admission, borrower, or identity card to gain access to the library, or if requested by any member of the library staff. Also, where applicable, a letter of introduction from their home library. Collection is catalogued online. See separate entry below for access requirements for SPECIAL COLLECTIONS. Photocopying and microform services available for a fee.

CONTACT

**Main Library**: Information Desk (tel. (01) 716 1148; fax (01) 716 1148; e-mail Library@ucd.ie)

**Branch Libraries**

- *Blackrock Library* (Graduate Business School and Business Information Centre, Michael Smurfit Graduate School of Business), University College Dublin, Carysfort Avenue, Blackrock, Co. Dublin, Ireland, tel. (01) 716 8069; fax (01) 716 8011; e-mail: library.blackrock@ucd.ie
- *Earlsfort Terrace Library*, Belfield Campus, tel. (01) 716 7471; fax (01) 475 4568; e-mail libetgen@ucd.ie
- *Richview Library*, University College Dublin, Richview, Clonskeagh Road, Dublin 4, Ireland, tel. (01) 716 2741; e-mail: richview.library@ucd.ie
- *Veterinary Medicine Library*, University College Dublin, Faculty of Veterinary Medicine, Belfield, Dublin 4, Ireland, tel. (01) 716 6028; e-mail: vetlib@ucd.ie

DESCRIPTION

UCD, which traces its origins to the Catholic University of Ireland founded in 1854 with John Henry Newman as its first Rector, has grown from modest beginnings to a ten-faculty (i.e. school) institution with over 18,000 students. In addition to the Main Library (humanities, social science, commerce, law, pure and applied sciences), the university operates four branch libraries: the Blackrock Library (business); the Earlsfort Terrace Library (medicine, civil engineering, agriculture and food engineering); the Richview Library (architecture and planning); and the Veterinary Medicine Library. The Main Library also houses Special Collections.

HOLDINGS

The library's holdings consist of just under 1,000,000 volumes, with substantial collections of microforms, growing electronic resources, and smaller collections in other print and non-print formats. Almost 80% of stock is on open access. Approximately 15,000 purchased monographs and 2,500 donations or legal deposit items are added to stock each year, and about 5,600 current periodicals titles are taken. The library is a European Documentation Centre and a national depository for United States government publications (now mainly in microform); it is also a legal deposit library for Republic of Ireland publications. The Main Library houses good research collections in the areas of the humanities, social science, commerce, law, and pure and applied sciences. Specific collections of note include: law and official publications; maps; music; newspapers, especially from Ireland, both national and regional, and Northern Ireland; periodicals; a Standards Collection; and theses. The library holds a full set of current British Standards on microfiche, updated monthly. Many international and European Standards are now included unchanged as British Standard implementations. The annual BSI Standards Catalogue and the monthly British Standards Service index allow identification of relevant standards and the location of the appropriate microfiche. Information about new standards is given in *BSI News*. Unique Irish Standards are held, but not implementations of International or European Standards. Details of Standards can be traced through the annual catalogue and the *NSAI Bulletin*. Ordnance Survey maps of Ireland ranging from 1:1,000 to 1:575,000 are available to UCD staff and students in Richview Library. Maps are available in a number of different formats (e.g. sheet, microfiche) and editions, both current and historical. In addition Richview Library has maps for the whole country available on disk at the scales of 1:1000, 1:2500, 1:10560 (latest editions).

The collections incorporate the libraries of older institutions, such as the Royal College of Science for Ireland and the Museum of Irish Industry. They include the gifts and bequests of many former members of the College, those who made their careers as teachers and researchers in UCD, and those who pursued careers elsewhere. The library has bought collections of value, and pursues a vigorous acquisition policy.

LOCATION

UCD is situated on a large modern campus about 2.5 miles to the south of the centre of Dublin. It is served by buses no. 3, 10, and 11B from the city centre, and 17, which crosses the south side.

## UNIVERSITY COLLEGE DUBLIN LIBRARY – SPECIAL COLLECTIONS

Main Library
University College Dublin
National University of Ireland
Belfield
DUBLIN 4
Ireland

TELEPHONE: (01) 716 7686/7149; FAX: (01) 716 1148
E-mail: norma.jessop@ucd.ie
Website: www.ucd.ie/library/collections/specoll.html#general

HOURS

M–F, 10:00am–12:55pm, 2:00–4:55pm; closed approximately ten days around Christmas; Good Friday, Easter Monday; and public holidays

ACCESS AND SERVICES

By appointment only. Letter of introduction required; students must have letter from supervisor. Charges for access: up to three working days, free. Up to ten working days, minor charge negotiable through Special Collections. Longer periods, users buy library admission card from the Main Information Desk. Laptops permitted; pencils only. Manuscripts may be consulted for research purposes and by prior appointment. Special Collections materials may only be consulted in the department's Reading Room. Photocopying is (rarely) undertaken, for a fee, depending on the condition of the item. Photography and scanning can be arranged. Almost all the printed material in SC is included in the Library's web catalogue. Manuscripts are variously listed.

CONTACT

Norma Jessop, Librarian for Special Collections

DESCRIPTION

The core collection is the library of the Catholic University of Ireland, founded 1854, to provide Irish Catholic young men with the possibility of getting a university degree or professional qualification without having to travel abroad. The university never received a charter, or enough support from professional/middle-class Catholic families. In the early 1880s it was put in the charge of the Jesuit Fathers, and became a College of the Royal University of Ireland. From then until 1909 the Catholic University Library was in storage. It was returned to UCD on the reconstitution of the college, in 1909, as a constituent college of the National University of Ireland.

Important collections include those of Archbishops Joseph Dixon (1806–66) and Daniel Murray (1768–1852); of Very Rev. Dr Flanagan, PP; and material, including manuscripts, from the library of Eugene O'Curry, Irish scholar and Professor of Irish History in the CUI. Subjects include theology, Bible studies, Catholic philosophy, Church history and devotional literature, mainly in 16th–18th century continental printings; Irish history, archaeology, language; classics; literature; and some oriental language items.

In 1909 University College inherited the library built up during its period as a college of the Royal University of Ireland. Acquisition continued with the Heinrich Zimmer collection (Celtica); law books and nominate reports, the library of Christopher Palles, the last Chief Baron of the Exchequer in Ireland (donation, in 1921). The majority of collections are, however, literary. Novelist Maeve Binchy and dramatist Frank McGuinness are depositing drafts and proofs of their work. The Constantine Curran collection includes James Joyce first editions and editions from the Irish literary revival; and manuscripts: principally some 400 letters, from writers and some painters, 1900s–1960s. The Patrick Kavanagh archive was bought in 1986. The library holds short stories and first editions of Mary Lavin; diaries, notebooks and papers of Seán Ó Riordáin, Irish-language poet; the letters of Gerard Manley Hopkins to his lifelong friend A.W.M. Baillie; the Tasso editions collected by David Nolan (at present on deposit); and the John Manning collection of children's books (by English authors mainly, in editions published from the 1880s to about 1920). The major modern printed collection is the bequest of John Lincoln Sweeney: English, Anglo-Irish and American literature in first and early editions, limited editions, and signed copies.

Francis J. O'Kelley collected Irish history, local history, and especially Irish printing and printing relating to Ireland, 17th–19th centuries, with particular emphasis on pamphlets, many scarce. The library of Colm Ó Lochlainn, printer, bookbinder, and bibliophile, includes early printings, handsome bindings, broadside and single ballads and songbooks, devotional literature and manuscripts.

There are small sections on engineering and science, the latter including a notable group of 19th-century palaeontology books. There is a pamphlet collection of some 8,000 items, including the O'Kelley pamphlets. Small collections and items individually acquired are usually of Irish interest, covering history, politics, religion, economy, local history, language, and literature.

Patrick Ferriter (d. 1928) collected and compiled manuscripts of Irish language songs, tales and poetry of the south-west of Ireland. Henry Morris collected a total of 39 manuscripts from the area of Co. Louth; his notes and correspondence were additional donations. 'Additional Irish mss' consists of individual Irish manuscripts in Irish; no. 14 is Dubhaltach Mac Firbisigh's *Leabhar genealach* (Book of genealogies). 'UCD mss' is a growing sequence of mainly English-language manuscripts, of which the most important is Thomas Hardy's *Return of the Native*. There is a small group of music scores by Sir Arnold Bax, in manuscript and corrected proof form, and 39 18th-century watercolour drawings of Irish antiquities, done by or for Gabriel Beranger.

Looking to the future, Irish publications for children and young adults are collected and kept as an archival collection. One copy of any Anglo-Irish literary work is acquired and kept in its original condition.

LOCATION

Special Collections is situated on Level 1 of the Main Library.

## VALUATION OFFICE IRELAND

Irish Life Centre
Lower Abbey Street
DUBLIN 1
Ireland

TELEPHONE: (01) 817 1000; FAX: (01) 817 1180
E-mail: info@valoff.ie
Website: www.valoff.ie

HOURS

M–F, 9:30am–12:30pm; 2:00–4:30pm; closed holidays and public holidays.

ACCESS AND SERVICES

Visitors welcome. The office's customer services team provides inspection facilities for members of the public to view all current and archive rating records and maps, provides certified extracts from maps, current valuation certificates, historical valuation certificates from current to 1850s, known as backdated certificates, and provisional valuations, required for licensing applications. The team also deals with archival queries, commonly for genealogical research. Fees may apply. Hourly charge for extracting information, 15.24 euro; 63c per sheet for photocopying.

CONTACT

Catherine English and/or Marion Richardson; e-mail: info@valoff.ie

DESCRIPTION

The Valuation Office is the State property valuation agency. The core business of the office is the provision of accurate, up-to-date valuations of commercial and industrial properties to ratepayers and local authorities as laid down by statute. The office also provides a valuation consultancy service to other government departments, local authorities, health boards, and the Revenue Commissioners.

HOLDINGS

The archive contains the original books of surveys carried out in the 1840s, books and maps of Griffith's Valuations in the 1850s, the original rating records, and documentation showing revisions up to the current position. Of special interest to genealogists, the archive holds a list of occupiers of property for the 26 counties in the Republic of Ireland dating back to 1846. The following details are held in relation to each property: occupier name, townland, address, description of property, acreage of holding, rateable value, and reference to its position on a valuation map. The archive is unique in that it can relate people to a particular property. In addition, the property location is outlined on a valuation map. The valuation maps are archived, so it may be possible to locate the exact position of a house or property of a particular family back to *c.*1850. The Valuation Office also holds valuations lists, valuation notebooks and files, maps, files, databases, manuals, and publications. The valuation lists contain details of the current rateable valuation of commercial properties, hereditaments and tenements, and of the rateable valuation of commercial, domestic and land properties from 1852. Note: rates on domestic property were abolished in 1978 and on agricultural land from 1984; consequently, there has been no need to update these categories. The valuations lists also contain information on those classes of property which have a rateable valuation but which have been identified by law and by legal decision as not required to pay rates. The lists are grouped geographically, corresponding to local authority areas, with administrative subdivisions in townland, ward or street. Valuation notebooks and files contain a report of the inspection by the valuer of each property that has a rateable valuation placed on it. Ordnance Survey maps show property boundaries for valuation purposes. Files contain papers, correspondence, briefings, submissions and reports produced in the performance of office functions. The databases – electronic, typed and manuscript – contain information associated with the establishment and revision of rateable valuations. Publications include *Guide to the Valuation Office Ireland.*

LOCATION

The Valuation Office is located diagonally across from the Abbey Theatre, two blocks east of O'Connell Street in city centre.

## DÚN LAOGHAIRE LIBRARY – LOCAL HISTORY DEPARTMENT

Lower George's Street
DÚN LAOGHAIRE, CO. DUBLIN
Ireland

TELEPHONE: (01) 280 1147; FAX: (01) 284 6141
E-mail: patwalsh@dlrcoco.ie
Website: www.dlrcoco.ie/library/lhistory.htm

HOURS

M, 10am–1:00pm; 2:00–5:00pm; Tu,Th, 1:15–8:00pm; W,F, 10:00am–5:00pm; Sat, 10:00am–1:00pm; 2:00–5:00pm; closed bank holiday weekends

ACCESS AND SERVICES

The Local History Department is based in the Dún Laoghaire Library, a branch of the Dún Laoghaire-Rathdown Public Library Service, headquartered at Duncairn House (1st floor),14 Carysfort Avenue, Blackrock, Co. Dublin; tel. (01) 278 1788; fax (01) 278 1792; e-mail libraries@dlrcoco.ie. Visitors welcome. Wheelchair-accessible. Photocopying and microfilm services available for a modest fee. Exhibitions are mounted on a regular basis. Recent showings include: *The Irish Civil War* (1997), *The 1848 Rebellion* (1998), *Dún Laoghaire Before The Railway* (1998), *Ships in the Bay* (2000), and *Ancient Places, Sacred Spaces* (2001).

CONTACT

Pat Walsh, Librarian

DESCRIPTION

On 1 January 1994 Dublin County Council and the Corporation of Dún Laoghaire were dissolved and replaced by three new administrative counties, South Dublin, Dún Laoghaire-Rathdown and Fingal. It is the aim of the Local History Department to collect, preserve, and make available for reference, material on the history of the administrative county.

HOLDINGS

The collection includes directories dating from 1798, council minutes from 1888, newspapers from 1819, and surveys and maps from 1730. The department also holds such genealogical resources as Griffith's Valuation, Census returns from 1813–1911 and the Tithe Applotment Books. The photograph collection covers prints and drawings from the 17th century to the present. Highlights include copies of the Lawrence Collection, the Civil War (Ireland 1922–3) series, and the Dún Laoghaire Harbour Collection.

LOCATION

By rail, take DART to Dún Laoghaire Station; the library is a ten-minute walk from the station. By bus, take No. 7, 7A, 8, 46A from Dublin city centre; 59

from Killiney; 75 from Tallaght; or 111 from Loughlinstown. No parking available at library.

## DÚN LAOGHAIRE-RATHDOWN HERITAGE CENTRE

Moran Park House
DÚN LAOGHAIRE, CO. DUBLIN
Ireland

TELEPHONE: (01) 230 1035; FAX: (01) 280 6969
E-mail: kcallery@dlrcoco.ie
Website: www.irishroots.net/DunLghre.htm

HOURS

M–Th, 9:00am–5:00pm

ACCESS AND SERVICES

Dún Laoghaire-Rathdown Heritage Centre offers a fee-based, partial genealogical service to persons wishing to trace their roots in South Co. Dublin. In addition, the centre holds a large collection of archival material covering the area's archaeology, geology, and ecology, with illustrations, photographs and maps, plus files on the area's maritime history. A copy of the centre's initial search form can be found on its website. Fees vary depending on amount of time and research required. Typically, an initial enquiry receives a reply from the centre within two weeks. Visitors are welcome and given immediate service. Publications include: *In the Mind's Eye – Memories of Dun Laoghaire*; *Dalkey – St Begnet's Graveyard*; and *Dalkey – Medieval Manor and Seaport*.

CONTACT

Catherine Malone

DESCRIPTION

Dún Laoghaire-Rathdown Heritage Centre is the Irish Family History Foundation's designated genealogical centre for South Co. Dublin. IFHF is the coordinating body for a network of government-approved genealogical research centres in the Republic of Ireland and in Northern Ireland that have computerized tens of millions of Irish ancestral records of different types. The centre focuses on Roman Catholic and Church of Ireland parish registers for South Co. Dublin. The area covered by this centre now lies in the hinterland of Dublin city but was, in the 19th century, a collection of rural towns and villages. The centre's archival holdings are an important research source for the history of this area. Chief surnames of South Dublin include: Byrne, Doyle, Kelly, Murphy, Kavanagh, O'Neill, O'Brien, O'Connor, O'Farrell and O'Toole.

HOLDINGS

The centre has computerized over 145,000 records. The main records include:

Roman Catholic records (baptismal and marriage) 1755–1900; Church of Ireland records, which include burial records as well as baptismal and marriage records, starting in 1694; and Presbyterian records that date from 1843. Also computerized are the pre-1900 gravestone inscriptions at the extensive Deansgrange Cemetery (from 1868) and St Begnet's Cemetery in Dalkey. Main towns in the Dún Laoghaire-Rathdown Heritage Centre's area include: Booterstown, Cabinteely, Dundrum, Dún Laoghaire (formerly Kingstown), Blackrock, Dalkey, Glasthule, Monkstown, and Donnybrook.

LOCATION

Dún Laoghaire, formerly named Kingstown after George IV (1820–30), is located on the coast about 7.2 miles south-east of Dublin city centre, conveniently serviced by the DART and by buses No. 7, 7A, 75, 45A, 46A, 59 and 111. Moran Park House is adjacent to the harbour, a few minutes' walk from the DART station, between the National Maritime Museum and the Royal Marine Hotel.

## FRANCISCAN LIBRARY

Dún Mhuire, Seafield Road
KILLINEY, CO. DUBLIN
Ireland

TELEPHONE: (01) 282 6091/6760; FAX: (01) 282 6993
E-mail: None
Website: None

HOURS

M–F, 10:00am–1:00pm, 2:30–4:30pm (usually, subject to staffing)

ACCESS AND SERVICES

Visitors welcome, but by appointment only. Disabled access facilities. Fees for photocopying by Librarian. There is a printed catalogue of Irish manuscripts that are now in the care of UCD (see above). Copies of *Dún Mhuire Killiney 1945–1995* are available from the Librarian. The collection is catalogued on computer.

CONTACT

Fr Ignatius Fennessy, Information Officer

DESCRIPTION

Private Franciscan library available to researchers.

HOLDINGS

The Collection includes some 22,000 volumes, 1,000 pamphlets, and 500 journal titles dealing primarily with Franciscan studies, the Irish language, and

Irish history, especially with respect to ecclesiastical and State history. Collections include the Papers of Eamon de Valera, Seán Mac Eoin, Muiris Ó Droighneáin, and George Gavan Duffy, all four now in the care of UNIVERSITY COLLEGE DUBLIN – ARCHIVES DEPARTMENT; the papers of Luke Wadding, OFM; and a rare book collection that includes 24 incunabula (15th-century printed books). The incunabula are also now in the care of UCD. The indexing of the papers of George Gavan Duffy, Seán Mac Eoin, and Muiris Ó Droighneáin is now complete, and the indexing of the papers of Eamon de Valera is expected to be completed shortly.

LOCATION

From Dublin city centre take the DART to Killiney; walk for ten minutes up Station Road (a hill) and down the other side on Seafield Road, around corner at bottom of the hill, first entrance on right-hand side, with a green postbox in the wall.

## FINGAL GENEALOGY

Swords Historical Society Co. Ltd
Carnegie Library
North Street
SWORDS, CO. DUBLIN
Ireland

TELEPHONE: (01) 840 0080; FAX: (01) 840 0080
E-mail: swordsheritage@eircom.net
Website: www.irishroots.net/Fingal.htm

HOURS

M–F, 1:00–4:30pm; other times by appointment

ACCESS AND SERVICES

Fingal Genealogy is a fee-based genealogical service centre that offers a complete range of genealogical research services, with a focus on North Co. Dublin. The centre is attached to a museum that reflects aspects of local and national culture. A copy of the centre's initial search form can be printed off its website. The initial fee is 25 euro (US$30).

CONTACT

Bernadette Marks, Coordinator

DESCRIPTION

Fingal Genealogy is a member of the Irish Family History Foundation, the coordinating body for a network of government-approved genealogical research centres in the Republic of Ireland and in Northern Ireland that have computerized tens of millions of Irish ancestral records of different types. Fingal

Genealogy focuses on North Co. Dublin. Main towns in the area include: Balbriggan, Baldoyle, Balrothery, Balscaden, Blanchardstown, Clontarf, Donabate, Fingal, Lusk, Malahide, Naul, Portmarnock, Rush, Skerries, and the 'county town', Swords. Publications currently available from the Fingal Heritage Group (prices are in US$ and do not include postage) include: *In Fond Remembrance – Headstone Inscriptions from St Columba's Church of Ireland, Swords*, $2.50; *Swords Heritage Trail*, $1.50; *Working Life in Fingal – Recollections from North County Dublin*, $6.00; *Swords Voices*, parts 3, 5, 6, 7 & 8 @ $6.00; *Sewn by Candlelight – History of the Act of Union and Education in Swords*, $6.00; and *A Great Benefit – Controversial History of Old Borough School, Swords*, $10.00.

HOLDINGS

Records include: Roman Catholic records, the earliest of which date from 1701; Church of Ireland records from 1705; Clontarf Methodist from 1874; and Census records available from as early as 1901. Fingal Genealogy also holds records of interment for all Church of Ireland cemeteries in its area, the earliest being Swords from 1705; vaccination records; school roll books; gravestone inscriptions for some local cemeteries; various trade directories; dog licence records; and 1916 Volunteer records.

LOCATION

Swords is located north of Dublin City, near Dublin Airport, and close to several sites of interest, including Newbridge House, Skerries Windmill, Ardgillen Castle, Swords Castle, and Malahide Castle.

# COUNTY FERMANAGH

## ENNISKILLEN LIBRARY

Hall's Lane
ENNISKILLEN, CO. FERMANAGH, BT74 7DR
Northern Ireland

TELEPHONE: (028) 6632 2886; FAX: (028) 6632 4685
E-mail: enniskillen_library@welbni.org
Website: www.welbni.org/libraries/homepage.htm

HOURS

M,W,F, 9:15am–5:15pm; Tu,Th, 9:15am–7:30pm; Sat, 9:15–1:00pm

ACCESS AND SERVICES

Visitors welcome. Borrowing privileges for visitors may be restricted. Disabled access facilities. Fees for photocopying, microfilm prints, faxes and e-mail. Only 5% of the collection is catalogued online. Printed finding aids available. Linked to the emigration database of the Ulster-American Folk Park.

CONTACT

Margaret Kane, Assistant Librarian for Local Studies
Marianna Maguire, Senior Librarian Assistant Local History

DESCRIPTION

Part of the Western Education and Library Board system, Enniskillen is the principal public library in Co. Fermanagh.

HOLDINGS

The library houses a general educational and recreational collection of some 21,000 books. Its Nawn Collection is one of the best and largest local studies collections at a public library in all of Ireland. This collection consists of some 30,000 books of Irish interest, plus prints, periodicals, paintings, photographs and an especially good collection of some 1,500 printed maps, including copies of Co. Fermanagh barony maps, a few county and Ulster maps from 1685, Ordnance Survey six-inch maps for Fermanagh and Tyrone (1835, 1859, 1908), and Ordnance Survey grid maps. Other special collections of note include: the W.B. Yeats Collection of some 400 volumes, including a considerable number of first editions; Fermanagh author Shan Bullock; an extensive Local Newspaper Collection on microfilm from 1738 to the present; a Railway History Collection, which consists of some 200 books, journals and maps on the history and development of railways in Ireland from the mid-1800s to recent times; and a Military History Collection, focusing on Irish regiments, especially the Royal Inniskilling Dragoon Guards and the Royal Inniskilling Fusiliers.

The Genealogy and Heraldry Collection focuses on Irish interests but also covers English and Scottish interests. The collection includes a number of rarities. The man for whom the collection is named, Frederick James Nawn, possessed an 'encyclopaedic knowledge of genealogy and family history', and the collection he built as Divisional Librarian reflects this interest, including a microfiche copy of the 1901 Census of Ireland and name index for Co. Fermanagh, plus various other important genealogical sources, including directories, indexes, and lists.

Other material includes Griffith's Valuation of Co. Fermanagh *c.*1862, microfilm copies of all Board of Guardians minute books for Enniskillen, Irvinestown (Lowtherstown) and Lisnaskea Poor Law Union workhouses *c.*1840–1894; Hearth Money rolls 1660s, Muster rolls, Militia lists; electoral registers for Co. Fermanagh, 1978, 1982–6, 1988–9; and periodicals, including *Familia* from 1987, *Irish Genealogical Research Society* (Ireland Branch Newsletter) from 1986; *Irish Genealogist* from 1939; *Irish Heritage Links*, 1981–90/91; *Irish Links* from 1984; *North Irish Roots* from 1984; *Ulster Link* 1987–8, odd numbers only; and *Ulster Origins* 1984–88 (5 vols).

The library also has a substantial collection of valuation revision lists for Co. Fermanagh. The earliest volumes cover the years 1864–5, 1869–70 and 1883–90. The larger section comprising *c.*110 vols covers the years 1910–30. The lists are bound individually by Poor Law Union, Rural District and Electoral Division with a list of townlands inside each cover. Some volumes are in need of repair and could not be produced to the public.

There is a small collection of records of public elementary schools in Co. Fermanagh. These are mainly roll books for schools mainly in the Clones area returned by the Public Record Office of Northern Ireland. For Lisroon there are roll books 1884–1954 (8 vols), Magheraveely 1908–1917 and Roslea 1921–7. For the public elementary school of Letter in Templecarn parish there is a pupils' register for the years 1951–7 bearing PRONI reference SCH 132/1/3. For that school PRO will have retained the earlier volumes in the series starting in 1865 (SCH 3/1/1–2).

LOCATION

Town centre, corner of Hall's Lane and Queen Street, opposite the bridge over the north branch of the River Erne (route to Enniskillen Airport).

# COUNTY GALWAY

## GALWAY CITY LIBRARY

St Augustine Street
GALWAY CITY, CO. GALWAY
Ireland

TELEPHONE: (091) 561 666; FAX: (091) 565 039
E-mail: info@galwaylibrary.ie
Website: www.galwaylibrary.ie

HOURS

M, 2:00–5:00pm; Tu–Th, 11:00am–8:00pm; F, 11:00am–5:00pm; Sat, 11:00am–1:00pm, 2:00–5:00pm
The Juvenile Library at Galway City closes at 5:00pm each day.

ACCESS AND SERVICES

Visitors welcome. Memberships available for a modest annual fee, allowing borrowing privileges. Identification required for application. Photocopying available for a fee; computers are provided for access to the Internet subject to conditions.

CONTACT

B. Kelly (Librarian with overall responsibility for Galway City Library services)
Public Library: Josephine Vahey; tel. (091) 561 666
Juvenile Library: Geraldine Mannion; tel. (091) 561 666

DESCRIPTION

The largest of the 21 branch libraries in the Galway Library Service.

HOLDINGS

The City Library offers a good general collection of educational and recreational material. The LOCAL HISTORY DEPARTMENT AND ARCHIVES has a separate entry below.

LOCATION

In St Augustine Street, city centre, off Lower Abbeygate St, one block south-west on William Street from Eyre Square/Kennedy Park.

## GALWAY CITY LIBRARY – LOCAL HISTORY DEPARTMENT AND ARCHIVES

Galway Public Library (County Library Headquarters)
Island House
Cathedral Square
GALWAY CITY, CO. GALWAY
Ireland

TELEPHONE: (091) 562 471; FAX: (091) 565 039
E-mail: info@galwaylibrary.ie
Website: www.galwaylibrary.ie

HOURS

Local History Department: M–F, 9:30am–1:00pm, 2:00–5:00pm

ACCESS AND SERVICES

It is advisable to make an appointment through the Local History Department by phoning (091) 562 471, or faxing (091) 565 039, as some of the material requires the use of microform readers, which may have to be reserved in advance.

CONTACT

Maureen Moran (Deputy County and City Librarian), tel. (091) 562 471

DESCRIPTION

The Galway Library Service was established in 1924 as an integral branch of the Galway Local Authority Service. The service now has purpose-built, full-time libraries in Galway City, Ballinasloe (tel. 0905 43464), Clifden (tel. 095 21092), Gort (tel. 091 631224), Athenry (tel. 091 845592), Portumna (tel. 0509 41261) and Tuam (which holds microfilm copies of the 1901 and 1911 Censuses, tel. (093) 24287); and sub-libraries in Ballygar, Carraroe (tel. 091 595733), Dunmore (tel. 093 38923), Glenamaddy (tel. 0907 59734), Inishbofin (tel. 095 45861), Inisheer (tel. 099 75008), Killimor (tel. 0905 76061), Kilronan, Letterfrack (tel. 091 845592), Loughrea (tel. 091 847778), Moylough, Oranmore (tel. 091 792117) Oughterard, Roundstone (tel. 095 35518), Spiddal (tel. 091 504028), Tiernea (091 551611) and Woodford. A mobile library brings books to many smaller towns and villages and a School Book Mobile services over 200 primary schools. The Headquarters Library houses the main local history collection and archives.

HOLDINGS

This collection includes a comprehensive collection of old local newspapers, Griffith's Valuation, local Poor Law Guardians minute books, local maps, local historical photographs, and the 1901 and 1911 Censuses.

There are virtually complete sets of Guardian minutes *c.*1840–1922 for the Poor Law Unions of Clifden, Galway, Gort, Loughrea, Mount Bellew and Tuam. There are substantial gaps in the series of Ballinasloe, and for Glenamaddy minutes survive only for the years 1894–5 and 1914–15. There are indoor relief registers for Gort 1914–20 and Tuam 1913–19.

Significant collections of records of administration are available for about a dozen estates, including:

- Blake estate, near Tuam 1666–1934 including agent's correspondence and land surveys.
- Ffrench of Rahasane, near Loughrea 1765–1897 including agents' correspondence and inventory of auctioned items 1830s.
- St George Mansergh, Headford 1775–1853; includes volume of maps and a rent roll giving tenants' names and their holdings.
- O'Kelly of Castle Kelly, Aghrane, Killeroran 1606–*c.*1880; includes wills and correspondence as well as marriage settlements.

The Newspaper Collection is of special interest because of its comprehensive coverage of the local area going back to 1823. Holdings (listed chronologically) include: *Galway Weekly Advertiser*, 1823–43; *Tuam Gazette*, 1824; *Western Argus*, 1828–33; *Galway Independent*, 1829–32; *Galway Free Press*, 1832–5; *Galway Patriot*, 1835–9; *Tuam Herald*, 1837–78; *Connacht Journal*, 1839–40; *Galway Vindicator*, 1841–99; *Galway Standard*, 1841–3; *Galway Mercury & Connacht Weekly Advertiser*, 1844–60; *Western Star*, 1845–69; *Galway Packet & Connacht Advocate*, 1852–4; *Galway Express*, 1853–1920; *Warden of Galway*, 1853; *Connacht Patriot and Tuam Advertiser*, 1859–69; *Galway Press*, 1860–61; *Galway American*, 1862–3; *Tuam News*, 1871–3; *Western News & Weekly Examiner*, 1878–92; *Tuam Herald*, 1883–1923; *Connacht People & Ballinasloe Independent*, 1884–6; *Western Advertiser*, 1884–96; *Western Star*, 1888–1902; *Galway Observer*, 1889–1923; *Western News & Galway Guardian*, 1899–1901; *Western News*, 1901–3; *Connacht Champion*, 1904–11; *Western News*, 1905–20; *Loughrea Nationalist*, 1905; *Galway Pilot*, 1905–18; *Connacht Tribune*, 1909–96; *East Galway Democrat*, 1913–21; *Western News & Galway Leader*, 1921–6; *Galway Observer*, 1925–66; *Connacht Sentinel*, 1927–45; *East Galway Democrat*, 1936–49; *Tuam Herald*, 1938–99; *Connacht Sentinel*, 1950–99; and *City Tribune*, 1984–99.

LOCATION

City centre, across the Salmon Weir Bridge, near the New Cathedral (the Cathedral of Our Lady Assumed into Heaven).

## GALWAY FAMILY HISTORY SOCIETY WEST

Unit 3, Venture Centre, Liosbaun Estate
Tuam Road
GALWAY CITY, CO. GALWAY
Ireland

TELEPHONE: (091) 756 737; FAX: (091) 756 737
E-mail: galwaywestroots@eircom.net
Website: www.mayo-ireland.ie/Geneal/WtGalway.htm

HOURS

M–Th, 9:30am–3:30pm; F, 9:30–1:00pm

ACCESS AND SERVICES

The West Galway centre offers a full range of fee-based genealogical services to people interested in researching their Galway roots. Initial enquiries are answered within four weeks and the centre has access to over a million records. An initial assessment payment of 40 euro is required with application, a copy of which can be found on the society's website. Fees are based on the time and expense involved in carrying out a thorough assessment. Cost of commissioning a family history report will normally be in the range 190 euro–320 euro depending on the amount of information located. Research consultation by prior appointment only at 60 euro per hour (or part thereof). In addition to providing a full service for those who wish to have their family roots traced, the society offers publications for sale including: the journals *Galway Roots* (Vols 1–5); *Forthill Cemetery*; *Castlegar Graveyard Inscriptions*; *Inishbofin through Time and Tide*. Prices range from 7 euro to 15 euro plus postage. Write, phone or e-mail for an exact quotation, including postage costs. The centre is not disabled-accessible.

CONTACT

Dee Goggin, Researcher

DESCRIPTION

One of the Irish Family History Foundation's two designated family research centres for Galway, the other being EAST GALWAY FAMILY HISTORY SOCIETY, Woodford. The main towns and villages in West Galway are Galway City, Tuam, Clifden, Oughterard, Athenry, and Kinvara. The Aran Islands and Inishbofin are also in this centre's catchment area. Parishes covered are: Abbeyknockmoy, Annaghadown, Aran Islands, Ardrahan, Athenry, Ballyconneely, Carraroe, Carna, Castlegar, Claregalway, Clarinbridge, Clifden, Clonbur, Cummer, Donaghpatrick, Dunmore, Galway City, Headford, Inishbofin, Kilconly/Kilbennan, Kilcummin/Oughterard, Kilannin, Killererin, Kinvara, Lackagh, Moycullen, Oranmore, Omey/Ballindoon, Rahoon, Rosmuc, Roundstone, Spiddal, and Tuam.

HOLDINGS

The centre has access to the following records containing over 2,000,000 entries in the Galway West area: Roman Catholic, Church of Ireland, Methodist and Presbyterian Church records up to 1900; civil records of births, deaths, and marriages from their inception in 1864 up to 1900; electors' lists; gravestone inscriptions; indexed directories (Slater's, Pigott's, and Thom's); parochial censuses (the oldest of which dates from 1821); newspaper obituaries; Encumbered Estates Court rentals; Workhouse Census search forms for Pension Applications; Tithe Applotment Records; Griffith's Valuation (1848–55); 1901 and 1911 Censuses of Population; Ordnance Survey maps showing townlands. The centre has also built up an extensive collection of local family history publications.

LOCATION

From Eyre Square, take N17 towards Tuam (North Galway). At roundabout at cemetery/Statoil station continue straight on the N17, first turn left at AIB bank, continue left at Corporate Express and straight on – across the road from Castle Print. Approximately one mile from Eyre Square (but difficult to find).

## NATIONAL UNIVERSITY OF IRELAND, GALWAY – JAMES HARDIMAN LIBRARY

GALWAY CITY, CO. GALWAY
Ireland

TELEPHONE: (091) 524 411, ext. 2540; FAX: (091) 522 394
E-mail: library@nuigalway.ie
Website: www.library.nuigalway.ie

HOURS

Term: M–F, 9:00am–10:00pm; Sat, 9:00am–1:00pm; extended opening hours apply close to examinations, while shorter hours apply outside term time. Hours differ for Special Collections (see separate entry below) and for the Medical and Nursing Libraries located at University College Hospital.

ACCESS AND SERVICES

Visitors welcome, but advance notice preferred and identification required. External service fees apply for visitors seeking self-service to library facilities and for those seeking borrowing privileges. The library also offers a customized information service tailored to the needs of businesses, industry professionals and individuals on a fee basis. Fees also apply for photocopying and microform prints. Disabled access facilities. The website is updated regularly and contains more detailed information. Free brochures, including one entitled 'Information Service for External Users', are available.

CONTACT

Marie Reddan, Librarian
Trish Finnan, Information Librarian, Commerce and External Liaison; tel. ext. 3564; e-mail: trish.finnan@nuigalway.ie

DESCRIPTION

The James Hardiman Library supports the teaching and research interests of NUI, Galway, originally founded in 1845 by Queen Victoria, along with universities in Cork and Belfast. NUI, Galway, formerly University College Galway, is part of the National University of Ireland system, which includes campuses in Dublin, Cork, Limerick, and Maynooth. The Galway campus has teaching and research interests in the sciences, engineering, law, commerce, medicine and humanities.

HOLDINGS

The library houses a collection of more than 270,000 volumes, 1,900 current periodicals, a range of electronic information products, a reference collection of Irish government publications, a European Documentation Centre, SPECIAL COLLECTIONS (see separate entry below), newspapers, health and safety publications, and an audiovisual collection.

LOCATION

Take N6 into Galway, follow signs for West Galway and Salthill. At junction of N6 and Newcastle Road, turn left. Take next left turn into campus.

## NATIONAL UNIVERSITY OF IRELAND, GALWAY – JAMES HARDIMAN LIBRARY – DEPARTMENT OF SPECIAL COLLECTIONS AND ARCHIVES

GALWAY CITY, CO. GALWAY
Ireland

TELEPHONE: (091) 524 411, ext. 2543, 3636; FAX: (091) 522 394
E-mail: marie.boran@nuigalway.ie; Kieran@sulacco.library.nuigalway.ie
Website: www.library.nuigalway.ie

HOURS

M–F, 9:00am–1:15pm, 2:30–5:00pm; closed for lunch, 1:15–2:30pm; Tu, 6:30–9:45pm (in term only)

ACCESS AND SERVICES

Visitors are welcome to consult material not available to them in their local repositories, but advance notice and identification required. Disabled access facilities. Laptops and photography permitted; pencils only. External service fees for visitors seeking borrowing privileges. Fees for photocopying and microfilm prints. Copying of archival material can only be done by the archivist, and at his discretion. Some 98% of the books in Special Collections are catalogued online. Printed and electronic finding aids are available for archival holdings. Exhibitions of material from the collections are held throughout the year. Free brochures, including one entitled 'Information Service for External Users', are available. The website is updated regularly and contains more detailed information.

CONTACT

Marie Boran, Special Collections Librarian; e-mail: marie.boran@nuigalway.ie
Kieran Hoare, Archivist; e-mail: Kieran@sulacco.library.nuigalway.ie

DESCRIPTION

NATIONAL UNIVERSITY OF IRELAND, GALWAY – JAMES HARDIMAN LIBRARY was founded in 1849 and has been developing special collections of both archival and printed material from its inception. Its areas of special interest include: Galway and West of Ireland studies; Irish literature in English; literature and publishing in the Irish language; history, particularly of the West of Ireland; and Irish theatre.

HOLDINGS

Special Collections houses some 40,000 volumes, plus significant holdings of journals, manuscripts, maps, microforms, newspapers, pamphlets, photographs, and recordings. Major book collections include: the Bairéad Collection of Irish language material, particularly ephemera from the early days of the Gaelic revival movements; the Cairnes Collection of works on 19th-century economy and society; the Coen Collection of local and Irish history, plus some religious and devotional material; the Déon Collection of modern French writing, including the publications of the donor, French author Michel Déon; the Delargy Collection of 20th-century Irish and European folklore; the Fanning Collection of Irish archaeology and history; the Freyer Collection of works by and about author Liam O'Flaherty (1896–1984); the Gregory Collection containing virtually all material published by and about Isabella Augusta, Lady Gregory (1852–1932), including associated works and biographies; the Hunt Collection of books on 20th-century psychology and related subjects, especially from an American perspective; the Irish Women's Publishing Collection, with a focus on feminist publishers in Ireland since 1980; the Killanin Collection of some 3,500 volumes on 20th-century Irish literature, art, and archaeology, plus world politics and horse racing; and the St Anthony's Collection of some 20,000 volumes from the library of St Anthony's College in Newcastle, Galway, with a concentration on devotional literature, theology, Irish and Cchurch history; and the Rare Book Collection. Note: The Killanin Collection, donated in 2000 in memory of Michael Morris, 3rd Baron Killanin, is still being processed and will not be available to readers until the work is completed.

Manuscript and Archive Collections of special importance include: The De hÍde Collection of manuscripts gathered by Doughláis de hÍde (Douglas Hyde), founder of the Gaelic League, who collected folklore and music in the Irish language; the Bairéad Collection of papers and correspondence relating to the Gaelic League and related Irish-language material; the LSB Manuscripts Collection of miscellaneous manuscripts on a variety of subjects, some in Gaelic; the Estate Papers Collection of material, such as rentals, marriage settlements, estate maps and household correspondence, relating to landed estates, principally in the West of Ireland; the Revolutionary Ireland Collection of papers pertaining to the period 1914–22 in Ireland, especially Co. Galway; the Co. Galway Collection, which includes the records of the Galway Municipal Authority dating back to its founding in 1484; the minute books for Galway Corporation, Galway Town Commissioners and the Galway Urban District Council; the Clifden Railway documents and the papers relating to LDF activity in Galway during the Second World War; the Academic Papers Collection containing the papers and books of distinguished faculty, members including John E. Cairnes, Mary Donovan O'Sullivan and Richard Doherty; the Theatre Archive containing the archives of Taibhdhearc na Gaillimhe, the Irish theatre founded in 1928; the Druid Theatre, founded in 1975, and the Galway Arts Festival, begun in 1977;

and the Photographic Archive, with special focus on Galway and UCG (University College Galway). Of special interest, two sets of papers relating to the Earls of Lucan have recently been made available for consultation. This Co. Mayo family goes back to the 16th century, and this archive holds special importance for 19th- and 20th-century Irish history, particularly dealing with land issues.

Though the library does not offer a family history enquiry service, Special Collections does house a variety of source materials for family history. These include the actual 1901 Census returns for Co. Galway, available on microfilm in the InfoMedia room; Griffith's Valuation (1848–57), available in hard copy for certain counties and on microfiche in the InfoMedia room for all of Ireland, where you may also find a searchable index on CD-ROM to the surnames found in Griffith's; Ordnance Survey Maps; and an extensive range of reference books. Special Collections houses bound volumes of an Index to Surnames in Griffith's for the counties of Connacht (Galway, Leitrim, Mayo, Roscommon, and Sligo), plus Donegal, Clare, Longford and Offaly. Though no countrywide census was done before 1821, local surveys were sometimes undertaken. See *Tracing Your Irish Ancestors* by John Grenham, copies of which are available in the library, for a listing of the surveys published in journals.

LOCATION

Take N6 into Galway, follow signs for West Galway and Salthill. At junction of N6 and Newcastle Road, turn left. Take next left turn into campus. Special Collections is located on the ground floor of the library.

## DIOCESE OF CLONFERT ARCHIVE

St Brendan's, Coorheen
LOUGHREA, CO. GALWAY
Ireland

TELEPHONE: (091) 841 560; FAX: (091) 841 818
E-mail: clonfert@iol.ie
Website: homepage.eircom.net/~clonfert

HOURS

By appointment only

ACCESS AND SERVICES

Visitors welcome but by appointment only. Advance notice and references required. Only pencils may be used. Photography not permitted. No disabled access facilities. No photocopying or microfilm facilities available.

CONTACT

Bishop John Kirby

DESCRIPTION

Small diocesan archive, with few documents dating before 1900. There was no permanent residence until 1907. Some bishops, on transfer, took their papers with them to their new assignments. Clonfert is one of the smallest dioceses in Ireland, with just 24 parishes.

HOLDINGS

Records and documents relating to the administration of the Roman Catholic Diocese of Clonfert.

LOCATION

St Brendan's Cathedral is in Loughrea town centre, just off the N6, south-east of Galway. Signposted.

## EAST GALWAY FAMILY HISTORY SOCIETY

Woodford Heritage Centre
WOODFORD, CO. GALWAY
Ireland

TELEPHONE: (0509) 49309; FAX: (0509) 49546
E-mail: galwayroots@eircom.net
Website: www.irishroots.net/EtGalway.htm; www.galwayroots.com (under construction)

HOURS

M–Th, 9:00am–4:30pm; F, 9:00am–1:00pm

ACCESS AND SERVICES

The East Galway centre offers a full range of fee-based genealogical services to people interested in researching their East Galway roots. Initial enquiries are answered promptly, and a family history report usually takes about four weeks. An initial assessment payment of $45 is required with application, a copy of which can be found on the society's website. Fees are based on the time and expense involved in carrying out a thorough assessment. Cost of commissioning a family history report will normally be in the range of $100–$250, depending on the amount of information located. The East Galway Family History Society offers a range of publications relating to the area for sale. These include: *A Forgotten Campaign*, which details the Land War in East Galway, at $20.00; *Clanrickarde Country* at $20.00; *Lough Derg – the Westside Story* (map) at $6.00; and *Woodford: a Guide to its Sights* at $2.50. Prices quoted exclude postage and packing.

CONTACT

Angela Canning

DESCRIPTION

One the Irish Family History Foundation's two designated family research centres for Co. Galway, the other being GALWAY FAMILY HISTORY SOCIETY WEST, Galway City. Chief towns and villages of East Galway include: Ballinasloe, Loughrea, Gort, Portumna, Glenamaddy, and Mountbellew.

HOLDINGS

The earliest Roman Catholic parish records computerized at this centre start in 1747. Earliest Church of Ireland records date from 1747 for Loughrea. For the parish of Ballinalsoe only, the society has computerized Presbyterian records, 1846–1900, and Wesleyan Methodist records, 1834–1900. Altogether, the centre has computerized about 1,000,000 pre-1901 records. Other major sources held at the East Galway Centre include: civil records of birth, death and marriage; the Book of Survey and Distribution; gravestone inscriptions; and the Woodford Parish Census. The earliest surviving Census for East Galway is that of 1901.

LOCATION

Woodford is 14.5 miles south of Loughrea on the R351. Loughrea is 21.5 miles south-east of Galway City on the N6.

# COUNTY KERRY

## KERRY ARCHAEOLOGICAL AND HISTORICAL SOCIETY

*See* KERRY LOCAL HISTORY AND ARCHIVES COLLECTION, Tralee

## KILLARNEY GENEALOGICAL CENTRE

Cathedral Walk
KILLARNEY, CO. KERRY
Ireland

Note: service currently suspended. Expected to reopen following completion of computerization of records. Until then, contact Rev. G. Walsh, Diocesan Secretary, Bishop's House, Killarney, Co. Kerry.

## KERRY LOCAL HISTORY AND ARCHIVES COLLECTION

Kerry County Library
Moyderwell
TRALEE, CO. KERRY
Ireland

TELEPHONE: County Library: (066) 718 3507; FAX: (066) 712 9202
Local History and Archives Department: (066) 712 1200; FAX: (066) 712 9202
E-mail: info@kerrycolib.ie or localhistory@kerrycolib.ie
Website: www.kerrycolib.ie

HOURS

Tralee Library: M,W,F,Sat, 10:00am–5:00pm; Tu,Th, 10:00am–8:00pm
Local History and Archives Department: M–F, 10:00am–1:00pm, 2:00–5:00pm; Sat, 10:00am–12:30pm, 2:30–5:00pm

ACCESS AND SERVICES

Visitors welcome. Membership available on application at no charge. Identification required. Charges are levied, however, on the borrowing of books (30c per each item borrowed; children up to and including second-level students are exempt from these charges). Online catalogue. The library is a focal point for cultural and educational activities in the community. Services include Internet workstations, with free access for public use. The Kerry Archaeological and Historical Society, established in 1967 for the collection, recording, study and preservation of material relating to the history and antiquities of Co. Kerry, also operates out of the library.

CONTACT

Kathleen Browne, County Librarian; e-mail: kabrowne@eircom.net
Ann Ferguson, Information/Reference Services Librarian; tel: (066) 712 1200; fax (066) 712 9202; e-mail: annferguson@eircom.net

Michael Costello, Local History Librarian
Michael Lynch, Archivist

DESCRIPTION

The Kerry County Library is the flagship library in the nine-library county system that also includes branch libraries in Killarney, tel. (064) 32655; fax (064) 36065; Ballybunion, tel. (068) 27615; Caherciveen, tel. (066) 947 2287; Castleisland, tel. (066) 714 1485; Dingle, tel. (066) 915 1499; Kenmare, tel. (064) 41416; Killorglin, tel. (066) 976 1272; and Listowel, tel. (068) 21491. The new Local Studies/Archives Department at Kerry County Library Headquarters, Tralee, was officially opened on 25 March 2002.

HOLDINGS

The library houses approximately 38,000 volumes of general educational and recreational interest. It is also home to the Kerry Local History Collection. This section aims to collect and make available as comprehensive as possible a collection of material relating to the history of the county, including published books, manuscripts, photographs, newspapers, and sound recordings. The collection includes: a comprehensive collection of local newspapers dating back to 1820s; a collection of books on Kerry and by Kerry authors; local maps (six-inch Ordnance Survey); local historical photographs (Lawrence and Eason Collections); Board of Guardian Minute Books (1840s–); periodicals, e.g. *Journal of the Royal Society of Antiquaries of Ireland*, *Journal of the Cork Historical and Archaeological Society*; Irish Folklore Commission Schools Collection (1937–8) on microfilm; Tithe Applotment Books (1820–30); Griffith's Valuation (*c.*1850); Census of Population 1901 (microfilm); Tralee Gaol Register (1833–4); and specialized collections of papers and family histories, including the Reidy family, Ferris family, Antarctic explorer Tom Crean, Thomas Ashe, and material on Roger Casement. Local newspaper holdings include: *Chutes Western Herald*, 1812–35; *Kerry Advocate*, 1914–15; *The Kerry Champion*, 1928–58; *Kerry Evening Post*, 1829–1917; *Kerry Evening Star*, 1902–14; *The Kerry Examiner*, 1840–56; *Kerry's Eye*, 1974 to present; *Kerry Independent*, 1880–84; *The Kerryman*, 1904 to present; *Kerry News*, 1924–41; *Kerry People*, 1902–22; *The Kerry Press*, 1914–16; *Kerry Reporter*, 1924–35; *Kerry Sentinel*, 1878–1917; *Kerry Star*, 1861–3; *Kerry Weekly Reporter and Commercial Advertiser*, 1883–1920; *Killarney Advertiser*, 1974 to present; *Killarney Echo and South Kerry Chronicle*, 1889–1920; *The Kingdom*, 1984 to present; *An Lóchrann*, 1913–20; *Munster Life*, 1897; *Raymond's Kerry Herald*, 1856; *Tralee Chronicle and Killarney Echo*, 1843–75; *Tralee Chronicle and Killarney Chronicle*, 1860–67; *Tralee Liberator*, 1914–39; *Tralee Mercury*, 1829–39; and *Weekly Chronicle*, 1873. The collection also includes a good representation of national newspapers, including *Freeman's Journal*, 1763–1860.

LOCATION

Town centre, corner of Dean's Lane and Moyderwell.

# COUNTY KILDARE

## NATIONAL UNIVERSITY OF IRELAND, MAYNOOTH – JOHN PAUL II LIBRARY

MAYNOOTH, CO. KILDARE
Ireland

TELEPHONE: (01) 708 3884; FAX: (01) 628 6008
E-mail: Reader.Services@may.ie
Website: www.may.ie/library

HOURS

Term: M–F, 8:30am–9:30pm; Sat, 10:00am–1:00pm; extended hours near exam time
Vacation: M–F, 9:00am–5:00pm

ACCESS AND SERVICES

Visitors admitted at the discretion of the Librarian. External readers welcome when material is not available elsewhere. Annual membership fee for borrowing privileges. Wheelchair-accessible. Photocopying and microform prints available for a fee. Leaflets and booklets describing services available. For access to early printed books and archives, both housed in the Russell Library, see ST PATRICK'S COLLEGE MAYNOOTH ARCHIVES and ST PATRICK'S COLLEGE MAYNOOTH – RUSSELL LIBRARY NUI. Maynooth provides the library service in the John Paul II Library and the Russell Library. There is a branch library of the University at the Kilkenny Campus, tel. (056) 75919.

CONTACT

Agnes Neligan, Librarian; tel. (01) 708 3879; e-mail: Agnes.Neligan@may.ie
Sallyanne Knowles, Executive Assistant; tel. (01) 708 3881; e-mail: Sally.A.Knowles@may.ie

DESCRIPTION

Maynooth is a constituent university of the National University of Ireland, having been a recognized college of that body since 1910. The seminary, St Patrick's College, was founded in 1795 to educate and train men in Ireland for the Catholic priesthood. In 1966 St Patrick's College opened its doors to lay students, and today the university has an enrolment of over 6,000 students. The library supports the teaching and research interests of students and faculty, with special interests in the areas of education, theology and the humanities. The John Paul II Library was opened in 1984, replacing the Russell Library as the university's main library.

HOLDINGS

The library houses a collection of more than 250,000 volumes, with significant collections built up by scholar professors from the mid-19th century onwards. Particular strengths are in theology, religion and history. Early printed books, manuscripts and archives are housed in the Russell Library.

LOCATION

Maynooth is 15 miles west of Dublin, off the M4. Served by buses (66, 66X, and 67A) from Dublin city centre and by trains from Dublin's Connolly Station. The campus is located in the village centre. The John Paul II Library is located in the South (old) Campus, across the footbridge *en route* to the North (new) Campus.

## ST PATRICK'S COLLEGE MAYNOOTH ARCHIVES

Russell Library
MAYNOOTH, CO. KILDARE
Ireland

TELEPHONE: (01) 628 5222; FAX: (01) 628 9063
E-mail: Penny.Woods@may.ie
Website: www.may.ie/library

HOURS

By appointment only.

ACCESS AND SERVICES

Visitors welcome, but advance notice and identification required. Wheelchair-accessible. Laptops permitted; pencils only. Leaflets and pamphlets available. For access to the College Archives permission must first be sought from the Archivist, Msgr Corish. Archival materials, including the Salamanca archives, may then be consulted in the Russell Library. Publications of interest include: Patrick J. Corish, *Maynooth College, 1795–1995* (Dublin, 1995); Patrick J. Hamell, *Maynooth Students and Ordinations, 1795–1984* (1982–4); and Patrick J. Corish, 'Maynooth College Archives', in *Catholic Archives*, 13 (1993):46–8.

CONTACT

Penelope Woods, Librarian, Russell Library; e-mail: Penny.Woods@may.ie

DESCRIPTION

St Patrick's College, Maynooth was founded in 1795 to educate and train Catholic clergy. In 1896 it was established as a Pontifical University, and in 1910 it also became a recognized college of the National University of Ireland. St Patrick's College is the National Seminary of Ireland and is administered separately from NUI, Maynooth.

HOLDINGS

The archive houses the original records of the college plus the historical archive of the Irish College of Salamanca in Spain. Though more than 11,000 priests have been ordained at Maynooth, a fire in 1940 destroyed the matriculation register for 1795–1940, removing an important family history record. This is a small domestic archive, of limited importance to genealogists. The Salamanca Archives of some 50,000 documents contains administration records not only of the Irish College in Salamanca, but also of the Irish Colleges of Alcala, Santiago, and Seville. They cover a period of three and a half centuries. The letters in the archives, which are kept in the library, have been listed on a database and in *The Salamanca Letters: a Catalogue of Correspondence (1619–1871)* (Maynooth, 1995).

LOCATION

Russell Library is located in St Patrick's House, the Gothic Quadrangle beyond St Joseph's Square, in the South Cloister.

## ST PATRICK'S COLLEGE MAYNOOTH – RUSSELL LIBRARY

MAYNOOTH, CO. KILDARE
Ireland

TELEPHONE: (01) 628 5222; FAX: (01) 628 9063
E-mail: Penny.Woods@may.ie
Website: www.may.ie/library

HOURS

Term and Vacation: M–Th, 10:00am–1:00pm, 2:00–5:00pm

ACCESS AND SERVICES

Researchers welcome, but advance notice and identification required. Visitors admitted at the discretion of the Librarian. Wheelchair-accessible. Laptops permitted; pencils only. Leaflets and pamphlets available. Publications of interest include: Agnes Neligan (ed.), *Maynooth Library Treasures* (Dublin, 1995). There are three catalogues, on cards, for the books in the Russell Library. These are also incorporated in the JOHN PAUL II LIBRARY card catalogue. There is a published catalogue for Irish manuscripts: Paul Walsh, *Catalogue of Irish mss in Maynooth College Library*. Part 1 (Má Nuad: Cuallacht Choilm Cille, 1943). Ó Fiannachta, Pádraig, *Clár lámhscríbhinní Gaeilge Mhá Nuad*. Fasc. 2–8. (Má Nuad: An Sagart, 1965–73). Ó Fiannachta, Pádraig, *Clár lámhscríbhinní Gaeilge. Leabhlarlanna na cléire agus mionchnuasaigh*. Fasc. 1–2. (Baile Átha Cliath: Institúid Árd-Léinn, 1978–80). Further additions to the ms collection are detailed in *Seanchas Ard Mhacha*, VII, 2 (1974), *Léachtai Cholm Cille*, XI (1980), XVI (1986), XVIII (1988), XX (1990); and De Brún, *Pádraig Lámhscríbhinní Gaeilge: treoirliosta* (Baile Átha Cliath: Institúid Árd-Léinn, 1988).

CONTACT

Penelope Woods, Librarian, Russell Library; e-mail: Penny.Woods@may.ie

DESCRIPTION

St Patrick's College, Maynooth was founded in 1795 to educate and train Catholic clergy. In 1896 it was established as a Pontifical University, and in 1910 it also became a recognized college of the National University of Ireland. St

Patrick's College is the National Seminary of Ireland and is administered separately from NUI, Maynooth. Lay students were first admitted to Maynooth in 1966, and today the National University of Ireland, Maynooth has an enrolment of more than 6,000 students. The library was completed in 1861, designed by A.W. Pugin (1812–52). In 1984 it was renamed for Charles Russell, President of Maynooth 1857–80; it served as the main college library until the opening of the John Paul II Library in 1984.

HOLDINGS

Russell Library houses the university's collection of rare and early printed books and manuscripts. The collection totals more than 22,000 books, plus maps, architectural records, illuminated manuscripts and some 300 volumes of Irish manuscripts. The pre-1851 books collection focuses on theological works, many of which were printed on the continent, but also includes significant holdings in history, geography, classics, antiquities, and science. Important holdings include: 59 incunabula, Maynoothiana, rare and interesting printings and bindings; 1,220 bound volumes of pamphlets, variously acquired on diverse subjects; a Bible collection, including the archive on permanent loan since 1986 of the National Bible Society of Ireland, formerly the Hibernian Bible Society, founded in 1806, containing over 2,000 bibles in numerous languages from the 16th century to the 1960s. The map collection includes a complete bound set of six-inch Ordnance Survey maps, 1833–45, a set of one-inch Ordnance Survey maps (1903) with ESB (Electrical Supply Board) lines and Catholic parish boundaries added, late 1940s, a map of Maynooth Castle (1636, copy), and 19th-century maps of college land and grounds. Architectural plans and drawings include drawings of college buildings by A.W. Pugin and Richard Pierce (1801–54); drawings of the College Infirmary, outbuildings, etc. by J.J. McCarthy (1817–82); and plans of the John Paul II Library by Hendy, Watkinson and Stonor (1984), and associated documentation.

The manuscript collection is especially strong in Irish-language materials. The Irish-language manuscripts represent in particular the collections of three men: John Murphy (1772–1847), Bishop of Cork; Eugene O'Curry (1796–1862), Professor of Irish History and Archaeology at the Catholic University of Ireland; and Laurence Renehan (1797–1857), President of Maynooth College and of the Celtic Society. The Murphy Collection contains 114 bound volumes bequeathed to the college in 1848. The O'Curry Collection contains 115 volumes of material, all collected or transcribed by him. The Renehan Collection contains material collected for an ecclesiastical history of Ireland, and, in addition to the Irish-language material, includes 79 bound volumes of manuscripts in English, French, and Latin. These manuscript collections are described and listed in a printed catalogue begun by Rev. Paul Walsh in 1943 and completed by An tAth. Pádraig Ó Fiannachta. The Irish language mss have been microfilmed and these may be consulted in the John Paul II Library. Much of the remaining manuscript holdings have Maynooth associations; they include: O'Hanlon mss, notes and correspondence of John, Canon O'Hanlon (1821–1905), with an index to the unpublished material for his *Lives of the Irish Saints* now available; Molloy mss, papers and lecture notes of Msgr Gerald Molloy (1834–1906); Shearman mss, papers of John Francis Shearman, antiquary and PP of Moone; material relating to the Irish Colleges of Paris and Bordeaux; and, of special importance, 12 Latin mss dating from the 11th to the 15th centuries, eight of which are illuminated. For the Salamanca Archives, *see* ST PATRICK'S COLLEGE MAYNOOTH ARCHIVES above.

LOCATION

Russell Library is located in St Patrick's House, the Gothic Quadrangle beyond St Joseph's Square, in the South Cloister.

## HISTORY AND FAMILY RESEARCH CENTRE

Riverbank
Main Street
NEWBRIDGE, CO. KILDARE
Ireland

Note: the History and Family Research Centre incorporates three related departments (ARCHIVES, KILDARE HERITAGE & GENEALOGY CO. LTD, and LOCAL STUDIES DEPARTMENT) under one roof. The facilities and premises have been redeveloped and the centre is now fully open to the public.

## HISTORY AND FAMILY RESEARCH CENTRE – ARCHIVES

History and Family Research Centre
Riverbank
Main Street
NEWBRIDGE, CO. KILDARE
Ireland

TELEPHONE: (045) 431 611; FAX: (045) 431 611
E-mail: kildarearchives@eircom.net
Website: kildare.ie/library/library

HOURS

By appointment only

ACCESS AND SERVICES

Visitors welcome, but strictly by appointment only.

CONTACT

Archivist; e-mail: kildarearchives@eircom.net

DESCRIPTION

Kildare County Council is developing a County Archive Service based at the History and Family Research Centre. In preparing for this, it was first necessary to identify and preserve the public archive collections held in various locations throughout the county. A specially adapted storage facility has now been assigned for the archives at Newbridge.

HOLDINGS

Quality archive collections have survived for Co. Kildare, but these are currently uncatalogued and therefore are not accessible.

LOCATION

Located in the County Library building, town centre, beside bridge crossing River Liffey.

## HISTORY AND FAMILY RESEARCH CENTRE – LOCAL STUDIES DEPARTMENT

History and Family Research Centre
Riverbank
Main Street
NEWBRIDGE, CO. KILDARE
Ireland

TELEPHONE: (045) 432 690; FAX: (045) 431 611
E-mail: kildarelocalhistory@eircom.net
Website: kildare.ie/library/library

HOURS

Tu–F, 9:00–1:00pm, 2:00–5:00pm; Sat, 10:00am–4:30pm

ACCESS AND SERVICES

Visitors welcome; appointments advisable. The facilities and premises at the History and Family Research Centre have been redeveloped and the centre is now fully open to the public. Because of staffing levels and ongoing projects, it is advised that all contact still be made by appointment only, although queries are being dealt with by phone, e-mail and post.

CONTACT

Librarian; e-mail: kildarelocalhistory@eircom.net

DESCRIPTION

The Local Studies Department forms an integral part of the County Library service and ultimately, in partnership with ARCHIVES and KILDARE HERITAGE AND GENEALOGY CO. LTD, will become an integral part of the Riverbank Cultural Campus. The Local Studies Collection has been extended and relocated in the History and Family Research Centre. It is the focal point for local history research in Co. Kildare for historians and enthusiasts alike. A new reading room provides a welcoming setting for users. The collection will be added to the computerized catalogue on the County Library's Genesis system, thus enhancing the service and making it more accessible.

HOLDINGS

Kildare Local Studies Department has a collection of books, periodicals, maps, photographs, and newspapers relating to all aspects of Kildare history. Among the most important items in the collection are the Ballitore manuscripts consisting of files of late 19th-century correspondence, school notebooks, drawings, etc. of the Shackleton and other Quaker families from Ballitore, Co. Kildare. The Teresa Brayton Collection of books, newspaper cuttings and personal items forms another important part of the local studies collection. Perhaps the most important source for the study of local history is the *Journal of the Kildare Archeological Society*, first published in 1891. In addition, Local Studies Department holds Griffith's Valuation; the six-inch Ordnance Survey (1837) and other maps of the county from the 18th century; Tithe Applotment Books; Minute Books of the Naas Board of Guardians (1843–*c.*1900); and photographs from the Lawrence Collection etc. Newspaper holdings include: *Leinster Leader* (*c.*1881–present) and the *Irish Times* (1859–95, 1912–18). Hard copies of the *Kildare Observer* are held, but are unavailable for public use because of condition.

LOCATION

Located in County Library Building, town centre, beside bridge crossing River Liffey.

## KILDARE HERITAGE & GENEALOGY COMPANY

History and Family Research Centre
Riverbank
Main Street
NEWBRIDGE, CO. KILDARE
Ireland

TELEPHONE: (045) 433 602; FAX: (045) 431 611
E-mail: capinfo@iol.ie
Website: www.kildare.ie/genealogy

HOURS

By appointment

ACCESS AND SERVICES

Visitors are welcome. The Kildare Heritage & Genealogy Company is a fee-based family history research centre for those interested in tracing their family roots in Co. Kildare. Fees are based on Irish Family History Foundation guidelines.

Consult website for fee schedule and application form. A minimum non-refundable charge of 20 euro must accompany all research requests. Currently, the company is compiling a computerized index to the local newspaper, *The Leinster Leader*, beginning in 1881, which will eventually be available to the public. For information on this project, contact the company.

CONTACT

Karel Kiely, Coordinator

DESCRIPTION

The Kildare Heritage and Genealogy Co. was established in partnership with Kildare County Council, to identify, collect and record historical, archaeological, and genealogical information for Co. Kildare for the purpose of establishing a County Heritage and Genealogical Centre. The Kildare Heritage Project, sponsored by the Kildare Heritage and Genealogy Co., co-funded by Kildare County Council and FÁS, has been running in Newbridge since late 1987. The project is computerizing Co. Kildare's genealogical records, including: Roman Catholic and Church of Ireland registers; graveyard inscriptions; Griffith's Valuation; Tithe Books; and the 1901 Census. A professional research service is provided to members of the public both at home and abroad.

HOLDINGS

The company has indexed church records for both Roman Catholic and Church of Ireland parishes in Co. Kildare. Roman Catholic parish registers generally consist of baptismal registers and marriage registers, although some burial registers also exist. Due to the fact that the Roman Catholic Church was officially suppressed from the 1690s to Catholic Emancipation in 1829, the parish registers of different parishes have varying start dates. The earliest registers that still survive start from about 1740. Church of Ireland parish registers generally consist of baptismal, marriage, and burial registers. These registers start much earlier than the Roman Catholic ones, with some Kildare registers going back as far as 1671. Lists of Catholic and Church of Ireland records can be found on the company's website. Work has been completed on the 1901 Census and Griffith's Valuation for Kildare.

LOCATION

Located in County Library Building, town centre, beside bridge crossing River Liffey.

# COUNTY KILKENNY

## KILKENNY ARCHAEOLOGICAL SOCIETY

Rothe House
16 Parliament Street
KILKENNY CITY, CO. KILKENNY
Ireland

TELEPHONE: (056) 22893; FAX: (056) 22893
E-mail: rothehouse@eircom.net
Website: www.irishroots.net/Kilknny.htm

HOURS

M–Sat, 10:30am–5:00pm

ACCESS AND SERVICES

KAS is a fee-based, not-for-profit organization that offers genealogical research services to persons interested in tracing their roots in Co. Kilkenny. It is a member of the Irish Family History Foundation, the coordinating body for a network of government-approved genealogical research centres in the Republic of Ireland and in Northern Ireland that have computerized tens of millions of Irish ancestral records of different types. Initial enquiries are usually replied to within one week. Record searches and partial searches usually take about one month and enquirers who commission full reports can anticipate a delay of about three months. The initial assessment costs 75 euro while a record search for one family unit over one generation costs 40 euro. A single record costs 15 euro. An application form is available through the society's website. Common surnames in Kilkenny City and County include: Murphy, Walsh, Brennan, Maher, Butler, Phelan (and O'Phelan), Grace, Fitzpatrick, Comerford, and Ryan. The main towns and villages in this county in addition to Kilkenny City are: Castlecomer, Callan, Freshford, Johnstown, and Thomastown. Kilkenny Ancestry offers a number of publications for sale. These include: *Old Kilkenny Review* for the years 1978, 1980, 1986, 1988, 1990–94; *Kilkenny Graveyard Inscriptions*, Knocktoper No. 1 and St Patrick's No. 2; W. Nolan and K. Whelan (eds) *Kilkenny: History and Society*; and *Kilkenny City and County – a photographic record*, paperback and hardback. See website for a more comprehensive listing and prices.

CONTACT

Researcher

DESCRIPTION

Kilkenny Ancestry is the primary genealogical research service for Co. Kilkenny, with some 2,000,000 genealogical records computerized.

HOLDINGS

Church records from 1754 to 1900 have been computerized. Kilkenny Ancestry also holds copies of: Indexed Pigott's and Slater's Directories; various estate rentals; a listing of some of the records of Kilkenny Corporation; and files of the *Kilkenny Journal* newspaper and some of the *Moderator*, neither of which is currently indexed, though the project has begun indexing the 18th-century items.

LOCATION

City centre, across from the courthouse, a ten-minute walk from Kilkenny Castle. The nearest car-park is on Parliament Street at the Market Cross Shopping Centre.

## KILKENNY COUNTY ARCHIVES

*See* KILKENNY COUNTY LIBRARY, Kilkenny

## KILKENNY COUNTY LIBRARY

NIB Building
6 Rose Inn Street
KILKENNY CITY, CO. KILKENNY
Ireland

TELEPHONE: (056) 91160; TAX: (056) 91168
E-mail: katlibs@iol.ie
Website: www.kilkennylibrary.ie

HOURS

M–F, 9:00am–1:00pm, 2:00–5:00pm; closed public holidays and bank holiday weekends.

ACCESS AND SERVICES

Visitors welcome, but advance notice preferred. Advance booking of microform reader–printers is required. Internet access available. No disabled access facilities. Fees for photocopying, microform prints and e-mail usage. Entire collection catalogued online. There is a printed catalogue for the Local History Collection. Free brochures are available, and an in-house guide and directory of services is available for consultation in the Local Studies Department. The library's website has a section devoted to local studies and provides a guide for researchers of genealogy in Kilkenny.

CONTACT

Declan McCauley, Assistant Librarian

DESCRIPTION

Headquarters library of Co. Kilkenny library system. The county's main local history collection is housed in the County Library.

## HOLDINGS

The library system houses a collection of some 300,000 books, plus journals, manuscripts, maps, microforms, newspapers, pamphlets, photographs, and recordings. The local history collection will be of special interest to visitors. It consists of important holdings of local history items, a local collection of material by Kilkenny authors or pertaining to Kilkenny, local newspapers, genealogical historical sources, and Kilkenny files collected from assorted publications.

The library also oversees the County Archives, but most of these records are held off premises so advance booking is essential. The archives include Board of Guardian minute books for the Poor Law Unions of Castlecomer, Thomastown and Urlingford *c.*1850–*c.*1900 and also Callan and Kilkenny 1842–1922 (some gaps in all series). The minutes detail the management of the workhouses where the destitute poor were accommodated.

Grand Jury records include printed presentments for the city and county of Kilkenny, 1839–1856.

Poll books survive for North Kilkenny 1897 and 1900 and registers of voters 1924–47 and 1964–.

Local authority records include those of the County Council and Rural District Councils from 1899 and there are also deposits of records of local business firms including indentures of apprentices.

Genealogical resources are especially strong. These include virtually all the standard sources for Kilkenny, such as Griffith's Valuation (microfilm and hard copy); Ordnance Survey maps; 1901 and 1911 Censuses; Tithe Applotment Books; lists, directories and various surveys; and a very strong local newspaper collection going back to 1767. See website for details.

## LOCATION

Kilkenny city centre. The Local Studies Department is still located at 6 John's Quay.

# COUNTY LAOIS

*for* KING'S COUNTY
*see* CO. OFFALY

## LAOIS AND OFFALY FAMILY HISTORY RESEARCH CENTRE

*See* IRISH MIDLANDS ANCESTRY, Tullamore, Co. Offaly

## LAOIS COUNTY LIBRARY – LOCAL STUDIES COLLECTION

Laois County Library Headquarters
Kea-Lew Business Park
Mountrath Road
PORTLAOISE, CO. LAOIS
Ireland

TELEPHONE: HQ: (0502) 72340/41; FAX: (0502) 64558
E-mail: library@laoiscoco.ie
Website: www.iol.ie/~libcounc/laois.htm

HOURS

Headquarters: M–F, 9:00am–1:00pm, 2:00–5:00pm
Portlaoise Branch Library, Dunamase House: Tu,F, 10:00am–5:00pm; W,Th, 10:00am–7:00pm; Sat 10:00am–1:00pm

ACCESS AND SERVICES

Visitors welcome. Modest membership fee required for borrowing privileges. Photocopying services available.

CONTACT

Gerry Maher, County Librarian

DESCRIPTION

Headquarters Library for Co. Laois, with branch libraries in: Abbeyleix, tel. (0502) 30020; Mountmellick, tel. (0502) 24733; Mountrath, tel. (0502) 56046; Portlaoise, tel. (0502) 22333; Portarlington, tel. (0502) 43751; Rathdowney, tel. (0502) 46852; and Stradbally, tel. (0502) 25065.

HOLDINGS

The Local Studies Collection, which is located at Headquarters, consists of manuscripts, local newspapers, books, pamphlets, photographs, maps, estate papers, and authors relating to Co. Laois and Ireland.

Estate papers include rentals for the Tipperary estate of the Countess of Milltown 1862–1969.

The Poor Law archive comprises minute books for the Poor Law Unions of Abbeyleix, Donamore and Mountmellick *c.*1844–*c.*1920.

The Laois County Council archive includes rate books 1934–57, microfilm copies of the tithe surveys for the county 1823–38, the tenement valuation *c.*1853 and the 1901 Census.

LOCATION

Kea-Lew Business Park, near town centre.

# COUNTY LEITRIM

## LEITRIM COUNTY LIBRARY

Main Street
BALLINAMORE, CO. LEITRIM
Ireland

TELEPHONE: (078) 44012; FAX: (078) 44425
E-mail: leitrimlibrary@eircom.net
Website: www.iol.ie/~libcounc/leitrim.htm

HOURS

M–F, 9:30am–5:30pm.

ACCESS AND SERVICES

Visitors welcome. No disabled access facilities. Photocopying and microform prints are available for a modest fee. The entire collection is catalogued, about half online.

CONTACT

Sean Ó Suilleabhain, County Librarian

DESCRIPTION

The library is the central public library for the County of Leitrim.

HOLDINGS

The library houses the usual range of public library material. Of principal interest to visitors would be its local history collection, which includes the Minutes of the Board of Guardians and oral interviews with local people. Of special genealogical interest are its holdings of Griffith's Valuation, Tithe Applotment Books, the 1901 and the 1911 Censuses, Ordnance Survey maps, estate papers, and its newspaper collection, all focusing on Co. Leitrim. There is also a collection of some 3,000 photographs, mostly after 1970.

LOCATION

Main Street, Ballinamore.

## LEITRIM GENEALOGY CENTRE

County Library
Main Street
BALLINAMORE, CO. LEITRIM
Ireland

TELEPHONE: (078) 44012; FAX: (078) 44425
E-mail: leitrimgenealogy@eircom.net
Website: www.irishroots.net/Leitrim.htm

HOURS

M–F, 10:00am–1:00pm, 2:00–5:00pm

ACCESS AND SERVICES

Visitors welcome. Disabled access facilities. Service fees apply. Genealogical research service, based on fees, as set by the Irish Family History Foundation, for the County of Leitrim. Local publications on sale.

CONTACT

Brid Sullivan

DESCRIPTION

Leitrim Genealogy Centre is the Irish Family History Foundation's designated genealogical research centre for Co. Leitrim. The centre is one of the longest established IFHF centres. Chief surnames found in Co. Leitrim include: Reynolds, McGowan, Rooney, Flynn, Kelly, Gallagher, Moran, Dolan, McLoughlin and McMorrow.

HOLDINGS

Main records include: Roman Catholic records, the earliest of which date from 1823; Church of Ireland records dating from 1783; Methodist records dating from 1840; and Presbyterian records dating from 1829. Records up to 1900 have been computerized. The centre also holds copies of: Griffith's Valuation; Tithe Applotment Books; the 1901 and the 1911 Censuses; Ordnance Survey maps; gravestone inscriptions; estate papers; and newspapers; plus indexes to church and civil records, all focusing on Co. Leitrim.

LOCATION

Located at rear of the County Library.

# COUNTY LIMERICK

## LIMERICK ANCESTRY

The Granary
Michael Street
LIMERICK CITY, CO. LIMERICK
Ireland

TELEPHONE: (061) 415 125; FAX: (061) 312 985
E-mail: None
Website: www.limerickancestry.com

HOURS

M–F, 9:30am–12:45pm, 2:00–3:30pm

ACCESS AND SERVICES

Limerick Ancestry provides a fee-based genealogical research service for persons interested in tracing their roots in Co. Limerick. Same-day/overnight search services are available to visitors. Application form/research questionnaire is available on LA's website or by post or fax from its office. LA also provides helpful leaflets on sources of information in the USA, Canada, and Australia. The initial search, which includes an assessment and information on the main generation being researched, costs 70 euro (but check website for current fees). Visa and Mastercard are accepted. Fees for further research will vary depending on amount of work possible. A quotation will be sent in advance.

CONTACT

Research Staff

DESCRIPTION

Limerick Ancestry is the Irish Family History Foundation's designated genealogical research centre for Limerick County and City. Limerick Ancestry is part of Limerick City Council and Limerick County Council. Previously it was supported by Shannon Development Company, a semi-state organization.

HOLDINGS

Staff have access to over 2,000,000 records. Church records include: Catholic registers with varying start dates from 1745 to 1867; Church of Ireland with start dates from 1692 to 1893; Presbyterian records from 1828; Methodist records from 1824; Quaker and Jewish records are also on file. Civil records include: non-Catholic marriages from 1845; births, marriages (Catholic), and deaths from 1864; Tithe Applotment Books 1824–35; Griffith's Valuation; and 1901/1911 Census returns for Limerick. Other sources include: trade directories; newspapers; Monteagle Estate Records; Limerick City Municipal Cemetery records; access to records in LIMERICK ARCHIVES; some graveyard inscriptions for Co. Limerick; and parish histories.

LOCATION

Limerick city centre, in a landmark 18th-century granary and bonded warehouse which also houses Limerick Archives and LIMERICK CITY PUBLIC LIBRARY, close to the Hunt Museum.

## LIMERICK ARCHIVES

The Granary
Michael Street
LIMERICK CITY, CO. LIMERICK
Ireland

TELEPHONE: (061) 415 125; FAX: (061) 312 985
E-mail: archives@limerickcity.ie or archives@limerickcoco.ie
Website: www.limerickcity.ie

HOURS

M–F, 9:30am–1:00pm, 2:00–3:30pm; closed public holidays

ACCESS AND SERVICES

Visitors welcome, but by appointment only. Advance notice, identification, and registration required. Readers must agree to observe the regulations of the Archives. Photocopying and microfilm print services available, but reproductions (including photographs) supplied by the office may be made only with the permission of the Senior Archivist.

CONTACT

City and County Archivist

DESCRIPTION

Incarnated as Limerick Regional Archives in the late 1970s, Limerick Archives developed largely into a genealogy-driven operation until 1998, when Limerick local authorities (Limerick City Council and Limerick County Council) took over the day-to-day administration of the service. A qualified archivist was appointed to oversee the records side of the operation, and the genealogy function carried on as a separate but linked activity (*see* LIMERICK ANCESTRY above). Limerick Archives focuses on collecting the administrative record for the city and county of Limerick, but accepts collections of local interest that are offered to it. A more aggressive and proactive collections policy will be adopted once the service is well established. Resources are shared with Limerick Ancestry's genealogy service.

HOLDINGS

Holdings include administrative records for the city (from 1841, with some older material related to St Michael's Parish back to 1809), and county (from 1899, plus older Poor Law Board of Guardians material, and Grand Jury Presentments).

There are almost complete collections of minute books for the Boards of Guardians of the Poor Law Unions of Kilmallock, Limerick and Newcastle West *c.*1840–1922. There are minutes 1850–1922 for Croom Poor Law Union and 1870–1891 for Glin. For Rathkeale only a single volume survived a fire at the workhouse; this covers the period January – November 1921.

Kilmallock Poor Law Union also has rate books 1842–73 (BG 106/N).

For St Michael's parish in the city of Limerick there is another series of rate books 1811–41 (with gaps; microfilm copies available in PRONI) and rent books *c.*1815. These are part of the archive of the Commissioners for the improvement of the parish.

There are also the following records with specific information about individuals:

- Register for Limerick house of industry 1774–94, some 2,000 names and addresses, details of age, occupation, etc.
- Register for St John's Fever and Lock Hospital 1816.
- Microfilm copy of a census of Shanagolden and Foynes area of Co. Limerick 1846 giving names and occupations, numbers in each household, several thousand names. This census was organized by Lord Monteagle and other local landlords. The original manuscript is held in the National Library of Ireland (MS 582). The MS runs to about 50 pages A3 size.
- Estate Papers: rent book for Lord Monteagle's estate 1831–50.
- The archive of the old Limerick Corporation includes records of the Mayor's Tholsel or small debtors' court 1773–95 and 1811–13, a Court of Claims register 1823–41, a register of admissions 1832–41, and paying orders 1777–1801.

Among private records, the Archives holds solicitors' records (some 4,000 property deeds); Encumbered Estate Court rentals; Monteagle Estate records (1800–1949); Limerick Chamber of Commerce; Limerick Harbour Commissioners; various company records; Limerick newspapers (hard copy and microfilm); maps (hard copy and microfilm); and microfilm collections of Limerick material held elsewhere. Property deeds have been fed to a local database, as have microfilm holdings. Handlists (short) of the various private collections also exist. The Archives collects anything to do with the administrative, social, economic, and cultural history of Limerick, and administrative collections for the city and county, e.g. P14/Monteagle Estate papers; PO1/Limerick Chamber of Commerce; PO2/Limerick Harbour Commissioners; PO9/ Limerick Water Works Company; P10/Limerick County Militia financial records, 1803–29; P11/Geary's Biscuit Factory papers; P12/Cannock & Company; P16/ Limerick Custom House papers; P21/ Coote family papers; and P22/ De Vere Papers.

LOCATION

Limerick city centre, in a landmark 18th-century granary and bonded warehouse which also houses Limerick Ancestry and LIMERICK CITY PUBLIC LIBRARY, close to the Hunt Museum.

## LIMERICK CITY PUBLIC LIBRARY

The Granary
Michael Street
LIMERICK CITY, CO. LIMERICK
Ireland

TELEPHONE: (061) 314 668; FAX: (061) 411 506
E-mail: citylib@limerickcity.ie
Website: www.limerickcity.ie

### HOURS

M,Tu, 10:00am–5:30pm; W–F, 10:00am–8:00pm, Sat, 10:00am–1:00pm; closed Saturdays of bank holiday weekends

### ACCESS AND SERVICES

Visitors welcome. Modest fees for photocopying and microfilm prints. Borrowing privileges may be restricted. Disabled access facilities. There is a searchable database of the Limerick Trade Directories from 1769 to 1879 (work in progress) that is currently available only in-house. Staff are happy to run searches and produce reports from this database.

### CONTACT

Dolores Doyle, City Librarian; e-mail: ddoyle@limerickcity.ie
Michael Maguire, Reference & Local History Librarian;
e-mail: mmaguire@limerickcity.ie

### DESCRIPTION

The Central Library at the Granary, along with one branch library at the Thomond Shopping Centre, Roxboro, Limerick, is funded by Limerick City Council. It provides a host of library services to the community, including a Local Studies Collection.

### HOLDINGS

The Local Studies Collection contains books, manuscripts, journals, newspapers, photographs, articles, maps, reports, and ephemera relating to Limerick City and County past and present. Of special interest is the extensive collection of books relating to the history, antiquities and society of the city and county, including the Kemmy Collection of books relating to Irish history, religion, and politics. Other collections include the Seamus Ó Ceallaigh Collection containing the research files, journals and books of the deceased GAA columnist of the *Limerick Leader* and renowned GAA historian. The collection includes material dating to the early years of the GAA in the Limerick area. The newspaper collection includes microfilm of the *Limerick Chronicle* (1782–1975, 1982 onwards), *Limerick Leader* (1893–1904, 1925 onwards), *General Advertiser or Limerick Gazette* (1806–20), *Munster Journal* (1749–84), and *Limerick Evening Post* (1811–19). Other material includes: the *Journal of the Association for the Preservation of the Memorials of the Dead in Ireland* (1888–1931); Memorial

Records of Irish soldiers who died in the First World War; business directories from 1769; Griffith's Valuation for Counties Limerick and Clare; list of landowners of one acre and upwards for the whole of Ireland (1876); Seamus Pender's 1659 Census of Ireland; Tithe Applotment Books for Co. Limerick; and Registers of Electors in Limerick City (1923, 1931 onwards).

LOCATION

Limerick city centre, in a landmark 18th-century granary and bonded warehouse which also houses LIMERICK ANCESTRY and LIMERICK ARCHIVES, close to the Hunt Museum.

## LIMERICK COUNTY LIBRARY – LOCAL STUDIES COLLECTION

Limerick County Library Headquarters
58 O'Connell Street
LIMERICK CITY, CO. LIMERICK
Ireland

TELEPHONE: (061) 214 452/318 477; FAX: (061) 318 570
E-mail: colibrarlimerickcoco.ie
Website: www.limerickcoco.ie/library

HOURS

Local Studies Department: M–F, 9:30am–1:00pm, 2:00–4:30pm
Dooradoyle Branch (main lending library): Tu,W, 10:00am–5:30pm; Th,F, 10:00am–8:30pm; Sat., 11:00am–5:30pm

ACCESS AND SERVICES

Visitors welcome. No membership fee. Photocopying and microfiche print services available at a cost of 10c per sheet. Books cannot be borrowed from Local Studies Collection.

CONTACT

Damien Brady, County Librarian
Margaret Franklin, Local Studies Librarian

DESCRIPTION

The Local Studies Collection houses a very strong Local History Collection and is based in the headquarters of the Limerick County Library. The Headquarters Library oversees a 25-branch county library system. Full-time, computerized branch libraries with Internet access include: Abbeyfeale (Bridge Street, Abbeyfeale, tel. (068) 32488, contact: Michael McInerney, Senior Library Assistant); Adare (Adare, tel. (061) 396 822, contact: Margaret O'Reilly, Assistant Librarian); Dooradoyle (Crescent Shopping Centre, Dooradoyle, tel. (061) 301 101, contact: Noreen O'Neill, Executive Librarian); and Newcastle West (Gortboy, Newcastle West, tel. (069) 62273, contact: Aileen Dillane, Executive

Librarian). Please note that Headquarters Library does not lend books. Its main lending library is the Dooradoyle Branch, located about two miles from headquarters in a Limerick City suburb.

HOLDINGS

The library houses the standard collection of educational and recreational reading material, including fiction, non-fiction, local history, and children's stock. The bulk of the local studies material is housed in the Headquarters Library, with a scattering of local history materials deposited in most of the branch libraries. Local Studies Department houses a very good collection of books, manuscripts, journals, newspapers, photographs, maps, CD-ROMs, reports, and archival resources of local interest. Collecting focuses on works that document any aspect of Limerick, works written by Limerick authors, and works published in Limerick. Priority is given to county history and antiquities, traditional areas of collecting interest. Sources of special genealogical interest include: Griffith's Valuation; Ordnance Survey Letters; Civil Survey 1654; the Bealoideas Collection for schools 1937–8; and *Baronies, Parishes and Townlands in Co. Limerick*, compiled by the Ballyhoura Architectural Survey. The collection also includes a good run of local newspapers and journals, mostly on microfilm, dating back to 1749. There are special collections on the Joyce brothers of Glenosheen, and on local scholar Mainchin Seoighe.

LOCATION

Located towards the crescent end of O'Connell Street (not the city end) on the block before the Belltable Arts Centre, same side.

## UNIVERSITY OF LIMERICK LIBRARY AND INFORMATION SERVICES

University of Limerick, Plassey
LIMERICK CITY, CO. LIMERICK
Ireland

TELEPHONE: (061) 202 166; FAX: (061) 213 090
E-mail: libinfo@ul.ie
Website: www.ul.ie/~library

HOURS

Term: M–F, 8:30am–9:00pm, Sat, 9:00am–12:45pm; Special Collections: M–F, 9:00am–5:00pm; Out of Term: M–F, 9:00am–5:00pm; Closed at 5:00pm on Fridays and on all Saturdays of Irish bank holiday weekends

ACCESS AND SERVICES

Visitors welcome, but advance notice preferred and identification required. For access to Special Collections advance notice especially appreciated. Disabled access facilities. Photocopying and microform prints available for a fee. Leaflets and booklets describing services and special collections are available.

CONTACT

Mary Dundon, Head of User Services; e-mail: mary.dundon@ul.ie
Patricia O'Donnell, Head, Information Services; e-mail: patricia.odonnell@ul.ie

DESCRIPTION

The University of Limerick is part of the National University of Ireland system, which also includes campuses in Cork, Dublin, Galway and Maynooth. The library supports the teaching and research interests of students and faculty, with special interests in the areas of engineering, science, business, computing and information sciences, education, and the humanities.

HOLDINGS

The library houses some 260,000 volumes, plus significant holdings of journals, manuscripts, maps, newspapers, pamphlets, photographs, and recordings. These represent general academic subjects, with special concentrations in engineering, business, and computing/information services. Special collections include: a regional collection; the Dunraven Estate Papers; the Glinn Estate Papers; the Eoin O'Kelly collection of early 19th-century Irish banknotes; and the Norton Collection. The last of these consists of more than 12,000 volumes mostly of an Irish interest, with a special focus on the Shannon River Valley. Highlights of the Norton Collection include: collections on Charles Stewart Parnell, Daniel O'Connell, Oliver Goldsmith, and Eamon de Valera; early Irish grammars and catechisms; 19th-century reports, commissions and inquiries; Ordnance Survey letter-books and maps; photograph albums; and travel literature.

LOCATION

The university is located two miles east of Limerick City and is easily accessible by taxi or by bus. Ample parking is available in designated areas.

# COUNTY LONDONDERRY

## IRISH ROOM

County Hall
Castlerock Road
COLERAINE, CO. LONDONDERRY, BT1 3HP
Northern Ireland

TELEPHONE: (028) 7035 1026; FAX: (028) 7035 1247
E-mail: elvacooper@hotmail.com
Website: www.neelb.org.uk

HOURS

M–F, 10:00am–12:00 noon, 1:30–4:30pm

ACCESS AND SERVICES

Visitors welcome. Special accommodations can be made for the disabled. Borrowing privileges not available. Fees for photocopying, microform prints and fax services.

CONTACT

Elva Cooper, Group Librarian, Coleraine Group; e-mail: elvacooper@hotmail.com

DESCRIPTION

The Irish Room is one of 38 libraries in the North Eastern Education and Library Board system. Its focus is local history.

HOLDINGS

The Irish Room houses a collection of more than 13,000 volumes, plus journals, maps, microforms, pamphlets and photographs focusing on the history of Coleraine and the surrounding area. The collection has remained largely static since 1973, except for donations, local newspapers and some current journal titles. Newspapers include: the *Coleraine Chronicle* (1844 to present), the *Northern Constitution* (1877–) and the *Ballymoney Free Press* (1870–). It boasts a strong collection of books illustrated by the Coleraine-born illustrator Hugh Thomson (1860–1920).

Genealogical Resources include: the printed copies of Griffith's Valuation for Ballycastle and Ballymoney Poor Law Unions, Co. Antrim 1861 and Coleraine and Magherafelt Poor Law Unions, Co. Londonderry 1859; microfilm copies of the Tithe Applotment books, Co. Londonderry 1826–38; extracts from 1831 census returns giving names of heads of households; index of 'protestant' householders in Counties Londonderry (most parishes), Antrim and Donegal (some parishes) 1740; flaxgrowers' award list 1796; Ordnance Survey memoirs and maps, 1830, 1857 for Co. Londonderry; Board of Guardians extracts for Ballymoney, Coleraine and Larne; and a special family history collection including mss and notebooks of Dr Hugh Mullin, local historian.

LOCATION

The library is housed in County Hall. Park in the Waterside Car-park, walk up past the Road Tax Office and follow the signs to the Irish Library. If disabled, please call ahead, and special arrangements for parking will be made.

## UNIVERSITY OF ULSTER LIBRARY, COLERAINE CAMPUS

Cromore Road
COLERAINE, CO. LONDONDERRY, BT52 1SA
Northern Ireland

TELEPHONE: (028) 7032 4345; FAX: (028) 7032 4928
E-mail: dj.mcclure@ulst.ac.uk
Website: www.ulst.ac.uk/library

HOURS

Term: M–F, 9:00am–10:00pm; Sat, 10:00am–5:00pm
Out of Term: M–F, 9:00am–5:00pm

ACCESS AND SERVICES

Visitors welcome but advance notice is preferred. Borrowing privileges and database searching are not usually extended to visitors. Application for access to special collections preferred. Disabled access facilities. The entire University of Ulster shares a common catalogue database. Fees apply for photocopying and microform print services, with advance notice preferred.

CONTACT

David McClure, Campus Library Manager

DESCRIPTION

The Coleraine campus is part of the four-campus University of Ulster system, which also includes Belfast, Jordanstown (in Newtownabbey), and Magee (in Derry). Coleraine maintains two libraries: the Central Buildings Library, which houses material for the sciences and arts, and the South Buildings Library, which houses material for business and management, social sciences, informatics, and health sciences.

HOLDINGS

The library houses a collection of some 280,000 bound volumes, plus significant holdings of journals (1,600 titles), manuscripts, microforms, newspapers, pamphlets, and photographs. It boasts major collections in the areas of social sciences, health sciences, business and management, informatics, arts, and education. It also houses a European Documentation Centre. Special Collections, located in the Central Buildings Library, houses a number of important research collections, including the Henry Davis gift of early printed books and fine bindings, featuring 80 incunabula (books printed before 1501); the Irish Collection, including folklorist Henry Morris' collection of Irish material, the library of Belfast poet John Hewitt, the library and archive of writer Francis Stuart, the papers of playwright George Shiels, and the Headlam-Morley Collection on the First World War. The library also contains the natural history collections of A.W. Stelfox and E.N. Carrothers.

LOCATION

The campus is located on the north coast of Northern Ireland, 34 miles east of Derry City.

## CENTRAL LIBRARY

35 Foyle Street
DERRY CITY, CO. LONDONDERRY, BT48 6AL
Northern Ireland

TELEPHONE: Tel: (028) 7127 2300; FAX: (028) 7126 1374
E-mail: centrallibrary_librarian@welbni.org; local-studies@welbni.tfnet.org
Website: www.welbni.org/libraries

HOURS

M,Th, 9:15:00am–8:00pm; Tu,W,F, 9:15am–5:30pm; Sat, 9:15am–5:00pm

ACCESS AND SERVICES

Visitors welcome, but identification required. Borrowing privileges for visitors may be restricted. Disabled access facilities. General stacks open, but stacks in Special Collections closed. Entire collection catalogued online.

CONTACT

Maura Craig, Senior Librarian in charge of Local History Collection

DESCRIPTION

Opened in 1990, this handsome facility is the main branch library for the City of Derry, located just outside the city walls. It has an important local studies department, with strong holdings of a genealogical interest. The library has an electronic link to the emigration database of the ULSTER-AMERICAN FOLK PARK, Omagh, Co. Tyrone.

HOLDINGS

The library houses more than 75,000 volumes, with access to a total stock of some 500,000 volumes in the Western Education and Library Board system. Its special collections department is one of the finest of its kind to be found in a branch library. The Irish and local studies collections include more than 15,000 volumes, 2,500 photographs, and 2,000 maps with special emphasis on the west of Co. Londonderry, including Limavady and Dungiven. Of special genealogical interest are: holdings of local newspapers on microfilm dating back to 1829; Griffith's Valuation (1860); Ordnance Survey maps for 1834, 1854, 1907 and *c.*1948 series; 1901 Census data; local history files; and an index to Hearth Money rolls for Co. Antrim 1669, Co. Londonderry 1663, and Co. Tyrone 1666.

LOCATION

On the west bank of the River Foyle, just south of the entrance to the city walls. City car-park nearby.

## CO. DERRY OR LONDONDERRY GENEALOGY CENTRE

Heritage Library
14 Bishop Street
DERRY CITY, CO. LONDONDERRY, BT48 6PW
Northern Ireland

TELEPHONE: (028) 7126 9792; FAX: (028) 7136 0921
E-mail: Not available to the public
Website: www.irishroots.net/Derry.htm

HOURS

M–F, 9:00am–5:00pm

ACCESS AND SERVICES

Visitors welcome. Derry Genealogy provides a fee-based genealogical research service for those interested in tracing their roots in Co. Londonderry or Co. Derry and in the Inishowen Peninsula, Co. Donegal. No direct access to database. Application may be made by letter, telephone, fax, e-mail or in person. The centre publishes books of genealogical and local history interest. These include: *Irish Passenger Lists, 1803–1806*; *A New Genealogical Atlas of Ireland*; and *The Making of Derry: An Economic History.*

CONTACT

Brian Mitchell, Director

DESCRIPTION

The Genealogy Centre in Derry City is the designated Irish Family History Foundation centre for Co. Derry (also known as Londonderry). These centres aim to create a comprehensive database of genealogical sources that are known to exist, including church records of all denominations, civil records, land valuations, Census records, gravestone inscriptions, and various other local sources. The Derry Centre offers a genealogical research centre for Co. Londonderry and the Inishowen Peninsula, Co. Donegal.

HOLDINGS

The centre collects copies of birth, marriage, and death certificates, church registers, gravestone inscriptions, Griffith's Valuation, Tithe Applotment Books, and the 1901 Census for Co. Londonderry to input them on the database. The reference collection also includes emigration books and some passenger lists.

LOCATION

City centre, within the walls, one block off the Diamond.

## DERRY CITY COUNCIL ARCHIVES

*See* HERITAGE & MUSEUM SERVICE, Derry

## HARBOUR MUSEUM

*See* HERITAGE & MUSEUM SERVICE, Derry

## HERITAGE & MUSEUM SERVICE

Harbour Square
DERRY CITY, CO. LONDONDERRY, BT48 6AF
Northern Ireland

TELEPHONE: (028) 7137 7331; FAX: (028) 7137 7633
E-mail: museums@derrycity.gov.uk
Website: www.derrycity.gov.uk/visitor_folder/visitor_index.htm (a dedicated website is in development)

HOURS

M–F, 10:00am–1:00pm, 2:00–4:30pm

ACCESS AND SERVICES:

Visitors welcome. No admission charge. This museum is sponsored by Derry City Council and is housed in the former Londonderry Port & Harbour Commissioner's Office in the city centre. Displays feature shipbuilding, emigration, and the wartime naval port. A permanent exhibition of historic artwork is on display. The museum also serves as the research centre for the Civic Archives, and material from the archives is regularly exhibited. First floor has no disabled access facilities. Informal application procedures for access to archives, but appointment required. Consult with Programme Organizer. Photocopying services available for a modest fee.

CONTACT

Bernadette Walsh, City Archivist

DESCRIPTION

Museum is located in an 1880 building converted for museum/archive use in 1993. The Civic Archives collects materials documenting the local history of Derry City and surrounding region.

HOLDINGS

Of special interest is the Derry City Council Archive detailing the growth and development of the city from the late 17th century onwards. Private collections include the archives of various local businesses, including transportation companies; community organizations, such as the Northern Ireland Civil Rights Association (NICRA), 1969–75; and the papers of prominent Derry citizens.

LOCATION

City centre, on the Waterside, close to the city walls.

## UNIVERSITY OF ULSTER LIBRARY, MAGEE CAMPUS

Northland Road
DERRY CITY, CO. LONDONDERRY, BT48 7JL
Northern Ireland

TELEPHONE: (028) 7137 5264; FAX: (028) 7137 5626
E-mail: sa.mcmullan@ulst.ac.uk
Website: www.ulst.ac.uk/library

HOURS

Term: M–F, 9:00am–9:00pm; Sat, 10:00am–5:00pm
Vacation: M–F, 9:00am–5:00pm

ACCESS AND SERVICES

Visitors welcome but advance notice is preferred. Borrowing privileges and database searching are not usually extended to visitors. Application for access to special collections preferred. Disabled access facilities. The entire University of Ulster shares a common catalogue database. About 90% of the Magee Campus collection is catalogued online. Fees apply for photocopying and microform print services, with advance notice preferred.

CONTACT

Stephanie McMullan, Campus Library Manager

## DESCRIPTION

The Magee campus is part of the four-campus University of Ulster system, which also includes Belfast, Coleraine, and Jordanstown (in Newtownabbey). Magee was founded in 1865 to prepare entrants for the Presbyterian Ministry, and in 1984 Magee University College became part of the University of Ulster. The existing library was opened in 1990. A new learning resources centre is due to open in September 2002.

## HOLDINGS

The library houses a collection of some 63,000 bound volumes, plus significant holdings of journals (600 titles), microforms, newspapers, pamphlets, and photographs. It specializes in the areas of informatics, art and design, business and management, social sciences, life sciences, and engineering. It has an important Irish Collection, consisting of some 6,000 volumes and 900 pamphlets, including a rare collection on the Siege of Derry in 1689. There is a rare book collection, with a particular strength in 18th-century Irish printing. Other collections of interest include the Spalding Collection on Eastern Civilizations, a small collection of manuscripts on Irish Presbyterianism, and a collection of some 3,000 photographic negatives of local interest. Journals in the collection include the *Derry Almanac*, the *Journal of the Royal Society of the Antiquaries of Ireland* (1890–1992), and the *Ulster Journal of Archaeology* dating back to 1853.

## LOCATION

From south of the city approach by the Foyle Bridge and follow directions to the Magee Campus.

# COUNTY LONGFORD

## LONGFORD BRANCH LIBRARY – LOCAL STUDIES

Business Centre
LONGFORD, CO. LONGFORD
Ireland

TELEPHONE: (043) 41124/41125; FAX: (043) 41124/41125
E-mail: longlib@iol.ie
Website: www.iol.ie/~libcounc/longford.htm

HOURS

M,W, 10:00am–1:00pm, 2:00–8:30pm; Tu,Th, 10:00am–1:00pm, 2:00–5:30pm; F, 10:00am–1:00pm, 2:00–5:00pm

ACCESS AND SERVICES

Visitors welcome. Free Internet access available. Modest fees for photocopying and microfilm print services. Membership required for borrowing privileges. Disabled access facilities.

CONTACT

Mary Reynolds, County Librarian

DESCRIPTION

Local Studies is based in the Longford Branch Library, which is one of six libraries operated by Longford County Library Headquarters. The others are: Ballymahon, Edgeworthstown, Granard, Drumlish, and Lanesboro. The library system is funded by the County Council. The Longford Branch Library also offers a business information service.

HOLDINGS

Local Studies houses several special collections of note, including collections on local writers Oliver Goldsmith, Padraic Colum, and Maria Edgeworth. It also holds strong collections of estate maps of Co. Longford, Tithe Applotment Books, and local newspapers (microfilm and hard-bound). It houses a substantial collection of archival and manuscript material of historical and genealogical interest. These include Poor Law Union Archives; Returns of Boards of Guardians, Officers etc., Ballymahon, Drumlish, Granard, and Longford; Rural District Council Archives; Longford County Council Archives; Urban District Council Archives; Petty Sessions material; and Grand Jury Presentments for Co. Longford (1817–95). Private material includes: Regulation & Record Book of the Longford Militia (1793–1855); Maria Edgeworth Collection of letters (1815–94); and the Honorable L.H. King Harman Collection of estate records, account books and scrapbooks. For a detailed listing of the contents of each of these collections, see library's website.

LOCATION

Town centre

## LONGFORD RESEARCH CENTRE

Longford Roots
1 Church Street
LONGFORD, CO. LONGFORD
Ireland

TELEPHONE: (043) 41235; FAX: (043) 41279
E-mail: longroot@iol.ie
Website: www.longford.com2.info

HOURS

M–Th, 9:00am–4:30pm; F, 9:00am–1:00pm

ACCESS AND SERVICES

Longford Research Centre offers a fee-based genealogical research service for persons interested in tracing their roots in Co. Longford. An application form can be obtained from the centre's website, by e-mail or by contacting the centre directly. An initial search fee of 65 euro (or equivalent) is required. The centre tries to keep its fees to a minimum, and the initial search fee charge is also the maximum amount charged. Success cannot be guaranteed in any search, however, and an unsuccessful search is usually more time-consuming than a successful one. Please allow six to eight weeks for our reply.

CONTACT

Mary Boland

DESCRIPTION

Longford Research Centre is the Irish Family History Foundation's designated research centre for the County of Longford. The IFHF is the coordinating body for a network of government-approved genealogical research centres in the Republic of Ireland and in Northern Ireland that have computerized tens of millions of Irish ancestral records of different types. Common Co. Longford surnames include: O'Farrell or Farrell, Quinn, Kenny, Kiernan, Mulvey, Smith, Leavy, Kelly, Glennon, Keenan, Casey and Murphy.

HOLDINGS

The centre has computerized church records of baptisms, marriages and burials for the majority of Catholic parishes as early as 1779 and some Church of Ireland, Methodist and Presbyterian parishes. Also available to the centre are: Griffith's Valuation; Tithe Applotment Books; the 1901 Census; and civil records.

LOCATION

Town centre. Longford Town, with a population of 6,500, is the administrative headquarters for Co. Longford.

# COUNTY LOUTH

## LOUTH COUNTY LIBRARY

Roden Place
DUNDALK, CO. LOUTH
Ireland

TELEPHONE: (042) 935 3190; FAX: (042) 933 7635
E-mail: library@louthcoco.ie
Website: www.louthcoco.ie/louth/html/library.htm

HOURS

Tu–Sat, 10:00am–1:00pm, 2:00–5:00pm; closed Saturdays of bank holiday weekends

ACCESS AND SERVICES

Visitors welcome, but borrowing privileges restricted. Disabled access facilities. Fees for photocopying and microfilm copy services. Approximately 85% of the collection is catalogued online, including the holdings of the branch libraries. The library offers a free Internet service to members, but visitors are also welcome to use this service within reason. The library also offers a basic genealogical research service. The wait is approximately 2–3 weeks, depending on volume of requests. There is no index to newspaper archives. The county has a separate archives service – LOUTH LOCAL AUTHORITIES ARCHIVES SERVICE, Dundalk. The library also provides a basic genealogical service for a fee.

CONTACT

Isabell Murphy; e-mail: Isabell.Murphy@louthcoco.ie

DESCRIPTION

The library is the flagship library in a five-library county system.

HOLDINGS

The holdings reflect the general educational and recreational reading interests of a public library, but there are several special collections of interest to visitors, especially genealogists, including the Lawrence Collection of photographs of Co. Louth; the *Louth Archaeological and Historical Journal* (1904–99); *Tempest Annual* (1863–1976), the local directory of Dundalk; local newspapers, including the *Dundalk Democrat* (1849–1996) and the *Argus* (1973 to present); and an extensive collection of local history books and books on Irish history. Holdings of special genealogical interest include: a database for Roman Catholic Church Records for Co. Louth that is not accessible to the public; a printed copy of Griffith's Valuation; 1835 Ordnance Survey maps for Louth, plus Taylor and Skinner maps (1777) and various other early maps of Louth and Dundalk; and a microfilm copy of the 1901 Census for Co. Louth.

LOCATION

Town centre, next door to St Patrick's Cathedral. Car parking facilities (fees apply) available at the rear of the building. Entrance to the car-park is from the Ramparts Road.

## LOUTH LOCAL AUTHORITIES ARCHIVES SERVICE

Old Gaol, Ardee Road
DUNDALK, CO. LOUTH
Ireland

TELEPHONE: (042) 933 9387; FAX: (042) 932 0427
E-mail: archive@louthcoco.ie
Website: www.louthcoco.ie/louth/html/archive.htm

HOURS

M, 2:00–5:00pm; Th, 9:30am–1:00pm

ACCESS AND SERVICES

An appointment should be made beforehand, preferably one week in advance. Readers are required to complete an application form on their first visit and pay a yearly subscription fee (concessions for students, unemployed, and under-16s). Only listed collections are available. Not all collections are listed due to service still in process of being established. Material cannot be borrowed. Reproduction fees apply. A research service is available for long-distance researchers – queries are catered for. Free Internet use for subscribers. Partial wheelchair accessibility.

CONTACT

Lorraine Buchanan, County Archivist; e-mail: Lorraine.Buchanan@louthcoco.ie

DESCRIPTION

Louth Local Authorities Archives Service was founded only recently (in 2000), as a result of the passing of the Local Government Act 1994, and is still in the process of being established. It is a repository for the public archives of Co. Louth. This means that it currently holds or seeks the acquisition of archives of Louth local authorities and their predecessor bodies. The mission statement of the Archives Service is: 'The identification, preservation and availability of the valuable public and private archives of Co. Louth.'

HOLDINGS

Holdings include complete series of minute books for the Boards of Guardians of the Poor Law Unions of Ardee and Dundalk *c.*1841–1924 and also Drogheda (with gaps). There are a few admission registers for Ardee workhouse *c.*1880–*c.*1910.

Rate books survive for the Dundalk area *c.*1840–*c.*1940 with a complementary set of manuscript 'valuation records' *c.*1855–*c.*1940 (these may be Grand Jury county cess records up to 1899). There is some coverage for all of Co. Louth in these series.

Fortunately for Louth, a county in the Pale region, exceptionally early records of Corporations survive including Drogheda 1503–1970, Dunleer 1683–1773, Carlingford 1694–1835, Dundalk 1831–41, followed by Dundalk Town Commissioners 1840–99 and Dundalk Urban District Council 1899–1971. There are records *c.*1650–*c.*1850 for Ardee Town Commissioners and Louth County Council and Rural District Council Records from 1899.

Grand Jury presentments are available for the years *c.*1780–*c.*1820.

LOCATION

Entrance is on the Ardee Road, behind the Garda Station. Car-parking facilities available adjacent to the building. Entrance to the car-park is from St Malachy's Villas. Five minutes' walk from Dundalk train station.

# COUNTY MAYO

## MAYO NORTH FAMILY HERITAGE CENTRE

Enniscoe, Castlehill
BALLINA, CO. MAYO
Ireland

TELEPHONE: (096) 31809; FAX: (096) 31885
E-mail: normayo@iol.ie
Website: www.mayo.irish-roots.net

HOURS

Genealogy: M–F, 9:00am–4:00pm

ACCESS AND SERVICES

Mayo North Family Heritage Centre offers a fee-based genealogical research service for persons interested in tracing their roots in North Mayo. An application form is available on the centre's website, and an initial search fee of 75 euro (or equivalent) is required. See website for sample report and explanation of terms and sources used in the reports. General enquiries answered immediately; otherwise response depends on type of research commissioned. Average cost of full report is 300 euro. This centre and SOUTH MAYO FAMILY RESEARCH CENTRE (Ballinrobe) have worked closely together for ten years and share resources, including a common website. The two centres have also worked together to develop a range of genealogical products to suit those interested in learning about their Mayo ancestry, and they have embarked on an international marketing campaign to this end. There is a museum, gardens and shop at the centre. Seasonal operating hours: telephone for details. Disabled access facilities.

CONTACT

Bridie Greavy, Supervisor

DESCRIPTION

Mayo North Family Heritage Centre is one of the Irish Family History Foundation's two designated research centres for Co. Mayo. The IFHF is the coordinating body for a network of government-approved genealogical research centres in the Republic of Ireland and in Northern Ireland that have computerized tens of millions of Irish ancestral records of different types. Common North Mayo surnames include: Gallagher, Durkan, McHale, Barrett, Kelly, Loftus, Gaughan, and Lavelle.

HOLDINGS

The two Mayo centres have jointly compiled and input almost 2,000,000 genealogical records onto a computer database, relying chiefly on church and civil records. These sources include: Griffith's Valuation (1856); the parochial registers of baptism and marriage for the Roman Catholic parishes; parochial registers of baptism and marriage for the Roman Catholic Catholic parishes including Kilconduff from 1808 and Church of Ireland parishes including Killala with registers from 1704. For Methodist churches in the Castlebar circuit there are registers from 1829 and for the Presbyterian church at Turlough the registers date from 1819. The earliest burial register is for Kilfian parish (probably Church of Ireland) from 1826. Other sources indexed include the civil registers of births, marriages and deaths beginning in 1864; the 1901 and 1911 Censuses of population; all pre-1950 gravestone inscriptions; and Tithe Applotment Books (1825–42).

LOCATION

On the grounds of the Enniscoe Estate, 3.5 miles south of Crossmolina on the R315 route to Castlebar.

## SOUTH MAYO FAMILY RESEARCH CENTRE

Main Street
BALLINROBE, CO. MAYO
Ireland

TELEPHONE: (092) 41214; FAX: (092) 41214
E-mail: soumayo@iol.ie
Website: mayo.irishroots.net/Mayo.htm

HOURS

M–F, 9:30am–12:00 noon, 1:30–4:00pm

ACCESS AND SERVICES

South Mayo Family Research Centre offers a fee-based, genealogical research service for persons interested in tracing their roots in South Mayo. An application form is available on the centre's website, and an initial search fee of 75 euro (or equivalent) is required, but is discountable from the cost of a comprehensive family history report. See website for sample report and explanation of terms and sources used in the reports. General enquiries answered immediately; otherwise response depends on type of research commissioned. Average cost of full report is 300 euro. Several other searches, e.g. gravestone search, birth search, marriage search, location search, are available for 15 euro–40 euro per search. These results are usually provided to visitors to the centre within two hours. This centre and MAYO NORTH FAMILY HERITAGE CENTRE (Ballina) have worked closely together for ten years and share resources, including a common website. The two centres have also worked together to develop a range of genealogical products to suit those interested in learning about their Mayo ancestry, and have embarked on an international marketing campaign to this end.

CONTACT

Gerard M. Delaney, Manager

DESCRIPTION

South Mayo Family Research Centre is one of the Irish Family History Foundation's two designated research centres for Co. Mayo. The IFHF is the coordinating body for a network of government-approved genealogical research centres in the Republic of Ireland and in Northern Ireland that have computerized tens of millions of Irish ancestral records of different types. Common South Mayo surnames include: Walsh, Burke, Gibbons, Prendergast, Joyce, Murray, Gallagher, Lydon, Heneghan, Murphy, O'Malley, Kelly, Moran, Duffy, O'Connor, Waldron, Farragher.

HOLDINGS

The two Mayo centres have jointly compiled and input almost 2,000,000 genealogical records onto an electronic database, relying chiefly on church and civil records. These sources include: Griffith's Valuation (1855–7); the parochial registers of baptism and marriage for Roman Catholic parishes including Crossboyne and Tagheen with registers from 1794. For Church of Ireland parishes the earliest registers are for Kilmaine and date from 1744. The earliest Presbyterian registers surviving are for Aughavale church dating from 1853.

Other sources indexed include the civil registers of births, marriages and deaths beginning in 1864; the 1901 and 1911 Censuses of population; all pre-1950 gravestone inscriptions; and Tithe Applotment Books (1825–42).

LOCATION

Town centre, in a refurbished schoolhouse on Main Street.

## CASTLEBAR CENTRAL LIBRARY – LOCAL STUDIES DEPARTMENT

Pavilion Road
CASTLEBAR, CO. MAYO
Ireland

TELEPHONE: (094) 20234; FAX: Not available to public
E-mail: ihamrock@mayococo.ie
Website: www.mayolibrary.ie/localstudies.html

HOURS

Tu,W, 10:00am–8:00pm; Th,F, 10:00am–1:00pm, 2:00–5:00pm; Sat, 10:00am–4:00pm

ACCESS AND SERVICES

Visitors welcome. Free Internet access available. Photocopying and microfilm copies available for a modest fee. Membership required for borrowing privileges. Disabled access facilities.

CONTACT

Ivor Hamrock, Librarian, Castlebar Library; e-mail: ihamrock@mayococo.ie
Austin Vaughan, County Librarian; e-mail: avaughan@mayococo.ie

DESCRIPTION

The Local Studies Department is located in Castlebar Central Library and is the central repository for a wealth of material on the history and heritage of Co. Mayo from earliest times to the present. Mayo County Library collects comprehensively material of local interest, including books, manuscripts, journals, newspapers, photographs, maps, CD-ROMs, microfilm, and ephemera. It is part of the County Library system, headquartered at Mountain View, Castlebar, Co. Mayo, tel. (094) 20253. Mayo County Library Service operates 12 branch libraries. The Castlebar Central Library also offers a Business Information Centre.

HOLDINGS

All the Co. Mayo branch libraries hold collections relating to the local history of their surrounding area. The Local Studies Department offers one of the strongest collections of its kind in all of Ireland. Special collections include: Michael Davitt (1846–1906) – complete works and related biographical and historical material; George Moore (1852–1933) – literary works, related biographical and critical material; George A. Birmingham (1865–1950) – collected literary works; and the 1798 Rebellion – events in Mayo. The department also maintains a collection of books, articles, maps, and illustrations on Co. Mayo. Archival materials include: Ballinrobe Poor Law Union Records (1844–1926), including Minute Books, financial records, outdoor relief records, and outgoing letter books. These records have been digitized and are now available in CD-ROM format at the Ballinrobe and Castlebar Libraries. The department also maintains a collection of all journals published locally, including: *Cathair na Mart*; *Journal of the Westport Historical Society* (annually, from 1982); *North Mayo Historical and Archaeological Society Journal* (annually, 1982–95); *Mayo Association Yearbook* (annually, from 1984); *Castlebar Parish Magazine* (annually, from 1971); *Journal of the South Mayo Family Research Centre* (annually, from 1989); and *Muintir Acla: Achill Island Journal* (quarterly, from 1995). Official publications of special local interest include: *Report of Her Majesty's Commissioners of Inquiry into the working of the Landlord and Tenant (Ireland) Act*, 1870 (Bessborough Commission); *British Parliamentary Papers, Famine Series*, Vols 1–8, Irish University Press 1968–70; *Digest of Evidence Taken before Her Majesty's Commissioners of Inquiry into the State of the Law and Practice in Respect to the Occupation of Land in Ireland*; HMSO 1847 (Devon Commission); *Congested Districts Board for Ireland*; and *Socio-economic Reports on 21 Districts in Co. Mayo 1892/9*. The Photographic Archive includes: the Wynne Collection, containing approximately 2,000 photographs taken by Thomas Wynne, Castlebar and his descendants dating from 1870, that cover the west of Ireland, landscapes, architecture, streetscapes, studio portraits, historical events, etc.; selected views of Mayo subjects from the Lawrence Collection of the National Library; a collection of 28 glass photographic plates showing views of Co. Mayo *c.*1920s; postcards of Co. Mayo scenes *c.*1900; and a collection of postcards from the 19th century. The Newspaper Collection includes extensive holdings of local and national papers dating from pre-Famine times to the present. See website for listing. The Map Collection is also noteworthy, and includes: a map of the Maritime County of Mayo in 25 sheets that began in 1809 and ended 1817, by William Bald FRSE, printed in 1830 (scale two inches); Ordnance Survey six-inch maps of Co. Mayo 1839 and 1900 edns; Recorded Monuments protected under Section 12 of the National Monuments (amendment) Act 1994; and the Co. Mayo Archaeological Constraint Maps, Office of Public Works, 1999. Of special genealogical interest are the department's holdings of: Tithe Applotment Books (*c.*1830) on microfilm; Griffith's Valuation (1855–7); Census of Ireland 1901 and 1911, Co. Mayo on microfilm; Parish Records for Oughaval, Burrishoole, Achill, and Ballycroy; and gravestone inscriptions for Castlebar Old Cemetery, Meelick Old and Meelick New Cemeteries and Bushfield; and a manuscript of Galway and Mayo Families by Father Munnelly. The department also boasts a strong collection of Land Surveys, drawn mostly from Ordnance Survey and Irish Manuscript Commission publications. Finally, the Department houses an impressive Folklore Collection, including microfilm copies of most of the material collected by schools in Co. Mayo for the 'The Schools' Scheme of 1937–1938' project, an 18-month effort by schoolchildren to document a wide range of Irish folk tradition, including folk tales and folk legends, riddles and proverbs, songs, customs and beliefs, games and pastimes, and traditional work practices and crafts.

LOCATION

Town centre.

## NATIONAL MUSEUM OF COUNTRY LIFE, Castlebar, Co. Mayo

*See* **NATIONAL MUSEUM OF IRELAND**, Dublin

## MICHAEL DAVITT MUSEUM

Straide
FOXFORD, CO. MAYO
Ireland

TELEPHONE: (094) 31942/31022; FAX: None
E-mail: davittmuseum@eircom.net
Website: museumsofmayo.com/davitt

HOURS

Sun–Sat, 10:00am–6:00pm; closed Christmas, St Stephen's Day, New Year's Day and Good Friday

ACCESS AND SERVICES

Visitors welcome. Disabled access facilities. Admission fees apply. Pencils only in archives. Internet access. Photocopying services for a modest fee. The museum also offers guided tours, a permanent exhibit, and an audiovisual presentation.

CONTACT

Curator

DESCRIPTION

The museum celebrates the life and work of the 19th-century Irish nationalist and radical land reformer Michael Davitt (1846–1906). It is housed in the restored pre-penal church in the village of Straide, Co. Mayo, where Michael Davitt was baptized in 1846. Davitt is buried nearby in the grounds of the 13th-century Straide Abbey.

HOLDINGS

The museum contains an extensive collection of documents, photographs, Land Acts, correspondence, postcards, and other material connected with the life of Davitt.

LOCATION

On the N58, between the towns of Castlebar and Ballina, north-west of Knock.

# COUNTY MEATH

## MEATH COUNTY LIBRARY

Meath County Library Headquarters
Railway Street
NAVAN, CO. MEATH
Ireland

TELEPHONE: (046) 21451/21134; FAX: (046) 21463
E-mail: colibrary@meathcoco.ie
Website: www.meath.ie/library.htm

### HOURS

M, 1:30–5:00pm; Tu,Th, 1:30–5pm, 7:00–8:30pm; W, 10:30am–6:30pm; F 10:30–4:00pm; Sat, 10:00am–12:30pm

### ACCESS AND SERVICES

Visitors welcome. Wheelchair-accessible. Photocopying at 10c per sheet and microfilm at 25c per print. Free membership and free Internet access.

### CONTACT

Ciaran Mangan, County Librarian; e-mail: cmangan@meathcoco.ie
Andy Bennett, Local Studies Librarian; tel. (046) 21134

### DESCRIPTION

The library is the headquarters library for the county system, which includes 11 branch libraries.

### HOLDINGS

In addition to the normal educational and recreational materials found in a county library, Meath maintains a special collection on local history and genealogy.

Of special interest to family history researchers are Dr Beryl Moore's recordings of gravestone inscriptions. Dr Moore was an indefatigable worker and she recorded all the inscriptions in more than 100 graveyards in Co. Meath. She ranged all over the county, except perhaps in the north-east part near the border with Co. Monaghan. Her recordings are available in typescript. Some examples of her work have been published in the journal of the Meath Archaeological and Historical Society.

Meath is exceptionally fortunate to have available some 50 volumes of records of the Meath County Infirmary including a register of patients *c.*1780–*c.*1800 (damaged) and also diet books listing the names of patients.

With regard to the large landed estates in the county there are rentals of the Bligh estate at Nobber *c.*1850 and rent books and letter books for the Mountainstown estate near Navan *c.*1850.

Minute books for the Boards of Guardians of the Poor Law Unions of Dunshaughlin, Kells, Navan and Trim survive for the period *c.*1840–*c.*1920 and there is also an incomplete series for Oldcastle. The Poor Law archive includes some rate books *c.*1925–*c.*1940.

For the towns of Kells and Navan there are records of Town Commissioners from *c.*1830 and Urban District Council records from 1899.

Other items of interest include newspapers, including the *Meath Herald*, 1845–96; *Meath Chronicle*, 1904– (microfilm and hard copy), the *Irish Peasant*, Feb. 1904 (one issue), 1903–6 (on microfilm); and the *Drogheda Independent* (1924–48 on microfilm).

The 1901 Census for Co. Meath is available on microfilm; also the surviving fragments of the 1821 census for 19 parishes in the baronies of Upper and Lower Navan and a register of persons planting trees in the county 1814.

LOCATION

Town centre, across from the bus stop. Public car-park on Circular Road.

## MEATH HERITAGE AND GENEALOGY CENTRE

Town Hall
Castle Street
TRIM, CO. MEATH
Ireland

TELEPHONE: (046) 36633; FAX: (046) 37502
E-mail: meathhc@iol.ie
Website: www.iol/~meathhc

HOURS

M–Th, 9:00am–5:00pm; F, 9:00am–2:00pm

ACCESS AND SERVICES

The Meath Heritage and Genealogy Centre offers a fee-based record search service for those interested in tracing their family roots in Co. Meath. Enquirers to this centre can expect a reply within about two weeks. A copy of the centre's application form can be found on its website. A 30 euro (or equivalent) fee is required for the initial search. Common surnames in Meath include: Reilly, Smith, Lynch, Brady, Farrell, Farrelly, Kelly, O'Brien, Daly and Maguire. Chief towns include: Navan, Trim, Kells, Slane, and Dunshaughlin. The centre offers a range of publications, including: *Trace your Meath Ancestors*; *The Boyne*; *The Battle of the Boyne*; *Trim*; and *Wellington*.

CONTACT

Noel E. French

DESCRIPTION

Meath Heritage and Genealogy Centre is the IFHF's designated research centre for the County of Meath. The IFHF is the coordinating body for a network of government-approved genealogical research centres in the Republic of Ireland and in Northern Ireland that have computerized tens of millions of Irish ancestral records of different types.

HOLDINGS

The centre has computerized over 400,000 records to date. Church records computerized include: Roman Catholic from 1742; Church of Ireland from 1698; and Presbyterian for Kells from 1873. Census returns also computerized.

LOCATION

Town centre, across from Trim Castle.

# COUNTY MONAGHAN

## MONAGHAN COUNTY LIBRARY

The Diamond
CLONES, CO. MONAGHAN
Ireland

TELEPHONE: (047) 51143; FAX: (047) 51863
E-mail: moncolib@eircom.net
Website: homepage.eircom.net/~monaghan/libbra.htm

HOURS

M, 2:00pm–5:00pm; 6:00–8:00pm; W–F, 2:00–5:00pm

ACCESS AND SERVICES

Visitors welcome, but identification required. Borrowing privileges for visitors available but limited. Consult with Librarian. The library provides a genealogical reference service.

CONTACT

Joe McElvaney, County Librarian; e-mail: jmcelvaney@monaghancoco.ie

DESCRIPTION

Headquarters library for Co. Monaghan, with branch libraries in Ballybay, Carrickmacross, Castleblayney, and Monaghan Town.

HOLDINGS

Good local history collection, supported by a general collection of Irish interest.

LOCATION

Town centre. Clones is the most ancient of the towns in Co. Monaghan, built around the site of a 6th-century monastery founded by St Tiarnach.

## THE HERITAGE CENTRE

St Louis Convent
MONAGHAN TOWN, CO. MONAGHAN
Ireland

TELEPHONE: (047) 83529; FAX: (047) 84907
E-mail: None available to the public
Website: No official site. *See*
homepage.eircom.net/~monaghan/museum.htm#heritage

HOURS

M,Tu,Th,F, 10:00am–12:00 noon, 2:00–4:00pm; Sat, Sun, 2:00–4:00pm

ACCESS AND SERVICES

Privately funded heritage centre open to the public for a modest admission fee. Disabled access facilities. The centre offers a permanent exhibition, which features documents, books, artefacts, crafts, newspapers, paintings, tapestries, and photographs tracing the history of the St Louis women and their work. The Sisters have been an integral part of Co. Monaghan and surrounding areas for almost 150 years, and this exhibit documents not only their lives but also the life of this broader community, especially its social, educational and religious heritage. The exhibit also features documents and photographs of its overseas missions, including its schools in California, Brazil, Ghana, and Nigeria.

CONTACT

Sister Mona Lally, Director

DESCRIPTION

The Heritage Centre is dedicated to the conservation and preservation of the historical, artistic and cultural heritage of the St Louis Sisters, a Catholic religious order of women founded in France in 1842. The origins of the community date back to the end of the French Revolution. The Sisters formerly operated an industrial school and a boarding school for girls, and continue to operate a junior school and a large secondary day-school.

HOLDINGS

The centre maintains a special collection that includes documents; liturgical and devotional items; crafts, including 19th-century Belleek china and some magnificent Carrickmacross lace; antiques; and archival material, including records of members of the religious community, students and industrial-school children. Records may be restricted. Consult with Director.

LOCATION

The centre is located on the grounds of the Monaghan convent, founded in 1859 by Mother Genevieve Beale (1820–78), near the town centre.

## MONAGHAN ANCESTRY

Clogher Historical Society
6 Tully Street
MONAGHAN TOWN, CO. MONAGHAN
Ireland

TELEPHONE: Mobile: (087) 631 0360 (for appointment only)
E-mail: Not available to public
Website: www.irishroots.net/Monaghan.htm

HOURS

By appointment only

ACCESS AND SERVICES

Visitors welcome by appointment, but postal enquiries are preferred. Monaghan Ancestry offers a fee-based genealogical research service for those interested in tracing their Monaghan roots. Estimates of costs are made based on availability of records, the estimated time involved in preparing a report, and the format in which the information is required. Monaghan Ancestry publishes the annual *Clogher Record*, the journal of the Clogher Historical Society. The Diocese of Clogher covers Counties Monaghan, Fermanagh, South Tyrone, and a small portion of Co. Donegal around Bundoran and Ballyshannon. The journal, issued worldwide, is devoted to the religious, social, economic, genealogical, archaeological, and political history of the diocese. Other publications include: *Old Monaghan 1785–1995*; Denis Carolan Rushe, *History of Monaghan for Two Hundred Years, 1660–1860* (reissue); and James Murnane and Peadar Murnane, *History of Ballybay*. Works currently in progress include a new book on Clones parish and a book on the civil parishes of Co. Monaghan.

CONTACT

Theo McMahon

DESCRIPTION

Monaghan Ancestry is the designated Irish Family History Foundation research centre for Co. Monaghan. The IFHF is the coordinating body for a network of government-approved genealogical research centres in the Republic of Ireland and in Northern Ireland that have computerized tens of millions of Irish ancestral records of different types.

HOLDINGS

Monaghan Ancestry has computerized all Roman Catholic baptismal and marriage records, from their commencement up to and including 1880. Other sources include Tithe Applotment Books for 22 of the 23 civil parishes. Only one parish, Tydavnet, does not have a detailed return in this series. Other records include: Griffith's Valuations of the 1858–61 period; the 1901 Census for Counties Monaghan, Fermanagh and Tyrone; gravestone inscriptions; International Genealogical Index, 1988 and 1992; Royal Irish Constabulary records, 1816–1921; civil records (non-Roman Catholic) of marriages from 1845 to 1900 for most parishes; Old Age Pension claims, some with abstracts from the 1841 and 1851 Censuses; rentals of the Rose Estate, Tydavnet, 1839–47 (these compensate to some extent for the loss of the Tithe Applotment Book for certain townlands in this parish); the Templeton Estate (mostly in Muckno parish) for 1805; the Forster Estate Rentals for certain townlands, 1802–8; the Murray Ker Estate (Kileevan/Newbliss), 1881–1911 and 1937; Rentals of the Kane Estate, 1764; the Famine Relief Books for Donagh and Errigal Truagh parishes by townland, Jan.–May 1847; Dunaghmoyne Vaccination Register, 1869–84; Index to Clogher Wills, 1659–1857; Lennard Barrett Estate Records and Rentals for Clones, 1682–1845; etc. In addition, the Centre maintains a reference library, which includes all publications of the Clogher Historical Society, 1953, to the present.

LOCATION

Near town centre, in private home.

## MONAGHAN BRANCH LIBRARY

North Road
MONAGHAN TOWN, CO. MONAGHAN
Ireland

TELEPHONE: (047) 81830; FAX: None
E-mail: None
Website: homepage.eircom.net/~monaghan/libbra.htm

HOURS

M,W,F, 11:00am–1:00pm, 2:00–5:00pm, 6:00–8:00pm; Tu,Th, 11:00am–1:00pm, 2:00–5:00pm

ACCESS AND SERVICES

Visitors welcome. Borrowing privileges are available to visitors for a modest annual fee. Limited disabled access facilities. Internet access available.

CONTACT

Mary McKenna, Senior Library Assistant

DESCRIPTION

Community-based library, part of the county system headquartered in Clones.

HOLDINGS

Contains a good if modest local and Irish history collection, with many of the standard genealogical reference sources available.

LOCATION

Town centre.

## MONAGHAN COUNTY MUSEUM

1–2 Hill Street
MONAGHAN TOWN, CO. MONAGHAN
Ireland

TELEPHONE: (047) 82928; FAX: (047) 71189
E-mail: comuseum@monaghancoco.ie
Website: www.monaghan.ie/html2/musuem.htm

HOURS

Tu–F, 10:00am–1:00pm, 2:00–5:00pm; Sat, 11:00am–1:00pm, 2:00–5:00pm

ACCESS AND SERVICES

Visitors welcome. Free admission. Limited disabled access facilities. Access to archives by appointment only. Photocopying services available for a modest fee. The museum offers an award-winning exhibits programme, featuring material dating from *c*.5000BC to the present. Of special interest is the Cross of Clogher, a 14th-century oak cross decorated with bronze and semi-precious metals. The museum also houses a fine collection of early medieval crannog (lake dwelling) artefacts.

CONTACT

Roisin Doherty, Curator

DESCRIPTION

Monaghan County Museum was established in 1974 by Monaghan County Council. It moved into its present quarters in 1986. It was the first local authority county museum in the Irish Republic and gained distinction in 1980 and 1993 by winning two European and Irish museum awards. The museum collects the material heritage of Co. Monaghan, has a mainly Irish art collection and keeps some limited archive material that may be consulted by prior appointment.

HOLDINGS

In addition to artefacts and paintings, the museum has a small archive focusing on Co. Monaghan records. These include estate papers, some of which extend beyond the boundaries of Monaghan; Monaghan County Council minutes, rate books, and ledgers from 1899 to 1959; Monaghan Urban District Council records; and personal papers, including those of Charles Gavan Duffy (1816–1903). *See also* FRANCISCAN LIBRARY, Killiney, Co. Dublin, for more information about Duffy records (specifically those of George Gavan Duffy, son of Charles), in the care of UNIVERSITY COLLEGE DUBLIN – ARCHIVES DEPARTMENT.

LOCATION

Town centre. Located on a hillside, across from Market House. Public car-parks nearby.

# COUNTY OFFALY

## IRISH MIDLANDS ANCESTRY (LAOIS AND OFFALY FAMILY HISTORY RESEARCH CENTRE)

Bury Quay
TULLAMORE, CO. OFFALY
Ireland

TELEPHONE: (0506) 21421; FAX: (0506) 21421
E-mail: ohas@iol.ie
Website: www.irishmidlandsancestry.com; www.irishroots.net/LaoisOff.htm; Offaly Historical & Archaeological Society: www.offalyhistory.com

HOURS

M–F, 9:00am–4:00pm

ACCESS AND SERVICES

The centre offers a fee-based, full-range genealogical research service. Appointments preferred for consultations at 25 euro per hour (deductible from further fees). Reports range from 149 euro to 300 euro plus postage. Initial enquiries are answered promptly; research usually takes from four to six weeks. The centre has indexed some 750,000 records in its database. An application form is available on the centre's website. Main surnames associated with Counties Laois and Offaly include: Kelly, Dunne, Molloy, Carroll, Egan, Dempsey, O'Connor, Daly, Fitzpatrick and Lalor. Principal towns include: (Offaly) Tullamore, Birr, Clara, Edenderry; (Laois) Portarlington, Portlaoise, Mountmellick and Mountrath. Publications offered by the centre include: *Annals of Clonmacnois*, $35; *Tullamore Town Album*, $25; *The Long Ridge* (Killeigh), $18; *Clara – A Pictorial Record*, $25; *Offaly Placenames*, $12; and *Quakers of Mount Mellick*, $16. Prices are exclusive of shipping and handling.

CONTACT

John Kearney, Coordinator

DESCRIPTION

Irish Midlands Ancestry, under the aegis of Offaly Historical & Archaeological Society, is the Irish Family History Foundation's designated research centre for the counties of Laois (formerly called Queen's Co.) and Offaly (formerly called King's Co.). The IFHF is the coordinating body for a network of government-approved genealogical research centres in the Republic of Ireland and in Northern Ireland that have computerized tens of millions of Irish ancestral records of different types.

HOLDINGS

The centre has indexed all available church records in the Laois and Offaly area. The earliest Roman Catholic parish records start at 1763. The earliest Church of Ireland records date from 1699 and the latest from 1876. Methodist records begin in 1830. Other material indexed includes: the Birr Workhouse register; births, marriages and deaths recorded in the *King's County Chronicle* newspaper

(1845–65) and the *Leinster Express* (1831–51); entries in trade directories for the period 1788 to 1908; and the Geashill Estate rental (1883).

LOCATION

Town centre, next to Tullamore Dew Heritage Centre.

## OFFALY COUNTY LIBRARY – LOCAL STUDIES SECTION

O'Connor Square
TULLAMORE, CO. OFFALY
Ireland

TELEPHONE: (0506) 46834; FAX: (0506) 52769
E-mail: libraryhq@offalycoco.ie
Website: www.offaly.ie/librariesartsandculture/libraries.asp

HOURS

By appointment only

ACCESS AND SERVICES

Visitors welcome, but by appointment only. Advance notice required. Fees for photocopying and microfilm printing services. Advance notice required for special services. Free Internet access available.

CONTACT

Mary Butler, Executive Librarian

DESCRIPTION

The Local Studies Section was established to collect and preserve all materials relating to Co. Offaly or written by persons from Co. Offaly.

HOLDINGS

The collection includes books, artefacts, films, journals, manuscripts, maps, microforms, newspapers, pamphlets, photographs, recordings and ephemera on the history, geography, culture, archaeology, geology, local government, sport, and architecture of the county. Special collections include: Poor Law and local government records from *c.*1830s; newspapers (on microfilm) from *c.*1845 including the *Midland Tribune*, *King's County Chronicle*, *Westmeath Independent*, and the *Tullamore & King's County Independent*; and photographs relating to all aspects of the county. Additional resources of special genealogical interest include: Tithe Applotment Books (on microfilm, 1823–38); Griffith's Valuation (including maps); 1901 Census (on microfilm); Ordnance Survey maps, 1st and 2nd editions; Taylor & Skinner Maps of the roads of Ireland (1778); John O'Donovan's Ordnance Survey Letters and Field Books describing King's Co. parishes in the 1840s; Grand Jury Presentment Books for the King's Co. (1830–78); and the Irish Folklore Commission Schools Collection (1937/8).

The Poor Law records are mainly the usual series of minute books for the Boards of Guardians *c.*1840–*c.*1920 but for Parsonstown (Birr) Poor Law Union there are at least two workhouse admission registers.

LOCATION

Town centre.

## OFFALY HISTORICAL & ARCHAEOLOGICAL SOCIETY

*See* IRISH MIDLANDS ANCESTRY, Tullamore, Co. Offaly

# COUNTY ROSCOMMON

*for* QUEEN'S COUNTY
*see* CO. LAOIS

## ROSCOMMON COUNTY LIBRARY

Abbey Street
ROSCOMMON TOWN, CO. ROSCOMMON
Ireland

TELEPHONE: (0903) 37271; FAX: (0903) 37101
E-mail: roslib@iol.ie
Website: www.iol.ie/~roslib

HOURS

Tu,Th, 1:00–8:00pm; W, 1:00–5:00pm; F,Sat, 10:00am–1:00pm, 2:00–5:00pm

ACCESS AND SERVICES

Visitors welcome, but borrowing privileges may be restricted. Photocopying services available.

CONTACT

Helen Kilcline, County Librarian

DESCRIPTION

Headquarters Library for the county system, which also includes branches in Castlerea, Boyle, Elphin, Strokestown, Ballaghaderreen, and Ballyforan.

HOLDINGS

In addition to the usual collection of educational and recreational material, the library houses a very fine local history and genealogy collection and archive. Archival material includes: Boards of Guardians Minutes for Boyle, Castlerea, Roscommon, Strokestown; Rural District Council Minutes for Athlone No. 2, Boyle, Carrick-on-Shannon, Castlerea, Roscommon, Strokestown; Minutes of the Boyle Dispensary District, Roscommon Board of Health (inc. acting for Athlone RDC), Roscommon County Council, Roscommon Pension Committee and Roscommon Town Commissioners; Strokestown RDC Labourers' Acts (acting as Rural Sanitary Authority); and Roscommon Grand Jury Records. Newspapers on microfilm include: *Boyle Gazette and Roscommon Reporter*, 1891; *Dublin Penny Journal*, 1832–6; *Irishman*, 1819–25; *The Nation*, 1842–52; *Roscommon Constitutionalist*; 1889–91; *Roscommon Herald*, from 1882; *Roscommon Journal and Western Impartial Reporter*, 1828–1927; *Roscommon Weekly Messenger* and *Roscommon Messenger*, 1848–1935; *Western Nationalist* (later continued as the *Roscommon Champion*), 1907–20; and the *Strokestown Democrat*, 1913–48. Several of the newspapers are available in hardbound copies. The library also houses microfilm copies of other material of local interest, including History of Roscommon – 1 reel; Irish Topographical Prints and Original Drawings – 3 reels; Monasteries of Roscommon – 1 reel; Moran Manuscripts 1548–50 – 2 reels; Reverend John Keogh's Statistical Account of Co. Roscommon (originally drawn up for Sir William Petty's Down Survey 1683); and the Irish Folklore Commission Schools Collection (1937/8) for Roscommon – 14 reels.

LOCATION

Town centre.

## CO. ROSCOMMON HERITAGE AND GENEALOGY COMPANY

Church Street,
STROKESTOWN, CO. ROSCOMMON
Ireland

TELEPHONE: (078) 33380; FAX: (078) 33398
E-mail: info@roscommonroots.com
Website: www.irishroots.net/Roscmmn.htm; www.roscommonroots.com

HOURS

M–F, 2:30–4:30pm

ACCESS AND SERVICES

The Co. Roscommon Heritage and Genealogy Company offers a fee-based, full-range genealogical research service to persons interested in tracing their family roots in Co. Roscommon. Enquiries to this centre are usually answered in about four weeks but at this time there is a large backlog of enquiries and delays of up to three months can be anticipated. An application form is available through the society's website. An initial research fee of $45.00 is required. Common surnames in Co. Roscommon are: Hanley, Beirne, Kelly, Brennan, Connor, Flynn, Cox, McDermott, Brady and Farrell. Chief towns and villages in Co. Roscommon include: Roscommon, Strokestown, Boyle, Elphin, Loughlynn, Ballaghadereen, Castlerea, and Knockcroghery.

CONTACT

Mary Skelly

DESCRIPTION

The Co. Roscommon Heritage and Genealogy Company is the designated Irish Family History Foundation centre serving Co. Roscommon. The IFHF is the coordinating body for a network of government-approved genealogical research centres in the Republic of Ireland and in Northern Ireland that have computerized tens of millions of Irish ancestral records of different types.

HOLDINGS

The company has access to over 1,000,000 genealogical records relating to the county. Main records include: Roman Catholic records that begin between 1789 and 1865 depending on the parish; Church of Ireland records starting between 1796 and 1877 depending on the parish; Presbyterian records that start between 1857 and 1861; and Methodist records that start in the early 1840s. The company has also computerized Griffith's Valuation; Tithe Applotment Books; a list of '40 Shilling Freeholders' for 1876; Pakenham–Mahon Eviction Lists from 1847; and RIC (Royal Irish Constabulary) records. The earliest census available that covers a large part of Co. Roscommon dates from 1749.

LOCATION

Town centre.

# COUNTY SLIGO

## CO. SLIGO HERITAGE AND GENEALOGY SOCIETY

Aras Reddan
Temple Street
SLIGO TOWN, CO. SLIGO
Ireland

TELEPHONE: (071) 43728
E-mail: heritagesligo@eircom.net
Website: www.mayo-ireland.ie/roots.htm; www.sligoroots.com

HOURS

M–F, 9:15am–4:45pm

ACCESS AND SERVICES

Visitors welcome. Full research enquiries might take up to two months to complete, but initial enquiries are answered as soon as possible. See website for application form. An initial search fee of 30 euro is required. The centre offers for sale a large selection of books of genealogical and local history interest.

CONTACT

John McTernan

DESCRIPTION

The society is the designated Irish Family History Foundation centre for Co. Sligo. These centres aim to create a comprehensive database of genealogical sources that are known to exist, including Church records of all denominations, civil records, land valuations, Census records, gravestone inscriptions, and various other local sources. The Sligo centre offers a genealogical research service for Co. Sligo. Common surnames in Co. Sligo include Gallagher, Brennan, MacGowan, Kelly, Gilmartin, Healy, Walsh, Hart, Feeney and MacDonagh. Towns in Co. Sligo include Sligo Town, Ballymote, Tobercurry, and Collooney.

HOLDINGS

The society has collected more than 400,000 records relating to Co. Sligo. These have been computerized and are available on the database at the centre. These records include church records: Roman Catholic dating back to 1796, Church of Ireland back to 1762, Presbyterian back to 1806, and Methodist back to 1819; the 1901 Census; 1858 Griffith's Valuation; Tithe Applotment Books (1823–37); the Elphin Diocesan Census of 1749; gravestone inscriptions; and various other genealogical sources.

LOCATION

In North-West Tourism Complex in Sligo town centre.

## SLIGO COUNTY LIBRARY

Westward Town Centre Complex
Bridge Street
SLIGO TOWN, CO. SLIGO
Ireland

TELEPHONE: (071) 47190/55060; FAX: (071) 46798
E-mail: sligolib@sligococo.ie
Website: www.iol.ie/~libcounc/sligo.htm

HOURS

M–F: 10:00am–12:45pm, 2:00–4:45pm

ACCESS AND SERVICES

Visitors welcome. No admission fees. Disabled access facilities. Collection catalogued online in 2002. Printed catalogue and finding aids available. Publications include: John C. McTernan (ed.), *Sligo: Sources of Local History: A Catalogue of the Local History Collection, with an Introduction and Guide to Sources*, new edn (Sligo: Sligo County Library, 1994); D. Tinney (ed.), *Jack B. Yeats at the Niland Gallery Sligo*; and Hilary Pyle, *The Sligo–Leitrim World of Kate Cullen*.

CONTACT

Donal Tinney, County Librarian; e-mail: dtinney@sligococo.ie

DESCRIPTION

This is the main library for Sligo Town and Co. Sligo, with four additional service points.

HOLDINGS

In addition to the standard general collection, the library offers a good local history collection focusing on Sligo, the Yeats family, Countess Markievicz and the Gore-Booth family, and the archaeology of Sligo. There is also a collection of newspapers published in Sligo from 1822 to the present. Special collections include: W.B. Yeats, Jack B. Yeats, Countess Markievicz, Autographs, and Local Authors.

Genealogical holdings for Co. Sligo include recordings of all gravestone inscriptions in some 150 graveyards in the county.

The Sligo Corporation archive includes rate books *c.*1842–1977.

For landed estates there are some 90 vols in the archive of an estate agent named Robinson who managed many estates in the county. This includes rentals for various estates from *c.*1850.

There are also parish records (not complete), directories and details of First World War dead. There are microfilm copies of the 1901 Census for Co. Sligo, tithe survey 1823–38, and also a set of the printed Griffith valuation for the county *c.*1855.

LOCATION

Ground floor section of the Westward Town Centre Complex on Bridge Street in Sligo town centre.

# COUNTY TIPPERARY

## BRÚ BORÚ HERITAGE CENTRE

Rock of Cashel
CASHEL, CO. TIPPERARY
Ireland

TELEPHONE: (062) 61122; FAX: (062) 62700
E-mail: bruboru@comhaltas.com
Website: www.irishroots.net/STipp.htm; www.comhaltas.com

HOURS

M–F, 9:00am–5:00pm

ACCESS AND SERVICES

The Brú Ború Heritage Centre offers a fee-based full genealogical service to enquirers, with access to church, civil, land, and Census returns for South Tipperary. Initial enquiries usually receive a reply within one month. An application form is available on the centre's website. The initial search fee, to accompany the form, is 40 euro. Fees vary.

CONTACT

Deirdre Walsh

DESCRIPTION

Brú Ború Heritage Centre is the designated Irish Family History Foundation centre serving South Tipperary. The IFHF is the coordinating body for a network of government-approved genealogical research centres in the Republic of Ireland and in Northern Ireland that have computerized tens of millions of Irish ancestral records of different types. Brú Ború, which means The Palace of Ború, is a cultural and interpretative village designed around a village green dedicated to the study and celebration of Irish music, song, dance, storytelling, theatre, and Celtic studies. Surnames in South Tipperary include: Ryan, Dwyer, Maher, O'Brien, Hayes, Quirke, Treacy, O'Meara, Macken, Maloney, Lonergan, and Kearney. Main towns in South Tipperary include: Cashel, Cahir, Tipperary, Clonmel, and Carrick-on-Suir.

HOLDINGS

The centre holds Roman Catholic records, the earliest of which date from 1778. These records, up to 1921, have been computerized. The centre also holds non-Catholic civil marriage records from 1845, plus copies of: 1901 Census; Tithe Applotment Books; Griffith's Valuation; and Hearth Money Rolls of 1666. It has access to approximately 400,000 records.

LOCATION

Brú Ború is a national heritage centre at the foot of the 'Rock of Cashel', historic castle ruins just outside the town of Cashel.

## GPA BOLTON LIBRARY

GPA Building
John Street
CASHEL, CO. TIPPERARY
Ireland

TELEPHONE: (062) 61944; FAX: (062) 61944
E-mail: boltonlibrary@oceanfree.net
Website: www.tipp.ie/stjohn.htm

### HOURS

Mar.–Oct.: Tu–Sat, 9:30am–5:30pm, Sun, 12:30–5:30pm
Oct.–Feb.: M–F, 9:30am–5:30pm

### ACCESS AND SERVICES

Visitors welcome, but advance notice preferred, especially for access to the collections. Tours available: 9:45am–4:45pm (Sun, 12:45–4:45pm). Admission fees apply. No disabled access facilities. About 90% of the library's holdings are catalogued in a printed catalogue, available within the library only.

### CONTACT

The Very Rev. Dr Philip Knowles, Dean of Cashel and Curator of the Bolton Library, The Deanery, Cashel, Co. Tipperary, tel. (062) 61222; Ms Mary Mulvey, tel. (062) 63175

### DESCRIPTION

The library is housed in a small but handsome 18th-century building near the Church of Ireland's Cathedral Church of St John the Baptist and St Patrick's Rock. The library was restored with a large grant from GPA. More recently the library has entered into a management arrangement with the University of Limerick. The library has been in its current quarters since 1836. Some of its greatest treasures are on exhibit.

### HOLDINGS

The library primarily houses the 18th-century private libraries of Archbishop Bolton of Cashel (d. 1744) and Archbishop William King of Dublin (1650–1729). It also houses portions of the collections of Archbishop Narcissus Marsh of Dublin (1638–1713), of Bishops Jephson and Foley, and of the Abbé Bignon. The collection totals some 12,000 volumes, plus a small but significant collection of manuscripts, bound pamphlets, and artefacts. It also includes maps and newspapers. Though the focus of the collection is on religion and theology, it covers a wide range of interests, including literature, the physical sciences, law, medicine, philosophy, astronomy, and Irish history and politics. The rare book collection contains some real gems. These include the 'smallest book in the world', a collection of some 20 incunabula, including a copy of the Nuremburg Chronicle (1493) and the 1473 Strasbourg edition of Vincent of Beauvais' *Speculem Historical*; a good representation of early presses, including Estienne,

Koberger, Froben, Caxton, and Aldus Manutius; and a collection of more than 200 bound volumes of pamphlets and broadsides dealing primarily with politics and controversies. The manuscript holdings include several medieval codices, the oldest dating from the 12th century; three Irish manuscripts, including a *c.*1716 copy of Geoffrey Keating's *Foras Feasa ar Eirin* in the hand of Dermot O'Connor; and a 1717 Hebrew manuscript of the translation of the Irish Book of Common Prayer, one of only four copies extant. The collection also houses about 900 early Irish imprints. Of special genealogical interest are the diocesan records of births, marriages and deaths going back to 1668. Also there are minute books of the diocesan council and account books; a printed copy of Griffith's Valuation and printed books of the Cashel Diocese dating from 1855 to 1891.

LOCATION

Town centre, just down to the right of the Church of Ireland Cathedral Church of St John the Baptist and St Patrick's Rock.

## TIPPERARY NORTH FAMILY HISTORY RESEARCH CENTRE

Governor's House
Kickham Street
NENAGH, CO. TIPPERARY
Ireland

TELEPHONE: (067) 33850; FAX: (067) 33586
E-mail: tippnorthgenealogy@eircom.net
Website: www.irishroots.net/NTipp.htm

HOURS

M–F, 9:30am–5:00pm

ACCESS AND SERVICES

Tipperary North Family History Research Centre offers a fee-based full genealogical service to persons interested in tracing their roots in North Tipperary. Initial enquiries usually receive a reply within one month. Visitors to the centre are given priority. An application form is available on the centre's website. There is an initial search fee of 100 euro. The centre offers a number of interesting publications for sale, including: *The Two Tipperarys* (the division of the county into two ridings in 1838), 12.63 euro; *The Great Famine in Nenagh Poor Law Union*, 19 euro; *A Trip Through Tipperary Lakeside*, 2.54 euro; *Blazing Tar Barrels* (first local government elections of 1899 in Tipperary North), 5 euro; *Co. Tipperary Guide* – eight suggested tours covering the whole county, 2.54 euro. Prices quoted are approximate and do not include postage and packing.

CONTACT

Nora O'Meara, Genealogy Officer

DESCRIPTION

Tipperary North Family History Research Centre is the designated Irish Family History Foundation centre serving North Tipperary. It is a company limited by guarantee with charitable status and managed by a Board of Directors who give their time voluntarily. The IFHF is the coordinating body for a network of government-approved genealogical research centres in the Republic of Ireland and in Northern Ireland that have computerized tens of millions of Irish ancestral records of different types. Common surnames in North Tipperary include: Ryan, O'Brien, Kennedy, O'Meara, Maher/Meagher, Burke, Gleeson, Carroll, Hogan and Kelly. Towns in Tipperary North include: Nenagh, Templemore, Thurles, and Roscrea. Villages include: Borrisokane, Borrisoleigh, Cloughjordan, and Newport.

HOLDINGS

The centre currently has computerized about 600,000 genealogical records. Main records include: Roman Catholic records, the earliest of which date from 1792; Church of Ireland records, some of which date from 1755; Methodist records from 1834; Tithe Applotment and Griffith's Valuation Lists; civil births, deaths and marriages 1864–1911; gravestone inscriptions for all of Tipperary North; 1901 Census. Note: church and civil records terminate in 1900 or 1911. In addition to the main sources, the centre has also computerized Civil Survey and Hearth Money Rolls (17th century); street directories (19th and 20th century); Encumbered Estate records for Nenagh, 1854; Vestry Book for Borrisokane (19th century); Poor Law rate books for Nenagh and Thurles Poor Law Unions, 1840s; and births, deaths and marriages in the *Nenagh Guardian*, 1838–66.

LOCATION

The Family History Research Centre is located in the former residence of the County Gaol governor (1842–86), which has since been a convent, a secondary school and, since 1984, a heritage centre.

## CASHEL AND EMLY ARCHDIOCESAN ARCHIVES (Roman Catholic)

Archbishop's House
THURLES, CO. TIPPERARY
Ireland

TELEPHONE: (0504) 21512; FAX: (0504) 22680
E-mail: cashelemly@eircom.net
Website: homepage.eircom.net/~cashelemly/genealog.htm

HOURS

Closed to visitors. *See* ACCESS AND SERVICES.

ACCESS AND SERVICES

Visitors are advised to consult the microfilm copies located in the National Library of Ireland. Permission to consult these copies is required but is readily given to bona fide researchers. Originals are made available only in exceptional circumstances. Parish records are available through TIPPERARY FAMILY HISTORY RESEARCH, Tipperary Town.

CONTACT

Tipperary Family History Research, Excel Heritage Centre, Mitchell Street, Tipperary Town

DESCRIPTION

Not applicable

HOLDINGS

Archives houses archdiocesan records, including parish records of marriages and baptisms, for the Roman Catholic Archdiocese of Cashel and Emly. The archdiocese includes parishes in parts of North and South Tipperary and south-east Limerick. There are 46 parishes in all, with some records dating back to the late 1700s.

LOCATION

Archbishop's House, Thurles.

## TIPPERARY LIBRARIES

Castle Avenue
THURLES, CO. TIPPERARY
Ireland

TELEPHONE: (0504) 21555; FAX: (0504) 23442
E-mail: tipplibs@iol.ie
Website: www.iol.ie/~tipplibs

HOURS

M–F, 9:30am–5:00pm; closed bank holidays

ACCESS AND SERVICES

Visitors welcome. Disabled access facilities. Laptops permitted. A small fee is charged for photocopies and microfilm copies. Advisable to book microfilm equipment in advance. Certain archival material may not be copied. Internet and e-mail services also available.

CONTACT

Mary Guinan-Darmody
Pat Bracken

DESCRIPTION

Tipperary Libraries is the main public library for Co. Tipperary. It also serves as the headquarters for the Co. Tipperary Historical Society. Back issues of the Society's *Tipperary Historical Journal* are available for purchase; the years 1988–91 are no longer available.

HOLDINGS

In addition to its general educational and recreational collection, the library houses a very good collection of local history materials focusing on Co. Tipperary. This collection includes Co. Tipperary published newspapers and a large collection of books and journals about the county and by Tipperary authors. Newspapers include *The Tipperary Star* since 1909; *The Nationalist* (Clonmel) since 1890; *The Guardian* (Nenagh) since 1968; *Midland Tribune* (1920–53); *Tipperaryman and Limerick Recorder* (1928–31); and the *Tipperary Vindicator* (1844–9); plus extracts and scattered copies of numerous other papers.

Among holdings of special genealogical interest are workhouse admission registers for the Poor Law Unions of Roscrea 1899–1924 and Thurles 1849–1924, and Poor Law Union rate books for Thurles 1842–*c.*1899 and Nenagh 1842–52. There are also Board of Guardians minute books *c.*1839–*c.*1923 for the Poor Law Unions of Cashel, Clogheen, Clonmel, Borrisokane, Nenagh, Roscrea and Thurles.

Also available is a printed version of the Hearth Money rolls 1665–7, and the printed version of the valuation of all properties which took place in Co. Tipperary as early as *c.*1849–51. There is also a complete set of Ordnance Survey maps for Tipperary, 1840 on the scale of six inches to one mile, copies of surviving parts of the 1766 religious census and some recordings of gravestone inscriptions. Microfilm copies of the 1901 Census for Co. Tipperary are available, and also for the tithe applotment surveys of parishes 1823–38. For North Tipperary there are Grand Jury Presentments from *c.*1800.

LOCATION

Town centre.

## TIPPERARY FAMILY HISTORY RESEARCH

Excel Heritage Centre
Mitchell Street
TIPPERARY TOWN, CO. TIPPERARY
Ireland

TELEPHONE: (062) 80555/80556; FAX: (062) 80551
E-mail: research@tfhr.org
Website: www.tfhr.org

HOURS

M–F, 9:30am–5:30pm; closed bank holidays

ACCESS AND SERVICES

Visitors welcome. Fees for research services.

CONTACT

Patrick McDonnell

DESCRIPTION

Tipperary Family History Research, established in April 2001 as successor to Tipperary Heritage Unit, conducts research within the records of the CASHEL AND EMLY ARCHDIOCESAN ARCHIVES (Roman Catholic), Thurles, Co. Tipperary.

HOLDINGS

Over 600,000 marriage and baptismal records, representing all 46 parishes that make up the archdiocese, have been indexed to date. The archdiocese includes parishes in parts of North and South Tipperary and south-east Limerick. Some records date back to the late 1700s, but the vast majority date from the 1800s.

LOCATION

Excel Heritage Centre, town centre. From Main Street turn onto St Michael's Street and take first left onto Mitchell Street.

# COUNTY TYRONE

## IRISH WORLD

formerly **IRISH WORLD FAMILY HISTORY CENTRE**

Family History Suite
51 Dungannon Road
COALISLAND, CO. TYRONE, BT71 4HP
Northern Ireland

TELEPHONE: (028) 8774 6065; FAX: (028) 8776 1306
Website: www.Irish-World.com

Just re-opened at time of publication; no further information available.

## CENTRE FOR MIGRATION STUDIES

Ulster-American Folk Park
2 Mellon Road
Castletown
OMAGH, CO. TYRONE, BT78 5QY
Northern Ireland

TELEPHONE: (028) 8225 6315; FAX: (028) 8224 2241
E-mail: uafp@iol.ie
Website: www.qub.ac.uk/cms

HOURS

M–F, 9:30am–4:30pm; closed weekends and public holidays and Christmas Day through New Year's Day

ACCESS AND SERVICES

Visitors welcome at no charge. Reference-only library collection. Disabled access facilities. The collection is catalogued on cards. The centre offers a master's programme on Irish migration studies through Queen's University Belfast, plus courses for visiting groups tailored to individual needs. It also hosts conferences, seminars and programmes on migration-related topics. Staff respond to enquiries and offer advice on family history research involving migration records. Fees for photocopying and microform prints. No charge for Internet access. Publications include the autobiography of Thomas Mellon, whose family home is the nucleus of the Ulster-American Folk Park, entitled *Thomas Mellon and His Times* (1994); *The Hungry Stream: Essays on Emigration and Famine* (1997), edited by E. Margaret Crawford; and *Atlantic Crossroads: Historical Connections between Scotland, Ulster and North America* (2001), edited by Patrick Fitzgerald and Steve Ickringill. Booklets about the ULSTER-AMERICAN FOLK PARK and the Mellon House are also available. The park offers a restaurant.

CONTACT

B.K. Lambkin, Director
Christine McIvor, Principal Librarian
Patrick Fitzgerald, Lecturer and Development Officer

DESCRIPTION

The Centre for Migration Studies aims to serve the community as a leading international institution for the study of human migration, focusing on the peoples of Ireland worldwide. Migration studies is about advancing the understanding of the movement and settlement of people (including immigration, internal migration, seasonal migration and emigration) through multidisciplinary approaches (including history, politics, economics, language, literature, art, and religion). The centre is a project of the Scotch-Irish Trust of Ulster, which supports the work of the Ulster-American Folk Park through partnership with the Department of Culture, Arts and Leisure, the five Education and Library Boards of Northern Ireland, Queen's University Belfast, the University of Ulster, and Enterprise Ulster. CMS is a member of the Association of European Migration Institutions (www.aemi.dk) and has close links with the Irish Centre for Migration Studies at University College Cork (www.migration. ucc.ie).

HOLDINGS

The CMS Library contains some 10,000 volumes, 1,340 maps, plus significant holdings of journals, microforms and recordings. The focus of the collection is on Ireland and North America in the 18th and 19th centuries, and the links between the two. The collection was organized originally to support the activities of the Ulster-American Folk Park, and to this end the library developed strengths in the fields of agriculture, architecture, crafts and industry, social customs, biography, politics, and religion. More recently the collection has expanded to cover the 17th and 20th centuries and all aspects of Irish migration worldwide. Special Collections of note include the CMS Irish Emigration Database, which contains some 30,000 primary source documents on all aspects of Irish emigration to North America, including Canada, from the early 1700s to the 1900s. Begun in 1988, new documents are being added to this database on a regular basis. Types of documents include ship passenger lists, emigrant letters, family papers and diaries of emigrants, shipping advertisements, newspaper reports, death and marriage notices of former emigrants, birth notices of children of Irish parentage, government reports and statistics of Irish emigration to North America, and illustrated material showing ship types, ports, routes and maps, shipboard conditions, and the cost of the voyage. Another collection of special note is 'The Art of European Migration', an image database designed to promote comparative study of the migration themes of 'departure', 'arrival', and 'return'. This database is accessible through the CMS website and is also available at certain public libraries in Northern Ireland.

LOCATION

Situated at the Ulster-American Folk Park, five miles outside Omagh in Co. Tyrone on the A5 from Omagh to Strabane.

## OMAGH LIBRARY

Spillars Place
OMAGH, CO. TYRONE, BT78 1HL
Northern Ireland

TELEPHONE: (028) 8224 4821; FAX: (028) 8224 6716/8224 6772
E-mail: Omagh_library@welbni.org
Website: www.welbni.org

HOURS

M,W,F, 9:15am–5:30pm; Tu,Th, 9:15am–8:00pm; Sat, 9:15–1:00pm, 2:00–5:00pm

ACCESS AND SERVICES

Visitors welcome, but advance notice preferred. Borrowing privileges for visitors may be restricted. Disabled access facilities. Fees for photocopying and microform prints. Free leaflets and brochures available. The library is electronically linked to the emigration database of the ULSTER-AMERICAN FOLK PARK, Omagh, Co. Tyrone.

CONTACT

Gerry McSorley, Senior Librarian

DESCRIPTION

Part of the Western Education and Library Board system, Omagh is the branch library for the largest town in Co. Tyrone. Located in an attractive building, it has a strong Irish and Local Studies department.

HOLDINGS

The library houses a general educational and recreational collection, with access to some 500,000 volumes in the WELB system. Its Irish and Local Studies collection includes more than 5,000 volumes, with strong holdings of maps, microforms, journals and newspapers, focusing on Co. Tyrone. It has all the standard genealogical reference sources for the area, including: microform copies of the 1901 Census; the printed Griffith's Valuation 1860; Board of Guardians minutes for Castlederg, Clogher, Omagh, and Strabane (*c.*1840–1900).

It is not generally known that the Omagh Library also holds significant collections of school records and duplicates of valuation records which have been returned from PRONI. The local valuation records now held in the Omagh Library cover the Rural District Council areas of Omagh, Castlederg, Clogher, Strabane. These volumes cover the years 1920–30, 1934–5 and 1957.

Records have also been transferred for at least six 'national' schools in West Tyrone, including Calkill in Cappagh parish for which there are roll books 1903–83, daily report books 1909–81, boys' and girls' registers 1931–52 and a register 1944–84. There are also roll books for this school for special subjects such as domestic economy and horticulture, a minute book and inspector's reports.

Other schools for which records are available are Beltany, Deverney (Recarson townland) and Edenderry in Cappagh parish, Carnkenny and Erganagh in Ardstraw and Tattykeeran in Clogherny parish.

LOCATION

Town centre, between Dublin Road and the Drumragh River.

## ULSTER-AMERICAN FOLK PARK

2 Mellon Road
Castletown
OMAGH, CO. TYRONE, BT78 5QY
Northern Ireland

TELEPHONE: (028) 8224 3292; FAX: (028) 8224 2241
E-mail: education@uafp.co.uk
Website: www.folkpark.com

HOURS

Apr.–Sept.: M–Sat, 10:30am–4:30pm, Museum closes at 6:00pm; Sundays and public holidays, 11:00am–5:00pm, Museum closes at 6:30pm
Oct.–Mar.: M–F, 10:30am–3:30pm, Museum closes at 5:00pm; closed weekends and public holidays and Christmas Day through New Year's Day

ACCESS AND SERVICES

Visitors welcome. Admission fees apply: adults, £4; children, seniors and disabled persons, £2.50; family, £10; reduced rates available for groups. Disabled access facilities. Free parking. Craft and Gift Shop. Restaurant.

CONTACT

Evelyn Cardwell, Education Officer
Phil Mowat, Curator

DESCRIPTION

Large and sophisticated outdoor museum and indoor galleries devoted to Ireland and the New World in the 18th and 19th centuries. Restored and replicated structures, including a full-scale emigrant ship, offer the visitor an opportunity to visit Ireland in 18th- and 19th-century times, board an emigrant ship and emerge in the New World. Exhibits trace the history of the times, with special attention to agriculture, crafts, transportation, and society. Original homesteads of the Mellon, Campbell, Devine, Hupp, Hughes, and Fulton families. A wonderful place to entertain and educate children and adults. The park is part of the Museums and Galleries of Northern Ireland (MAGNI) service, which also includes the ULSTER FOLK AND TRANSPORT MUSEUM, Cultra, Co. Down; the ULSTER MUSEUM, Belfast, Co. Antrim; and its branch, the ARMAGH COUNTY MUSEUM, Armagh City, Co. Armagh.

HOLDINGS

*See* CENTRE FOR MIGRATION STUDIES, Omagh. The museum itself features exhibits focusing on emigration, folklife of Ireland and America, agriculture, crafts, education, religion, shops, shipping, all with relevance to the 18th and 19th centuries.

LOCATION

Situated five miles outside Omagh, on the A5 from Omagh to Strabane.

## ULSTER HISTORY PARK

150 Glenpark Road
Cullion, Lislap
OMAGH, CO. TYRONE, BT79 7SU
Northern Ireland

TELEPHONE: (028) 8164 8188; FAX: (028) 8164 8011
E-mail: uhp@omagh.gov.uk
Website: www.omagh.gov.uk/historypark.htm

HOURS

Apr.–June, Sept.: M–Sun, 10:00am–5:30pm; July–Aug.: M–Sun, 10:00am–6:30pm; Oct.–Mar., M–F: 10am–5:00pm; last admission one hour before closing

ACCESS AND SERVICES

Visitors welcome. Admission fees apply: adults, £3.75; children, students, seniors and disabled persons, £2.50; group and family rates available. Disabled access facilities. Indoor exhibition gallery; audiovisual programme; conference facilities; cafeteria; shop; picnic area and ample free parking.

CONTACT

Elizabeth Harkin, Education/Promotions Officer; e-mail: elizabeth.harkin@omagh.gov.uk

DESCRIPTION

The Ulster History Park is a 35-acre outdoor museum that traces the history of settlement in Ireland from the arrival of the first Stone Age hunters and gatherers up to the Plantation period of the early 17th century. Full-scale replicas of homes and monuments through the ages include megalithic tombs, a church and a round tower of the early Christian period, timber houses of the Stone Age farmers, and reconstructions of a 'rath' and crannog, homes of farmers in the first millennium AD. An indoor exhibition develops the theme of settlement and an audiovisual presentation explores the legacy of the past still visible in the landscape.

HOLDINGS

Plans to develop a library have not materialized as yet, but visitors to the Centre for Migration Studies at the Ulster-American Folk Park may want to make time for a visit to this very interesting history park.

LOCATION

Situated seven miles north of Omagh, on the B48 Omagh to Gortin Road.

# COUNTY WATERFORD

## WATERFORD COUNTY ARCHIVES SERVICE

Dungarvan Library
Davitt's Quay
DUNGARVAN, CO. WATERFORD
Ireland

TELEPHONE: (058) 23673/41231; FAX: (058) 42911
E-mail: archivist@waterfordcoco.ie
Website: www.waterfordcoco.ie

HOURS

Tu, 10:00am–2:00pm; F, 1:00–5:00pm; or by appointment

ACCESS AND SERVICES

Visitors welcome. For detailed description of holdings and services, visit the website. The Archives Service is located in the library building; while no parking is available immediately outside the library, parking is available nearby.

CONTACT

Archivist

DESCRIPTION

The Archives Service is housed in Dungarvan Library and holds records of local authorities in Co. Waterford, past and present, plus private collections relating to Waterford.

HOLDINGS

The County Archives hold: Grand Jury Records; Board of Guardian Records; Rural District Council Records; Waterford County Council Records; Dungarvan Town Council Records; and private papers.

There are virtually complete sets of minute books of the Boards of Guardians for the Poor Law Unions of Dungarvan, Kilmacthomas, Lismore and Waterford *c.*1843–1923. There is also an unusual set of 'valuation' books recording payments of Grand Jury cess from 1869. Up to 1875 these are in annual volumes but a single large volume covers the years *c.*1876–*c.*1900. Since these volumes record the names of tax payers annually, a search can show the probable year of death of a person when the name disappears. These records are arranged by barony, townland and parish.

On some estates payment of county cess was the responsibility of the landlord, in which case the names of occupiers of holdings are not given. These books thus contain fewer names of occupiers than surviving Poor Law rate books or the valuation revision books held in the Valuation Office, Middle Abbey Street, Dublin.

There is also a collection of Grand Jury records up to 1899 including presentments from 1865 and contract books 1829–67.

The archive also holds Rural District Council records from 1899.

The private papers include the Chearnley Papers (1671–1915), relating to lands predominantly in West Waterford; and the Hugh Ryan Papers, containing an important collection of political pamphlets relating to Irish nationalism and records relating to a survey carried out by Ryan of the gravestones of Mothel and Rathgormack. The Villiers-Stuart Papers are available on microfilm, as are papers from the Lismore (Devonshire) estate held in the National Library of Ireland. The County Archive holds the 19th-century records for the Lismore estate including rentals, tenants' application books and agents' correspondence but these are not yet available to researchers as they are still being cleaned, sorted, and listed. Also on microfilm are the Tithe Applotment Books for Co. Waterford. The Census records for 1901 and 1911 are shortly to be added to the microfilm holdings.

LOCATION

Dungarvan Library Building, town centre. Dungarvan lies between Cork City and Waterford City on the N25. There is a frequent bus service between Cork City and Dungarvan and between Waterford City and Dungarvan.

## WATERFORD COUNTY LIBRARY HEADQUARTERS

LISMORE, CO. WATERFORD
Ireland

TELEPHONE: (058) 54128; FAX: (058) 54877
E-mail: libraryhq@waterfordcoco.ie
Website: www.waterfordcoco.ie

HOURS

Library Headquarters: M–F, 9:00am–5:00pm

ACCESS AND SERVICES

Visitors welcome. Disabled access facilities. Laptops permitted. A fee is charged for photocopies.

CONTACT

Donald Brady, County Librarian

DESCRIPTION

Library Headquarters mainly deals with administrative issues pertaining to the seven libraries in the county system: Cappoquin, Dungarvan, Dunmore, Lismore, Portlaw, Tallow, and Tramore. The WATERFORD MUNICIPAL LIBRARY, Waterford City is administered separately. Each library in the system offers the usual educational and recreational collections, plus access to the library system's online database.

HOLDINGS

The library holds an impressive local studies and family history collection, of which core resources are all accessible online. Of special genealogical interest are: Civil Records for Co. Waterford, including all deaths registered from 1 January 1864 to 31 December 1901; Griffith's Valuation (1848–64); gravestone memorials; historical trade directories (1824–1910); war memorials; and Ordnance Survey maps and photographs.

LOCATION

Town centre.

## WATERFORD CITY ARCHIVES

Waterford City Council
City Hall, The Mall
WATERFORD CITY, CO. WATERFORD
Ireland

TELEPHONE: (051) 843 123; FAX: (051) 879 124
E-mail: archives@waterfordcity.ie
Website: www.waterfordcity.ie/archives.htm

HOURS

By appointment, M–F, 9:00am–5:00pm

ACCESS AND SERVICES

Visitors welcome, but by appointment only. Readers are required to complete an application form on their first visit and are issued with a reader's ticket valid until the end of the calendar year. Photocopying facilities are available, but at the discretion of the Archivist and depending on copyright restrictions as well as the nature and condition of the material in question. Much of the material has been listed and searchable databases for some categories of records are being prepared on an ongoing basis. In general Waterford City Archives cannot undertake detailed genealogical and historical searches, although it does contain material of genealogical interest. Each query will be dealt with on an individual basis, however, and where the City Archivist can help, he will do so.

CONTACT

Donal Moore, City Archivist

DESCRIPTION

Waterford City Council was the first local authority to appoint an Archivist under the terms of Section 65 of the 1994 Local Government Act encouraging the establishment of local archives. A building in the centre of the medieval city was provided as a home for the City Archives and has been converted on a phased basis to provide work areas, secure storage spaces, and a reading room.

HOLDINGS

The core of the archives' collections comprises material originating within Waterford City Council (formerly Waterford Corporation) dating back to the 17th century. Nevertheless, a conscious decision was made that the new facility would be a city archives and not just a repository for the Council's own records. The archives has been given or lent a substantial number of items and collections by groups, individuals, companies and institutions in the city and there is an active acquisitions policy. At present the transfer or purchase of several significant collections of archival material created in the city is being negotiated. It is an objective also to 'repatriate' at least some of the material that left the city over the years and is now housed in repositories outside the city. Principal holdings include: Minute Books, Waterford Corporation, 1654–1990s (59 volumes); Committee Records, Waterford Corporation, 1778–1940s (19 committees); Records of Town Clerk's Office, 1700–1990s; Records of Finance Office, 1796–1980s; Records of City Engineer's Office, 1700–1990s, including over 2,500 maps and plans (drawings) for the city and its environs from the 18th century to the present, plus many reports and photographs of completed and proposed works; Estate Records, 1670s–1970s including searchable database of expired leases of Corporation property, 1670s–1970s (1,100+ entries); motor registration files from 1923; over 2,500 photographic prints of buildings, streets, events and people in the city from the 1870s to the present; school records (Mount Sion, St Patrick's, and Manor (St John's) Primary Schools, 1909–1990s); and over 70 small, private and institutional collections.

LOCATION

The City Archives building occupies a prominent position in the centre of the medieval city. Part of the building dates back at least as far as the 17th century.

## WATERFORD HERITAGE SERVICES

St Patrick's Church
Jenkin's Lane
WATERFORD CITY, CO. WATERFORD
Ireland

TELEPHONE: (051) 876 123; FAX: (051) 850 645
E-mail: mnoc@iol.ie
Website: www.waterford-heritage.ie; www.irishroots.net/Waterfrd.htm

HOURS

M–Th, 9:00am–5:00pm; F, 9:00am–2:00pm

ACCESS AND SERVICES

The Waterford Heritage and Genealogy Centre offers a fee-based, full-range genealogical research service for enquirers interested in tracing their roots in Waterford City and County. A copy of the application form can be found on the centre's website. The Waterford Centre does commissioned work and does not have reading rooms available for the public. Chief surnames of Co. Waterford include Power, Walsh, O'Brien, Murphy, Ryan, McGrath, Foley, Flynn, Morrissey, Kelly, Phelan, and Sullivan. Main towns include: Waterford, Dungarvan, Lismore, Cappoquin, Clonmel, and Carrick-on-Suir (Clonmel and Carrick-on-Suir straddle the Tipperary–Waterford border). Publications include (prices quoted are in US$, inclusive of postage and handling): *The Connerys: Making of a Waterford Legend* (145 pp.), $16; *Waterford History and Society*, price on application; *Discover Waterford* by Eamon McEneaney (109 pp.), $20; *Sliabh Rua: a History of its People & Places*, ed. J. Walsh (612 pp.), $40; and *The O'Briens of Déise* by Frank O'Brien (230 pp.), $25.

CONTACT

Carmel Meehan

DESCRIPTION

The Waterford Heritage and Genealogy Centre is the designated Irish Family History Foundation centre serving Waterford City and County. The IFHF is the coordinating body for a network of government-approved genealogical research centres in the Republic of Ireland and in Northern Ireland that have computerized tens of millions of Irish ancestral records of different types.

HOLDINGS

Church records form the major source of electronic data. Roman Catholic records in Co. Waterford start in the year 1706; the latest parish to begin keeping records did so in 1852. Church of Ireland records in Waterford have various starting dates, depending on the parish, from 1655 and 1870. Earliest surviving and complete Census for Waterford is that of 1901. Some Census extracts for the period 1766 to 1851 also survive. Other genealogical sources available for Co. Waterford include: Polling Lists from 1755 and 1775; The Civil Survey of Ireland compiled in the years 1654–6; Subsidy Rolls for Co. Waterford of 1662; Householders of Waterford City of 1663; Carrick-on-Suir Census of 1799; Freemen of Waterford list of 1542; street and trade directories from 1788; gravestone inscriptions; local newspapers from 1771 to present; biographical entries in local newspapers from 1770s to 1820s; and a local history collection.

LOCATION

Town centre, in the former 18th-century priest's residence next to St Patrick's Church.

## WATERFORD MUNICIPAL LIBRARY

31 Ballybricken
WATERFORD CITY, CO. WATERFORD
Ireland

TELEPHONE: (051) 309 975; FAX: (051) 850 031
E-mail: library@waterfordcity.ie
Website: www.waterfordcorp.ie

HOURS

Tu,Th,Sat, 10:00am–5:30pm; W,F, 1:30–8:00pm

ACCESS AND SERVICES

Visitors welcome. Disabled access facilities. Borrowing privileges available only if membership is taken out. Fee for photocopying services. Note: work has commenced on the renovation and extension of the Central Library in Lady Lane. At present, City Library services are operating from the temporary library premises in Ballybricken.

CONTACT

K. Moran, Librarian; e-mail: kmoran@waterfordcity.ie

DESCRIPTION

This is the main city library, with one branch library, operated by Waterford Corporation. Waterford County Council operates six branch libraries elsewhere in the county. *See* WATERFORD COUNTY LIBRARY HEADQUARTERS, Lismore.

HOLDINGS

In addition to its educational and recreational collection, the library has a solid local history and genealogical collection that includes most of the standard reference sources, such as Waterford newspapers with indices to a certain point, Griffith's Valuation in hard copy and on microfilm, Ordnance Survey maps for Kilkenny and Waterford City and County, the 1901 and 1911 Censuses, city maps and Infirmary Records.

LOCATION

Town centre.

# COUNTY WESTMEATH

## ATHLONE PUBLIC LIBRARY

Father Mathew Hall
ATHLONE, CO. WESTMEATH
Ireland

TELEPHONE: (0902) 92166; FAX: (0902) 96900
E-mail: gobrien@westmeathcoco.ie
Website: No direct website; several links, including www.athlone.ie/genealogy

HOURS

M,W, 10:00am–1:00pm, 2:00–5:30pm; Tu,Th, 10:00am–8:00pm; F, 10:00am–1:00pm, 2:00–5:00pm; Sat, 10:00am–1:30pm

ACCESS AND SERVICES

Visitors welcome. Membership required for borrowing privileges. No disabled access facilities. Nine public computer terminals available with Internet access.

CONTACT

Gearoid O'Brien, Executive Librarian

DESCRIPTION

Municipal library with a strong local history and genealogy collection.

HOLDINGS

In addition to the usual educational and recreational collections of a public library, Athlone Public Library houses a large number of relevant genealogical sources and will help with advice and information where possible.

LOCATION

Opposite Athlone Castle.

## DÚN NA SÍ HERITAGE CENTRE

Knockdomney
MOATE, CO. WESTMEATH
Ireland

TELEPHONE: (0902) 81183; FAX: (0902) 81661
E-mail: dunnasimoate@eircom.net
Website: www.irishroots.net/Wstmeath.htm

HOURS

M–Th, 10:00am–4:00pm; F, 10:00am–3:00pm

ACCESS AND SERVICES

Dún na Sí Heritage Centre offers a fee-based partial genealogical service to enquirers and has access to church, civil, land and Census returns for Co. Westmeath. Enquirers may expect a delay of up to two months before receiving a reply from the centre. There is an assessment fee of 75 euro. An application form is available on the website.

CONTACT

Caroline Ganley

DESCRIPTION

Dún na Sí Heritage Centre is the Irish Family History Foundation's designated research centre for Co. Westmeath. The IFHF is the coordinating body for a network of government-approved genealogical research centres in the Republic of Ireland and in Northern Ireland that have computerized tens of millions of Irish ancestral records of different types. Chief surnames in Co. Westmeath include: (Mc)Geoghegan, O'Growney, Brennan, O'Coffey, O'Mulleady, O'Malone, O'Daly, McAuley, McCormack. Main towns and villages include: Mullingar, Athlone, Castlepollard, Moate, and Kilbeggan.

HOLDINGS

The centre has access to approximately 750,000 records. Main records include the following: Roman Catholic records for Co. Westmeath start in 1737; earliest Church of Ireland records date from 1710 (some available); earliest Presbyterian records date from 1800 (some available). Other sources include: Griffith's Valuation; Pigott's Directory; Slater's Directory; Estate Lists; Voters' Lists; and the 1911 Census.

LOCATION

On the Mount Temple Road, 0.6 miles from the Gap House pub.

## WESTMEATH COUNTY LIBRARY HEADQUARTERS – LOCAL STUDIES COLLECTION

Dublin Road
MULLINGAR, CO. WESTMEATH
Ireland

TELEPHONE: (044) 40781/2/3; FAX: (044) 41322
E-mail: mfarrell@westmeathcoco.ie
Website: www.iol.ie/~libcounc/westmeath.htm

HOURS

M–F, 10:00am–1:00pm, 2:00–5:00pm

ACCESS AND SERVICES

Visitors welcome. Reference only. Fees for photocopying.

CONTACT

Mary Farrell, County Librarian

DESCRIPTION

The Local Studies Collection is one of the strongest of its kind in Ireland, in terms of both the breadth and the depth of its holdings. It is part of the Co. Westmeath library system, and is located in Library Headquarters, Mullingar.

HOLDINGS

The Local Studies Collection contains a wealth of books, maps, journals, newspapers, photographs, and ephemera relating to every aspect of life in Co. Westmeath, past and present. All books in the collection have a connection to Westmeath, in terms of authorship or subject matter. Authors represented in the library collections include: John Broderick, Leo Daly, Alice Dease, J.P. Donleavy, Desmond Egan, Lawrence Ginnell, Josephine Hart, Marian Keaney, Thomas Pakenham, Brinsley MacNamara, T.P. O'Connor, Padraic O'Farrell, A.J. Stanley; Michael Walsh, Fr Paul Walsh, Oliver Goldsmith, and Christopher Nolan. The collection also includes directories, almanacs, topographical dictionaries, parish histories, GAA histories, and unpublished works such as thesis and project material. There are some 3,500 items in this collection.

The Irish Collection is also housed at Library Headquarters and comprises 12,000 volumes on all aspects of Irish society. The library houses a number of special collections, from local newspapers to author collections. Newspaper holdings include: *Westmeath Journal*, 1813, 1823–34; *Midland Chronicle and Westmeath Independent*, 1827; *Athlone Independent*, 1833–6; *Athlone Sentinel*, 1834–61; *Westmeath Guardian*, 1835–96; *Athlone Conservative Advocate*, 1837; *Athlone Mirror*, 1841–2; *Westmeath Herald*, 1859–61; *Westmeath Independent*, 1860–82; *Westmeath Examiner*, 1882–1920, 1989–95; *Athlone Times*, 1889–1902; and *Midland Reporter and Westmeath Nationalist*, 1891–1939. The Photographic Collection contains some 2,500 prints of Westmeath including copies of the Lawrence Collection, 1870–1914. Maps include: Petty Maps for Co. Westmeath; Revised Ordnance Survey maps (1837) and their accompanying letters and Name Books, compiled under the direction of John O'Donovan; Geological Survey of Ireland, Westmeath (1860, one-inch; 1913, six-inch); Mullingar (1911, revised 1953, scale 1:2,500); Irish Historical Town Atlas No. 5, Mullingar (RIA); and Irish Historical Town Atlas No. 6, Athlone (RIA).
Local government records include the following. Grand Jury Presentment Books outlining the construction of roads in the county are available for the period 1802–87; Board of Guardian Minute Books, which detail the operation of the Poor Law System in the 19th and early 20th centuries for Athlone (1849–1920) and Mullingar (1857–1921); Rural District Council Minute Books for Athlone (1899–1925), Ballymore (1900–25), Delvin (1919–23), Kilbeggan (1914–17), and Mullingar (1899–1925); Valuation Lists (1878–1972); Board of Health and

Public Assistance Minute Books (1922–42); Westmeath County Council Minute Books (1899–1986); and Mullingar Commissioners' Books (1923–57).

Other records of special genealogical interest include: Census records for the 19th century in addition to Pender's Census 1659; 1901 and 1911 Census manuscript forms that provide detailed information on each resident of the county are available on microfilm. Gravestone inscriptions are available for the following parishes: Athlone Abbey Graveyard; Mount Temple Churchyard; Templecross Cemetery, Tisternagh Ballynacargy; All Saints, Mullingar; Lynn Church, Mullingar; Kilbixby Graveyard, Ballinacargy; Quaker Graveyard, Moate; St Mary's Church of Ireland, Moate, Kilcleigh and Killomenaghan.

The Kirby Collection contains approximately 250 different editions of *The Vicar of Wakefield* by Oliver Goldsmith (1728–74), a native of Westmeath. All the editions are illustrated and represent the work of the main Irish, British and continental illustrators of the day. The collection contains a number of fine bindings. The Howard Bury Collection, on permanent loan to the library, ranges from personal accounts of the diaries and tours at the beginning of the 19th century to details of local politics and electioneering in the mid-19th century. It also includes prisoner-of-war diaries and accounts of the geographical and mountaineering expeditions of Col. Howard Bury, and papers relating to the Belvedere Estate. The collection is named after Col. Howard Bury, the former owner of Belvedere House. The Burgess Collection was assembled by Dr John B. Burgess (1885–1960) of Athlone. It contains: Athlone directories; wills and deeds; registers of Kiltoom Parish Church, St Mary's Parish Church and several other churches in the Athlone area; Athlone newspapers; dictionary of Athlone biography; and vestry minutes of the Franciscan Abbey, Athlone. The John Broderick Collection contains an extensive collection of books, reviews, typescripts, etc. by John Broderick (1927–89), the Athlone-born novelist and critic. Private papers include the following: the Fr Paul Walsh Papers containing notes and unpublished material relating to this distinguished historian and scholar, born at Ballinea, Mullingar; the Laurence Ginnell Papers containing a selection of papers relating to this North Westmeath MP who was born in Delvin, Co. Westmeath.

LOCATION

Dublin Road, Mullingar.

# COUNTY WEXFORD

## WEXFORD COUNTY LIBRARY – LIBRARY MANAGEMENT SERVICES

Kent Building
ARDCAVAN, CO. WEXFORD
Ireland

TELEPHONE: (053) 24922; FAX: (053) 21097
E-mail: libraryhq@wexfordcoco.ie
Website: www.wexford.ie/library

HOURS

Vary from library to library. See website.

ACCESS AND SERVICES

Visitors welcome, but advance notice essential and preferably in writing for special services. Disabled access facilities. A fee is charged for photocopying, microfilm prints and fax services.

CONTACT

Librarian

DESCRIPTION

This is the headquarters library for Co. Wexford, which operates branch libraries in Bunclody, Enniscorthy, Gorey, New Ross, and Wexford Town.

HOLDINGS

In addition to its general educational and recreational collection of more than 200,000 volumes, the library system maintains special collections in local and Irish history, genealogy, local authors, local prints and photographs, archives, local newspapers (19th century), a map collection, and a 1798 collection. For the bicentennial of the 1798 rebellion, the Library Service compiled a brochure entitled *Mightier than the Sword*, which lists various sources held by the libraries documenting the history and culture of Wexford. These resources include all the standard genealogical reference sources.

LOCATION

Town centre.

## CO. WEXFORD HERITAGE AND GENEALOGY CENTRE

Yola Farmstead
TAGOAT, CO. WEXFORD
Ireland

TELEPHONE: (053) 32611; FAX: (053) 32612
E-mail: wexgen@iol.ie
Website: www.geocities.com/wexgen

HOURS

M–F, 9:00am–4:30pm

ACCESS AND SERVICES

Co. Wexford Heritage and Genealogy Centre currently offers a fee-based, partial genealogical service to those interested in tracing their roots in Co. Wexford. Service to enquirers and the indexation of genealogical records continues. There is a 75 euro initial search fee. An application form is available on the website. The centre is based at the Yola Farmstead, a folk and theme park. It documents the history of the Yola people, descendants of the first Norman settlers in south-east Ireland. These settlers intermarried with the native Irish and developed their own unique farming methods, customs, style of dress, hairstyle, and language. In addition to providing enquirers with information on their Wexford ancestors, the centre retails heraldic plaques, coasters, and crystal items.

CONTACT

Pat Stafford

DESCRIPTION

Co. Wexford Heritage and Genealogy Centre is the Irish Family History Foundation's designated research centre for Co. Wexford. The IFHF is the coordinating body for a network of government-approved genealogical research centres in the Republic of Ireland and in Northern Ireland that have computerized tens of millions of Irish ancestral records of different types. Common surnames in Co. Wexford include: Murphy, Sinnott, Doyle, Furlong, Walsh, Rossiter, Scallan, O'Brien, Brown, Stafford, Devereux, and Kavanagh. Main towns include: Wexford, Enniscorthy, Gorey, and New Ross.

HOLDINGS

Records include: Roman Catholic Records for Co. Wexford starting in 1671, and Church of Ireland records dating from 1779. Also computerized are: Cantwell's Tombstone Inscriptions (partial); Royal Irish Constabulary records; Griffith's Valuation (*c.*1853); Bassett's Directory (1885); Thom's Directory; Pigott's Directory; and the complete set of *Hore's History of Wexford.*

LOCATION

Yola Farmstead, a folk and theme park located 2.5 miles south of Rosslare on the R736.

## WEXFORD TOWN LIBRARY

*See* WEXFORD COUNTY LIBRARY – LIBRARY MANAGEMENT SERVICES, Ardcavan

# COUNTY WICKLOW

## WICKLOW COUNTY ARCHIVES

*See* WICKLOW COUNTY LIBRARY – LOCAL HISTORY COLLECTION AND ARCHIVES, Bray

## WICKLOW COUNTY LIBRARY – LOCAL HISTORY COLLECTION AND ARCHIVES

Wicklow County Library Headquarters
Boghall Road
BRAY, CO. WICKLOW

TELEPHONE: (01) 286 6566; FAX: (01) 286 5811
E-mail: wcclhq@eircom.net; library@wicklowcoco.ie
Website: www.iol.ie/~libcounc/wicklowsc.htm

HOURS

Local History Collection and Archives by appointment

ACCESS AND SERVICES

Visitors welcome. Membership required for borrowing privileges.

CONTACT

Brendan Martin, County Librarian

DESCRIPTION

The Local History Collection is housed in the Wicklow County Library Headquarters in Bray. The County Library operates branch libraries in Arklow (Station Road, tel. (0402) 39977); Baltinglass (The Courthouse, tel. (0508) 82300); Blessington (Baltinglass Road, tel. (045) 897 1700); Carnew (tel. (055) 26088); Dunlavin (Market House, tel. (045) 401 111); Enniskerry (tel. (01) 286 4339); Greystones (Church Road, tel. (01) 287 3548); Rathdrum (10 Gilbert's Row, tel. (0404) 43232); Tinahely (The Court House, tel. (0402) 38080); and Wicklow (Killmantin Hill, tel. (0404) 67025).

HOLDINGS

The Local History Collection includes books, journals and files on topics pertaining to Co. Wicklow, its people and places. There are several special collections, most notably the J.M. Synge Collection, the Charles Stewart Parnell Collection, and the 1798 Collection. Newspapers on microfilm include: *Wicklow Newsletter*, 1858–99 (incomplete); *Arklow Reporter*, Aug.–Dec. 1890 (incomplete), 1891, and Jan.–June 1893; *Wicklow Star* Oct. 1895–Feb. 1900. Local History also houses the archives for Wicklow County. Important records include: Wicklow Borough and Town Commission Minutes 1663–1888; Grand Jury Presentment Books (1819–98); Public Health Committee and Electric Light Committee, late 1880s–1930s; Poor Law Election return of votes cast 1886;

Rural District Council Minute Books (1899–1925); Register of Licences Issued (Motor Car Act) from 1904; Rate Books from 1924 (Wicklow County Council); correspondence relating to the Council, the Harbour & Esplanade Committee, and the General Purpose Committee; Sanatorium Benefit Register, *c.*1930; Proceedings of the Township Commissioner's Court (19th century); legal material 1880s; miscellaneous hospital documents from the 1930s; motor tax files from the 1920s; labourer's cottage rentals from the 1920s; County Council Correspondence from 1899; valuation lists from late 19th century; Agenda Books from the 1890s; Minute Books & Committee Minute Books of Bray Urban District Council from 1857; Poor Law Minute Books for Rathdrum Union & Shillelagh Poor Law Unions; Rate Books from 1860 (Bray UDC); Indoor Registers for Rathdrum Union (1842–1921); press letter books (1867–1917); Indoor Register for Shillelagh Poor Law Union (1842–1910); Workmen's Account Books (1868–1960s); Manuscript Assizes Payments Books (1856–93); Collector's Rate Books from 1876 (Bray UDC); and the Rathdrum Poor Law Union Burial Board Minute Book 1875.

LOCATION

Town centre. Bray is easily reached from Dublin city centre using the DART.

## THE WICKLOW FAMILY HISTORY CENTRE

Wicklow's Historic Gaol
WICKLOW TOWN, CO. WICKLOW
Ireland

TELEPHONE: (0404) 20126; FAX: (0404) 61612
E-mail: whf@eircom.net
Website: www.wicklow.ie

HOURS

M–F, 10:00am–1:00pm, 2:00–5:00pm

ACCESS AND SERVICES

The centre offers a fee-based partial genealogical research service to persons interested in tracing their roots in Co. Wicklow. There is an initial search fee of 95 euro. A three- to four-month delay in reporting on the initial search should be anticipated. An application form can be found on the website. Services offered include: assessment (stage 1), family history report (stage 2), mini-reports, single record search, and location search and certificate. The initial search fee covers the assessment. A description of each of these services can be found on the website. The cost of the family history report, an attractively bound, comprehensive and customized report, is 444 euro.

CONTACT

Joan Kavanagh, Manager

DESCRIPTION

The Wicklow Family History Centre is a genealogy research service established in 1987 by Wicklow County Council.

HOLDINGS

Records computerized to date include Roman Catholic and Church of Ireland parish records, baptisms and marriages in Presbyterian churches and baptisms within the circuit of Methodist churches in the county. In all, the centre holds over 275,000 baptismal, 50,600 marriage, and 40,000 burial records. Roman Catholic records do not normally include burial records. The earliest parish records for Co. Wicklow are Church of Ireland records, dating from the 17th century. The records for Roman Catholic parishes as a rule do not start until the early 19th century, although Wicklow Town records commence in 1747 – a distinction shared by only a few parishes in all of Ireland. Other sources held include: Tithe Applotment Books; Griffith's Valuation printed reports and the accompanying maps; tombstone inscriptions; Census returns of 1901; Ordnance Survey townland maps; parish maps, placename histories; Hearth Money Rolls of 1669; Religious Census of 1766; Poll Book 1745–59; Corn Growers, Carriers & Traders List, 1788–90; material relating to the 1798 rebellion; Wicklow Gaol records; convict records; commercial directories; electoral registers; school lists; and lists of landowners.

LOCATION

Town centre.

## APPENDIX 1

# TRACING YOUR COUNTY KILDARE ANCESTORS

*Karel Kiely*

For those who wish to do their own family history research, sources are available in the following places:

- National Library of Ireland, Kildare Street, Dublin 2
- National Archives, Bishop Street, Dublin 8
- General Register Office, Joyce House, Lombard Street East, Dublin 2
- Kildare County Library Local Studies Department, Newbridge, Co. Kildare.
- Local parishes.

## NATIONAL LIBRARY

### PARISH REGISTERS

For most family history researchers, parish registers provide the earliest direct source of family information. Unlike most early records, parish registers provide evidence of direct links between one generation and the next (via baptismal registers) and one family and another (via marriage registers). Because of their importance for family history research, in the 1950s and 1960s the National Library of Ireland carried out a programme of microfilming all the Catholic parish registers available for filming at that time. As a result, the National Library holds microfilm copies of the registers of most Catholic parishes in Ireland up to 1880 (including the counties of Northern Ireland).

The registers are handwritten and include records of baptisms and marriages, but only rarely include records of deaths. The start dates of the registers can vary from the 1740s/1750s in some city parishes in Dublin, Galway, Waterford, Cork, and Limerick to the 1780s/1790s in counties such as Kildare, Wexford, Waterford, and Kilkenny. The year 1880 was taken as the cut-off for the microfilming of parish registers, as, by that year, civil registration was well under way (it began in 1864). Post-1880 genealogical information should be available from the records in the General Register Office.

The *List of Parish Registers on Microfilm* includes a list of parishes (by diocese), the covering dates of the registers in each parish, and the National Library call number of each film. This list is available from the History and Family Research Centre Local Studies Department and Kildare Heritage & Genealogy Co.

### ACCESS TO THE MICROFILMS OF THE REGISTERS IN THE NATIONAL LIBRARY

Microfilms of registers for the following dioceses are freely available for consultation (counties or parts thereof in each diocese are given in parentheses):

- **Dublin** (Dublin, Wicklow, Carlow, Kildare, Laois, Wexford)
- **Kildare and Leighlin** (Kildare, Offaly, Laois, Kilkenny, Carlow, Wicklow, Wexford).

The quality of the information may vary from parish to parish. In general, baptismal registers contain: date of baptism; child's name; father's name; mother's name and maiden name; names of godparents (place of residence is often included). Marriage registers contain the names of the bride and groom and their witnesses. In some cases place of residence is also recorded.

Church of Ireland records are held in a variety of locations including the National Archives, the Representative Church Body Library and local parishes. Please consult 'A Table of Church of Ireland Parish Records', available from the local studies department of Kildare County Library to establish where records are held.

## NATIONAL ARCHIVES

The National Archives holds microfilm copies of some Church of Ireland Parish Registers; Tithe Applotment books; Griffith's Valuation; 1901 and 1911 Census; Wills and Testamentary records.

## GENERAL REGISTER OFFICE

Civil registration commenced in 1864. Births, deaths and marriages for Co. Kildare are available from that date.

## HISTORY AND FAMILY RESEARCH CENTRE – LOCAL STUDIES DEPARTMENT

The following can be inspected (by appointment with the librarian only):

- Alphabetical Index to Townlands of Co. Kildare
- 1641 Book of Survey & Distribution
- 1654 Civil Survey
- 1659 Pender's Census
- Hearth Money Rolls, 1662
- Tithe Applotment Books (1820s–1830s)
- Griffith's Valuation (1850s)
- Index to Surnames of Griffith's Valuation & Tithes
- 1840 Castledermot Census
- 1901 Census
- Graveyard Inscriptions
- Directories

## LOCAL PARISHES

Names and addresses of parish priests/rectors are given in the Catholic Directory and the Church of Ireland Directory, available in Newbridge library.

APPENDIX 2

# TITHE AND VALUATION RECORDS *c.*1823

*Brian Trainor*

Farmers of most agricultural land in Ireland were liable to pay to the rector of the established Church of Ireland a tithe or tax of one tenth of the yearly produce of the land and stock. This tax was especially unpopular with Presbyterians and Roman Catholics. Agitation against the tax forced the Government to change the law and make the tithe charge a financial one (instead of crops etc.) and levied on the landlord rather than on the tenant. In order to determine the amount of money to be charged in lieu of tithe all agricultural land liable to tithe had to be surveyed and valued. This work was done by local surveyors and the detail given is variable; unfortunately there are no maps accompanying the survey showing the locations of farms. The surveys provide the names of lease-holding tenants in each townland and thus serve as a sort of a farm census for the whole country. The tithe surveys for parishes in Northern Ireland for the years 1823–38 are deposited in the Public Record Office of Northern Ireland (FIN/5A) and those for the Republic of Ireland are available in the National Archives, Dublin (OL4). In order to conserve the original documents only microfilm copies of these surveys are produced to the public.

The earliest full valuation of property in Ireland was carried out in the 1830s. This valuation was carried out in each townland and parish and the surveyor's manuscript field books of this 'townland valuation' for parishes in Northern Ireland are deposited in the Public Record Office of Northern Ireland (VAL/1B) and those for the Republic are in the National Archives (OL4). No detail is given of buildings unless these were valued at £3.00 or more and this lower limit was raised to £5.00 in 1838 thus excluding most rural houses. Most of Ulster was valued before the threshold was raised to £5.00. with the result that many buildings in the North around £2.00 valuation are included. In towns many houses were substantial enough to reach the valuation of £3.00 or £5.00 and in these cases detailed measurements of rooms and outbuildings are sometimes given as well as names of occupiers. For the town of Downpatrick the names of 330 occupiers are given in the field book for the parish of Down *c.*1838 (VAL/1B/378 and OL4.0459).

The National Archives, Dublin has another set of these valuation field books 1830s for most parishes in Northern Ireland except for Co Tyrone.

The first detailed valuation of all properties in Ireland began in the province of Leinster during the Great Famine in 1846, and the valuation was completed in Northern Ireland 1858–64. The manuscript field books of this valuation for Northern Ireland with annotated maps showing the precise location of holdings are held in PRONI (VAL/2B) and also the annual revisions recording changes in occupancy, consolidation of farms and the upheavals resulting from the Land Acts from the 1880s up to *c.*1950 (VAL/12B). Similar records exist for all parishes in the Republic of Ireland but these are held in the Valuation Office, Middle Abbey Street, Dublin.

Sir Richard Griffith, the great Commissioner of Valuation who was responsible for these massive surveys by central government arranged that a summary version of the valuation of 1846–64 for the whole country be made available in print. Some 200 volumes were published as official papers, one for each Poor Law Union or part. This printed valuation popularly known as 'Griffith's Valuation' appeared in the period 1847–1865. It is doubtful if any country in the world has such ready access in printed form to records detailing the value and acreage of farms and buildings, usually with the names of landlords and the exact locations marked on official maps held in the Public Record Office of Northern Ireland and in the Valuation Office, Dublin. A microfiche copy of the printed version of the valuation is available in the National Archives, Dublin.

The following tables provide the exact references for each parish for the tithe and valuation records that are held in PRONI and the National Archives, Dublin. This will be of particular use to family and local historians researching in these institutions.

In the National Archives cataloguing work is proceeding with their valuation records of the 1830s. The present staff inherited difficulties in dealing with large counties such as Cork and Tipperary, since these had been subdivided into two or three sections for the cataloguing of their holdings of Tithe Applotment books 1823–1838. For County Cork over twenty parishes are divided between N[orth], S[outh] and E[east], and since parishes can still be further divided between two or three baronies it will be appreciated that no exact positioning of particular records (census searches, house books, etc.) can be readily achieved. Tom Quinlan, Senior Archivist in the National Archives, has been my indispensable support as I toiled with catalogues. He saved me from many errors. I take responsibility for those that remain in this present text which can only be considered, in part, as a report on work in progress.

| PARISH/TOWN/ VILLAGE | TITHES 1823–38 FIN 5A/ | VALUATION 1830S VAL 1B/ FIELD BOOK (NA) OL4. | TENEMENT VALUATION c.1861–2 VAL 2B/1/ | VALUATION REVISIONS c.1860–c.1930 VAL 12B/ |
|---|---|---|---|---|
| Aghagallon | 3 | 165A-B, 0069 | 54 | 9/1A-E |
| Aghalee | 4 | 166, 0070 | 58B | 9/2 A-E |
| Ahoghill | 10 | 15D, 176, 179, 0001, | 64 A-C | 3/1 A-E, 3A-D, |
| | | 0059, 0080, 0082 | | 4A, 5A-J, |
| | | | | 9A-D, 14A-F, |
| | | | | 18A-E, 19A-D |
| Antrim | 13 | 16, | 5A-C, 51, | 1/1A- F, 2A-C, |
| | | 0083, | | 3A-C, 11A, 12A |
| | | 180 | 69 | 22A-E, 28A-E |
| Ardclinis | 15 | 147A-B, 0050 | 38 | 7/1A-E |
| Armoy | 21 | 130, 0032 | 23A-B | 2/1A-E |
| | | 141, 0044 | 37 | 4/1A-D |
| Ballinderry | 26 | 167, 0071 | 55A-B, 58B | 9/3A-C |
| Ballintoy | 27 | 131, | 24A-B | 2/2A-E, 6A-D, |
| | | 0033 | | 8/1A-E, 8A-E, |
| | | | | 9/3A-E, 9A-E, |
| | | | | 10A-F, 17A-E |
| Ballycastle | | 280 | 2B, 1/28C | 2/4A, 5A-C |
| (Ramoan) | | | | |
| Ballyclare | | | 7B | 5A-B, 6A-B |
| (B'linny & B'nure) | | | | |
| Ballyclug | 30 | 11, 0002 | 1 | 3/2A-E, 4A, 5A-V |
| Ballycor | 24 | 0007/8 | 6, 11 | 4A-E, 7/2A-D |
| Ballyeaston | 24 | | | |
| (B'cor & Rashee) | | | | |
| Ballylinny | 38 & 67 | 112, 0014 | 7A | 1/4A-E, 7A-F |
| Ballymartin | 39 & 67 | 113, 0015, 124, 0025 | 11 | 1/14A-F, 29A-F |
| Ballymoney | 40 | 142A-D | 35A-F | 4/3A-G, 5A-E, |
| | | 154 | 50A | 12A-E, 14A-F, |
| | | 0045 | | 23A-F, 24A-D |
| Ballymena | | | 66A-F | 3/5K-V |
| (Kirkinriola) | | | | |
| Ballynure | 44 | 114, 0016 | 11, 12 | 1/4A-E, 7/3A-E |
| Ballyrashane | 46 | 137, 0039 | 30A | 4/4 A, 5A-E, |
| | | 30/14A-D | 6/1A-C | |
| Ballyscullion | 47 | 181, 0084 | 72B | 3/4A, 6A-E |
| Ballyscullion | Nil | 182, 0089 | | 3/4A, 6A-E |
| Grange of | | | | |
| Ballywillin | 51 | 137, 0040 | 30A | 4/4A; 6/1A-C, |
| | | | | 2A-E |
| Belfast | 36 | see Shankill | 18, 21A-D | 43/ |
| Billy | 56 | 132, 0034 | 24B | 2/6A-D, 9A-E, |
| | | 138, 0041 | 25A-B | 10A-F, 4/5A-E, |
| | | | 31 | 6A-C, 7A-E, |
| | | | | 30/8A-D |
| Blaris | 57 | 168, 0072 | 56A-B | 8/9A-T, 10A-C, |
| | | | | 11A, 12A-E, |
| | | | 3 | 20/6A-G, 16A-E |
| Broughshane | | | 3C | 3/7A-E |
| (Racavan) | | | | |
| Bushmills | | | 26 | 4/6A-C; 30/8A-D |
| (Billy) | | | | |

| PARISH/TOWN/ VILLAGE | TITHES 1823–38 FIN 5A/ | VALUATION 1830S VAL 1B/ FIELD BOOK (NA) OL4. | TENEMENT VALUATION c.1861–2 VAL 2B/1/ | VALUATION REVISIONS c.1860–c.1930 VAL 12B/ |
|---|---|---|---|---|
| Camlin | 63 | 169, 0073 | 52 | 1/16A-F |
| Carncastle | 66 | 150, 0055 | 42 | 7/4A-E |
| Carnmoney | 67 | 115A-B, 0017 | 13A-B | 5/7A-G, 12A-K |
| Carrickfergus | 70 | 187, 0031 | 22A-E, | 7/5A-F, 6A-D, 7A-C |
| Connor | 83 | 12, 0003 | 2A-B, 8A | 1/13A-E, 3/4A, 18A-E |
| Craigs (Ahoghill) | 10 | 155 176 178 A-B | 45, 65A-B | 3/3A-D, 4A, 13A-E, 14A-F, 19A-D 20A-D |
| Cranfield | 85 | 183, 0085 | 70 | 1/15A-F |
| Crumlin (Camlin) | | | 51 | 1/16A-F |
| Culfeightrin | 87 | 133, 0035 | 27A-B | 2/8A-D, 11A-F, 15A-D, 16A-D |
| Derryaghy | 91B | 125, 0026 170, 0074 | 19A-B 57 | 8/2A-G, 5A-E |
| Derrykeighan | 93 | 134, 0042, 139A-B | 32 | 4/5A-E, 10A-E |
| Dervock (Derrykeighan) | | | 33 | 4/10A-E |
| Doagh, Grange of | 102 | 17A-B, 0009 | 7A | 1/4A-E |
| Doagh, Village | | 7B | | |
| Donegore | | 18, 0010 | 8A-B | 1/17A-E |
| Drumbeg | 117 | 126 | 20 | 8/15A-J, 20/3A-E |
| Drummaul (Randalstown) | 124 | 184, 0086 | 71A-D | 1/10B-E, 3/9A-D, 11A-D, 22A-F; 23A, 24A, 27A-E, 28A-E |
| Drumtullagh, Grange of | Nil | 25B | 2/9A-C | 2/9A-E |
| Dunaghy | 128 | 156, 0060 | 46A-B | 3/4A, 8A-D, 22A-D |
| Dundermot, Grange of | 130 | 157, 0062 | 46B | 3/4A, 12A-D |
| Duneane | 132 | 185, 0087 | 71D 72A-B | 3/4A, 25A-E 10A-E, 15A-F |
| Dunluce | 134 | 140 | 34A-B | 4/4A, 5A-E, 21A-C, 6/1A-C, 2A-E |
| Finvoy | 142 | 158A-C 0061 | 47A-B | 4/11A-E, 12A-E, 25A-E |
| Glenavy | 147* | 171, 0075 | 58A-B | 8/4A-D; 9/3A-E |
| Glenarm (Tickmacrevan) | | | 41B | 7/9A-H, 10A-E |
| Glenwhirry | Nil | 13, 0004 | 3A | 3/4A, 17A-D |
| Glynn | 149 | 116 | 14 | 7/11A-D |
| Gracehill (Ahoghill) | | | 64D | |
| Inispollan, Grange of | Nil | 0051 | 39 | 2/14A-E |
| Inver | 158 | 117, 0019 | 14 | 7/14A-G, 15B-M |
| Island Magee | 159 | 118, 0020 | 15 | 7/12A-G |
| Kilbride | 162 | 19, 0011 | 8B | 1/4A-E, 20A-F |

| PARISH/TOWN/ VILLAGE | TITHES 1823–38 FIN 5A/ | VALUATION 1830S VAL 1B/ FIELD BOOK (NA) OL4. | TENEMENT VALUATION c.1861–2 VAL 2B/1/ | VALUATION REVISIONS c.1860–c.1930 VAL 12B/ |
|---|---|---|---|---|
| Killagan | 172 | 144, 159, 0047 | 48 | 4/15A-F |
| Killdollagh | 169 | 0063, 0046 | | 30/14A-D |
| Killead | 174 | 164A-C<br>0068 | 53A-C | 1/8A-F, 9A-F,<br>19A-E, 26A-E |
| Killyglen, Grange of | 181 | 151, 0056 | 44A | 7/4A-E |
| Kilraghts | 188 | 145, 0048 | 36 | 4/18A-E |
| Kilroot | 190 | 119, 0021 | 16 | 7/18A-E |
| Kilwaughter | 192 | 152A-B, 0057 | 43 | 7/13A-F |
| Kirkinriola | 194 | 177, 66B-F,<br>0081 | 66A* | 3/4A, 5A-V,<br>14A-F, 19A-D |
| Lambeg | 196 | 127, 0028<br>172, 0076 | 59 | 8/7A-D, 9L<br>20/10A-F |
| Larne | 197 | 153, 0058 | 44A-C | 7/14A-G, 15A-M,<br>16A |
| Layd | 198 | 148A-D, 0053 | 40A-B, 19A-F | 2/7A-E, 14A-F, |
| Layd, Grange of | Nil | 0052 | 39 | 2/14A-D |
| Lisburn | (See Blaris) | | 61A-D | |
| Loughguile | 208 | 146A-D, 0049<br>160, 0064 | 37 & 48 | 4/1A-D, 2A-D,<br>8A-E, 9A-D,<br>15A-F |
| Magheragall | 217 | 174, 0077 | 55B<br>62A-B | 8/6A-F, 13A-E |
| Magheramesk | 221 | 175, 0078 | 62B | 8/14A-D |
| Mallusk Grange of | 259 | 0067 | | |
| Muckamore Grange of | Nil | 163 | 52 | 1/1A-F, 2A-C,<br>3A-C |
| Newtown Crommelin | 228 | 161, 0065 | 49, 21A | 3/22A-D |
| Nilteen Grange of | 110 | 9, 0012 | 17A-E | |
| Portglenone | 232 | 178A-B | 67A-C | 3/1A-E, 4A,<br>20A-D, 23A-E |
| Portrush (Ballywillin) | | | 30B | 4/22A-D |
| Racavan | 250 | 14A-B, 0005 | 3A-B | 3/4A, 7A-E, 24A-D |
| Raloo | 234 | 120, 0022 | 17A-B | 7/17A-E |
| Ramoan (Ballycastle) | 235 | 135, 0037 | 28A-B | 2/3A-G, 16A-D,<br>17A-E |
| Randalstown (Drummaul) | | | 71E | 23A, 24A |
| Rasharkin | 236 | 162, 0066 | 50A-B | 3/4A, 13A-E,<br>15A-D, 4/16A-F,<br>17A-E |
| Rashee | 24 | 111, 0013 | 10 | 1/25A-F |
| Rathlin Is | 238 | 136, 0038 | 29 | 17A-E, 18A-D |
| Shankill | 36<br>247 | 121A-B, 0023<br>128 A-B, 0028 | 18<br>21A-D | 5/3A-F, 4A-D,<br>5A-E, 6A-E, 8A-F |
| Shilvodan Grange of | 83 | 186, 0088 | 73 | 28A-E |

| PARISH/TOWN/ VILLAGE | TITHES 1823–38 FIN 5A/ | VALUATION 1830S VAL 1B/ FIELD BOOK (NA) OL4. | TENEMENT VALUATION c.1861–2 VAL 2B/1/ | VALUATION REVISIONS c.1860–c.1930 VAL 12B/ |
|---|---|---|---|---|
| Skerry | 250 | 15A-C, 0006 | 4A-C | 3/7A-E, 16A-D, 21A-D |
| Stranocum (Ballymoney) | | | 33 | |
| Templecorran | 257 | 122 | 16 | 7/18A-F |
| Templepatrick | 259 | 123A-B, 0024 129A-B, 0030 | 7B, 10, 11, 18, 21C | 1/14A-F, 29A-F |
| Tickmacrevan (Glenarm) | 263 | 149, 0054 | 41A, | 7/9A-H, 10A-E |
| Tullyrusk | 269 & 147 | | 173A-B | 63 8/16A-D |
| Whitehead | | | | 7/19A |

* Includes mill book

| PARISH/TOWN | TITHES 1823–38 FIN 5A/ | VALUATION 1830S VAL 1B/ FIELD BOOK (NA) OL4. | TENEMENT VALUATION c.1864 VAL 2B/2/ | VALUATION REVISIONS c.1860–c.1930 VAL 12B/ |
|---|---|---|---|---|
| Acton | | | 32D | |
| Armagh | 20 | 21A & B, 224 234, 0090 0110 | 1A-G, 22 | 10/4A-H, 5A-C, 6A-C, 7A-C, 8A-C, 9A-E, 25A-E |
| Ballymore | 41 | 214, 248 0120 | 32A-C, 32E | 11/1A-C, 11/5A-G, 15/23A-D, 15/24A-D |
| Ballymyre | 42 | 239, 0102 | 13 | 15/2A-D |
| Blackwatertown (Clonfeacle) | | 249 | 2B | |
| Camlough (Killevy) | | 178 | | |
| Charlemont (Loughgall) | | 249 | 2B | |
| Clonfeacle | 79 | 22, 225A & B 234, 0111 | 2A, 23 | 10/12A-F, 23A-E, 30A-E, 38A-D, |
| Creggan | 86 | 240A & B 0103 | 14A-G | 12/2A-E, 3A-4E, 5A-E, 6A-E, 7A-D, 13/1A-F |
| Crossmaglen (Creggan) | | | 14G | |
| Derrynoose | 95 | 23, 235, 248 0091, 0131 | 3A-C, 40 | 10/11A-E, 17A-E, 19A-D, 26A-C, 28A, 39A-E |
| Drumcree | 119 | 226A & B, 234, 0112 | 24A-H | 14/2A-C, 6A-C, 12A-13B, 14A |
| Eglish | 136 | 24, 236, 248 0092, 0132 | 4, 41 | 10/10A-D, 22A-E |
| Forkill | 143 | 215, 247, 248 0121, 0126 | 32E, 35A-C | 12/5A-C,15/13A-B, 18A-D, 24A-C |
| Grange | 150 | 25, 227, 234 0093, 0113 | 5, 25 | 10/23A-E, 25A-E, 31A-E, 33A-E |
| Jonesborough | 160 | 243, 248, 0127 | 36 | 15/15A-C |
| Keady | 161 | 26A-D, 237 248-9, 0094 0133 | 6A-D, 3B-C, 42 | 10/3A-B, 17A-E, 19A-D, 26A-C, 27A-C, 28A-B |
| Kilclooney | 225 | 210A & B 216, 248, 249 0098, 0122 | 9A-C | 10/13A-D, 29A-D, 34A-E |
| Kildarton | 20 etc | | | 10/24A-D, 25A-E, 29A-C |
| Killevy | 178 | 217, 244A & B 248, 0123 0128 | 32E, 34C, 37A-J | 12B, 15/1A-D, 1F, 1H, 3A-E, 6A-J, 15A-C, 17A-C, 18A-D, 22A-24C |
| Killylea (Tynan) | | 249 | | |
| Killyman | 183 | 228, 234, 0114 | 27 | 10/30A-C |
| Kilmore | 186 | 218, 248 229A & B 0115, 0124 | 26A-D, 33 | 10/25A-E, 11/4A-F, 31A-E, 33A-E, 37A-F |

| PARISH/TOWN | TITHES 1823–38 FIN 5A/ | VALUATION 1830S VAL 1B/ FIELD BOOK (NA) OL4. | TENEMENT VALUATION c.1864 VAL 2B/2/ | VALUATION REVISIONS c.1860–c.1930 VAL 12B/ |
|---|---|---|---|---|
| Lisnadill | 202 | 27, 211, 241 0095, 0099 0104 | 8A, 10A-B 12B, 15 | 10/3A-D, 9A-E, 11A-E, 29A-D, 32A-E |
| Loughgall | 206 | 28, 230, 234 249, 0096 | 7, 28A-C | 10/2A-E, 10/25A-E, 31A-E, 33A-E, 38A-D |
| Loughgilly | 207 | 212, 219 245A & B, 248 0100, 0125 | 11, 29, 34A-C, 38A-B | 10/34A-C, 11/3A-D, 15/3A-E,19A D, 23A-D, 24A-D |
| Lurgan (Shankill) | | | 20C-G | 14/9A-H |
| Magheralin | 219 | 220, 234, 0106 | 17 | 14/5A-C |
| Markethill (Mullaghbrack) | | | 12C | |
| Middletown (Tynan) | | | | 43D |
| Montiaghs | 223 | 221, 234, 0107 | 18 | 14/11A-C |
| Mountnorris (Loughgilly) | | | | 32D |
| Mullaghbrack | 225 | 213, 231, 234 0101, 0117 | 12A-B, 29 | 10/24A-D, 34A-E, 11/3A-E |
| Newry | 226 | 232, 234, 246A-E, 248 0118, 0130 | 39A-C | 10/33A-D, 15/1A-H, 22/16A-C 17A-C, 18A-D |
| Newtownhamilton | 229 | 242A & B 0105 | 16A-D | 12/1A-D, 5A-E, 6A-E, 8A-E |
| Poyntzpass (Ballymore) | | | | 32D |
| Portadown (Drumcree etc) | | | 24E-H | 14/13A-N |
| Richhill (Kilmore) | | | 26E | |
| Seagoe | 245 | 222, 234, 0108 | 19A-D | 14/3A-C, 4A-C, 7A-C |
| Shankill | 248 | 223A & B 234, 0109 | 20A-G | 14/5A-C, 9H |
| Tandragee (Ballymore) | | | 11 | 11/5A-G |
| Tartaraghan | 255 | 233A & B 234, 0119 | 21A-C | 10/2A-C, 30A-C, 14/15A-D |
| Tynan | 270 | 29A & B 238, 248 0097, 0134 | 8A, B 43A-D | 10/11A-E, 17A-E, 22A-E, 35A-E, 39A-E |

| PARISH/TOWN/ VILLAGE | TITHES 1823–38 FIN 5A/ | VALUATION 1830S VAL 1B/ FIELD BOOKS OL4. (NATIONAL ARCHIVES) | TENEMENT VALUATION c.1861–4 VAL 2B/3/ | VALUATION REVISIONS c.1861–c.1930 VAL 12B/ |
|---|---|---|---|---|
| Aghaderg | 1 | 337, 351, 0419 | 42, 55B-D | 16/14A-D, 18A-E, 22A-D |
| Annaclone | 11 | 352, 0438, 0439 | 56 | 16/1A-F |
| Annahilt | 12 | 338A & B, 383, 0445 | 35 | 20/1A-E |
| Ardglass | 16 | 368, 311B, 0451 | 70A-B | 18/1A-F, 27A |
| Ardkeen | 17 | 35, 0388 | 7A-B, 23, 27 | 28/2A-F, 23/19A-F |
| Ardquin | 18 | 36, 0389 | 8 | 18/2A-F |
| Ballee | 23 | 369, 311B, 0452 | 71 | 18/1A-F, 22A-E |
| Ballyculter | 32 | 370, 311B, 0453 | 72 | 18/11A-E, 22A-E, 25A-F |
| Ballyhalbert (St Andrew's) | 33 | 0312, 0395 | 7B, 9 | 23/1A-4F, 19A-F |
| Ballykinler | 35 | 376A & B, 311B | 76 | 18/5A-F |
| Ballynahinch | | | 28B | |
| Ballyphilip Slanes & Witter (Portaferry) | 45 & 49 | 37, 0390 | 10 | 18/20A-F, 23/27A-D |
| Ballytrustan | 45 & 49 | 38, 0391 | 11 | 18/20A-D, 23/27A-D |
| Ballywalter | 50 | 39, 0392 | 9 | 23/6A-F |
| Banbridge (Seapatrick) | | | 64B, C | 16/7A-C, 8B-D |
| Bangor | 54 | 31, 315, 0384, 0398 | 1A-C, 7B | 23/7A-K, 8A |
| Blaris | 57 | 324, 339 0406, 0420, | 24A, 43 | 9A-S, 20/6A-D, 16A-G |
| Bright | 62 | 377, 311B, 0458 | 77 | 18/15A-E |
| Castleboy | exempt | 310, 0393 | 12 | 18/2A-F |
| Castlewellan (Kilmegan) | | | 63B | 18/4G |
| Clonallan | 75 | 353, 0440 | 57A-C, 60A | 22/5A-D, 23A-G, 25A-C |
| Clonduff | 77 | 354, 0432 | 49A-C | 22/6A-D, 10A-D, 12A-D, 20A-B, 20D, 20F-H |
| Clough (Loughinisland) | | | 66D | 18/5A-E |
| Comber | 82 | 316A-C, 0407 | 2, 16A & B 25A | 18/5A-E, 11A-F, 20A-E, 20/11A E, 23/3A-F |
| Crossgar (Kilmore) | | | 28B | 16/9A-E, 18/6A-F, 27A |
| Donaghadee | 104 | 32, 0385 | 3A-C | 23/10A-C, 13A-E 15A-B |
| Donaghcloney | 105 | 340, 0423 | 44A-B 46C | 21/4A-F, 9A-F |
| Donaghmore | 108 | 355, 0441 | 58A-B | 22/9A-E, 11A-E |
| Down | 111 | 378, 0459 | 78A-D | 18/7A-K, 12A-E, 26A-E |
| Dromara & Magherahamlet | 112 | 341, 356, 384, 0421, 0433, 0446 | 36, 37, 50A-B | 16/2A-E, 9A-E, 20/9A-D |
| Dromore | 113 | 342, 0422 | 38A-F | 16/10A-F, 21A-E, 23A-E, 20/2A-D |

| PARISH/TOWN/ VILLAGE | TITHES 1823–38 FIN 5A/ | VALUATION 1830S VAL 1B/ FIELD BOOKS OL4. (NATIONAL ARCHIVES) | TENEMENT VALUATION c.1861–4 VAL 2B/3/ | VALUATION REVISIONS c.1861–c.1930 VAL 12B/ |
|---|---|---|---|---|
| Drumballyroney | 116 | 357A & B | 59A-C | 16/4A-E, 24A-E, 22/20A-B, 20D, 20F-H |
| Drumbeg | 117 | 326, 0408 | 25B-C | 20/3A-E, 10B-E |
| Drumbo | 118 | 327, 0409 | 25A-C | 20/3A-E, 7A-F, 11A-E |
| Drumgath | 120 | 358 & A B | 59C 20C, | 22/10A-D, 20A, 20E-H |
| Drumgooland | 122 | 359, 0434 | 51A-D | 16/5A-F, 15A-D, 20A-E |
| Dundonald | 131 | 317, 0399 | 17 | 17/8A-G, 23/5A-F |
| Dundrum (Kilmegan) | | | 79 | 18/9A-E, 27A |
| Dunsfort | 135 | 371, 311B, 0454, 2360 | 73 | 18/11A-11E |
| Garvaghy | 146 | 343, 360 | 39, 52 | 16/3A-E, 12A-E |
| Gilford (Tullylish) | | 0424, 0435 | 48E-F | 16/13A-B |
| Greyabbey | 151 | 33, 0386 | 4 | 23/16A-F, 21A-E |
| Groomsport | | | 5 | |
| Hillsborough | 152 | 344A & B | 45A-C | 20/5A-D, 14A-E |
| Holywood | exempt | 318 | 18A-D | 10A-G, 11A-E, 17/2A-J, 10A-D, 43L/1-2, 43N/1-2 |
| Inch | 154 | 372, 0456 | 74 | 18/13A-D |
| Inishargy | 155 | 311A & B, 0394 | 13 | 23/4A-F, 19A-F |
| Kilbroney | 163 | 361, 0442 | 61A-B, 65A | 19/15A-E, 21A-F |
| Kilclief | 164 | 373, 379, 311B,0460 | 70A | 18/25A-F |
| Kilcoo | 166 | 362, 0436 | 53A-B, 62 | 19/7A-F, 11A-E |
| Kilkeel | 171 | 390A & B 0464 | 81A-H | 19/4A-E, 13A-E, 14A-J, 18A-E, 19A-F |
| Killaney | Nil | 328, 0410 | 26 | 20/15A-D |
| Killinchy | 179 | 319, 329, 335 0400, 0411, 0417 | 19, 23, 27, 33 | 18/14A-E, 19A-E 23/3A-F, 18A-E, 28A-E |
| Killyleagh | 182 | 331, 336 | 34A-C | 18/6A-F, 16A-F |
| Killough | | 0412, 0418 | 80B | 18/15A-E, 27A |
| Kilmegan | 184 | 363A & B 380, 311B 385,0447, 0461 | 63A, 66B-C 79 | 18/4A-G, 9A-E, 24A-E |
| Kilmood | 185 | 320, 0401 | 20 | 23/18A-E |
| Kilmore | 187 | 330, 386 0413, 0448 | 28A, 66A 68 | 18/6A-F, 18A-E, 19A-E, 23A-D |
| Kircubbin (Inishargy) | | | 5 | |
| Knockbreda | 195 | 321, 332 0402, 0414 | 18D, 21, 29 | 17/3A-B, 6A-H 20/7A-D |
| Knockbreda (Belfast Co. Borough) | | | 43A/5-10, 15-23, 43K/1 | 43A/28-34, 38-39 |
| Knockbreda (Ballymacarrett ED) | | | 43A/28-34, 38-39 | 43A/28-34, 38-39 |
| Lambeg | 196 | 333, 0415 | 30 | 20/10A-F |

| PARISH/TOWN/ VILLAGE | TITHES 1823–38 FIN 5A/ | VALUATION 1830S VAL 1B/ FIELD BOOKS OL4. (NATIONAL ARCHIVES) | TENEMENT VALUATION c.1861–4 VAL 2B/3/ | VALUATION REVISIONS c.1861–c.1930 VAL 12B/ |
|---|---|---|---|---|
| Lisburn (Blaris) | | | 24B | |
| Loughbrickland (Aghaderg) | | | 55A | |
| Loughinisland | 209 | 387, 0449 | 66A-C | 18/5A-F, 23A-D, 24A-E |
| Maghera | 211 | 364, 0437 | 54 | 19/17A-F |
| Magheradrool | 215 | 388A & B 0450 | 67A-B 68 | 18/3A-G, 10A-E 20/13A-E |
| Magherahamlet | 112 | | 68 | 18/10A-E, 20/9A-D |
| Magheralin | 219 | 346, 0425 | 46A-C, 47C | 21/1A-E, 6A-F, 7A-E |
| Magherally | 220 | 345, 0426 | 40 | 16/19A-E |
| Moira | 222 | 347, 0427 | 47A-C | 21/7A-E |
| Newcastle (Kilmegan) | | | 53A | 19/20A-D |
| Newry | Nil | 365, 389 0465 | 69A-K | 16/3A-E, 22/7A-F, 14A-L, 16A-C, 17A-C, 19A-F |
| Newtownards | 227 | 34, 322 0387, 0403 | 6A-D, 22A-B | 23/21A-E, 22A-E, 23A-C, 24A-F, 25A-N |
| Newtownbreda (Knockbreda) | | | 31 | |
| Portaferry (See Ballyphilip) | | | 14 23/26A | 18/20A-F, 27A, |
| Rathfriland (Drumballyroney) | | | 60B-C | 22/21A-B, 22A-B |
| Rosstrevor (Kilbroney) | | | 61C | |
| Rathmullan | 239 | 374, 381, 311B, 0395 | 72, 80A | 18/11A-E, 15A-E, 26A-E |
| St Andrew's (Ballyhalbert) | 241 | 312, 0462 | | |
| Saintfield | 242 | 334 | 32A-C | 18/19A-E, 20/18A-E |
| Saul | 244 | 375, 311B, 0416, 0457 | 75 | 18/7A-K, 22A-E |
| Seaforde | | | 66D | |
| Seapatrick | 246 | 348A & B, 366, 0428/9 | 41, 64A 44A | 16/6A-H, 8A-D, 19A-E |
| Shankill | | 349, 0430 | 46A, 47B | 21/5A-D |
| Slanes | 45 | 313, 0396 | 15 | 23/27A-D |
| Strangford | | | 14 | |
| Tullylish | 266 | 350, 0431 | 44B, 48A-D | 16/25A-H, 21/4A-F, 8A-F |
| Tullynakill | 267 | 323, 0404/5 | 23 | 23/28A-E |
| Tyrella | 271 | 382, 311B, 0463 | 80A | 18/26A-E, 27A |
| Waringstown (Donaghcloney) | | | 44C | |
| Warrenpoint | 75 | 367, 0443/4 | 65A-B | 23A-G, 25A-C |
| Witter (Ballyphilip) | 45 | 314, 0397 | | |

| PARISH/TOWN/ VILLAGE | TITHES 1823–38 FIN 5A/ | VALUATION 1830S VAL 1B/ FIELD BOOKS OL4. (NATIONAL ARCHIVES) | TENEMENT VALUATION c.1861–2 VAL 2B/4/ | VALUATION REVISIONS c.1861–c.1930 VAL 12B/ |
|---|---|---|---|---|
| Aghalurcher | 6<br>also D998/ 22/1 | 428A-B,<br>0502-4 | 19A-E | 28/5A-D, 6A-D, 7A-E, 10A-E, 11 A-E, 19A-E, 20A-E, 21A-E, 22A-F, 23A-F, 24A-E |
| Aghavea | 8 | 429, 0505-7 | 20A-C | 28/6A-E, 11A-E, 13A-E, 19A-E, 22A-F |
| Belleek | 55 | 415A-B, 0490 | 10 | 24/1A-E, 2A-E, 7A-E |
| Boho | 60 | 41, 422, 0466<br>0496 | 1 & 15 | 24/6A-E, 26/1A-E, 22A-E, 37A-D |
| Cleenish | 72 | 42, 432,<br>430A & B,<br>432, 0467-9<br>0497, 0508-9<br>0511<br>430A-B | 1, 2A-D<br>7E<br>21 | 24/6A-E; 26/7A-E, 10A-E, 19A-D, 20A-E, 23A-E, 24A-F, 30A-F, 31A-E, 32A-E, 37A-E |
| Clones* | MIC 442/10 | 46, 0474 | 5A-D<br>6 | 25/1A-D, 2A-E 3A-E, 5A-E, 7A-E, 8A-D, 10A-E |
| Currin* | MIC 442/10 | 47A-D, 49<br>0475 | 6 | |
| Derrybrusk | 92 | 431, 433<br>0510, 0512 | 22 | 26/4A-E, 26A-E, 28/5A-E |
| Derryvullen | 96 | 419<br>0491<br>0498<br>434<br>0513 | 11A-B<br><br><br>21, 22, 23A-C | 26/2A-E, 3A-F, 5A-F, , 10A-E, 17A-K, 31A-E 27/9A-E, 11A-E, 13A-E, 15A-E, |
| Devenish | 101 | 424 A-D<br>0498 | 16A-D | 24/4A-E, 8A-E, 26/12A-F, 16A-E, 17A-K, 33A-E, 35A-E, 36A-E, 37A-E |
| Drumkeeran | 123 | 416 A-B<br>0492, 3819 | 12A-C | 27/3A-E, 4A-E, 5A-E, 6A-E, 7A-F, 8A-E, 16A-E |
| Drummully | 125 | 410A-C | 6, 7B | 25/2A-E, 4A-E |
| Ederny (M'culmoney) | | 0476-9 | 13D | |
| Enniskillen | 137 | 425A-B<br>435A-B<br>0499, 0514<br>3820/1 | 20C, 23A & B<br>24A-H | 26/3A-F, 4A-E, 5A-F, 6A-F, 17A-K, 18A-H, 25A-E, 28/11A-E, 31A-E, 38A-F |
| Galloon | 145 | 48, 411, 412<br>0478-81 | 5B, 7A-E | 25/3A-E, 4A-E, 6A-E, 7A-E, 8A-E, 9A-E, 28/3A-E, 7A-E, 8A, 14A-E |
| Inishmacsaint | 156 | 426A-C<br>0500 | 17A-D | 24/3A-E, 5A-E, 26/12A-F, 36A-E |

| PARISH/TOWN/ VILLAGE | TITHES 1823–38 FIN 5A/ | VALUATION 1830S VAL 1B/ FIELD BOOKS OL4. (NATIONAL ARCHIVES) | TENEMENT VALUATION c.1861–2 VAL 2B/4/ | VALUATION REVISIONS c.1861–c.1930 VAL 12B/ |
|---|---|---|---|---|
| Kesh (M'culmoney) | | | 13D | |
| Killesher | 177 | 43<br>0472, 0482-6 | 3A-C | 26/9A-E, 11A-E, 13A-F, 19A-F, 27A-E |
| Kinawley | Nil | 44, 413 | 4A-B<br>8A-E | 26/9A-E, 11A-E, 28A-F, 29A-E, 28/1A-E, 2A-E, 12A-E, 15A-E, 16A-E, 17A, 25A-E |
| Lack (M'culmoney) | | | 13D | |
| Lisnaskea (Aghalurcher) | | | 27 | |
| Magheracross | 213 | 417, 436<br>0515 | 25A-B | 26/2A-E, 3A-F, 34A-F, 27/2A-E, 9A-F |
| Magheraculmoney | 214 | 418<br>0493 | 13A-D | 27/7A-F, 10A-E, 12A-E, 14A-E, 15A-E |
| Newtownbutler (Galloon) | | | 7F | |
| Pettigoe (T`carn) | | | 12D | |
| Rosslea (Clones) | | | 5E | |
| Rossory | 240 | 45, 427A-B<br>0473, 0501 | 18 & 24B | 26/7A-E, 16A-E, 17A-K, 30A-F, 32A-E |
| Templecarn | MIC 442/9 | 421 A-B<br>0494 | 14 | 27/3A-E |
| Tempo (Enniskillen) | | | 28 | |
| Tomregan | MIC 442/2 | 414, 0487-9 | 9 | 28/2A-E |
| Trory | 265 | 420<br>437A-B, 0495, 0516 | 23C, 26 | 26/2A-E, 27/11A-E |

* For border parishes, original records, were retained in Dublin and are now in the National Archives; microfilm copies MIC 442 in PRONI. Parishes include Clones, Currin, Templecarn and Tomregan.

| PARISH/TOWN/ VILLAGE | TITHES 1823–38 FIN 5A/ | VALUATION 1830S VAL 1B/ FIELD BOOKS OL4. (NATIONAL ARCHIVES) | TENEMENT VALUATION c.1858–9 VAL 2B/5/ | VALUATION REVISIONS c.1860–c.1930 VAL 12B/ |
|---|---|---|---|---|
| Aghadowey | 2 | 51 | 1A-C, 2 | 30/1A-E, 2A-E, 6A-F, 11A-E, 13A-F, 15A-E, 18A-E |
| Aghanloo | 7 | 511, 520, 1071 | 17A-B | 31/1A-E |
| Agivey | nil | 52 | 2 | 30/2A-F, 34/2A-E |
| Arboe | 14 | 522, 1079, 1079A | 25, 43A | 34/26A-F |
| Artrea | 22 | 523 | 26A-C, 43A | 34/4A-E, 9A-G, 16A-E, 20A-F, 24A-F, 26A-F |
| Ballinderry | 25 | 525, 1081 | 27, 43A | 9/3A-C |
| Ballyaghran (Agherton) | 28 | 539A & B 546A | 10, 15A-B | 30/4A-F, 17A-H |
| Ballymoney | 40 | 540, 546A | 11, 15B | 4/3A-G |
| Ballynascreen | 43 | 524, 1082 | 28A-C, | 34/5A-E, 8A-E, 43A & C, 12A-F, 25A-F |
| Ballyrashane | 46 | 53, 546A & B, 1068 | 12, 15B | 30/14A-F |
| Ballyscullion | 47 | 526, 1083 | 29A-B, 43B | 34/6A-G, 9A-G |
| Ballywillin | 51 | 541A-C, 546A | 13, 15B | 13A-G, 19A-E, 30/4A-F |
| Balteagh | 52 | 513A & B 516, 1072 | 18 | 31/13A-G, 19A-E, 21A-E |
| Banagher | 53 | 512A-E 548A & B 1073, 1095 | 19, 44 | 31/11A-E, 12A-F, 21A-F |
| Bellaghy (B'scullion) | | | 29C | |
| Bovevagh | 61 | 514A-C, 516 1074 | 17B, 20A-B, 21C | 31/6A-E, 14A-E, 23A-D |
| Camus (Macosquin) | 64A | | | |
| Carrick* | | 515 | 17B, 24A | 31/13A-G, 14A-E, 23A-E, 24A-E |
| Castledawson (Magherafelt) | | | 37H | |
| Clondermot (Glendermot) | 76 | 549A-D | 45A-D, 50 | 32/1A-G, 12A-F, 14A-F, 33/4A-C |
| Coleraine | 81 | 53, 542A-D, 546A & C, 1069 | 3B-F, 14, 15B | 30/4A-G, 9A-D, 14A-D, 17A-H |
| Cumber Lower | 88 | 552, 1096 | 46, 50 | 32/1A-G, 4A-F, 13A-F |
| Cumber Upper | 89 | 554, 1097 | 47A-B 50 | 31/12A-F, 32/2A-F, 5A-F |
| Derry, Deanery of | 91A | | | |
| Derryloran | 94 | 527, 1084 | 30, 43A | 34/19A-F |
| Desertlyn | 98 | 528, 1085 | 31A-B, | 34/2A-E, 7A-E, 43A & C, 20A-F |
| Desertmartin | 99 | 529, 1086 | 32A-B, 42 | 34/2A-E, 7A-E, 43A, 11A-F, 14A-E |
| Desertoghill | 100 | 54A-C | 4A-B | 29/1A-D, 30/6A-F, 12A-F, 19A-F |

| PARISH/TOWN/ VILLAGE | TITHES 1823–38 FIN 5A/ | VALUATION 1830S VAL 1B/ FIELD BOOKS OL4. (NATIONAL ARCHIVES) | TENEMENT VALUATION c.1858–9 VAL 2B/5/ | VALUATION REVISIONS c.1860–c.1930 VAL 12B/ |
|---|---|---|---|---|
| Drumachose | 115 | 517A-F | 17B, 22A-C | 31/13A-G, 16A-E, 18A-G |
| Draperstown (Ballynascreen) | | | 42 | |
| Dunboe | 129 | 55A & B | 5A-C | 30/3A-G, 5A-F, 10A-F |
| Dungiven | 133 | 518A-C, 1075 | 21A-D | 31/9A-F, 14A-E, 15A-F |
| Errigal | 140 | 56 | 5C, 6A | 30/12A-F, 13A-F, 31/12A-F, 13A-F, 18A-E, 19A-F |
| Faughanvale | 141 | 550A & B 1098 | 48A-B, 50 | 31/3A-G, 10A-E, 32/6A-F, 12A-F |
| Fermoyle** | 129 | | 7 | 30/3A-E, 10A-E, 15A-E |
| Garvagh (Errigal) | | | 6B | |
| Kilcronaghan | 167 | 530, 1087 | 33A, 43A | 34/8A-E, 14A-E, 28A-E |
| Kildollagh | 169 | 543, 546A | 15A-B | 30/14A-F |
| Killelagh | 196 | 532A & B 1070 | 34, 37A & D 43B | 34/27A-E, 29A-E |
| Killowen | 180 | 57 | 8 | 30/5A-F, 9A-D |
| Kilrea | 189 | 58, 544, 1088 | 35, 43B | 29/3A-F; 30/21A-21D |
| Learmont*** | 53 | 551 | 49A-B, 50 | 32/2A-F, 3A-F |
| Limavady (Drumachose) | | | 22B-C | |
| Lissan | 203 | 533A & B 1089 | 36A-B 43A & C | 34/15A-F, 19A-F, |
| Londonderry (Templemore) | | | 16C-H | |
| Macosquin | 64A | 59 | 5C, 9A-B | 30/5A-F, 11A-F, 15A-E, 20A-F |
| Maghera | 212 | 534A & B 1090 | 37A-G, 43B & C | 34/8A-E, 11A-F, 13A-E, 17A-G, 23A-F, 27A-E, 29A-E |
| Magherafelt | 216 | 535 1091 | 38A-C, 43A | 34/2A-E, 9A-G, 18A-F |
| Magilligan | 252 | 519A-C, 520 1076 | 17B, 23 | 31/1A-E, 3A-G, 4A-D, 5A-E |
| Moneymore | | | 31B | |
| Swatragh (Maghera) | | | 37G | |
| Tamlaght | 251 | 536, 1092 | 39, 43A | 34/26A-F |
| Tamlaghtard (Magilligan) | 252 | | | 31/1A-E, 3A-G, 4A-F, 5A-E |
| Tamlaght Finlagan | 253 | 521A-C 1077 | 24A-C | 31/3A-G, 18A-G, 20A-G, 24A-E |
| Tamlaght O'Crilly | 254 | 510, 537 545, 1093 | 40A-C, 43B | 29/1A-D, 2A-D, 30/21A-D, 34/10A-F |

| PARISH/TOWN/ VILLAGE | TITHES 1823–38 FIN 5A/ | VALUATION 1830S VAL 1B/ FIELD BOOKS OL4. (NATIONAL ARCHIVES) | TENEMENT VALUATION c.1858–9 VAL 2B/5/ | VALUATION REVISIONS c.1860–c.1930 VAL 12B/ |
|---|---|---|---|---|
| Templemore | 91A | 547A-F, 553A-D 1078 | 16A-J | 32/8A-G, 10A-G, 11A-ZD, 33/1A-B, 2A-F, 3A-C, 5A-C |
| Termoneeny | 261 | 538A & B 1094 | 41, 43B-C | 34/17A-G, 23A-F, 28A-E |
| Upperlands (Maghera) | | | | 34/30A |

* This parish was created in 1846 from parts of Balteagh, Bovevagh and Tamlaght Finlagan.
** This parish was created in 1843 out of Dunboe.
*** This parish was created in 1831 from parts of Banagher and Cumber Upper and Lower.

| PARISH/TOWN/ VILLAGE | TITHES 1823–38 FIN 5A/ | VALUATION 1830S VAL 1B/ | TENEMENT VALUATION c.1860 VAL 2B/6/ | VALUATION REVISIONS c.1860–c.1930 VAL 12B/ |
|---|---|---|---|---|
| Aghaloo | 5 | 66B | 6A-C | 36/3A-D, 4A-B 38/3A-F, 8A-F, 21A-F |
| Aghalurcher | 6 | 61A & B | 1 | 36/11A-F, 14A-F |
| Arboe | 14 | 618 | 18A-E 27 | 37/1A-F, 4A-G, 10A- F, 13A-G |
| Ardstraw | 19 | 633A-F | 35 | 35/5A-F, 8A-F, 17A-F |
| | | 637A-F | 40A 47C | 19A-F, 39/10A-E 41/27A-F, 42/ 1A-F, 2A, 7A-F, 12A-F, 17A-F, 27A-H |
| Artrea | 22 | 619 | 19 | 37/4A-G, 21A-F |
| Ballinderry | 25 | 620A & B | 20 | 37/13A-G |
| Ballyclog | 29 | 621A & B | 21 | 37/1A-F |
| Beragh (Clogherny) | | 626A | | |
| Bodoney Lower | 58 | 643 | 45A-B | 39/1A-E, 2A-E, 4A-D, 6A-E, 13A-D |
| Bodoney Upper | 59 | 644 A & B | 46 A-C | 30/3A-E, 5A-F, 7A-G, 9A-G, 11A-G |
| Camus | 64B & C | 638 A-C | 41 | 42/10A-G, 31A-M |
| Cappagh | 65 | 626B | 28 645A & B | 41/6A-F, 17A-F, 47A-C 19A-F, 24A-F, 26A-F, 31A-F, 32A-G |
| Carrickmore (T'maguirk) | | 626A | | |
| Carnteel | 68 | 68 | 6C, 7A-B | 36/3A-D, 4A-B, 5A-B, 7A-F, 18A-F, 38/1A-F, 3A-F, 10A-F |
| Castlederg (Urney) | | 626A | | 35/1A, 6A-F |
| Coagh (Tamlaght) | | 66A | | |
| Coalisland (D'henry) | | 66A | | |
| Clogher | 73 | 62A-K 647 | 2A-F | 36/1A-F, 2A-F, 6A-F, 8A-F, 9A-F, 10A-F, 11A-F, 14A-F, 16A-G |
| Clogherney | 74 | 627 | 29 | 41/4A-G, 6A-F, 14A-F, 35A-F, 39A-F |
| Clonfeacle | 79 | 610 | 9A-D | 38/4A-F, 5A-F, 6A-F, 14A-F, 22A-F |
| Clonoe | 80 | 69 | 10A-B | 38/20A-F, 23A-F |

| PARISH/TOWN/ VILLAGE | TITHES 1823–38 FIN 5A/ | VALUATION 1830S VAL 1B/ | TENEMENT VALUATION c.1860 VAL 2B/6/ | VALUATION REVISIONS c.1860–c.1930 VAL 12B/ |
|---|---|---|---|---|
| Cookstown (Derryloran) | | 66A | | |
| Cumber Upper | | 641 | | 37/7A-C |
| Derryloran | 84 | 622A & B | 22A -B | 37/5A-K, 7A-C, 11A-F, 15A-F, 21A-F |
| Desertcreat | 97 | 623 | 24A-D | 37/16A-F, 17A-F, 18A-F, 21A-F |
| Donacavey | 103 | 63A & B, 628 | 2B, 3A-B 30 | 41/8A-F, 13A-E, 15A-F, 22A-F, 23A-F, 39A-F, 42A-E |
| Donaghedy | Nil | 639A & B | 42A-D | 39/8A-E, 12A-E, 42/6A-G, 18A-G, 19A-G, 22A-F, 26A-G |
| Donaghenry | 107 | 611 | 11A-B 18E | 37/20A-G, 21A-F, 38/25A-F |
| Donaghmore | 109A | 612 | 12A-C | 38/2A-F, 9A-F, 11A-F, 13A-F, 14A-F, 15A-F, 17A-N |
| Dromore | 114 | 626A, 629 | 31A-B 33B | 40/4A-F, 5A-F, 41/5-F, 16A-F, 25A-F, 43A-F |
| Drumglass | 121 | 613 | 13 | 38/5A-F, 15A-F, 17A-N |
| Drumquin (Longfield E &W) | | 626A | | |
| Drumragh | 126 | 630A & B | 32A -B | 41/6A-F, 10A-F, 29A-F, 34A-M, 36A-M, 39A-F |
| Dungannon Middle | 617 | | 38/17A-N | |
| Errigal Keerogue | 139 | 64A & B | 4A-B | 36/7A-F, 12A-F, 13A-F, 15A-F, 38/1A-F |
| Errigal Trough | MIC 442/10 | 65A-C | 5 | |
| Gortalowry (Derryloran) | | 66A | | |
| Irishtown | | 626A | | |
| Kildress | 170 | 624 | 24A 25A-C | 37/2A-F, 9A-F, 14A-F, 15A-F |
| Killeeshil | 175 | 67 | 6C, 8 | 38/1A-F, 10A-F |
| Killyman | 183 | 614 | 15A-C | 38/5A-F, 16A-F |
| Kilskeery | 191 | 631A & B | 33A-B | 40/1A-E, 2A-F, 4A-E, 5A-F |
| Learmount* | | | 42D | |
| Leckpatrick | 201 | 640 | 43A-B | 42/5A-G, 22A-F, 31A-M |
| Lissan | 203 | 625 | 26 | 37/3A-F, 11A-F |
| Longfield East | 204 | 633A-F | 36 | 41/18A-F, 34A-F |

| PARISH/TOWN/ VILLAGE | TITHES 1823–38 FIN 5A/ | VALUATION 1830S VAL 1B/ | TENEMENT VALUATION c.1860 VAL 2B/6/ | VALUATION REVISIONS c.1860–c.1930 VAL 12B/ |
|---|---|---|---|---|
| Longfield West | 205 | 633A-F | 37A-B | 35/4A-F, 9A-F, 11A-F, 21A-F |
| Loy (Derryloran) | | 66A | | |
| Omagh (Drumragh) | | | | 41/37A-G |
| Magheracross | 213 | | 33B | 40/1A-E, 42/27A-H |
| Newtownstewart (Ardstraw) | | | 40B | |
| Pomeroy | 231 | 66A, 615 | 16A-D | 37/16A-F, 38/2A-F, 13A-F |
| Stewartstown (Donaghenry) | | 66A | | |
| Strabane (Camus & Urney) | | | | 42/31E-M |
| Tamlaght | 251 | | 27 | 37/4A-G |
| Termon Rock (Carrickmore) | | 626A | | |
| Termonamongan | 260 | 633A-F | 38A-C | 35/10A-F, 13A-F, 14A-F, 16A-F, 20A-F |
| Termonmaguirk | 262 | 632, 646 | 34A-C | 41/2A-F, 7A-F, 12A-F, 28A-F, 35A-F, 40A-F |
| Trillick (Kilskeery) | | 626A | | |
| Tullyniskan | 268 | 616 | 17 | 38/25A-F |
| Urney | MIC442/8B | 633A-F 642 | 39, 44 | 35/6A-F, 13A-F, 16A-F, 42/1A-F, 20A-G, 31A-M |

* One townland only in Co Tyrone parish created 1831 from parts of Banagher and Cumber Upper and Lower.

There are two volumes containing valuations of properties in towns and villages in Co. Tyrone.
Val 1B|66A includes Coagh, Coalisland, Cookstown (including the townlands of Gortalowry and Loy which are both partly within Cookstown), Pomeroy and Stewartstown.
Val 1B|626A includes Beragh, Castlederg, Dromore, Drumquin, Fivemiletown, Termon Rock (Carrickmore), Irishtown (an unofficial name probably for an area on the outskirts of Omagh), and Trillick.

| PARISH | TITHES 1823–38 TAB 3/ | FILM | VALUATION FIELD BOOK 1830s OL4./ HOUSE BOOK [OL5.] | TENEMENT VALUATION FICHE C.1852–3 | 1841/1851 CENSUS SEARCH Cen /S/3 |
|---|---|---|---|---|---|
| Agha | 32 | 1 | 0163, 2016 | 2.G.12. | 23-26 |
| Aghade | 43 | 2 | 0147 | 3.F.10. | 12 |
| Ardoyne | 23 | 1 | 0148/53, 0179, 2036 | 2.B.4., 3.F.13 | 13-15 |
| Ardristan | 25 | 1 | 0180, 2037 | 2.B.4. | 48 |
| Ballinacarrig | 6 | 1 | 0135, 1994, | 1.B.4. | |
| Ballon | 42 | 2 | 0154 | 3.G.2. | |
| Ballycrogue | 7 | 1 | 0136, 1995 | 1.B.7. | |
| Ballyellin | 36 | 1 | 0155, 0164, 0194, 2017 | 3.A.6., 3. G.9., 4.C.8. | 16-17, 72-73 |
| Baltinglass | 13 | 1 | 0181, 2038 | 2.B.6. | 49 |
| Barragh | 45 | 2 | 2005, 0197, 2010, 2059 | 3.G.10. | 82 |
| Carlow | 4 | 1 | 0137, 1996 | 1.B.8. | 1-5 |
| Clonmelsh | 5 | 1 | 0138, 1997 | 1.D.13. | |
| Clonmore | 22 | 1 | 0182, 2039 | 2.B.7. | 50-51 |
| Clonygoose | 37 | 2 | 0165, 2018 | 3.A.10. | 27-28 |
| Cloydagh | 26 | 1 | 0174, 0139, 1998, 2028 | 1.E.1., 1.F.8. | 42-43 |
| Crecrin | 21 | 1 | 2040, 0183 | 2.C.1. | |
| Dunleckny | 33 | 1 | 0166, 2019 | 3.B.6. | 29-30 |
| Fennagh | 24 | 1 | 0184, 0167, 2020, 2041, 0156 | 2.C.2., 3.C.9., 4.A.12. | 18, 31 |
| Gilbertstown | 40 | 2 | 0157 | 4.A.13. | |
| Grangeford | 9 | 1 | 0140, 1999 | 1.E.1. | |
| Hacketstown | 19 | 1 | 0185, 2042 | 2.C.8. | 52-54 |
| Haroldstown | 18 | 1 | 0186, 2043 | 2.D.5. | 55 |
| Kellistown | 8 | 1 | 0141, 00158, 2000 | 1.E.6., 4.B.2. | 6 |
| Killerrig | 3 | 1 | 0142, 2001 | 1.E.8. | 7-9 |
| Killinane | 30 | 1 | 2029, 0168, 0175, 2021 | 1.F.12., 3.D.5. | 44 |
| Kiltegan | 15 | 1 | 0187, 2045 | 2.D.8. | |
| Kiltennell | 38 | 2 | 0169, 2022 | 3.D.5. | 32-34 |
| Kineagh | 12 | 1 | 0188, 2044 | 2.D.9. | |
| Lorum | 35 | 1 | 2023 | 3.E.4. | 35-39 |
| Moyacomb | 46 | 2 | 0198 | 2.G.3. | 83-84 |
| Myshall | 44 | ? | 0159, 0170, 2011 | 3.E.10., 4.B.4. | 19-22 |
| Nurney | 31 | 1 | 0143, 0160, 0171, 2002, 2024 | 1.E.11., 3.E.11., 4.C.4. | 10 |
| Oldleighlin | 28 | 1 | 0176, 2030 | 1.G.1. | 45-47 |
| Painestown | 1 | 1 | 0144 | 1.E.12. | |
| Rahill | 11 | 1 | 0189, 2046 | 2.D.12. | 57 |
| Rathmore | 17 | 1 | 0190, 2047 | 2.D.14. | 58 |
| Rathvilly | 14 | 1 | 0191, 2048 | 2.E.1. | 59-63 |
| Sliguff | 34 | 1 | 0172 | 3.E.13. | 40-41 |
| St.Mullin's | 47 | 2 | 0195, 2056 | 4.C.10. | 74-77 |
| Straboe | 16 | 1 | 0192, 2049 | 2.E.12. | 64 |
| Templepeter | 41 | 2 | 0161 | 4.C.4. | |
| Tullowcreen | 27 | 1 | 0177, 2031 | 2.A.4. | |
| Tullowmagimma | 10 | 1 | 0145, 0162, 2003 | 1.E.4., 4.C.6. | 11 |
| Tullowphelim | 20 | 1 | 0193, 2050 | 2.E.13. | 65-71 |
| Ullard | 39 | 2 | 0196, 0173, 2025 | 3.E.10. | 78-81 |
| Urglin | 2 | 1 | 0146, 2004 | 1.F.3. | |
| Wells | 29 | 1 | 0178, 2032 | 2.A.11. | |

| PARISH | TITHES 1823–38 TAB 4/ | FILM | VALUATION FIELD BOOKS 1830s OL4./ HOUSE BOOKS [OL5.] | TENEMENT VALUATION FICHE C.1857 | 1841/1851 CENSUS SEARCH Cen /S/4 |
|---|---|---|---|---|---|
| Annagelliff | 13 | 5 | 0224, [0061], [3787] | 5 G 6 | 516-540 |
| Annagh | 16 | 5 | 0219, 0220, 0233, [0060 0069/70] | 5.A.6., 5.F.2. 7.C.8. | 470-482, 782-803 |
| Bailieborough | 23 | 5A | 0199, 0206, [3772/5, 3798/9] | 1.D.6., 1.A.14. | 162-195 |
| Ballintemple | 26 | 5B | 0212, [0047] | 4.B.8. | 284-341, 469 |
| Ballyconnell (Tomregan) | | | [3800/01] | | |
| Ballyjamesduff (Castlerahan) | | | [3802] | | |
| Ballymachugh | 28 | 5B | 0213, [0048/9] | 4.C.14. | 342-3 |
| Belturbet (Annagh & Drumlane) | | | [2387] | | |
| Castlekeeran (Loughan) | | | [3764] | | |
| Castlerahan | 32 | 5B | 2028A, [3764], [0037] | 10.B.2. | 2-40 |
| Castleterra | 11 | 4 | 0225, [0062/3] | 6.A.6. | 541-581 |
| Cavan (Urney) | | | [3803] | | |
| Crosserlough | 30 | 5B | 0200, [0038], 0214, [0050/1], 0226, [0064], 2029A, [3764], [3788], | 6.C.3., 4.D.10. 4.F.10., 10.C.11. | 41-86, 344-359, 582-584 |
| Denn | 14 | 5 | 0201, [0039], 0215, [0052/3], 0227, [3770], 2030A, 2033A, [3789/90] | 6.C.4. 10.G.12. 4.E.5., 5.A.4. 10.C.13. | 87-91, 360-365, 412, 585-631 |
| Drumgoon | 19 | 5A | 0207, [0071], 0234 | 7.D.4., 8.D.8. | 196-214, 632, 804-824 |
| Drumlane | 6 | 4 | 0221 | 2.D.12., 5.C.4. | 483-513 |
| Drumlumman | 27 | 5B | 0216, [0054/5] | 4.E.9., 9.D.4. | 366-440 |
| Drumreilly | | | 0238, [0079], 0239 | 2.E.4. | 932-935 |
| Drung | 17 | 5 | 0235, [0072/3] | 7.F.3. | 825-857 |
| Enniskeen | 24 | 5A | 0208, [3776/8] | 1.E.13. | 215-229 |
| Kilbride | 29 | 5B | 0217, [0056], [3786] | 4.E.9., 10.F.14. | 441-449 |
| Kildallan | 7 | 4 | 0245 | 3.C.8., 3.E.12. | 119-1134 |
| Kildrumsherdan | 18 | 5 | 0236, [0074/6] | 7.G.12. | 858-885 |
| Killashandra | 8 | 4 | 0246, [3804] | 3.D.10., 3.F.2. | 1135-1210, 1212 |
| Killinagh | 1 | 3 | 0240, [0080] | 8.G.12. | 936-1007 |
| Killinkere | 31 | 5B | 0202, [0040], 0228, [3766], 2034A, [3791/2] | 6.D.6., 1.B.9. 10.D.2. | 92-120, 635-645 |
| Kilmore | 12 | 4 | 0218,[0057/8], 0229, [0065], [3793] | 6.D.8., 4.E.11. | 450-468, 646-675 |
| Kinawley | 3 | 4 | 0241, [0081/2], 0242 | 2.E.6., 9.B.6. | 1008-1032 |
| Knockbride | 21 | 5A | 0209, [3779/81], [3813] | 2.B.8., 8.E.11. | 231-257 |
| Larah | 20 | 5A | 0230, [0066], 0237, [0077/8], [3794/6] | 6.E.12., 5.G.3., 8.C.4. | 676-704 887-931 |
| Lavey | 15 | 5 | 0231, [0067], [3795/6] | 6.F.7. | 705-757, 886 |
| Loughan or Castlekeeran | | | [0041], [3767], [3764] | 9.G.10. 10.D.3. | 121-123 |
| Lurgan | 33 | 5B | 0203, [0042], [3768] | 10.D.8. | 124-136 |
| Moybolgue | 25 | 5A | 0210, [3782/3] | 1.G.13. | 258-262 |
| Mullagh | | | 0204, [0043], 2031A, [3771], [3806] | 1.A.14., 9.G.10., 10.F.2. | 137-154 |

| PARISH | TITHES 1823–38 TAB 4/ | FILM | VALUATION FIELD BOOKS 1830s OL4./ HOUSE BOOKS [OL5.] | TENEMENT VALUATION FICHE C.1857 | 1841/1851 CENSUS SEARCH Cen /S/4 |
|---|---|---|---|---|---|
| Munterconnaught | | | 0205, [0044], 2032A, [3769] | 10.F.4. | 155-161 |
| Scrabby | 9 | 4 | 0247, 2037A | 4.B.5., 9.F.2. | 1211, 1213-1227 |
| Shercock | 22 | 5A | 0211, [0045], [3784/5], [3897] | 2.A.4. | 263-283 |
| Swanlinbar (Kinawley) | | | [3808] | | |
| Templeport | 2 | 3 | 0243, [0083/4] | 2.F.8., 9.B.7. | 1033-1105 |
| Tomregan | 5 | 4 | 0222, [0059] 0244, [0085/6] | 3.B.10., 2.D.13., 5.E.13. | 514-515, 1106, 118 |
| Urney | 10 | 4 | 0223, [0068] 0232, [3797] | 5.E.14., 6.G.10. | 758-781 |
| Virginia (Lurgan) | | | [3806] | | |

| TOWNS | VALUATION HOUSE BOOK 1830s [OL5.] |
|---|---|
| Belturbet | [2387] |
| Kingscourt | [3799] [3805] |

The 1821 census is available in the National Archives for 16 parishes: Annagelliff, Ballymachugh, Castlerahan, Castleterra, Crosserlough, Denn, Drumlumman, Drung, Kilbride, Kilmore, Kinawley, Larah, Lavey, Lurgan, Mullagh, Munterconnaught.

| PARISH | TITHES 1823–38 TAB 5/ | FILM | VALUATION FIELD BOOK 1830s OL4./ HOUSE BOOK [OL5.] | TENEMENT VALUATION FICHE 1855 | 1841/1851 CENSUS SEARCH Cen /S/5 |
|---|---|---|---|---|---|
| Abbey | 3 | 6 | 0268, 3818 | 1.A.12. | 96-100 |
| Bunratty | 76 | 11 | 0248 | 2.D.10. | 1 |
| Carran | 10 | 6 | 0269 | 1.B.5., 1.F.6. | 101-106 |
| Clareabbey | 45 | 9 | 0304 | 3.D.8., 6.E.2. | 638-640 |
| Clondagad | 46 | 9 | 0305 | 6.C.14. | 641-664, 689 |
| Clonlea | 49 | 10 | 0314, 3840 | 9.D.4., 11.C.14. | 874-878 |
| Clonloghan | 71 | 11 | 0249 | 2.D.14. | 2 |
| Clooney | 18 | 7 | 0286 | 1.F.8., 4.G.4. | 30-38, 303-311 |
| Clooney | 30 | 8 | 0262 08, 3807/08, 3809 | 2.G.10., 11.A.12. | 30-38, 303-311 |
| Doora | 31 | 8 | 0263 8, 3809/10 | 2.G.12. | 39-40 |
| Drumcliff | 43 | 9 | 0306 | 3.F.13. | 665-677 |
| Drumcreehy | 2 | 6 | 0270, 3819 | 1.B.11. | 107-110 |
| Drumline | 72 | 11 | 0250 | 2.E.3. | 3 |
| Dysert | 25 | 8 | 0297, 3834 | 1.F.14., 3.C.6. | 554-560 |
| Feakle | 33 | 8 | 0322 | 10.D.11., 11.E.2. | 994-1042 |
| Feenagh | 73 | 11 | 0251 | 2.E.6., 11.C.8. | |
| Gleninagh | 1 | 6 | 3820, 0271 | 1.C.7. | 111-113 |
| Inagh | 24 | 7 | 0298 | 4.F.2. | 561-594 |
| Inchicronan | 27 | 8 | 0264, 3811/2 | 3.A.6., 11.B.5. | 41-71 |
| Inishcaltra | | | 0323 | 10.E.10. | |
| Kilballyowen | 57 | 10 | 0309 | 7.D.6. | 694-724 |
| Kilchreest | 63 | 11 | 0279, 3828 | 5.F.10. | 146-155 |
| Kilconry | 75 | 11 | 0252 | 2.E.9. | 4-5 |
| Kilcorney | 9 | 6 | 0272 | 1.C.9. | 114 |
| Kilfarboy | 39 | 9 | 0294 | 4.C.12. | 407-435 |
| Kilfearagh | 56 | 10 | 0310 | 8.F.5. | 725-758 |
| Kilfenora | 16 | 6 | 0287, [2412] | 1.F.9., 4.G.13. | 312-318 |
| Kilfintinan | 77 | 11 | 0254 | 9.B.5. | 6-12 |
| Kilfiddane | 62 | 10 | 0280, 3829 | 5.G.6., 6.F.4. | 173-191 |
| Kilfinaghta | 74 | 11 | 0253 | 2.E.11., 9.A.12., 11.C.8. | |
| Kilkeedy | 20 | 7 | 0299 | 1.F.14. | 595-606 |
| Killadysert | 64 | 11 | 0281, 3831 | 6.A.6. | 156-172 |
| Killaloe | 53 | 10 | 0315, [0087], [2420/22] | 9.D.8., 10.B.12. | 879-880 |
| Killard | 41 | 9 | 0295 | 7.A.6. | 436-496 |
| Killaspuglonane | 14 | 6 | 0288 | 5.A.9. | 319-324 |
| Killeany | 8 | 6 | 0273, 3821/22 | 1.C.12. | 115-116 |
| Killeely | 78 | 11 | 0255 | 9.C.1. | 13-15 |
| Killilagh | 12 | 6 | 0289 | 5.A.13. | 325-354 |
| Killimer | 65 | 11 | 0282, 3832 | 6.F.4. | 192-216 |
| Killinaboy | 21 | 7 | 0300, 3836 | 2.A.1. | 607-613 |
| Killofin | 66 | 11 | 0283, 3830 | 6.B.9. | 291-302 |
| Killokennedy | 51 | 10 | 0316, 3841/42 | 9.D.10. | 881-888 |
| Killonaghan | 5 | 6 | 0274, 3823 | 1.C.14. | 117-129 |
| Killone | 44 | 9 | 0307 | 3.E.4. | 692-693 |
| Killuran | 48 | 10 | 3845, 3846, 0317 | 9.E.8., 11.D.7. | |
| Kilmacduane | 55 | 10 | 0311, 3833 | 7.B.9., 8.A.12. | 759-800 |
| Kilmacrehy | 13 | 6 | 0290 | 5.B.12. | 355-369 |
| Kilmaleery | 70 | 11 | 0256 | 2.F.2. | 16-17 |
| Kilmaley | 42 | 9 | 0308 | 3.E.11., 6.E.2. | 678-688 |
| Kilmanaheen | 17 | 7 | 0291 | 5.C.12. | 370-389 |

| PARISH | TITHES 1823–38 TAB 5/ | FILM | VALUATION FIELD BOOK 1830s OL4./ HOUSE BOOK [OL5.] | TENEMENT VALUATION FICHE 1855 | 1841/1851 CENSUS SEARCH Cen /S/5 |
|---|---|---|---|---|---|
| Kilmihil | 60 | 10 | 0284 | 3.C.4., 6.F.12. | 217-274 |
| Kilmoon | 6 | 6 | 0275, 3824 | 1.D.5., 5.E.10. | 130-131 |
| Kilmurry | 61 | 10 | 0285 | 6.C.5., 6.G.12. | 18-23, 275-290, 497-553, 690 |
| Kilmurry | 40 | 9 | 0296 | 4.E.10., 7.B.9. | 18-23, 275-290, 497-553, 690 |
| Kilmurry | 69 | 11 | 0257 | 11.C.10. | |
| Kilnamona | 26 | 8 | 0301, 3837 | 3.C.14. | |
| Kilnasoolagh | 67 | 11 | 0258 | 2.F.5. | 24-25 |
| Kilnoe | 37 | 9 | 0324 | 10.E.10., 11.E.10. | 691-693, 1043-1044 |
| Kilraghtis | 29 | 8 | 0265, 3813/14 | 3.B.2. | 72-74 |
| Kilrush | 59 | 10 | 0312 | 8.D.3. | 801-815 |
| Kilseily | 50 | 10 | 0318, 3847, 3848 | 9.E.9. | 889-898 |
| Kilshanny | 15 | 6 | 0292 | 5.E.2. | 390-406 |
| Kiltenanlea | 54 | 10 | 0319, 3849 | 9.F.9. | 899-926 |
| Kiltoraght | 19 | 7 | 0293 | 1.F.10., 5.E.8. | 406 |
| Moyarta | 58 | 10 | 0313 | 8.C.2. | 817-873 |
| Moynoe | 35 | 8 | 0325 | 10.F.6. | 1045-1053 |
| Noughaval | 11 | 6 | 0276, 3825 | 1.D.7., 1.F.6. | 132-134 |
| O'Briensbridge | 52 | 10 | 0320, 3850 | 9.G.8., 10.C.14. | 927-938 |
| Ogonnelloe | 47 | 10 | 0321, 3851 | 10.C.14. | 939-943 |
| Oughtmama | 4 | 6 | 0277, 3826 | 1.D.9. | 135-144 |
| Quin | 32 | 8 | 0266, 3815 | 3.B.9., 11.B.11. | 75-89 |
| Rath | 22 | 7 | 0302, 3838 | 2.B.4., 4.G.2. | |
| Rathborney | 7 | 6 | 0278, 3827 | 1.E.1. | 145 |
| Ruan | 23 | 7 | 0303 | 2.B.10. | 629-637 |
| St Munchin | 79 | 11 | 0259 | 9.C.7. | |
| St Patrick's | 80 | 11 | 0260 | 9.C.10. | |
| Templemaley | 28 | 8 | 0267, 3816/17 | 1.F.4., 3.B.11. | 90-95 |
| Tomfinlough | 68 | 11 | 0261 | 2.F.9. | 26-29 |
| Tomgraney | 34 | 8 | 0326, [2439] | 10.F.11. | 1054-1064 |
| Tulla | 36 | 9 | 0327, [0088, 2440/42] | 11.E.2. | 1080-1084 |

| TOWNS | VALUATION HOUSE BOOK 1830s [OL5.] | TOWNS | VALUATION HOUSE BOOK 1830s [OL5.] |
|---|---|---|---|
| Ballyvaghan (Corranroo) | [2388/89] | Kilkishen | [2416] |
| | | Killadysert | [2417] |
| Broadford | [2391] | Kilrush | [2423/26] |
| Carrigaholt | [2392] | Labasheeda | [2427/29] |
| Clare | [2393/94] | Lahinch | [2411, 2412, 2430] |
| Cooraclare | [2395] | Liscannon | [2412] |
| Corofin | [2396/98] | Milltown Malbay | [2431/33] |
| Crusheen | [2399/400] | Newmarket-on-Fergus | [2434/35] |
| Ennis | [2401/09] | Scariff | [2436] |
| Ennistymon | [2410, 2411, 2412] | Sixmilebridge | [2437/38] |
| Kilkee | [2413/15] | | |

| PARISH | TITHES 1823–38 TAB/ | FILM | VALUATION FIELD BOOK 1830s OL4./ HOUSE BOOK [OL5.] | TENEMENT VALUATION FICHE 1851/3 | 1841/1851 CENSUS SEARCH Cen /S/6 |
|---|---|---|---|---|---|
| Abbeymahon | 6S/66 | 25 | 2203, [0470/71] | | |
| Abbeymahon | 6S/66 | 25 | 2203, [0470/71] | 21.C.10. | 932-938 |
| Abbeystrowry | 6S/52 | 24 | [0260/63] | 10.A.6. | 267-270 |
| Aghabulloge | 6N/48 | 19 | [0682/83] | 32.E.8. | 1082-1096 |
| Aghacross | 6E/32a | 13 | 2160, [0314/5] | 13.C.2. | |
| Aghada | 6E/105 | 16 | [0506/8] | 23.C.9. | 956-958 |
| Aghadown | 6S/55 | 24 | [0264/67] | 10.B.12. | 271-277 |
| Aghern | 6E/69 | 14 | [0658/60] | 27.D.2. | 1058a-1059 |
| Aghinagh | 6N/50 | 19 | [0684/87] | 32.F.13. | 1097-1102 |
| Aglish | 6N/56 | 20 | [0688/89] | 31.F.12., 32.G.9. | |
| Aglishdrinagh | 6N/24 | 18 | 2254, [0757/58] | 23.E.2. | |
| Ardagh | 6E/87 | 15 | [0509/10] | 22.D.10. | 959 |
| Ardfield | 6S/61 | 24 | 2204, [0472/73] | 21.D.8. | 939 |
| Ardnageehy | 6E/42 | 13 | [0009/11] | 2.D.4., 3.C.1. | 32-39 |
| Ardskeagh | 6E/2 | 12 | [0452/53] | 19.C.10. | |
| Athnowen | 6N/57 | 20 | [0699] | 31.F.13., 32.A.10. | 1103 |
| Ballinaboy | 6S/25 | 23 | 2220, [0370/72, 0597/98, 0599, 0570/72, 0690/91] | 14.G.8., 32.B.2., 25.F.4., 24.F.4., 24.F.10. | 973-974, 1104-1105 |
| Ballinadee | 6N/46 | 19 | [0181/3], [0720/21] | 33.F.10., 8.C.2., 8.C.4. | |
| Ballinadee | 6S/74 | 25 | 2104, 2244, [0181/3] | 33.F.10., 8.C.2., 8.C.4. | |
| Ballintemple | 6E/108 | 16 | [0511] | 23.D.6. | 960 |
| Ballyclogh | 6N/34 | 18 | 2255, [0410], [0759/61] [2445] | 18.C.2., 35.D.12., 35.E.6. | 1271 |
| Ballycurrany | 6E/53 | 14 | 2045a/46a, [0112/13] | 3.B.6. | 40 |
| Ballydeloher | 6E/59 | 14 | [0114/17] | 2.D.6. | |
| Ballydeloughy | 6E/12 | 12 | [0435A], 0446] | 19.C.12. | 891 |
| Ballyfeard | 6S/29 | 23 | 2221, [0600/02] | 25.E.14., 25.F.8. | 1021 |
| Ballyfoyle | 6S/35 | 23 | 2222, [0603/05] | 25.E.14., 25.F.12. | 1022 |
| Ballyhay | 6E/1 | 12 | [0452/53] | 19.D.2. | 892 |
| Ballyhay | 6N.20 | 18 | 2256, [0762/63] | 35.E.14. | |
| Ballyhooly | 6E/27 | 13 | [0436/37], [2448/49] | 19.C.2., 19.D.4. | 893 |
| Ballymartle | 6S/26 | 23 | [0599, 0606, 0672, 0673] | 25.F.1., 25.G.2., 27.G.2. | 1023-1025 |
| Ballymodan | 6S/20 | 22 | 2105, 2233 [0184/5, 0638/40] | 26.E.14., 8.C.2., 8.C.14. | 234-236, 1037-1050 |
| Ballymoney | 6S/70 | 25 | 2106, [0186/7] | 8.C.2., 8.D.12. | 237 |
| Ballynoe | 6E/70 | 15 | [0661/63] | 27.D.6. | 1060-1062 |
| Ballyoughtera | 6E/94 | 15 | [0512/13] | 23.D.10. | |
| Ballyspillane | 6E/62 | 14 | 2047a/48a, [0118/19] | 3.G.11. | |
| Ballyvourney | 6N/38 | 19 | 2245, [0722/23] | 33.F.10. | 1135-1170 |
| Barnahely | 6S/41 | 23 | [0573/75] | 24.F.4, 24.G.2. | 975-981 |
| Bohillane | 6E/99 | 16 | [0514] | 23.E.2. | |
| Bregoge | 6N/31 | 18 | 2257, [0764/66] | 35.F.4. | |
| Bridgetown | 6E/25 | 12 | [0440] | 19.D.10. | 894 |
| Brigown | 6E/33 | 13 | 2161/62, [0316/23], | 13.C.4. | 465-470 |
| Brinny | 6S/17 | 22 | 2107, 2223, 2234 [0188, 0644/45, 0607/08] | 26.G.4., 25.F.1., 25.G.8., 8.E.12. | 1051-1052 |

| PARISH | TITHES 1823–38 TAB | FILM | VALUATION FIELD BOOK 1830s OL4./ HOUSE BOOK [OL5.] | TENEMENT VALUATION FICHE 1851/3 | 1841/1851 CENSUS SEARCH Cen /S/6 |
|---|---|---|---|---|---|
| Britway | 6E/50 | 14 | 2049a/51a, [0664/66, 0120/21] | 3.C.13., 3.G.13., 27.D.13. | 41-42 |
| Buttevant | 6N/32 | 18 | 2258, [0767/69], [2461] | 35.D.12. | 1272-1280 |
| Caheragh | 6S/46 | 24 | [0268/73], 2139/43, 2157 | | 278-288 |
| Caherduggan | 6E/87 | 12 | [0438/39], | 19.E.2. | |
| Caherlag | 6E/60 | 14 | 2051a/52a, [0122/23] | 2.D.10., 4.A.1. | 43-44 |
| Cannaway | 6N/55 | 19 | [0695/96] | | 1110 |
| Carrigaline | 6E/84 | 15 | 2189, [0373/74, 0609/12, 0576/78] | 14.C.9., 25.G.10., 24.F.4., 24.G.10. | 493-509, 982-998 |
| Carrigaline | 6S/38 | 23 | [0373/74, 0609/12, 0576/78] | 14.C.9., 25.G.10., 24.F.4., 24.G.10. | |
| Carrigdownane | 6E/13 | 12 | [0446/47] | 19.E.8. | |
| Carrigleamleary | 6E/15 | 12 | [0441/42] | 19.E.10. | |
| Carrigrohane | 6E/77 | 15 | [0375/76, 0697/98] | 15.A.7., 32.B.4. | 1106-1109 |
| Carrigrohane | 6N/64 | 20 | [0375/76, 0697/98] | 15.A.7., 32.B.4. | |
| Carrigrohanebeg | 6N/58 | 20 | [0699], [0700] | 32.B.10. | |
| Carrigtohill | 6E/61 | 14 | 2053a, [0124/26] | 2.E.3., 4.A.2. | 45-50 |
| Castlehaven | 6S/53 | 24 | 2144, [0274/77] | 10.D.7. | 289-330 |
| Castlelyons | 6E/44 | 14 | 2054a/55a, 2163/64 [0324/25, 0127/30] [2460] | 13.E.4., 3.C.14. | 51-54 |
| Castlemagner | 6N/10 | 18 | [0411], [2462] | 16.D.12. | |
| Castletownroche | 6E/17 | 12 | [0443], [2466/68], | 19.C.2., 19.E.4. | 895 |
| Castleventry | 6S/13 | 22 | 2205, [0189/91, 0474/75] | 6.D.4., 21.E.4. | 331, 940 |
| Churchtown | 6N/27 | 18 | 2259, [0412/13], [0770/71] [2472] | 16.E.9., 35.D.13., 35.G.8. | 1281 |
| Clear Island | 6S/58 | 24 | [0278/80] | 10.E.11. | 332 |
| Clenor | | | [0444/45] | 19.F.10. | |
| Clondrohid | 6N39 | 19 | 2246, [0724/27] | 33.G.14. | 1171-1190 |
| Clondulane | 6E/38a | 13 | [0326] | 13.E.8. | 471 |
| Clonfert | 6N/1 | 17 | [0414, 0420, 0431] | 16.E.10. | 710-733 |
| Clonmeen | 6N/13 | 18 | [0415] | 17.B.10. | 734-740 |
| Clonmel | 6E/66 | 14 | 2056a, 2058a, [0131/33] | 2.E.3. | 55-62 |
| Clonmelsh | 6E/66 | 14 | | 2.E.3. | |
| Clonmult | 6E/58 | 14 | 2059a, 2060a, [0515/16, 0664/66, 0134/35] | 4.B.3., 27.D.13., 23.E.4. | |
| Clonpriest | | | [0517/18] | 22.E.4. | |
| Clontead | 6S/83, 84 | 26 | [0672/73, 0679] | 27.G.3. | 1074 |
| Cloyne | 6E/98 | 16 | [0519, 0530/31] | 23.E.4. | 961 |
| Coole | 6E/45 | 14 | [0136/38] | 3.D.13. | |
| Cooliney | 6N/23 | 18 | 2260, [0772/73] | 36.A.2. | |
| Corbally | 6N/66 | 20 | [0699], [0700] | 32.B.12. | |
| Corcomohide | 6N/18 | 18 | 2261, [0774/75] | 36.A.4. | |
| Cork City Parishes | 6E/80 | 15 | | 30.F.4., 30.D.8., 29.A.12., 29.G.14., 28.F.4., 28.G.3. | |
| Corkbeg | 6E/107 | 16 | [0528/29] | 23.F.12. | |
| Courtmasherry | | | [0476] | | |
| Creagh | 6S/56 | 24 | [0281/84] | 10.F.2. | 333-336 |

| PARISH | TITHES 1823–38 TAB | FILM | VALUATION FIELD BOOK 1830s OL4./ HOUSE BOOK [OL5.] | TENEMENT VALUATION FICHE 1851/3 | 1841/1851 CENSUS SEARCH Cen /S/6 |
|---|---|---|---|---|---|
| Cullen | 6N/11 | 18 | [0416, 0599, 0613] | 18.F.10., 25.G.12. | 741-780, 1026 |
| Cullen | 6S/27 | 23 | 2224, [0416, 0599, 0613] | 18.F.10., 25.G.12. | |
| Currykippane | 6E/75 | 15 | 2190, [0377/78] | 15.A.10. | |
| Dangandonovan | 6E/88 | 15 | [0526/27] | 22.F.1., 23.G.3. | |
| Derryvillane | | | 2165/66 [0327/29], [0446/47] | 19.G.2., 13.F.2. | 472, 896 |
| Desert | 6S/79 | 26 | 2108, 2206 [0192/3, 0477/78] | 21.E.6., 8.E.14. | |
| Desertmore | 6N/61 | 20 | [0701/02] | 31.F.14. | 1111-1112 |
| Desertserges | 6S/71 | 25 | 2109, 2131, 2235 [0194/6, 0646/47] | 26.G.8., 8.F.4. | 238-241, 1053-1054 |
| Donaghmore | 6S/68 | 25 | 2207, [0479/80, 0092/94], [3807] | 33.A.7., 1.G.8., 21.E.8. | |
| Donaghmore | 6N/49 | 19 | [0479/78, 0092/94] [0703/04], [3807] | 33.A.7., 1.G.8., 21.E.8. | 1113-1114 |
| Doneraile | 6E/5 | 12 | [2595/97] | 19.C.3., 19.G.4. | 897-900 |
| Drinagh | 6S/51 | 24 | [0197/8, 0285/87] | 6.D.12., 7.F.8., 10.G.13. | 337-339 |
| Drishane | 6N/36 | 19 | 2247, [0417/18], [0728/29] [2599] | 18.G.12., 34.G.12 | 781, 1192-1236 ? |
| Dromdowney | 6N/35 | 19 | 2262, [0776/77] | 36.A.6. | |
| Dromdaleague | 6S/50 | 24 | [0288/91] | 11.A.8. | 340-341 |
| Dromtarriff | 6N/12 | 18 | [0419] | 17.D.3. | 782-784 |
| Dunbulloge | 6E/41 | 13 | 2061a, 2191 [0139/40, 0379] | 2.E.10., 15.A.14. | 62-65 |
| Dunderrow | 6N/68 | 20 | [0614/15, 0672, 0674] [0705/06] | 25.F.1., 26.A.4., 27.G.11. | |
| Dunderrow | 6S/24 | 23 | 2225, [0614/15, 0672, 0674] | 25.F.1., 26.A.4., 27.G.11. | 1075, 1115-1117 |
| Dungourney | 6E/57 | 14 | 2062/63a [0525, 0141/42] | 4.B.6., 23.G.6. | |
| Dunisky | 6N/44 | 19 | 2248, [0730/31] | 34.B.10. | 1236-1237 |
| Dunmahon | 6E/20 | 12 | 2167, [0449] | 20.A.12., 13.F.4. | 901 |
| Durrus | 6S/45 | 24 | 2038a, 2039a, 2145/46, [0292, 0089/90] | 1.A.14., 12.F.14. | 342-350 |
| Fanlobbus | 6S/9 | 22 | 2110, 2132, [0199/201] | 7.A.4. | 351-356 |
| Farahy | 6E/7 | 12 | 2168, [0330/32, 0450] | 20.B.2., 13.F.6. | 902 |
| Fermoy | 6E/38 | 13 | 2169, 2201/2, [0333/37] | 13.F.8. | 473-474 |
| Garranekinnefeake | 6E/97 | 16 | [0524] | 23.G.8. | 972 |
| Garrycloyne | 6N/54 | 19 | [0095/97, 0697/98] | 32.C.2., 2.A.2. | 1118-1123 |
| Garryvoe | 6E/100 | 16 | [0523] | 23.G.12. | |
| Glanworth | 6E/18 | 12 | 2170/71, [0338/40, 0451] | 19.C.3., 20.B.8., 14.A.6. | 903-905 |
| Glenor | 6E/16 | 12 | | | |
| Grenagh | 6N/72 | 20 | [0098/100, 0697/98] [3808] | 32.C.9., 2.A.4. | 22-27 |
| Gortroe | 6E/49 | 14 | 2064/65, [0143/44] | 3.D.14. | 66 |
| Hackmys | 6N/22 | 18 | 2263, [0778/79] | 36.A.8. | |
| Ightermurragh | 6E/95 | 15 | [0520/22] | | 963 |

| PARISH | TITHES 1823–38 TAB | FILM | VALUATION FIELD BOOK 1830s OL4./ HOUSE BOOK [OL5.] | TENEMENT VALUATION FICHE 1851/3 | 1841/1851 CENSUS SEARCH Cen /S/6 |
|---|---|---|---|---|---|
| Inch | 6E/103 | 16 | [0539/40] | 24.A.11. | |
| Inchigeelagh | 6N/42 | 19 | 2249, [0732/37] | 33.D.12., 34.B.11. | |
| Inchigeelagh | 6S/6 | 21 | [0202/4] | 33.D.12., 34.B.11., 7.D.8. | 1238-1246 |
| Inchinabacky | 6E/65 | 14 | 2065a, [0145] | 4.B.13. | |
| Inishcarra | 6N/52 | 19 | [0707/08] | 32.C.9. | 1124 |
| Inishkenny | 6N/69 | 20 | [0380/83], [0699], [0700] | 15.A.14. | 510 |
| Inishkenny | 6E/83 | 15 | 2192, [0380/83] | 32.D.6., 15.A.4. | |
| Inishannon | 6S/22 | 23 | 2111, 2226 [0205/6, 0616/18] | 25.F.1., 26.A.8., 8.G.8. | 242-243, 1027-1029 |
| Imphrick | 6E/41 | 12 | | | 906 |
| Imphrick | 6N/29 | 18 | 2264, [0452/53], [0780/81] | 36.A.10., 20.C.6. | |
| Island | 6S/62 | 24 | 2112, 2208 [0207/8, 0481/82] | 21.E.10., 8.G.14. | |
| Kilbolane | 6N/17 | 18 | 2265, [0782/83] | 35.D.13., 36.A.12., 31.G.3. | 1282-1288 |
| Kilbonane | 6N/60 | 20 | [0709/10] | | 1127 |
| Kilbrin | 6N/7 | 17 | [0421/22] | 17.D.12. | 788-791 |
| Kilbrittain | 6S/73 | 25 | 2113, [0209/10] | 9.A.4. | |
| Kilbrogan | 6S/19 | 22 | 2236, [ 0641/45, 0648/51] | 26.G.12. | 1055 |
| Kilbroney | 6N/30 | 18 | 2266, [0784/85] | 36.B.12. | 1289 |
| Kilcaskan | 6S/2 | 21 | 2090/93, [0175] | 4.E.4. | 90-129 |
| Kilcatherine | 6S/1 | 21 | 2094/96, [0176/77] | 5.A.4. | 130-188 |
| Kilcoe | 6S/48 | 24 | 2147, 2158/59, [0293] | 11.G.10. | 358-366 |
| Kilcorcoran | 6N/6 | 17 | [0423/24] | 17.E. 10. | |
| Kilcorney | 6N/37 | 19 | [0738/40] | 35.C.1. | 1247-1251 |
| Kilcredan | 6E/101 | 16 | [0537/38] | 24.B.2. | |
| Kilcrohane | 6S/44 | 23 | 2148, [0294/95] | 12.A.10. | 357, 367-374 |
| Kilcrumper | 6E/21 | 12 | 2172/73, [0341/42] | 19.C.3., 20.C.10., 14.A.10. | |
| Kilcully | 6E/74 | 15 | [0384/85] | 15.B.5. | |
| Kilcummer | | | [0454/56] | 20.C.14. | |
| Kildorrery | 6E/30 | 13 | 2174/75, [0343/45, 0457/58] | 20.D.4., 14.A.12. | |
| Kilfaughnabeg | 6S/14 | 22 | 2114, 2133 [0211/13] | 6.D.10., 7.F.11. | 375-378 |
| Kilgarriff | 6S/75 | 25 | 2115, 2209 [0214, 0483/84] | 9.A.12., 21.E.14., 8.C.3. | 244 |
| Kilgrogan | 6N/28 | 18 | 2267, [0786/87] | 36.C.2. | |
| Kilgullane | 6E/34 | 13 | 2176, [0346/47, 0449] | 20.D.6., 14.B.6. | 479 |
| Kilkerranmore | 6S/59 | 24 | 2210, 2216 [0215/17, 0485/87] | 6.D.12., 21.F.2. | 941-942 |
| Killaconenagh | 6S/4 | 21 | 2097/100, [0178/79] | 5.C.8. | 218-233 |
| Killanully | 6S/39 | 23 | [0386], [0579/81] | 25.A.14., 15.B.6. | 999 |
| Killanully | 6E/86 | 15 | 2193, [0386] | 25.A.14., 15.B.6. | |
| Killaspugmullane | 6E/51 | 14 | 2066, [0146/47] | 2.F.14. | 68-69 |

| PARISH | TITHES 1823–38 TAB | FILM | VALUATION FIELD BOOK 1830s OL4./ HOUSE BOOK [OL5.] | TENEMENT VALUATION FICHE 1851/3 | 1841/1851 CENSUS SEARCH Cen /S/6 |
|---|---|---|---|---|---|
| Killathy | 6E/28 | 13 | [0458a] | 20.D.8. | |
| Killeagh | 6E/90 & 91 | 15 | [0532/36], [2615] | 22.F.1., 24.B.4. | 964-966 |
| Killeenemer | 6E/19 | 12 | [0449] | 20.D.12. | |
| Killowen | 6S/18 | 22 | 2237, [0652/53] | 27.B.2. | |
| Killowillan | 6E/110 | 16 | | 27.B.2. | |
| Kilmacabea | 6S/11 | 22 | 2117, 2134 [0218/20, 0296/97] | 7.G.7., 11.B.14. | 380-384 |
| Kilmacdonogh | 6E/96 | 16 | [0544/45] | 22.F.11., 24.B.4. | |
| Kilmaclenine | 6N/33 | 18 | 2268, [0788/89] | 36.C.4. | 1290 |
| Kilmahon | 6E/104 | 16 | [0541/43] | 24.B.5. | |
| Kilmaloda | 6S/72 | 25 | 2119, [0221/3] | 8.C.3., 9.C.8. | 245-246 |
| Kilmeen | 6S/10 | 22 | 2120, 2135, [0224/27, 0488/89, 0425/26] | 17.E.12., 19.A.9., 6.D.12., 7.D.11., 21.F.12. | |
| Kilmeen | 6N/5 | 17 | 2211, [0224/27, 0488/89, 0425/26] | 17.E.12., 19.A.9., 6.D.12., 7.D.11., 21.F.12. | 247-249, 785-787, 792-813, 943 |
| Kilmichael | 6N/45 | 19 | 2250, [0741/44] | 33.E.9., 34.D.1., 7.E.4. | |
| Kilmichael | 6S/7 | 21 | 2121, 2136, [0228/31] | 33.E.9., 34.D.1., 7.E.4. | 1252-1253 |
| Kilmocomoge | 6S/5 | 21 | 2042a, 2043a 2118, 2149, [0232/33, 0298/99, 0091] | 1.B.3., 6.D.2., 12.A.6. | 1-21, 379 |
| Kilmoe | 6S/49 | 24 | 2150/52, [0300/303] | 12.G.10. | 385-409 |
| Kilmoney | 6S/42 | 23 | [0582/83] | 25.B.2. | |
| Kilmonogue | 6S/32 | 23 | 2227, [0091], [0619] | 25.F.1., 26.B.2. | 1030-1032 |
| Kilmurry | 6N/47 | 19 | 2251, [0718/19], [0745/47] | 34.D.3., 31.G.9. | 1254-1255 |
| Kilnaglory | 6N/63 | 20 | [0387/88], [0699], [0700] | 15.B.7., 32.D.10. | |
| Kilnaglory | 6E/82 | 15 | 2194, [0387/88] | 15.B.7., 32.D.10. | |
| Kilnagross | 6S/77 | 26 | 2122, [0234] | 9.D.6. | |
| Kilnamanagh | 6S/3 | 21 | 2101/03, [0180] | 5.F.5. | 189-217 |
| Kilnamartery | 6N/40 | 19 | 2252 [0748/50] | 34.D.13. | 1256-1257 |
| Kilpatrick | 6S/31 | 23 | [0620/22, 0584/85] | 26.B.8., 25.B.6. | 1000 |
| Kilphelan | 6E/35 | 12 | 2177/78, [0348/49] | 14.B.10. | |
| Kilquane | 6E/52 | 14 | 2067, 2069/70, [0452/3] | | |
| Kilquane | | 12 | 2067, [0148] | 2.G.6., 20.D.14. | |
| Kilroan | 6S/82 | 26 | [0404/05, 0672, 0674] | 16.B.2., 27.G.14. | |
| Kilroe | 6N/8 | 18 | [0427] | 17.G.10. | 814 |
| Kilsillagh | 6S/69 | 25 | 2212, [0490/91] | 21.F.14. | 944 |
| Kilshanahan | 6E/48 | 14 | 2070/71, [0149/50] | 3.E.9. | 67 |
| Kilshannig | 6N/16 | 18 | 2200, [0428] | 18.C.8. | 815-843 |
| Kilworth | 6E/36 | 13 | 2179, [0350/51] [2616] | 14.B.12. | 475-478 |
| Kinneigh | 6S/8 | 22 | 2137, [0235/37] | 6.C.6., 7.E.8. | 250-253 |
| Kinsale | 6S/85 | 26 | [0675/76, 0677] | 28.A.1. | 1077-1078, 1298 |
| Kinure | 6S/33 | 23 | [0623/25] | 25.F.1., 26.B.12. | 1033 |
| Knockavilly | 6S21 | 23 | [0626/27] | 25.F.2., 26.C.2., 31.G.10. | |

| PARISH | TITHES 1823–38 TAB | FILM | VALUATION FIELD BOOK 1830s OL4./ HOUSE BOOK [OL5.] | TENEMENT VALUATION FICHE 1851/3 | 1841/1851 CENSUS SEARCH Cen /S/6 |
|---|---|---|---|---|---|
| Knockavilly | 6N/67 | 20 | [0626/27], [0711/12] | 25.F.2., 26.C.2., 31.G.10. | 1126 |
| Knockmourne | 6E/68 | 14 | 2072, 2180 [0352, 0667/68, 0151] | 14.C.10., 3.E.13., 27.D.14. | 70, 480-482, 1063-1066 |
| Knocktemple | | | [0429] | 17.G.14, 18.E.13. | 844-851 |
| Lackeen | 6N/26 | 18 | 2269, [0790/90a] | 36.C.6. | |
| Leighmoney | 6S/28 | 23 | 2228, [0628, 0629] | 26.C.6. | 1034 |
| Leitrim | 6E/39 | 13 | 2181/82, [0353/55] | 14.C.12. | |
| Liscarroll | 6N/25 | 18 | 2270, [0791/93], [2627] | 35.D.13., 36.C.8. | 1291-1293 |
| Liscleary | 6S/40 | 23 | [0586/88] | 25.B.8. | 1001-1002 |
| Lisgoold | 6E/54 | 14 | 2073/75, 0152/53 | 4.C.1. | |
| Lislee | 6S/67 | 25 | 2213, [0492/94] | 21.G.2. | 945-953 |
| Lismore & Mocollop | 6E/40 | 13 | 2185, [0356/57] | 14.D.4. | 483-485 |
| Litter | 6E/29 | 12 | [0358/59, 0459/60] | 20.E.2., 14.D.6. | 907 |
| Little Island | 6E/60 | 14 | 2075/76, [0154/56] | 2.G.9. | |
| Macloneigh | 6N/43 | 19 | [0751/52] | 34.E.11. | 1269-1270 |
| Macroney | 6E/37 | 13 | 2185, [0360/64] | 14.D.10. | 489-490 |
| Macroom | 6N/41 | 19 | 2253, [0753/56], [2628/30] | 34.F.2. | 1258-1268 |
| Magourney | 6N/59 | 19 | [0713/15] | 33.B.12. | 1128-1129, 1134 |
| Mallow | 6N/15 | 18 | [0461, 0430], [2631/37] | 19.C.3., 20.E.6., 18.E.14. | 908-923 |
| Mallow | 6E/14 | 12 | [0461, 0430] | 19.C.3., 20.E.6., 18.E.14. | |
| Marmullane | 6S/36 | 23 | [0589/91] | 24.F.5., 25.B.15. | 1003-1005 |
| Marshalstown | 6E/32 | 13 | 2186, [0365/67] | 14.E.6. | 486-488 |
| Matehy | 6N/53 | 19 | [0716/17] | 32.D.14. | 1130-1133 |
| Middleton | 6E/93 | 15 | [0546/50], [2638/39] | 24.B.10. | |
| Mogeely | 6E/71, 89 | 15 | [0551/55, 0669/71] | 27.E.7., 24.D.3. | 967, 1067-1073 |
| Mogeesha | 6E/64 | 14 | 2077/78 [0556/57, 0157] | 4.C.5., 24.D.13. | 968 |
| Monanimy | 6E/24 | 12 | [0462/63] | 19.C.3., 20.G.6. | 924-925 |
| Monkstown | 6S/37 | 23 | [0592/94] | 24.F.5., 25.C.8. | 1006-1016 |
| Mourneabbey | 6E/22 | 12 | [0464] | 21.A.2., 2.B.2. | 28-31 |
| Mourneabbey | 6N/71 | 20 | [0464, 0101/04] | 21.A.2., 2.B.2. | |
| Moviddy | 6N/59 | 20 | [0718/19] | 31.G.13. | |
| Murragh | 6S/15 | 22 | 2123, 2238/39, [0238/40, 0654/55] | 6.C.13., 27.B.4. | 1056-1057b |
| Myross | 6S/54 | 24 | [0304/8] | 11.C.5. | 410-441 |
| Nohaval | 6S/34 | 23 | 2229, [0630/32] | 26.C.10. | |
| Nohavaldaly | 6N/4 | 17 | [0432] | 18.A.5. | 852-876 |
| Rahan | 6E/23 | 12 | [0465/66] | 19.C.4., 21.A.4. | 926-929 |
| Rathbarry | 6S/60 | 24 | 2214, [0241/43 [0495/6] | 6.E.4., 22.A.8. | 954 |
| Rathclarin | 6S/78 | 26 | 2124, [0244/46] | 8.C.3., 9.D.14. | 254-256 |
| Rathcooney | 6E/73 | 15 | 2195, [0389/91] | 15.B.8. | 511-517 |

| PARISH | TITHES 1823–38 TAB | FILM | VALUATION FIELD BOOK 1830s OL4./ HOUSE BOOK [OL5.] | TENEMENT VALUATION FICHE 1851/3 | 1841/1851 CENSUS SEARCH Cen /S/6 |
|---|---|---|---|---|---|
| Rathcormack | 6E/43 | 13 | 2079/80, [0158/60] | 3.E.14. | 71-79 |
| Rathgoggan | 6N/21 | 18 | 2271, [0794/97] | 35.D.13., 36.D.2. | 1294-1297 |
| Ringcurran | 6S/86 | 26 | 2230, [0629, 0633, 0672, 0674, 0677/80] | 26.D.2. | 1076, 1079-1081 |
| Ringrone | 6S/81 | 26 | 2125, [0247, 0406/07, 0672, 0674, 0680] | 8.C.3., 9.E.12., 16.A.14., 16.B.6., 28.D.2. | 257, 707 |
| Ross | 6S/12 | 22 | 2126, 2138, 2215 [0248, 0250/52, 0497/98] | 6.E.5., 22.B.4. | 258-264 |
| Rosskeen | 6N/14<br>6N/70 | 18<br>20 | [04330] | 18.A.8. | 877 |
| Rostellan | 6E/102 | 16 | [0556/59] | 24.E.1. | 969 |
| Shandrum | 6N/19 | 18 | 2272, [0798/99] | 35.D.14. | |
| Skull | 6S/47 | 24 | 2153/56, [0309] | 12.B.14. | 442-463 |
| St Anne's (Shandon) | 6E/77 | 15 | [0392/94], [2497/515] | 15.C.8. | 518-520, 601-609, 610 |
| St Finbar's | 6E/79 | 15 | [0395/96], [2516/27] | 32.A.7., 15.D.3. | |
| St Finbar's | 6N/62 | 20 | [0395/96], [0699] | 32.A.7., 15.D.3. 611-649 | 521-534, |
| St Mary's (Shandon) | 6E/76 | 15 | 2196, [0397/98], [2428/47] | 15.F.8. | 535-539, 650-676 |
| St Michael's | 6E/46 | 14 | 2081, 2197, [0161/63, 0399] | 2.G.12., 15.F.14. | |
| St Nathlash | 6E/10 | 12 | [0467] | 21.B.12. | 930 |
| St Nicholas | 6N/65 | 20 | [0400/1], [0699], [0700] | 32.E.7., 15.G.1. | |
| St Nicholas | 6E/81 | 15 | 2198, [0400/01] [2548/64] | 32.E.7., 15.G.1. | 677 |
| Subutler | 6N/9 | 18 | [0434], [3809] | 18.A.10. | |
| Templebodan | 6E/55 | 14 | [0164], 2081 | 4.C.10. | 80 |
| Templebreedy | 6S/43 | 23 | [0595/96] | 24.F.5., 25.D.8. | 1017-1020 |
| Templebryan | 6S/76 | 26 | 2127, [0253/54 | 9.F.4. | |
| Templemartin | 6S/16 | 22 | 2240, [0656/57] | 27.B.12. | |
| Templemichael | 6S/23 | 23 | 2231, [0634/35] | 26.D.4. | |
| Templemolaga | 6E/31 | 13 | 2187, [0368/69] | 14.F.2. | 491-492 |
| Templenacarriga | 6E/56 | 14 | 2083/84, [0165] | 4.D.2. | |
| Templeomalus | 6S/63 | 24 | 2216, [0499/500] | 22.B.6. | |
| Templequinlan | 6S/64 | 25 | 2128/2217, [0255/56, 0501/02] | 22.B.12., 9.F.8. | |
| Templeroan | 6E/6 | 12 | [0468] | 19.C.4., 21.B.6. | 931 |
| Templerobin | 6E.67 | 14 | 2085/86, [0166/71] | 3.G.14. | 81-89 |
| Templetrine | 6S/80 | 26 | 2129, [0257/58, 0408/09] | 8.C.3., 9.F.10., 16.A.14., 16.C.6. | 708 |
| Templeusque | 6E/47 | 14 | 2087, [0172/73] | | |
| Timoleague | 6S/65 | 25 | 2130, 2218, [0259, 0503], [2657] | 22.C.2., 9.G.2. | 265-266, 955 |
| Tisaxon | | | 2241 | 28.D.7. | |
| Titeskin | 6E/106 | 16 | [0560/61] | 24.E.4. | |
| Trabolgan | 6E/109 | 16 | [0562/63] | 24.E.6. | |
| Tracton | 6S/30 | 23 | 2232, [0636/37a] | 25.F.2., 26.D.8. | 1035-1036 |

| PARISH | TITHES 1823–38 TAB | FILM | VALUATION FIELD BOOK 1830s OL4./ HOUSE BOOK [OL5.] | TENEMENT VALUATION FICHE 1851/3 | 1841/1851 CENSUS SEARCH Cen /S/6 |
|---|---|---|---|---|---|
| Tullagh | 6S/57 | 24 | [0310/13] | 11.D.1. | 464 |
| Tullylease | 6N/2 | 17 | 2273 [0435] [0800/01] | 18.A.11., 36.F.4. | 878-890 |
| Wallstown | 6E/9 | 12 | [0458a, 0469] | 21.B.12. | |
| Whitechurch | 6E/72 | 15 | 2199 [0105/08, 0174/74a, 0402/03] | 2.B.14., 3.B.13., 15.G.10. | |
| Whitechurch | 6N/73 | 20 | [0105/08, 0174/74a, 0402/03] | 2.B.14., 3.B.13., 15.G.10. | 541 |
| Youghal | 6E/92 | 15 | [0564/69], [2661/69] | 22.G.9. | 970-972 |

| TOWNS & VILLAGES | VALUATION HOUSE BOOK 1830s [OL5.] | TOWNS & VILLAGES | VALUATION HOUSE BOOK 1830s [OL5.] |
|---|---|---|---|
| Aghern Village | [2482] | Glanmire | [2607] |
| Bandon | [2454/58] [0641/43] | Glanworth | [2608/09] |
| Bantry | [2459] | Holy Trinity | [2483/96] |
| Ballincollig | [2443/44] [0693/94] | Inishannon | [2610] |
| Ballycottin | [2446, 2447] | Kanturk | [2611/13] |
| Ballyclogh | [2627] | Killawillin | [2614] |
| Ballymagooly | [2450] | Killeagh | [2615] |
| Ballynacorra | [2451/52] | Kilworth | [2616] |
| Ballyneen | [2453] | Kingwilliamstown | [2469] |
| Ballynoe Village | [2482] | Kinsale | [2617/21, 2623/24] |
| Berehaven | [2465] | Lady's bridge | [2625/26] |
| Boherboy | [2469] | Millstreet | [2640] |
| Bridebridge | [2460] | Miscellaneous | [2579/94] |
| Castlemartyr | [2463/64] [0520/22] | Mitchelstown | [2641/42] [0322?] |
| Castletown | | New Glanmire | [2643] |
| (Berehaven) | [2465] | Newmarket | [2644] |
| Castletownsend | [2658] [0304/8] | Newmarket | [2469] |
| Cecilstown | [2469] | Passage West | [2645] |
| Charleville | [2470/71] [0794/92] | Queenstown | [2646/49] [0166/71] |
| Churchtown | [2627] | Riverstown | [2650] |
| Clonakilty | [2473/78] | Rockmills | [2651] |
| Cloyne | [2479/80] | Ross Carbery | [2652/53] |
| Coachford | [2481] [0713/15] | Scartlea | [2447] |
| Cobh | | Shanagarry | [2447] |
| (See Queenstown) | [2481] | Shanagarry | [2654] |
| Conna Village | [2482] | Shanballymore | [2655] |
| Carraglass Village | [2482] | Skibbereen | [2656] |
| Douglas | [2598] | St Paul's | [2565/69] |
| Dunmanway | [2600/602] | St Peter's | [2570/78] |
| Farsid | [2660] | Union Hall | [2658] [0304/8] |
| Fermoy | [2603/06] | Watergrasshill | [2659] |
| Freemount | [2469] | Whitegate | [2660] |

| PARISH | TITHES 1823–38 TAB 7/ | FILM | VALUATION FIELD BOOKS 1830s OL4./ HOUSE BOOKS [OL5.] | TENEMENT VALUATION c. 1857 FICHE | 1841–1851 CENSUS SEARCHES Cen /S/7 |
|---|---|---|---|---|---|
| Aghanunshin | 18 | 29 | 0353, 2316, [0818] | 9.A.12. | 671-680 |
| Allsaints | 29 | 30 | 0365, [0832] | 9.G.6., 11.A.2. | 1345-1357 |
| Aughnish | 16 | 29 | 0354, 2317, [0819/20] | 9.B.4. 12.D.11. | 681-696 |
| Ballintra (Drumhome) | | | [2671] | | |
| Ballyshannon (Kilbarron) | | | [2671] | | |
| Bundoran (Inishmacsaint) | | | [2671] [3810] | | |
| Burt | 25 | 30 | 0346, 2310/11, [0816] | 10.C.10. | 563-583 |
| Carndonagh | | | 2306 | | |
| Clonca | 1 | 27 | 0340, 2307 | 7.B.4. | 487-502 |
| Clondahorky | 10 | 28 | 0355, 2318, [0821] | 3.F.10. | 697-747 |
| Clondavaddog | 7 | 27 | 0356, 2319, [0822] | 13.B.4. | 748-808, 1667 |
| Clonleigh | 35 | 31 | 0368, 2329/30, [0833] | 14.C.5. | 1358-1384, 1387-8, 1930 |
| Clonmany | 2 | 27 | 0341, 2308 | 7.C.13. | 503-517 [T550/37 in PRONI] |
| Convoy | 36 | 31 | 0366, [0834] | 14.F.2. | 1528-1558 |
| Conwal | 17 | 29 | 0357, 0367, 2320/21, 2331 | 9.D.1. 11.C.12. 15.F.10. | 809-882 1559-1580 |
| Culdaff | 4 | 27 | 0342, 2309, [0812/3] | 7.E.10. | 518-526 |
| Derry (Templemore) | | | | | |
| Desertegny | 20 | 29 | 0347 | 8.E.8. | 584-595 |
| Donagh | 3 | 27 | 0343 | 7.G.6. | 527-539 |
| Donaghmore | 39 | 31 | 0369, 2332, [0835] | 13.E.8. 14.G.12. | 1581-1621 1645 |
| Donegal | 49 | 32 | 0378-79, [2671] | 2.G.6. | 1668-1715 |
| Drumhome | 49 | 32 | 0380, [0842] | 1.A.12. | 1716-1799, 1847 |
| Fahan Lower | 21 | 30 | 0348 | 8.F.1. | 596-629 |
| Fahan Upper | 22 | 30 | 0349, 2312 | 10.D.8. | 630-644 |
| Gartan | 14 | 29 | 0358, 2322, [0823] | 4.A.7. 9.B.6. | 883-905 |
| Glencolumbkille | 42 | 32 | 0328, [0802] 2275, 2284 | 4.G.8. | 1-51 |
| Inch | 24 | 30 | 0350, 2313/14 | 10.E.5. | 645-653 |
| Inishkeel | 28 | 30 | 0329, 0336, 2276, 2285, 2289/90, 2300/02, 2305, [0803/04] | 5.G.2. 5.B.3. | 52-85 316-372 |
| Inishmacsaint | 52 | 32 | 0381 | 1.E.8. | 1800-1808 1814-1819, 1824 |
| Inver | 46 | 32 | 0330, [0805/06], 2277 | 2.B.2. | 86-187, 714 |

| PARISH | TITHES 1823–38 TAB 7/ | FILM | VALUATION FIELD BOOKS 1830s OL4./ HOUSE BOOKS [OL5.] | TENEMENT VALUATION c. 1857 FICHE | 1841–1851 CENSUS SEARCHES CEN S[7] |
|---|---|---|---|---|---|
| Kilbarron | 51 | 32 | 0379<br>0382 | 1.B.14.<br>7.A.4. | 1803, 1807-1813<br>1819-1885 |
| Kilcar | 42 | 32 | 0331, 2278 | 5.C.1. | 188-222 |
| Killaghtee | 45 | 32 | 0332, 2279-80,<br>2287, [0807] | 2.D.9.<br>5.D.9. | 223-245 |
| Killea | 33 | 31 | 0370,<br>[0836] | 11.B.2. | 1389-1393 |
| Killybegs Lower | 41 | 32 | 0333, 0337,<br>2281, 2285,<br>2292/3,<br>[0808/09] | 6.C.4.<br>5.D.12. | 246-261, 351<br>373-377 |
| Killybegs Upper | | | 0334, 2282,<br>2286-7, [0810] | 5.E.9. | 262-284 |
| Killygarvan | 13 | 29 | 0359, 2323,<br>[0824] | 12.G.13. | 562, 906-930, 786 |
| Killymard | 47 | 32 | 0335, 2283,<br>2288, [0811] | 2.E.12. | 278, 285-315, 714 |
| Kilmacrenan | 15 | 29 | 0360, 2324,<br>[0825] | 4.A.9., 9.C.7.<br>12.F.3. | 802, 931-993 |
| Kilteevoge | 37 | 31 | 0371 | 15.C.2. | 1384-6,<br>1622-1644 |
| Laghy (Drumhome) | | | [2671] | | |
| Leck | 30 | 31 | 0372 | 9.G.6. | 863, 1394-1409 |
| Letterkenny (Conwal) | | | [3811] | | |
| Lettermacaward | 27 | 30 | 0338, 2294/95,<br>2303 | 6.C.7. | 378-397 |
| Malin (Clonca) | | | [3812] | | |
| Mevagh | 11 | 28 | 0361, 2325 | 11.C.14. | 517, 994-1075 |
| Mintiaghs (Barr of Inch) | 19 | 29 | 0351 | 8.G.10. | 650-653 |
| Moville Lower | 5 | 27 | 0344,<br>[0814] | 8.A.14. | 540-550 |
| Moville Upper | 6 | 27 | 0345,<br>[0815] | 8.C.11. | 551-562 |
| Muff | 13 | 30 | 0352, 2315, [0817] | 10.E.8. | 654-670 |
| Raphoe | 34 | 31 | 0373, 2333-5,<br>[0837/8] | 10.B.3.<br>13.G.6. | 1410-1445<br>1532, 1547 |
| Raymoghy | 34 | 31 | 0374,<br>[0839/40] | 10.A.3.<br>11.B.6. | 1357-1667<br>1446-1486 |
| Raymunterdoney | 9 | 28 | 0362, 2326,<br>[0826] | 14.A.13.<br>4.A.11. | 1076-1094 |
| Stranorlar | 38 | 31 | 0375, 2336 | 15.D.8. | 1645-1660 |
| Taughboyne | 32 | 31 | 0376,<br>[0841] | 11.B.9.<br>14.B.3. | 506, 1487-1527<br>1373, 1470 |
| Templecarn | 50 | 32 | 0383 | 3.D.4. | 1886-1929 |
| Templecrone | 26 | 30 | 0339, 2304,<br>2296/9 | 6.D.4. | 398-486 |
| Templemore | 20 | 29 | 0364,<br>[0827/9] | | |

| PARISH | TITHES 1823–38 TAB 7/ | FILM | VALUATION FIELD BOOKS 1830s OL4./ HOUSE BOOKS [OL5.] | TENEMENT VALUATION c. 1857 FICHE | 1841–1851 CENSUS SEARCHES CEN S|7| |
|---|---|---|---|---|---|
| Tullaghobegley | 8 | 28 | 0363, 2327, [0827/29] | 4.B.8. | 433, 1095-1319 |
| Tullyfern | 12 | 29 | 0364, 2328, [0830/31] | 12.B.11. | 768, 794, 1320-1344 |
| Urney | 40 | 32 | 0377, 2337 | 13.F.10. | 1661-1667 |

| TOWNS | VALUATION HOUSE BOOK 1830s [OL5.] |
|---|---|
| Ballyshannon | [2671] |
| Bundoran | [3810, 2671] |
| Letterkenny | [3811] |
| Lifford | [2670] |
| Malin | [3812] |
| Pettigoe | [2671] |
| Killybegs | X.056 valuation book 1857 |

| PARISH | TITHES 1823–38 TAB 9/ | FILM | VALUATION FIELD BOOKS 1830s OL4./ HOUSE BOOKS [OL5.] | TENEMENT VALUATION 1848–52 FICHE | 1841–1851 CENSUS SEARCHES Cen /S/9 |
|---|---|---|---|---|---|
| Aderrig | 49 | 34 | | 4.G.2., 5.B.13 | |
| Artaine/Artane | | 34 | [0864/65], [2711] | 2.G.10 | |
| Baldongan | 5 | 33 | [0843] | 1.A.8., 1.G.7 | |
| Baldoyle | | 34 | | 2.G.12. | |
| Balgriffin | 34 | 34 | [0866/67], [2711] | 3.A.3. | |
| Ballyboghil | 14 | 33 | | 2.A.3., 2.A.6. | |
| Ballyfermot & Palmerstown | 59 | 34 | [0931] | 7.A.14., 8.A.7. | |
| Ballymadun | 10 | 33 | [0856] | 2.A.8., 2.C.10. | |
| Balrothery | 2 | 33 | [0844/45], [2673] | 1.A.9., 1.G.7. | 1-5 |
| Balscaddan | 1 | 33 | [0846/47] | 1.C.3. | |
| Booterstown | 71 | 35 | [2675], [0895] | 3.G.6., 4.C.7., 5.C.14. | 300-301 |
| Castleknock | 26 | 34 | [3814] | 2.D.6., 2.G.1. | 26 |
| Chapelizod | 27 | 34 | | 2.E.6., 2.G.1. | 27-28 |
| Cloghran | 31 | 34 | [0868/69], [2711] | 2.E.9., 2.G.1. | |
| Clondalkin | 58 | 34 | [0931a/34] | 4.G.2., 5.B.1., 7.B.1, 8.A.7. | 334-339 |
| Clonmethan | 12 | 33 | [0857] | 2.A.10., 2.C.10 | 20 |
| Clonsilla | 25 | 33 | [0862] | 2.E.10., 2.G.10 | |
| Clontarf | 46 | 34 | [0870/71] | 3.A.8. | 30-31 |
| Clonturk | | 34 | [0872/74] | 3.B.3. | 32 |
| Clorhran | | 33 | | | |
| Coolock | 35 | 34 | | 3.B.12. | 33-34 |
| Cruagh | 66 | 35 | | 7.B.13., 8.A.7. | 340 |
| Crumlin | 62 | 34 | [0935], [2676] | 7.C.1., 8.A.8. | 341 |
| Dalkey | 78 | 35 | [0896], [2677] | 5.D.12. | 302-305 |
| Donabate | 17 | 34 | | 4.C.14., 4.F.6. | 277-278 |
| Donnybrook (St. Mary's) | 68 | 35 | [0897], [0936], [2679/87] | 7.C.6., 8.A.8., 3.G.7., 5.E.7. | 41-52 |
| Drimnagh | 61 | 34 | | 7.C.7. | |
| Dublin city (No parish) | | | | | 54-77, 79-87, 89, 92-135, 137-165, 167, 169-188, 190-209, 211, 213-215, 217-242, 244-251, 255-270, 272-275, 349, 362-3, 374 |
| Esker | | 34 | | 4.G.2., 5.B.13., 7.C.8., 8.A.8. | 288-290 |
| Finglas | 24 | 33 | [2690] | 4.D.2., 4.F.6., 2.E.13., 2.G.1. | |
| Garristown | 7 | 33 | [0858] | 2.A.13., 2.C.10. | 21-23 |
| Glasnevin | 37 | 34 | [2691], [0875/76] | 3.C.2. | |
| Grallagh | 8 | 33 | | 2.B.13., 2.C.10. | |
| Grangegorman | 43 | 34 | [0877] | 3.C.8. | 35, 58, 212, 216 |
| Hollywood | 9 | 33 | [0859] | 2.B.14., 2.C.11. | |
| Holmpatrick | | 33 | [0848] | 1.C.9., 1.G.7 | 6-11 |
| Howth | 42 | 34 | [0878], [3818] | 3.C.11. | |
| Kilbarrack | 41 | 34 | [0879/80] | 3.D.5. | 36 |

| PARISH | TITHES 1823–38 TAB 9/ | FILM | VALUATION FIELD BOOKS 1830s OL4./ HOUSE BOOKS [OL5.] | TENEMENT VALUATION 1848–52 FICHE | 1841–1851 CENSUS SEARCHES Cen /S/9 |
|---|---|---|---|---|---|
| Kilbride | 53 | 34 | | 4.B.6. | 291 |
| Kilgobbin | 79 | 35 | [0898/99] | 5.E.9. | 306 |
| Kill | 77 | 35 | [0900] | 5.E.13. | 307-308 |
| Killeek | 20 | 33 | | 4.D.3., 4.F.6. | |
| Killiney | 80 | 35 | [0901/02] | 5.F.6. | 309-310 |
| Killossery | 15 | 33 | | 4.D.4., 4.F.6. | |
| Killester | 45 | 34 | [0881] | | |
| Kilmactalway | 51 | 34 | | 4.G.6., 5.B.13. | 292 |
| Kilmacud | 73 | 35 | | 5.F.10. | |
| Kilmahuddrick | 52 | 34 | | 4.G.9., 5.B.13. | |
| Kilsallaghan | 19 | 33 | | 4.D.6., 4.F.6. | 279 |
| Kiltiernan | 81 | 35 | [0903] | 5.F.11. | 311 |
| Kinsaley | 32 | 32 | [0882] | 3.D.8. | 37 |
| Leixlip | 47 | 34 | | 4.G.9., 5.B.13. | 293-294 |
| Lucan | | 34 | [2705] | 4.G.11., 5.B.14. | 295-296 |
| Lusk | 4 | 33 | [0849/53], [2706] | 1.D.11., 1.G.8. | 12-19 |
| Malahide | 28 | 34 | [0883/84] | 3.D.12. | 38-39 |
| Monkstown | 75 | 35 | [0904/21], [2707] | 4.B.8., 4.C.7., 5.F.14. | 312-318 |
| Naul | 6 | 33 | [0860] | 2.C.4., 2.C.11. | 24-25 |
| Newcastle | 54 | 34 | [2708] | 5.A.1., 5.B .14. | 297-298 |
| Old Connaught | 83 | 35 | [0922] | 6.D.4. | 319 |
| Palmerston | 59 | 34 | [0937], [2709] | 7.C.9., 8.A.8. | |
| Palmerstown | 11 | 33 | [0861] | 2.C.7., 2.C.11. | 342-344 |
| Portmarnock | 33 | 34 | [0885] | 3.E.4. | |
| Portraine | 18 | 33 | | 4.D.9., 4.F.7. | |
| Raheny | 40 | 34 | [0886/88], [2710/11] | 3.E.7. | |
| Rathcoole | 55 | 34 | [2715] | 5.A.8., 5.B.14. | 299 |
| Rathfarnham | 69 | 35 | [0863], [0923], [3815] | 7.C.14., 8.A.8., 6.D.12. | 320-325 |
| Rathmichael | 82 | 35 | [0924] | 6.E.13. | |
| Saggart | 56 | 34 | [2720] | 5.B.3., 5.C.1. | |
| Santry | 30 | 34 | [0894], [2711] | 3.F.5. | |
| St Brides's | | | | | 271 |
| St Brigid's | | | | | 78 |
| St Catherine's | 63 | 34 | [0938] | 7.C.14., 8.A.8. | 345-346 |
| St George's | 44 | 34 | [0889/91] | 3.E.11. | 252 |
| St James' | 60 | 34 | [0939/42] | 2.F.12., 2.G.1. | 29, 166, 347-348, 350 |
| St John's | | | | | 168 |
| St Jude's | | | | | 351 |
| St Kevin's | | | | | 88 |
| St Margaret's | | 34 | [0894] | 3.F.2. | 40 |
| St Mark's | | 35 | | 4.B.9., 4.C.7. | |
| St Michan's | | | | | 136, 243 |
| St Mary's | 85 | 36 | | | |
| St Nicholas Within | | | | | 210 |
| St Nicholas Without | | | [0943/44] | | |
| St Paul's | | | | | 254 |

| PARISH | TITHES 1823–38 TAB 9/ | FILM | VALUATION FIELD BOOKS 1830s OL4./ HOUSE BOOKS [OL5.] | TENEMENT VALUATION 1848–52 FICHE | 1841–1851 CENSUS SEARCHES Cen /S/9 |
|---|---|---|---|---|---|
| St Peter's | | 35 | [0945/47] | 7.D.14., 8.A.9., 4.B.9., 4.C.7. | 352-361 |
| St Patrick's | 84 | 36 | | | |
| St Thomas' | | | | | 90 |
| St Werburgh's | | | | | 276 |
| Stillorgan | 77 | 35 | [0925/26] | 6.F.4. | 326 |
| Swords | 16 | 33 | [2724/25] | 4.D.14., 4.F.7., 3.F.10. | 280-287 |
| Tallaght | 65 | 35 | [0948/51], [2726] | 7.G.3., 8.A.9. | 364-373 |
| Taney | 70 | 35 | [0927/28] | 4.C.6., 6.F.10. | 53, 327-328 |
| Tully | 76 | 35 | | 6.G.9. | 329-330 |
| Ward | | 33 | | 2.F.13. | |
| Westpalstown | 13 | 33 | | 2.C.9., 2.C.11. | |
| Whitechurch | 72 | 35 | [0929/30] | 6.G.12. | 331-333 |
| Williamstown | | | [3816/17] | | |

| TOWNS | VALUATION HOUSE BOOK 1830s [OL5.] | TOWNS | VALUATION HOUSE BOOK 1830s [OL5.] |
|---|---|---|---|
| Artaine | [2711] | Haroldscross | [2694, 2696, 2697] |
| Balbriggan | [2672/73] | Haroldcross E | [2695] |
| Balgriffin | [2711] | Islandbridge | [2698] |
| Ballybough | [2711] | Killester S. | [2711] |
| Balrothery | [2673] | Kilmainham | [2699] |
| Blackrock | [2674], [0904/21] | Kingstown | [2700/03] [0904/21] |
| Booterstown | [2675] | Little Bray | [2704] |
| Clontarf E | [2711] | Lusk | [2706] |
| Coolock | [2711] | Portobello | [2694] |
| Crumlin | [2676] | Raheny | [2710/11] |
| Dalkey | [2677] | Rathmines W | [2696] |
| Dolphin's Barn | [2678] | Richmond | [2711] |
| Donnybrook | [2679/87] | Ranelagh N | [2712] |
| Drumcondra | [2688] | Ranelagh S | [2713/14] |
| Dundrum | [2689] | Rathmines E | [2716/17] |
| Finglas | [2690] | Rathmines W | [2717] |
| Glasnevin | [2691] | Rush | [2718/19] [0854] |
| Glasthule | [2692] | Skerries | [2721/23] [0855] |
| Goldenbridge | [2693] | | |

| PARISH | TITHES 1823–38 TAB 11/ | FILM | VALUATION FIELD BOOKS 1830s OL4./ HOUSE BOOKS [OL5.] | TENEMENT VALUATION 1855–6 FICHE | 1841–1851 CENSUS SEARCHES Cen /S/11 |
|---|---|---|---|---|---|
| Abbey | 121 | 41 | | | |
| Abbeygormacan | 112 | 41 | [1026], [3833] | 11.A.2., 2.B.2., 10.G.14., 14.B.4. | 1624-1625, 1774-1794 |
| Abbeyknockmoy | 41 | 40 | 0540, 051 0542, [0964] | 6.A.2., 15.C.2., 17.B.12. | 2408-2427 |
| Addergoole | 10 | 37 | | 16.C.4. | 825-871 |
| Ahascragh | 78 | 40 | [0996], [2727/28] | 2.A.6., 11.G.2., 1.E.12., 11.E.12., 11.F.14. | 655-673, 702, 1184-1200, 1274-1280 |
| Annaghdown | 36 | 38 | 0543 /44, [0965] | 6.A .3., 15.C.2. | 471-508 |
| Ardrahan | 66 | 39 | 0588, [1018], [1037] | 8.G.2., 9.F.10., 7.G.10., 9.B.14., 10.C.14. | 703-712, 1438-1443, 1917-1919 |
| Athenry | 69 | 39 | 0520, 0545 0546, 0547 [0966], [3825], [2729/30] | 6.B.4., 5.E.4., 5.C.14., 9.D.12. | 49-67, 509-510, 713 |
| Athleague | | | | 11.G.4. | 1281-1290 |
| Augheart | 123 | 41 | | | |
| Aughrim | 77 | 40 | [0997/98], [2731/32] | 1.F.1., 1.B.9. | 674-675, 1201-1204 |
| Ballinchalla | No Tab | 37 | [1044] | 13.G.8., | 2292-2301 |
| Ballindoon | 4 | 37 | 0537, [0960], [3831] | 2.E.12. | 289-300 |
| Ballinrobe | No Tab | 37 | [1045] | 13.G.10. | 2302-2317 |
| Ballymacward | 46 | 39 | [0999/100] | 2.A.12., 10.B.12., 12.C.14., 1.F.7., 11.F.1. | 1205-1216, 2428-2452 |
| Ballynacourty | 56 | 39 | | 5.E.6. | 714-729 |
| Ballynakill | 19 | 38 | 0528 , [0952], [2739/40] | 7.D.10. | 79-117?, 1626-1718? |
| Ballynakill | | 39 | 0538 | 11.G.9. | 301-347? |
| Ballynakill | 105 | 41 | [0961], [3834] | 11.B.12., 14.F.10. | 1291-1295? |
| Beagh | 90 | 40 | [1019] | 8.A.1. | 1444-1494 |
| Belclare | 30 | 38 | 0548, [0967] | 15.C.7. | 511-518 |
| Boyounagh | 18 | 38 | 0529, [0953], [1047a] | 6.F.12., 6.D.12. | 118-127, 2453 |
| Bullaun | 91 | 40 | [1043] | 10.D.1. | 1920-1922 |
| Cargin | 31 | 38 | 0549, 0550, [0968] | 15.C.7. | 519-521 |
| Claregalway | 55 | 39 | 0551/52/53, [0969] | 6.B.8., 5.F.1. | 522-533, 728-735 |
| Clonbern | 22 | 38 | 0530 | 6.G.12., 17.D.8. | 128-169 |
| Clonfert | 111 | 41 | | 2.C.8., 14.B.4. | 1795-1821 |
| Clonkeen | 45 | 39 | | 10.B.13., 12.D.4. | 2454-2463 |
| Clonrush | 107 | 41 | | 17.G.12. | 1719-1726 |
| Clontuskert | 81 | 40 | | 1.B.10., 2.B.8. | 676-682 |
| Cong | 8 | 37 | [1046] | 13.E.4. | 2318-2351 |
| Cummer | 34 | 38 | 0554/55/56, [0970] | 15.D.13. | 534 |
| Derrymacloughney | 122 | 41 | | | |
| Donaghpatrick | 26 | 38 | 0557 /58, [0971] | 15.D.13. | 535-559 |
| Dunamon | 21 | 38 | 0532, [0955] | 17.F.1. | 177 |
| Donanaghta | 115 | 41 | [1027/29] | 14.B.5. | 1822-1834 |

| PARISH | TITHES 1823–38 TAB 11/ | FILM | VALUATION FIELD BOOKS 1830s OL4./ HOUSE BOOKS [OL5.] | TENEMENT VALUATION 1855–6 FICHE | 1841–1851 CENSUS SEARCHES Cen /S/11 |
|---|---|---|---|---|---|
| Dunmore | 11 | 37 | 0533, [0956/57], [2745] | 16.D.2., 7.A.7., 17.D.11., | 178-211, 872-967 |
| Drumatemple | 17 | 38 | 0531, [0954] | 7.A.5. | 170-176 |
| Drumacoo | 61 | 39 | 0592 | 5.F.10., 8.G.9. | 736-750 |
| Duniry | 103 | 41 | [1030], [3834], [3840] | 11.A.4., 14.G.13. | 1727-1739 |
| Fahy | 114 | 41 | | 14.B.11. | 1835-1843 |
| Fohanagh | 71 | 39 | [1001] | 1.F.12., 11.F.4., 1.C.8. | 1217-1236 |
| Grange | 74 | 40 | [1002/03] | 10.A.10., 10.D.3. | 1237-1243 |
| Inishcaltra | 106 | 41 | [3835] | 18.A.7. | 1740-1747 |
| Inisheer | 84 | 40 | 0517, [3822] | 5.D.4. | 1-7 |
| Inishmaan | 83 | 40 | 0518, [3823] | 5.D.5. | 8-21 |
| Inishmore | 82 | 40 | 0519, [3824] | 5.D.7. | 22-48 |
| Isertkelly | 93 | 40 | [3843] | 10.D.3. | 1923-1924 |
| Kilbarron | | 41 | | 18.A.14. | |
| Kilbeacanty | 89 | 40 | [1020] | 8.B.5. | 1495-1526 |
| Kilbegnet | 20 | 38 | [0958] | 7.E.10., 17.F.2. | 212-226 |
| Kilbennan | 13 | 37 | | 16.F.1. | 968-993 |
| Kilchreest | 95 | 40 | 0593, [0983], [3844] | 9.F.12., 10.D.4. | 1925-1927 |
| Kilcloony | 80 | 40 | | 1.C.8. | 683-691, 699 |
| Kilcolgan | 63 | 39 | 0594 | 8.G.13. | 751-762 |
| Kilconickny | 68 | 39 | 0521, 0595, [0984], [3826] | 9.F.14., 9.E.10., 10.D.6. | 763, 1928-1930 |
| Kilconierin | 68 | 39 | 0522, 0596, [0985], [3827] | 9.G.5., 9.E.11., 10.D.12. | 68-69, 764 |
| Kilconla | 12 | 37 | [0972] | 16.F.11. | 994-1032 |
| Kilconnell | 72 | 40 | [1004], [2774] | 1.F.13. | 1244-1250 |
| Kilcooly | 100 | 40 | [3836] | 11.A.7. | 1748-1750 |
| Kilcoona | 33 | 38 | 0559, 0560 | 15.E.7. | 560-567 |
| Kilcroan | 16 | 38 | [0959] | 7.B.4. | 227-241 |
| Kilcummin | 23 | 38 | [3846] | 5. B.4., 12.G.14. | 1964-2065 |
| Kilgerrill | 79 | 40 | [1005/06] | 1.G.6., 1.E.3. | 692-698 |
| Killinny | 86 | 40 | | | |
| Kilkerrin | 39 | 38 | [1047b/47c] | 6.E.2. | 2464-2527 |
| Kilkilvery | 29 | 38 | [0973/74] | 15.E.12. | 568-570 |
| Killaan | 75 | 40 | [1007] | 1.G.7., 10.B.7., 10.D.13. | 1931, 1251-1254 |
| Killallaghtan | 76 | 40 | 0587, [1008] | 1.G.11., 1.E.7. | 1255-1259 |
| Killannin | 24 | 38 | [3845] | 4.G.14., 13.C.7. | 2054-2241 |
| Killeany | 32 | 38 | 0562, 0563, [0975] | 15.F.1. | 571-579 |
| Killeely | 58 | 39 | | 9.A.4. | 765-773 |
| Killeenadeema | 96 | 40 | [1038] | 10.D.13. | 1932-1936 |
| Killeenavarra | 65 | 39 | | 9.A.12. | 774-785 |
| Killeeneen | 59 | 39 | [0986] | 9.B.3., 9.G.9. | 786-788 |
| Killererin | 35 | 38 | 0534, 0564, 0565, [0976] | 16.G.5., 17.C.11 17.D.12., 15.F.6., | 242-243, 580-598, 1033-1035, 2487 |

| PARISH | TITHES 1823–38 TAB 11/ | FILM | VALUATION FIELD BOOKS 1830s OL4./ HOUSE BOOKS [OL5.] | TENEMENT VALUATION 1855–6 FICHE | 1841–1851 CENSUS SEARCHES Cen /S/11 |
|---|---|---|---|---|---|
| Killeroran | 48 | 39 | [1017] | 11.G.12. | 1296-1353 |
| Killian | 47 | 39 | [1016] | 12.B.2. | 1354-1415 |
| Killimorbologue | 116 | 41 | [1031/32] | 14.B.14. | 1844-1849 |
| Killimordaly | 73 | 40 | 0523/25, [3828], [1010/11] | 10.C.5., 9.E.12., 10.A.13. | 70, 1260-1265, 2528 |
| Killinny | | | [1021] | 8.C.2. | 1527-1534 |
| Killinan | 94 | 40 | [0987], [1039] | 12.B.2. | 1937-1939 |
| Killogilleen | 67 | 39 | [0988], [1040] | 9.G.11., 10.E.14. | 789-791, 1940 |
| Killora | 60 | 39 | [0989] | 9.G.14. | 792-799 |
| Killoran | 109 | 41 | [1017], [3837] | 1.E.10., 11.A.9., 2.B.11. | 700-701, 1753 1850-1863 |
| Killoscobe | 42 | 40 | | 12.D.4. | 2529-2558 |
| Killosolan | 43 | 39 | [1009] | 12.D.13., 11.F.8. | 1266-1273, 2559-2581 |
| Killower | 27 | 38 | [0977] | 15.G.3. | 599-604 |
| Killursa | 28 | 38 | [0978] | 15.G.6. | 605-629 |
| Kilmacduagh | 88 | 40 | [1022] | 8.C.7. | 1535-1561 |
| Kilmalinogue (Portumna) | 120 | 41 | | 14.C.12. | 1864-1867 |
| Kilmeen | 99 | 40 | [3838], [1043] | 10.F.1., 11.A.9. | 1751-1752, 1941 |
| Kilmoylan | 37 | 38 | [0979] | | 630-631 |
| Kilquain | 113 | 41 | | 14.D.2. | 1868-1878 |
| Kilreekill | 98 | 40 | [3839] | 2.A.10., 11.A.12. | |
| Kiltartan | 87 | 40 | [1023] | 8.D.6. | 1563-1584 |
| Kilteskill | 101 | 40 | [1041], [3840] | 10.F.1., 11.B.2. | |
| Kilthomas | 97 | 40 | [1042] | 8.E.4., 10.B.10, 9.C.1. | 1585-1590 1942-1952 |
| Kiltormer | 110 | 41 | [1033] | 2.C.1. | 1879-1887 |
| Kiltullagh | 70 | 39 | 0526, [1012/13], [3829] | 9.E.13., 10.B.5. | 71-78 |
| Kinvarradoorus | 85 | 40 | [1025] | 8.E.7. | 1591-1623 |
| Lackagh | 38 | 38 | [0980] | 6.B.13., 16.B.4. | 632-642 |
| Leitrim | 102 | 41 | [3841] | 11.B.4. | 1754-1761 |
| Lickerrig | | 39 | [0990] | 10.A.7., 9.F.9. | |
| Lickerrig | 64 | 39 | 0527, [3830] | 10.F.4. | 800 |
| Lickmolassy (Portumna) | 119 | 41 | [1034/35] | 14.D.6. | 1888-1905 |
| Liskeevy | 12/9 | 37 | | 16.G.6. | 1036-1082 |
| Loughrea | 92 | 40 | [1043], [2778/81] | 10.F.5. | 1953-1963 |
| Meelick | 118 | 41 | | 14.E.9. | 1906-1911 |
| Monivea | 44 | 39 | [0981], [1014/15], [1047d] | 6.C.9., 5.G.14. 10.C.6., 17.C.13. | 2582-2606 |
| Moycullen | 25 | 38 | [3847] | 5.B.6. | 2242-2289 |
| Moylough | 40 | 39 | [2782/83] | 6.F.9., 12.E.10., 17.D.7., 12.C.6. | 1416-1422, 2607-2655 |
| Moyrus | 3 | 37 | [0962] | 3.A.8., 3.F.6. | 348-429 |
| Omey | 2 | 37 | 0539, [0963], [3832] | 3.D.7. | 430-470 |

| PARISH | TITHES 1823–38 TAB 11/ | FILM | VALUATION FIELD BOOKS 1830s OL4./ HOUSE BOOKS [OL5.] | TENEMENT VALUATION 1855–6 FICHE | 1841–1851 CENSUS SEARCHES Cen /S/11 |
|---|---|---|---|---|---|
| Oranmore | 52 | 39 | [2784/87] | 4.F.4., 4.G.10., 3.G.8., 4.B.2., 5.F.10. | 801-821, 1109-1111 |
| Rahoon | 53 | 39 | [3848] | 5.C.10., 4.F.8., 4.C.10. | 1112-1141, 2290-2291 |
| Ross | 7 | 37 | [1047] | 13.F.2., 14.A.1. | 2352-2407 |
| St Nicholas & Islands | 54 | 39 | | 4.F.7., 3.G.11., 4.B.3., 4.F.1. | 1142-1162 |
| Stradbally | 57 | 39 | | 5.G.9., 9.B.12 | 822-824 |
| Taghboy | | 39 | | 12.C.10. | 1423-1437 |
| Templetogher | 15 | 38 | 0535 | 7.B.11. | 244-287 |
| Tiranascragh | 117 | 41 | | 14.F.1. | 1912-1913 |
| Tuam | 14 | 37 | 0536, [0982], [2792/6] | 16.G.14., 17.D.12., 16.A.11 | 288, 643-654, 1083-1108 |
| Tynagh | 104 | 41 | [1036], [3840], [3842] | 11.B.10., 15.A.1., 14.F.4. | 1762-1773, 1914-1916 |

| TOWNS & VILLAGES | VALUATION HOUSE BOOK 1830s [OL5.] |
|---|---|
| Ballinasloe | [2733/36] |
| Ballygar | [2737/38] |
| Ballynakill (Woodford) | [2739/40] |
| Clarin Bridge | [2741] |
| Clifden | [2742/43] |
| Craughwell (Killora) | [2744] |
| Eyrecourt | [2746] |
| Portumna | [2746, 2788/89] |
| Killimor | [2746] |
| Galway City | [2747/67] [1163-1183] |
| Gort | [2768/70] |
| Headford | [2771/73] |
| Killimor | [2775] |
| Kinvarra | [2776/77] |
| Roundstone | [2790/91] |

| PARISH | TITHES 1823–38 TAB 12/ | FILM | VALUATION FIELD BOOKS 1830s OL4./ HOUSE BOOKS [OL5.] | TENEMENT VALUATION 1855–6 FICHE | 1841–1851 CENSUS SEARCHES Cen /S/12 |
|---|---|---|---|---|---|
| Aghadoe | | | [1135/38] | 5.D.10., 9.G.12. | |
| Aghavallen | 2 | 42 | [1111/12] | 6.F.12. | 487-528 |
| Aglish | 74 | 44 | [1139/43] | 10.A.14. | 935-945 |
| Annagh | 53 | 43 | 2571/2604, [1056/57], [1185] | 2.G.12., 11.E.14. | 1068 |
| Ardfert | 25 | 42 | 2572/2573/2605, [1048] | 1.B.2., 11.F.10. | 1-15, 1069-1074 |
| Ballincuslane | 56 | 44 | 2576/77/ 2606 | 11.F.14. | 1075-1114 |
| Ballinvoher | 40 | 43 | [1058/59] | 2.G.14. | 151-173 |
| Ballyconry | 8 | 42 | | 7.A.8. | |
| Ballyduff | 28 | 42 | [1060/61] | 3.A.13. | 174 |
| Ballyheige | 16 | 42 | | 1.C.2. | 16-21 |
| Ballymacelligott | 49 | 43 | 2578/2607 | 12.A.6. | 1115-1121 |
| Ballynacourty | 39 | 43 | [1062/63] | 3.B.2. | 175 |
| Ballynahaglish | 45 | 43 | 2579/2607a | 12.B.8. | 1122-11252 |
| Ballyseedy | 54 | 44 | 2580/81 | 12.B.14. | 1126 |
| Brosna | 52 | 43 | [1186] | 12.C.6. | |
| Caher | 65 | 44 | 2559, [1120/21] | 8.C.8. | 639-658, 660-672 |
| Castleisland | 51 | 43 | 2587, [2802/03] | 12.D.4. | 1173-1233 |
| Cloghane | 27 | 42 | [1064/65] | 3.B.9. | 191-196 |
| Clogherbrien | 46 | 43 | 2588/2609 | 12.F.4. | 1234 |
| Currans | 59 | 44 | 2589/2610, [1144/46] | 12.F.10., 10.B.6. | 1235-1241 |
| Dingle | 35 | 43 | [1066/67], [2806/07] | 3.C.3. | 197-210 |
| Drumod | 70 | 44 | 2560, [1122/23] | 8.E.7. | 673-731 |
| Duagh | 15 | 42 | [1113] | 7.A.12., 1.D.8. | 22-48, 529-530 |
| Dunquin | 41 | 43 | [1068/69] | 3.E.4. | 211-217 |
| Dunurlin | 32 | 43 | [1070/71] | 3.E.10. | |
| Dysert | 13 | 42 | 2590 | 7.B.2., 1.D.12. | 49-52, 531-534, 1242-1249 |
| Dysert | 61 | 44 | | 12.G.2. | |
| Fenit | 44 | 43 | 2591 | 12.G.8. | 1250-1252 |
| Finuge | 14 | 42 | [1049] | 1.F.2. | 53-60 |
| Galey | 6 | 42 | | 7.B.6. | 535-545 |
| Garfinny | 36 | 43 | [1072/73] | 3.E.14. | 218 |
| Glanbehy | 67 | 44 | 2561, [1124/25] | 8.G.9. | 732-771 |
| Kenmare | 84 | 45 | 2554, [2808] | 5.G.14. | 448-460 |
| Kilbonane | 74 | 44 | [1147/49] | 10.B.8. | 946-953 |
| Kilcaragh | 19 | 42 | [1050] | 1.F.8. | 61-68 |
| Kilcaskan | 87 | 45 | 2555 | 6.B.7. | |
| Kilcolman | 62 | 44 | 2592/93, [1150/51] | 12.G.10., 10.C.6. | 954-961, 1253-1267 |
| Kilconly | 1 | 42 | | 7.C.4. | 546-554 |
| Kilcredane | 76 | 44 | [1152/55] | 10.C.10. | |
| Kilcrohane | 82 | 45 | [1096/102] | 4.D.14. | 303-444 |
| Kilcummin | 77 | 45 | [1156/59] | 10.C.14. | 962-1013 |
| Kildrum | 43 | 43 | [1074/76] | 3.F.3. | 219-220 |
| Kilfeighny | 20 | 42 | | 1.F.12. | 69-83 |
| Kilflyn | 24 | 42 | [1051] | 1.G.8. | 84-85 |
| Kilgarrylander | 57 | 44 | 2611, [1187] | 13.A.8. | 1268-1273 |
| Kilgarvan | 85 | 45 | 2556 | 6.B.14. | 461-468 |
| Kilgobban | 31 | 43 | [1077/78] | 3.F.9. | 221-233 |
| Killaha | 81 | 45 | 2569/70, [1160/62] | 10.F.14. | 1014-1019 |
| Killahan | 17 | 42 | [1052] | 2.A.2. | 123-124 |

| PARISH | TITHES 1823–38 TAB 12/ | FILM | VALUATION FIELD BOOKS 1830s OL4./ HOUSE BOOKS [OL5.] | TENEMENT VALUATION 1855–6 FICHE | 1841–1851 CENSUS SEARCHES CEN S\|12\| |
|---|---|---|---|---|---|
| Killarney | 80 | 45 | [1163/66], [2809/14], [3850] | 10.F.14. | 1020-1027 |
| Killeentierna | 60 | 44 | 2594 /2612, [1167/70] | 13.B.8., 11.B.12. | 1037-1039, 1274-1292 |
| Killehenny | 4 | 42 | [1114] | 7.C.12. | 572-574 |
| Killemlagh | 68 | 44 | [1126/27] 2562 | 9.B.2. | 772-812 |
| Killinane | 66 | 44 | 2563, [1128/29] | 9.C.3. | 813-834 |
| Killiney | 30 | 42 | [1079/80] | 3.G.1. | 126-134, 234-245 |
| Killorglin | 63 | 44 | 2545/2546/2564, 2595/2613, [1130/31], [1171/73], [2815/16] | 13.C.2., 9.D.6 5.D.11., 11.B.14. | 248, 264-272, 1028-1036, 835-848, 1293-1332 |
| Killury | 11 | 42 | [1053] | 2.A.8. | 125 |
| Kilmalkedar | 34 | 43 | [1081/84] | 4.A.4. | 246-247 |
| Kilmoyly | 22 | 42 | | 2.B.12. | 86-104 |
| Kilnanare | 73 | 44 | [1174/77] | 11.C.3. | 1040-1046 |
| Kilnaughtin | 3 | 42 | [1115] | 7.D.10. | 555-571 |
| Kilquane | 26 | 42 | [1083/84] | 4.A.11. | |
| Kilshenane | 21 | 42 | 2542/2543, [1054] | 2.C.10. | 105-119 |
| Kiltallagh | 58 | 44 | 2596/97 | 13.D.12. | 1334-1335 |
| Kiltomy | 18 | 42 | | 2.D.6. | 120-122 |
| Kinard | 37 | 43 | [1085/87] | 4.B.2. | 249-253 |
| Knockane | 71 | 44 | 2549/2551, [1103/06] | 5.E.5., 5.B.1. | 273-301 |
| Knockanure | 10 | 42 | | 7.F.2. | 575-583 |
| Lisselton | 5 | 42 | [1117] | 7.F.6. | 584-591 |
| Listowel | 9 | 42 | [1118/19], [2817/18] | 7.F.14. | 592-618 |
| Marhin | 33 | 43 | [1088/89], [1116?] | 4.B.7. | |
| Minard | 38 | 43 | [1090/91] | 4.B.10. | 254-258 |
| Molahiffe | 72 | 44 | [1178/80] | 11.C.10. | 1047-1059 |
| Murher | 7 | 42 | | 8.A.6. | 619-637 |
| Nohaval | 55 | 44 | 2598/2614 | 13.E.8. | |
| Nohavaldaly | 78 | 45 | [1181/84] | 11.D.6. | 1060-1067, 1336-1340 |
| O Brennan | 50 | 43 | 2599 | 13.E.8. | 1341-1344 |
| O Dorney | 23 | 42 | [1055] | 2.E.2. | 135-143 |
| Prior | 69 | 44 | 2565, [1132], [3849] | 9.D.12. | 849-903 |
| Ratass | 48 | 43 | 2600/2615 | 13.E.14. | 1345-1353 |
| Rattoo | 12 | 42 | | 8.B.6., 2.E.12. | 144-150, 638 |
| Stradbally | 29 | 42 | [1092/93] | 4.C.3. | 259-261 |
| Templnoe | 83 | 45 | 2550/2552/2553, [1007/10] | 5.G.2., 5.B.2. | 302, 445-447 |
| Tralee | 47 | 43 | 2601/2616, [1188], [2823] | 13.F.10+14 [2824/33] | 1354-1361 |
| Tuosist | 86 | 45 | 2557/2558 | 6.D.1. | 469-486 |
| Valencia | 64 | 44 | 2566/2567/8, [1133/34] | 9.E.13. | |
| Ventry | 42 | 43 | [1094/95] | 4.C.9. | 262-263 |

| TOWNS | VALUATION HOUSE BOOK 1830s [OL5.] |
|---|---|
| Ballylongford | [2796a] |
| Blennerville | [2797/99] |
| Cahersiveen | [2800/01] |
| Castlemaine | [2804] |
| Chapelstown | [2805] |
| Milltown | [2819/20] |
| Sneem | [2821/22] |
| Tarbert | [2823] |

| PARISH | TITHES 1823–38 TAB 13/ | FILM | VALUATION FIELD BOOKS 1830s OL4./ HOUSE BOOKS [OL5.] | TENEMENT VALUATION 1851 FICHE | 1841–1851 CENSUS SEARCH Cen /S/13 |
|---|---|---|---|---|---|
| Ardkill | 10 | 46 | 0703 | 4.B.7. | 1 |
| Ardree (Tankardstown) | 104 | 49 | 0738, [3873] | 1.F.8. | |
| Ballaghmoon | 115 | 49 | 0739, [3874] | 1.F.9. | |
| Ballybought | 81 | 48 | 0763, [3887] | 4.E.14. | 77 |
| Ballybrackan | 86 | 48 | 0800 | 2.B.7. | |
| Ballymany | 63 | 47 | 0784, [3902] | 6.C.8. | |
| Ballymoreustace | 77 | 48 | 0762, [3888] | 4.F.1. | 79 |
| Ballynadrumny | 1 | 46 | 0704, [3851] | 4.B.11. | 2 |
| Ballynafagh | 30 | 46 | 0714, [3855] | 5.E.10 | 14-15 |
| Ballysax | 64 | 47 | 0785, [3903] | 2.E.14., 6.D.5. | 135 |
| Ballyshannon | 92 | 48 | 0786/0801, [3904] | 2.E.14., 6.C.8., 2.B.13 | |
| Balraheen | 16 | 46 | 0728, [3866] | 3.D.14. | 59 |
| Belan | 107 | 49 | 0740 | 1.F.10. | |
| Bodenstown | 36 | 47 | 0753, [3951] | 6.A.2. | |
| Brannockstown | 78 | 48 | 0764, [3889] | 4.F.11. | 80 |
| Brideschurch | 35 | 47 | 0715, [3856] | 5.E.13. | 17-18 |
| Cadamstown | 4 | 46 | 0705, [3852] | 4.C.1. | 3-5 |
| Carbury | 9 | 46 | 0706, [3853] | 4.C.6. | 6-8 |
| Carn | 65 | 47 | 0787, [3905] | 2.E.14., 6.C.9. | 136-137 |
| Carnalway | 75 | 48 | 0765, [3890] | 4.F.12. | 81-84 |
| Carragh | 34 | 47 | 0716 | 5.F.1. | 19-27 |
| Carrick | 5 | 46 | 0707 | 4.C.8. | |
| Castledermot | 111 | 49 | 0741, [3875], [2840/42] | 1.F.11., 2.F.2. | 67-74 |
| Castledillon | 46 | 47 | 0823, [3941] | 3.C.6. | |
| Churchtown | 96 | 48 | 0779, [3897] | 1.B.2. | 108-110 |
| Clane | 33 | 47 | 0717, [3857], [2845/46] | 5.F.4. | 16, 28 |
| Clonaghlis | 48 | 47 | 0824, [3942] | 3.C.7. | |
| Cloncurry | 12, 56 | 46, 47 | 0729/0788, [3867], [3906] | 3.E.6. | 60-61, 138-140 |
| Clonshanbo | 15 | 46 | 0730, [3868] | 3.E.2. | |
| Coghlanstown | 76 | 48 | 0766, [3891] | 4.G.3. | |
| Confey | 21 | 46 | 0813, [3919], [3920] | 2.G.7. | |
| Davidstown | 99 | 48 | 0772 | 1.D.12. | 111-114 |
| Donadea | 18 | 46 | 0731, [3869] | 3.E.12. | |
| Donaghcumper | 44 | 47 | 0814/0825, [3921] | 2.F.12., 3.C.8., 3.D.1. | |
| Donaghmore | 22 | 46 | 0815, [3922/23] | 3.A.2. | |
| Downings | 31 | 46 | 0718, [3858] | 5.G.1 | 29-31 |
| Duneany | 84 | 48 | 0802 | 2.C.1. | |
| Dunfierth | 7 | 46 | 0708, [3854] | 4.C.11. | |
| Dunmanoge or Monmahennock | 110 | 49 | 0742, [3876] | 1.G.7. | |
| Dunmurraghill | 17 | 46 | 0732, [3869] | 3.E.13. | |
| Dunmurry | 58 | 47 | 0789, [3907] | | |
| Feighcullen | 68 | 47 | 0721/0790, [3861], [3908] | 4.A .2., 5.A.4. | 37-39 |
| Fontstown | 93 | 48 | 0773/0803 | 2.C.3., 1.E.2. | 115-118 |
| Forenaghts | 52 | 47 | 0826, [3943] | 5.D.13. | |
| Gilltown | 79 | 48 | 0767, [3892] | 4.G.4. | 85-86 |
| Graney | 113 | 49 | 0743 | 1.G.10. | |
| Grangeclare | 58 | 47 | 0791, [3909] | 4.A.14., 6.C.13. | |
| Grangerosnolvan | 106 | 49 | 0744, [3878] | 1.G.14. | |

| PARISH | TITHES 1823–38 TAB 13/ | FILM | VALUATION FIELD BOOKS 1830s OL4./ HOUSE BOOKS [OL5.] | TENEMENT VALUATION 1851 FICHE | 1841–1851 CENSUS SEARCH Cen /S/13 |
|---|---|---|---|---|---|
| Greatconnell | 72 | 48 | 0722, [3862] | 5.A.8. | 40-49 |
| Haynestown | 53 | 47 | 0827, [3944] | 5.D.13. | |
| Harristown | 89 | 48 | 0804 | 2.C.6. | |
| Jago | 80 | 48 | 0768, [3893] | 4.G.7. | 87 |
| Johnstown | 41 | 47 | 0754, [3952] | 6.A.4. | |
| Kerdiffstown | 39 | 47 | 0755, [3953] | 6.A.5. | |
| Kilberry | 95 | 48 | [3898] | 1.B.13. | |
| Kilcock | 13 | 26 | 0733, [3870], [2847/49], [4255] | 3.F.1. | |
| Kilcullen | 94 | 48 | 0736, [2850/51] | 5.D.1. | 63-66 |
| Kildangan | 87 | 48 | 0805 | 2.C.11. | |
| Kildare & Bishopscourt | 61 | 47 | 0723/0792, [3910], [2852], [2853], [2854] | 4.B.3., 6.D.11., 5.A .14. | 141 |
| Kildrought | 26 | 46 | 0816, [3925], [3926/27] | | 147 |
| Kilkea | 109 | 49 | 0745, [3879] | 2.A.1. | |
| Kill | 50 | 47 | 0769/0828, [3945], [3894] | 5.D.13., 4.G.8. | |
| Killadoon | 27 | 46 | 0817, [3928], [3929] | 2.G.5. | |
| Killashee | 73 | 48 | 0756 /0770, [3895] | 6.A .6. | 88-90 |
| Killelan | 108 | 49 | 0746, [3880] | 2.A.3. | |
| Killybegs | 32 | 46 | 0719, [3859] | 5.G.6. | 32-35 |
| Kilmacredock | 23 | 46 | 0818, [3930] | 2.G.7. | |
| Kilmeage | 66 | 47 | 0724/0793, [3911] | 6.C.13. | 50-51 |
| Kilmore | 8 | 46 | 0709 | 4.C.14. | |
| Kilpatrick | 11 | 46 | 0710 | 4.D.2. | 9-10 |
| Kilrainy | 2 | 46 | 0711 | 4.D.5. | |
| Kilrush | 91 | 48 | 0806 | 2.C.11. | |
| Kilteel | 51 | 47 | [3946] | 5.E.3. | 148-149 |
| Kineagh | 112 | 49 | 0747, [3881] | 2.A.9. | |
| Knavinstown | 83 | 48 | 0807 | 2.C.14. | |
| Lackagh | 82 | 48 | 0808, [3918] | 2.D.1. | |
| Ladytown | 71 | 48 | 0725, [3864] | 5.B.14. | |
| Laraghbryan | 20 | 46 | 0819, [3931/32] | 3.A.2. | 150 |
| Leixlip | 24 | 46 | 0820, [2855/56], [3933/4], [3859] | 2.G.9. | 151-153 |
| Lullymore | 54 | 47 | [3912] | 4.A.4. | |
| Lyons | 47 | 47 | 0830, [3947] | 3.C.12 | 154 |
| Mainham | 19 | 46 | 0734, [3871] | 3.E.3. | 61 |
| Monasterevin | 85 | 48 | 0809, [2853], [2861/62] | 2.D.9. | 142 |
| Moone | 103 | 49 | 0748/0774/0794, [3882], [3913] | 6.C.14., 1.E.4., 2.A.11 | |
| Morristownbiller | 69 | 47 | 0726, [3865] | 5.C.1. | 52-55 |
| Mylerstown | 3 | 46 | 0712 | 4.D.7. | 11-13 |
| Narraghmore | 101 | 48 | 0749/0775/0781, [3883], [3899] | 1.C.7., 1.E.6. | 75-76, 119-124 |
| Naas | 40 | 47 | [3954], 0757, [2864] | 6.A.6. | 91-101 |
| Nurney | 6, 90 | 46, 48 | 0713, 0810 | 4.D.10., 2.E.8. | 143 |
| Oldconnell | 70 | 48 | [3863] | 5.C.7. | 56-58 |
| Oughterard | 49 | 47 | 0831, [3948] | 5.E.7. | |
| Painestown | 114 | 49 | 0750, [3884] | 2.B.2. | |
| Pollardstown | 62 | 47 | 0796, [3914] | 6.D.10. | |
| Rathangan | 55 | 47 | 0797/0811, [3915], [2853], [2868] | 6.C.14., 4.A.5., 2.E.12. | 144 |

| PARISH | TITHES 1823–38 TAB 13/ | FILM | VALUATION FIELD BOOKS 1830s OL4./ HOUSE BOOKS [OL5.] | TENEMENT VALUATION 1851 FICHE | 1841–1851 CENSUS SEARCH Cen /S/13 |
|---|---|---|---|---|---|
| Rathernan | 67 | 47 | 0727 | 5.C.11. | |
| Rathmore | 43 | 47 | 0758, [3955] | 6.B.10. | 102-105 |
| Relictstown | 116 | 49 | | | |
| Scullogestown | 14 | 46 | 0735, [3872] | 3.E.14. | |
| Sherlockstown | 38 | 47 | 0759, [3956] | 6.C.2. | |
| St John's | 98 | 48 | 0782, [3900] | | 77, 125 |
| St Michael's | 97 | 48 | 0751/0783, [3885], [3901] | | 126 |
| Stacumny | 45 | 47 | 0832, [3949/50] | | 155 |
| Straffan | 28 | 46 | 0821, [3935/36] | 3.A.14 | 156 |
| Taghadoe | 25 | 46 | 0822, [3937/38] | 3.B.3. | |
| Tankardstown Ardree | 105 | 49 | 0752/0776, [3886] | 1.E.13., 2.B.2. | |
| Thomastown | 57 | 47 | 0798, [3916] | 4.B.2. | |
| Timahoe | 29 | 46 | 0720 [3860] | 5.G.11. | 36 |
| Timolin | 102 | 49 | 0777, [2870] | 1.E.13. | 127-128 |
| Tipper | 42 | 47 | [3957] | 6.C.2. | 106-107 |
| Tipperkevin | 74 | 48 | 0771, [3896] | 4.G.13. | |
| Tully | 60 | 47 | 0737/0799, [3917] | 2.E.14., 6.D.2., 2.F.1., 5.D.12. | 145 |
| Usk | 100 | 48 | 0778 | 1.F.4., 6.E.11. | 129-134 |
| Walterstown | 88 | 48 | 0812 | 2.E.12., | |
| Whitechurch | 37 | 47 | 0761, [3958] | 6.C.5. | |

| TOWNS | VALUATION HOUSE BOOK 1830s [OL5.] |
|---|---|
| Athy | [2834/37] |
| Ballitore | [2837/38] |
| Ballymore Eustace | [2839, 2851] |
| Celbridge | [2843/44, 2860] |
| Johnstown | [2864, 2869] |
| Kildare | [2852, 2853, 2854] |
| Kill | [2864] |
| Kilmeage | [2865/67] |
| Leixlip | [2855/56] |
| Maynooth | [2857/59] [3961] |
| Newbridge | [2865/67] |
| Prosperous | [2846] |
| Robertstown | [2865/67] |
| Sallins | [2864, 2869] |

| PARISH | TITHES 1823–38 TAB 14/ | FILM | VALUATION FIELD BOOKS 1830s OL4./ HOUSE BOOKS [OL5.] | TENEMENT VALUATION FICHE 1849–50 | 1841–1851 CENSUS SEARCH Cen /S/14 |
|---|---|---|---|---|---|
| Abbeyleix | 14 | 50 | 0854, [3978] | 2.C.4. | 14 |
| Aghaviller | 104 | 54 | 0959, [3982] | 8.C.2. | 196-200 |
| Aglish | 140 | 55 | 0935 | 6.G.10. | 137-139, 138A |
| Aharney | 10 | 50 | 0872 | 3.E.2. | 67-69 |
| Arderra | 136 | 55 | 0936 | 6.G.12. | |
| Attanagh | 13 | 50 | 0855, [3962] | 2.C.5. | 15-17 |
| Balleen | 7 | 50 | 0873 | 3.E.8. | 70 |
| Ballycallan | 41 | 51 | 0836 | 1.D.9. | |
| Ballinamara | 38 | 51 | 0835 | 1.D.6. | |
| Ballybur | 52 | 52 | 0975 | 9.A.6. | |
| Ballygurrim | 119 | 54 | 0919 | 5.F.12. | |
| Ballylarkin | 32 | 51 | 0837 | 1.E.3. | 3-4 |
| Ballylinch | 83 | 53 | 0884 | 4.B.8. | |
| Ballytarsney | 135 | 55 | 0937 | 7.A.2. | 140 |
| Ballytobin | 97 | 54 | 0949 | 7.E.14. | |
| Blackrath | 66 | 52 | 0885 | 4.B.9. | 82 |
| Blanchvilleskill | 74 | 53 | 0886 | 4.B.10. | 83 |
| Borrismore | 6 | 50 | 0874 | 3.E.11. | |
| Burnchurch | 56 | 52 | 0976 | 9.A.6. | |
| Callan | 47 | 51 | 0833, [2875/77] | 1.A.4. | 1-2 |
| Castlecomer | 15 | 50 | 0856, [3963], [3878/9] [4000/01] | 2.C.7., 2.D.9. | 18-25 |
| Castleinch | 51 | 52 | 0977 | 9.A.10. | |
| Clara | 70 | 53 | 0877 | 4.B.11. | |
| Clashacrow | 36 | 51 | 0838 | 1.E.5. | |
| Clomantagh | 28 | 50 | 0839 | 1.E.6. | 5-8 |
| Clonamery | 112 | 54 | 0920 | 5.G.2. | |
| Clonmore | 131 | 55 | 0938 | 7.A.3. | 141 |
| Columbkille | 89 | 53 | 0888 | 4.B.14. | 84-87 |
| Coolaghmore | 93 | 54 | 0950 | 7.F.3. | |
| Coolcashin | 8 | 50 | 0875 | 3.E.12. | |
| Coolcraheen | 22 | 50 | 0857, [3964] | 3.B.8., 1.E.10. | |
| Danesfort | 57 | 52 | 0979 | 9.A.12. | 226 |
| Derrynahinch | 106 | 54 | 0960, [3983/84] | 8.C.11. | 201-206 |
| Donaghmore | 18/ | 50 | 0858 | 2.C.12. | 26-45 |
| Dunbell | 73 | 53 | 0889 | 4.C.6. | |
| Dungarvan | 81 | 53 | 0890 | | |
| Dunkitt | 121 | 55 | 0921 | 5.G.8. | 119-123 |
| Dunmore | 26 | 50 | 0859, [3965] | 3.B.9., 3.B.14. | 46 |
| Dunnamaggan | 98 | 54 | 0961 | 7.F.9., 8.D.5. | |
| Durrow | 11 | 50 | | 3.E.13. | |
| Dysart | 21 | 50 | 0860, [3966] | 2.G.6., 3.A.11., 3.B.1. | 47-49 |
| Dysartmoon | 113 | 54 | 0922 | 6.A.6. | |
| Earlstown | 59 | 52 | 0979 | 9.B.3. | |
| Ennisnag | 60 | 52 | 0980, [3985] | 9.B.5., 8.D.6. | |
| Erke | 1 | 50 | 0877 | 3.E.13. | 71-72 |
| Famma | 91 | 53 | 0891 | 4.C.14. | |
| Fertagh | 4 | 50 | 0841 | 3.F.11., 1.E.10. | 73-76 |
| Fiddown | 128 | 55 | 0963, [3986] | 8.D.6., 7.A.7. | 142-149 |
| Freshford | 33 | 51 | 0842, [2880], [4002] | 1.E.11. | 9-9a |
| Garranamanagh | 29 | 50 | 0843 | 1.F.7. | |

| PARISH | TITHES 1823–38 TAB 14/ | FILM | VALUATION FIELD BOOKS 1830s OL4./ HOUSE BOOKS [OL5.] | TENEMENT VALUATION FICHE 1849–50 | 1841–1851 CENSUS SEARCH Cen /S/14 |
|---|---|---|---|---|---|
| Gaulskill | 122 | 55 | 0923 | 6.A.14. | 124-126 |
| Glashare | 2 | 50 | 0879, 2695 | 3.G.6. | |
| Gowran | 71 | 53 | 0892, [2883] | 4.C.14. | |
| Graiguenamanagh | 86 | 53 | 0893, [2884/5] | 4.D.13. | 88-97 |
| Grange | 50 | 52 | 0981 | 9.B.7. | |
| Grangekilree | 58 | 52 | 0982 | 9.B.9. | |
| Grangemaccomb | 19 | 50 | 0861, [3967] | 2.D.7., 3.A.3., 3.B.10., 3.C.6., 3.C.8. | 50-51 |
| Grangesilvia | 76 | 53 | 0894, [2882] | 4.F.3. | 98-99 |
| Inistiogue | 92 | 53 | 0895, [2886] | 4.F.10. | 101-103 |
| Jerpointabbey | 88 | 53 | 0896, [3979] | 4.G.9. | |
| Jerpointchurch | 102 | 54 | 0964, [3987] | 8.D.7 | 207 |
| Jerpointwest | 108 | 54 | 0965, [3988] | 4.G.11., 8.D.13. | |
| Kells | 95 | 54 | 0984, 2696 | 9.B.10., 7.F.14. | 170-178 |
| Kilbeacon | 110 | 54 | 0966, [3989] | 8.E.1. | 208 |
| Kilbride | 117 | 54 | 0925 | 6.B.4. | |
| Kilcoan | 118 | 54 | 0926 | 6.B.8. | |
| Kilcolumb | 123 | 55 | 0927 | 6.B.12. | 127, 136 |
| Kilcooly | 34 | 51 | 0844 | 1.F.8. | |
| Kilderry | 67 | 52 | 0898 | 4.G.13. | |
| Kilfane | 85 | 53 | 0899 | 5.A.1. | |
| Kilferagh | 54 | 52 | 0985 | 9.B.11. | |
| Kilkeasy | 105 | 54 | 0967, [3990] | 8.E.9. | 209-212 |
| Kilkenny | 43-46 | 51 | 2694, [2889-2914], [4003-4007] | 9.D.14., 9.F.13. 9.G.11., 10.A.11. 10.B.2. | 185-195 |
| Kilkerril | 141 | 55 | | | |
| Kilkieran | 63 | 52 | 0900 | 5.A.5. | |
| Killahy | 35, 109 | 51, 54 | [3991] 0845 | 1.F.8., 8.E.12. | |
| Killaloe | 48 | 52 | 0986, 0834 | 1.F.9., 9.B.12. | |
| Killamery | 96 | 54 | 0953 | 7.G.7. | |
| Killarney | 79 | 53 | 0901 | 5.A.6. | |
| Kilmacahill | 72 | 53 | 0902 | 5.A.6. | 104 |
| Kilmacar | 20 | 50 | [3968] | 2.G.10., 3.A.6. | 52-54 |
| Kilmacow | 138 | 55 | 0940 | 7.D.8. | 150 |
| Kilmademoge | 27 | 50 | 0863, [3969] | 3.C.2. | |
| Kilmadum | 62 | 52 | 0903, [3970] | 3.A.2., 3.C.4., 5.A.11. | |
| Kilmaganny | 100 | 54 | 0954 | 7.G.14. | 179-183 |
| Kilmakevoge | 124 | 55 | 0928 | 3.C.2. | 128 |
| Kilmanagh | 40 | 51 | 0847 | 1.F.10. | |
| Kilmenan | 17 | 50 | 0865, [3971] | 2.D.8., 8.A.10 | 55-56 |
| Kilree | 99 | 54 | | 8.A.10 | 184 |
| Knocktopher | 103 | 54 | 0969, [3992] [2872] | 8.F.4. | 213-220 |
| Lismateige | 107 | 54 | 0970, [3994] | 8.F.13. | 221-223 |
| Listerlin | 115 | 54 | 0929, [3981], [3993] | 8.G.2. | 129 |
| Mallardstown | 94 | 54 | 0956 | 8.A.13. | |
| Mayne | 22 | 50 | 0866, [3972] | 3.B.10. | |
| Mothell | 24 | 50 | 0904 | 2.G.13., 3.A.13., 3.B.2., 5.A.14. | 57-59 |

| PARISH | TITHES 1823–38 TAB 14/ | FILM | VALUATION FIELD BOOKS 1830s OL4./ HOUSE BOOKS [OL5.] | TENEMENT VALUATION FICHE 1849–50 | 1841–1851 CENSUS SEARCH Cen /S/14 |
|---|---|---|---|---|---|
| Muckalee | 25 | 50 | 0868, [3973], [3995] | 2.G.14., 3.B.6. | 60-61, 224 |
| Muckalee | 130 | 55 | 0972 | 8.G.3., 7.C.3. | 60-61, 224 |
| Odagh | 39 | 51 | 0848, [3974] | 3.B.12., 3.C.6. | 10 |
| Outrath | 53 | 52 | 0987 | 9.C.2. | 227 |
| Owning | 127 | 55 | 0942 | 7.C.3. | 163 |
| Pleberstown | 90 | 53 | 0905 | 5.A.14. | |
| Pollrone | 134 | 55 | 0943 | 7.C.8. | 164-165 |
| Portnascully | 139 | 55 | 0944 | 7.D.2. | 166 |
| Powerstown | 82 | 53 | 0906 | 5.B.1. | 105-107 |
| Rossinan | 111 | 54 | 0973, [3996] | 8.G.5., 6.E.10. | |
| Rathbeagh | 30 | 50 | 0880, [3976] | 3.G.9., 2.D.8. | 62-65 |
| Rathcoole | 64 | 52 | 0907 | 5.B.8. | |
| Rathkieran | 133 | 55 | 0930 | 7.D.7. | 167 |
| Rathlogan | 5 | 50 | 0881 | 3.G.12. | |
| Rathpatrick | 125 | 55 | 0930 | 6.D.8. | 130 |
| Rathaspick | 16 | 50 | 0870, [3975] | 2.G.12. | |
| Rosbercon | 116 | 54 | 0931, [2917] | 6.E.2. | 131-133 |
| Rosconnell | 12 | 50 | 0871, [3977] | 2.C.10. | 66 |
| Shanbogh | 120 | 55 | 0933 | 6.E.12. | 134 |
| Shankill | 68 | 52 | 0911, [3980] | 5.C.9. | 108-110 |
| Sheffin | 9 | 50 | 0849 | 3.G.13., 1.G.7. | 77-78 |
| St Canice's | 42 | 51 | 0850 | 1.G.8., 9.C.7. | |
| St John's | 43 | 51 | 0908 | 5.B.10. | |
| St Martin's | 69 | 53 | 0909 | 5.C.6. | |
| St Mary's | 44 | 51 | [4003/05] | 9.G.11. | |
| St Maul's | 45 | 51 | [4006] | 5.C.8. | 111-112 |
| St Patrick's | 46 | 51 | 0991, [4007] | 9.C.9. | 228 |
| Stonecarthy | 61 | 52 | 0988, [3997] | 9.C.5. | 225 |
| The Rower | 114 | 54 | 0934 | | 135 |
| Thomastown | 84 | 53 | 0912, [2919/21] | 5.D.2. | 113-117 |
| Tibberaghny | 129 | 55 | 0945 | 7.D.12. | 168 |
| Tiscoffin | 65 | 52 | 0913 | 5.D.13. | |
| Treadingstown | 77 | 53 | 0914 | 9.D.1., 5.E.4. | |
| Tubbrid | 132 | 55 | 0946 | 7.D.13. | |
| Tubbridbritain | 31 | 51 | 0851 | 1.G.14. | 11 |
| Tullaghanbrogue | 49 | 52 | 0852 | 2.A.5. | 12 |
| Tullaherin | 80 | 53 | 0915 | 5.E.6. | |
| Tullahought | 101 | 54 | 0958 | 8.B.2. | |
| Tullamaine | 45 | 52 | 0993 | 9.D.4. | |
| Tullaroan | 37 | 51 | 0853 | 2.A.6. | 13 |
| Ullard | 87 | 53 | 0916 | 5.E.10. | 118 |
| Ullid | 137 | 55 | 0947 | 7.E.1. | |
| Urlingford | 3 | 50 | 0883, [2922] | 4.A.1. | 79-81 |
| Wells | 75 | 53 | 0917 | 5.F.1. | |
| Whitechurch | 126 | 55 | 0948 | 7.E.3. | 169 |
| Woolengrange | 78 | 53 | 0918 | 5.F.1. | |

| TOWNS | VALUATION HOUSE BOOKS 1830s [OL5] |
|---|---|
| Ballyhale | [2871/72] [3998/99] |
| Ballyragget | [2873] |
| Bennettsbridge | [2874] |
| Goresbridge | [2881/82] |
| Higginstown | [2872] |
| Johnstown | [2807/88] |
| Mullinvat | [2872] [2916] |
| St Canice | [2889/93, 2903/05] |
| St John's | [2894/96, 2906/08] |
| St Mary's | [2897/900, 2909/11] |
| St Maul's | [2901, 2912/13] |
| St Patrick's | [2902, 2914/15] |
| Stoneyford | [2872] [2918] [4008] |

| PARISH | TITHES 1823–38 TAB 24/ | FILM | VALUATION FIELD BOOKS 1830s OL4./ HOUSE BOOKS [OL5.] | TENEMENT VALUATION FICHE 1850/51 | 1841–1851 CENSUS SEARCH Cen /S/24 |
|---|---|---|---|---|---|
| Abbeyleix | 41 | 85 | 1537, 1550, 1564, [2932/35] | 3.F.10., 1.D.12., 3.B.2. | 44-47 |
| Aghaboe | 23 | 85 | 1528, 2702 | 2.C.6., 1.E.2. | 5-12, 29-32 |
| Aghmacart | 32 | 85 | 1538 | 1.F.2. | 33 |
| Aharney | 36 | 85 | 1539 | 1.G.2. | |
| Ardea | 5 | 84 | 1566, [2954/59] | 5.A.6. | 82-84 |
| Attanagh | 37 | 85 | 1540 | 1.G.4. | |
| Ballyadams | 43 | 85 | 1575, [4010] | 6.D.2., 1.A.8. | |
| Ballyroan | 38 | 85 | 1551, [2939] | 3.C.4. | |
| Bordwell | 29 | 85 | 1529, 1541 | 2.D.4., 1.G.7. | 34 |
| Borris | 10 | 84 | 1558, [2940] | 4.D.6. | 52-54 |
| Castlebrack | 1 | 84 | 1585 | 7.A.8. | |
| Clonenagh & Clonagheen | 9 | 84 | 1552, 1559, 1565 [2952/53] | 3.F.12., 4.F.1., 3.D.4. | 55, 59-81 |
| Cloydagh | 53 | 86 | 1569 | 5.F.6. | |
| Coolbanagher | 6 | 84 | 1567 | 5.B.12. | |
| Coolkerry | 31 | 85 | 1530, 1542 | 2.D.6., 1.G.10. | |
| Curraclone | 18 | 85 | 1576, [4011] | 6.D.4. | |
| Donaghmore | 25 | 85 | 1531, [2944] | 2.D.8. | |
| Durrow | 33 | 85 | 1543, [2945/47] | 1.G.14. | 35-39 |
| Dysartenos | 14 | 84 | 1560, 1577, [4012] | 4.F.6., 6.D.10. | 103 |
| Dysartgallen | 42 | 85 | 1553 | 3.D.5. | 48 |
| Erke | 27 | 85 | 1532, 1544 | 2.E.2., 2.A.12. | 13-15 |
| Fossy or Timahoe | 40 | 85 | 1554, 1578, [4013] | 4.F.8., 6.E.2., 3.E.7. | 49-51 |
| Glashare | 35 | 85 | 1545 | 2.B.2. | |
| Kilcolmanbane | 13 | 84 | 1555, 1561 | 4.F.12., 3.E.14. | |
| Kilcolmanbrack | 39 | 85 | 1556 | 3.F.1. | |
| Kildellig | 28 | 85 | 1546 | 2.B.4. | |
| Killabban | 49 | 86 | 1521, 1570, [2938, 4009] | 5.F.10. | 1, 88-93 |
| Killenny | 15 | 84 | 1579, [4015] | 6.E.4. | |
| Killermogh | 30 | 85 | 1547 | 2.B.6. | 40-41 |
| Killeshin | 51 | 86 | 1571 | 6.A.8. | 94-98 |
| Kilmanman | 2 | 84 | 1586, [2942/3] | 7.B.4. | 106-107 |
| Kilteale | 12 | 84 | 1562, 1580, [4014] | 4.F.8., 6.E.6. | |
| Kyle | 21 | 85 | 1533 | 2.E.6. | 16-21 |
| Lea | 7 | 84 | 1568, [1189] | 5.C.8. | 85-87 |
| Moyanna | 16 | 84 | 1581, [4016] | 6.E.10. | 104 |
| Mountrath | | | [2961/63] | | |
| Monksgrange | 48 | 86 | 1522 | 1.C.2. | 2-3 |
| Offerlane | 8 | 84 | 1589 | 7.F.14. | 111-135 |
| Rahan | | | [1189A] | | |
| Rathaspick | 47 | 85 | 1523, 1572 | 1.C.4., 6.B.14. | 4, 99-101 |
| Rathdowney | 24 | 85 | 1534, 1548, [2948, 2967/68] | 2.E.14., 2.B.10 | 22-25 |
| Rathsaran | 26 | 85 | 1535 | 2.G.14. | 26 |
| Rearymore | 3 | 84 | 1587 | 7.C.10. | |
| Rosconnell | 34 | 85 | 1549, 1557 | 2.B.12., 3.F.2. | 42-43 |
| Rosenallis | 4 | 84 | 1588, [2954/60] | 7.D.8. | 108-110 |
| Shrule | 50 | 86 | 1573 | 6.C.6. | 102 |
| Skirk | 22 | 85 | 1536 | 3.A.4. | 27-28 |
| Sleaty | 52 | 86 | 1574 | 6.C.8. | |

| PARISH | TITHES 1823–38 TAB 24/ | FILM | VALUATION FIELD BOOKS 1830s OL4./ HOUSE BOOKS [OL5.] | TENEMENT VALUATION FICHE 1850/51 | 1841–1851 CENSUS SEARCH Cen /S/24 |
|---|---|---|---|---|---|
| St John's | 44 | 85 | 1524 | 1.C.10. | |
| Straboe | 11 | 84 | 1563 | 4.G.1. | 56-58 |
| Stradbally | 27/17 | 84 | 1582, [4017], [2969/72] | 6.F.4. | 105 |
| Tankardstown | 46 | 85 | 1525 | 1.C.12. | |
| Tecolm | 45 | 85 | 1526 | 1.D.2. | |
| Timahoe/Fossy | | | [4018] | | |
| Timogue | 19 | 85 | 1583, [4018] | 6.G.4. | |
| Tullomoy | 20 | 85 | 1584, [4019] | 6.G.6., 1.D.4. | |

| TOWNS | VALUATION HOUSE BOOK 1830s [OL5.] |
|---|---|
| Abbeyleix | [2932/35] |
| Arless | [2951] |
| Ballickmoyler | [2951] |
| Ballinakill | [2936/37] |
| Ballybrittas | [2960] |
| Ballylynan | [2938, 2951] |
| Ballyroan | [2939] |
| Castletown | [2941, 2947] |
| Clonaslee | [2942/43, 2960] |
| Erril | [2948] |
| Graigue | [2949/50, 2951] |
| Maryborough | [2952/53] |
| Mountmellick | [2954/59, 2960] |
| Portarlington | [2964/66] |

| PARISH | TITHES 1823–38 TAB 16/ | FILM | VALUATION FIELD BOOKS 1830s OL4./ HOUSE BOOKS [OL5.] | TENEMENT VALUATION 1856 FICHE | 1841–1851 CENSUS SEARCH Cen /S/16 |
|---|---|---|---|---|---|
| Annaduff | 13 | 61 | 1057, 1062 | 3.A.2., 6.D.4., 4.A.8., 6.E.10. | 494-504, 675-680 |
| Carrigallen | 15 | 61 | 1047 | 1.E.14., 6.A.12. | 1-39 |
| Cloonclare | 5 | 60 | 1051, 1065, 2699, [4257] | 5.D.4., 4.B.8. | 137-193, 752-769 |
| Cloone | 17 | 61 | 1048, 2698, [4256], [2924] | 6.C.4., 6.F.5. | 40-60, 681-722 |
| Cloonlogher | 4 | 60 | 1052 | 4.D.8. | 194-202 |
| Drumlease | 3 | 60 | 1053 [4258] | 4.D.12. | 203-252 |
| Drumreilly | 9 | 60 | 1049, 1054, [4256], [4020], [4259] | 2.F.2., 1.F.13 | 61-92, 253-311 |
| Fenagh | 12 | 61 | 1050, 1058, 1063 | 6.D.5., 2.A.14., 7.B.13. | 93-94, 505-512, 723-727 |
| Inishmagrath | 8 | 60 | 2697, [4021], [4260] | 4.E.14. | 312-379 |
| Killanummery | 6 | 60 | 1055, [4261], | 5.A.8. | 380-426 |
| Killarga | 7 | 60 | 1056, [4022], [4262] | 5.B.11. | 427-493 |
| Killasnet | 2 | 59 | 1066, 2700 | 5.E.1. | 770-808 |
| Kiltubbrid | 11 | 61 | 1060 | 3.F.1. | 595-669 |
| Kiltoghert | 10 | 60 | 1059, [4023] | 3.A.12. | 513-594 |
| Mohill | 16 | 61 | 1061, 1064, [2931] | 4.A.6., 6.E.5. | 670-674, 728-751 |
| Oughteragh | 14 | 61 | [4256] | 2.A.14., 6.D.2. | 95-136 |
| Rossinver | 1 | 59 | 1067, 2701 | 1.A.12., 5.F.14. | 808-870 |

| TOWNS | VALUATION HOUSE BOOK 1830s [OL5.] |
|---|---|
| Ballinamore | [2923] |
| Drumahaire | [2925] |
| Drumkeeran | [2926] |
| Drumsna | [2927] |
| Keshkerrigan | [2928] |
| Manorhamilton | [2929/30] |

| PARISH | TITHES 1823–38 TAB 17/ | FILM | VALUATION FIELD BOOKS 1830s OL4./ HOUSE BOOKS [OL5.] | TENEMENT VALUATION FICHE 1850/52 | 1841–1851 CENSUS SEARCH Cen /S/17 |
|---|---|---|---|---|---|
| Abbeyfeale | 74 | 65 | 2749, [1252/54], [2973] | 6.B.14. | 318-352 |
| Abington | 61 | 64 | 2703-04, 2769-2771 | 1.A.14., 8.C.2. | 532-537 |
| Adare | 89 | 66 | 2757-58-59, [1221/22], [1250], [2974/75] | 7.E.8., 7.E.12., 11.G.5., 13.A.2. | 268-272, 446-448 |
| Aglishcormick | 60 | 64 | 2705, [1237] | 1.B.6., 3.E.2. | 1-3 |
| Anhid | 93 | 66 | | 13.B.1. | |
| Ardagh | 11 | 62 | 2790, [1255/56] | 10.F.12., 6.D.6. | 353, 583-586 |
| Ardcanny | 27 | 62 | 2760 | 7.E.8., 7.F.4. | 449-450 |
| Ardpatrick | 121 | 67 | 2728 | 4.D.6. | 182-183 |
| Askeaton | 14 | 62 | [1190/91], [1190/91] [2976/77] | 2.E.10. | 60-65 |
| Athlacca | 95 | 66 | | 13.B.3. | 273-276 |
| Athneasy | 131 | 67 | 2729, 2800, [1270] | 9.E.14., 4.D.8. | 184-185 |
| Ballinacurra | 131 | 67 | [3040] | | |
| Ballinard | 109 | 66 | 2801, [1271/72] | 9.F.4. | |
| Ballingaddy | 122 | 67 | 2730 | 4.D.14. | 186 |
| Ballingarry | 81 | 65 | [1223/25], [1243/44] | 11.G.6. | 66-67, 93-108, 187-191 |
| Ballingarry | 125 | 67 | 2731-32, [4024], [2978/81] | 4.E.6. | 66-67, 93-108,187-191 |
| Ballinlough | 111 | 66 | 2802, [1271/72] | 9.F.8. | 663 |
| Ballybrood | 57 | 64 | 2706 | 1.B.8. | 4 |
| Ballycahane | 38 | 63 | 2777, 2803, [1273/74] | 8.F.8., 8.F.12., 9.F.12 | 542-544 |
| Ballylanders | 126 | 67 | [1245], 4025/26 | 4.F.2. | 192-211 |
| Ballynamona | 110 | 66 | 2804, [1275] | 9.F.14. | |
| Ballynaclogh | 66 | 64 | | 3.E.4. | |
| Ballyscadden | 119 | 66 | 2734 | | |
| Bruff | 96 | 66 | [2982/83] | 13.B.8. | 277-283 |
| Bruree | 84 | 65 | [1226/28], [2983] | | 109-110, 284-285 |
| Caheravally | 50 | 63 | | 1.B.12. | |
| Caherconlish | 53 | 64 | [2985] | 1.C.4. | 5-15 |
| Cahercorney | 106 | 65 | 2805, [1271/72] | 9.G.2. | |
| Caherelly | 55 | 64 | 2707 | 1.D.4. | |
| Cahernarry | 51 | 63 | 2708 | 1.D.10. | |
| Cappagh | 17 | 62 | [1192/95], [1192/95] | 2.F.10. | 68-69 |
| Carrigparson | 49 | 63 | 2709 | 1.D.14. | |
| Castletown | 64 | 64 | [1238] | 3.F.4. | |
| Chapelrussell | 26 | 62 | 2761-62 | 7.E.8. | 451 |
| Clonagh | 19 | 62 | [1196], [1196a/97] | 2.F.13. | 70 |
| Cloncagh | 80 | 65 | [1229] | 12.C.8. | 111-115 |
| Cloncrew | 85,86 | 65 | | 12.C.14. | 116 |
| Clonelty | 73 | 65 | 2750, [1257/58] | 6.C.7. | 355-357 |
| Clonkeen | 47 | 63 | | 1.E.4. | |
| Clonshire | 18 | 62 | [1198/200] | 2.G.1. | |
| Colmanswell | 87 | 65 | | 12.D.2. | 117 |
| Corcomohide | 83 | 65 | [1230/31] | 12.D.5. | 118-132 |
| Crecora | 35 | 63 | 2778 | 8.G.2. | 545-546 |
| Croagh | 22 | 62 | 2721, [1201/02] | 2.G.2. | 71-74 |
| Croom | 91 | 66 | 2779, [1222], [1232], [2987/88] | 8.G.8. | 286-300 |
| Darragh | 129 | 67 | 2735 [1246] | 4.G.2. | 212-227 |

| PARISH | TITHES 1823–38 TAB 17/ | FILM | VALUATION FIELD BOOKS 1830s OL4./ HOUSE BOOKS [OL5.] | TENEMENT VALUATION FICHE 1850/52 | 1841–1851 CENSUS SEARCH Cen /S/17 |
|---|---|---|---|---|---|
| Derrygalvin | 46 | 63 | 2710 | 1.E.6. | |
| Donaghmore | 48 | 63 | 2711 | 1.E.10. | |
| Doon | 63 | 64 | 2772-73 | 8.E.2., 3.E.8., 3.F.6. | 172-177, 538 |
| Doondonnell | 20 | 62 | 2722, [1203] | 2.G.14. | 75 |
| Drehidtarsna | 90 | 66 | [1222] | 12.E.9., 13.D.9. | |
| Dromcolliher | | | [2989/90] | | 133-143 |
| Dromin | 97 | 66 | | 13.D.9. | 301-304 |
| Dromkeen | 58 | 64 | 2712 | 1.E.14. | |
| Dunmoylan | 7 | 62 | | 10.G.7. | 587-588 |
| Dysert | 92 | 66 | | 13.D.14. | |
| Effin | 102 | 66 | 2736, [4027/28] | 13.E.1., 4.G.10. | 228-230, 305-307 |
| Emlygrennan | 117 | 66 | 2737 | 4.G.14. | 231 |
| Fedamore | 104 | 66 | 2713, [1276/77], [2993] | 1.F.4., 9.E.8., 9.G.4. | 664-674 |
| Glenogra | 105 | 66 | 2806, [1278/79] | 10.A.4. | 675 |
| Galbally | 120 | 67 | 2738, [4029], [2991] | 5.A.6. | 232-237 |
| Grange | 72 | 65 | 2751, [1259] | 6.D.12. | 358-359 |
| Grean | 65 | 64 | 2714, [1239] | 1.F.6., 3.G.14. | |
| Hackmys | 100 | 66 | | 13.E.6. | 308-310 |
| Hospital | 112 | 66 | 2807-08, [1280], [4032], [2994] | 9.E.9., 10.A.10. | |
| Inch St Lawrence | 56 | 64 | 2715 | 1.F.10. | |
| Iveruss | 24 | 62 | 2763-64 | 7.E.9., 7.F.14. | 76, 452-455 |
| Kilbeheny | 130 | 67 | 2739, [4030] | 5.B.14. | 238-247 |
| Kilbolane | 88 | 65 | | 12.F.6. | |
| Kilbradran | 9 | 62 | 2791, [1196], [1203] | 10.G.12., 3.A.2. | |
| Kilbreedy | 101 | 66 | 2740 | 13.E.8. | 248-249 |
| Kilbreedy Major | 115 | 66 | 2809, [1247] | 10.B.8., 5.D.6. | |
| Kilcolman | 8 | 62 | 2792 | 11.A.2. | 589 |
| Kilcornan | 25 | 62 | 2765-66 | 7.E.9., 7.G.8. | 456-461 |
| Kilcullane | 108 | 66 | 2810, [1281] | 9.E.9. | 676-677 |
| Kildimo | 28 | 62 | 2767-68 | 7.E.9. | 462-468 |
| Kilfergus | 2 | 62 | 2793 | 11.A.5. | 590-611 |
| Kilfinnane | 124 | 67 | 2741, [1248], [4031], [2995] | 5.D.12. | 250-251 |
| Kilfinny | 79 | 65 | [1222], [1233/34] | 12.F.7. | 144 |
| Kilflyn | 128 | 67 | 2742, [1249] | 5.F.10. | 253-258 |
| Kilfrush | 113 | 66 | 2811, [1282] | 10.C.2. | |
| Kilkeedy | 29 | 62 | 2780-81, 2789 | 8.F.8., 8.G.14. | 547-552 |
| Killagholehane | 78 | 65 | 2752, [1260] | 6.E.1. | 360-366 |
| Killeedy | 77 | 65 | 2753, [1261] | 6.E.7. | 354, 367-412 |
| Killeely | 30 | 62 | [3011], [3035] | 14.B.2., 14.B.10., 13.G.8., 13.G.12. | 178 |
| Killeenagarriff | 43 | 63 | 2716 | 1.F.14. | 31-32 |
| Killeenoghty | 37 | 63 | 2782 | 9.B.6., 13.E.10. | 553 |
| Killonahan | 34 | 63 | 2783 | 8.F.8., 9.B.8., 13.E.11. | 311-313 |
| Kilmallock (Sts. Peter & Paul) | | | [2996/7] | | |

| PARISH | TITHES 1823–38 TAB 17/ | FILM | VALUATION FIELD BOOKS 1830s OL4./ HOUSE BOOKS [OL5.] | TENEMENT VALUATION FICHE 1850/52 | 1841–1851 CENSUS SEARCH Cen /S/17 |
|---|---|---|---|---|---|
| Kilmeedy | 82 | 65 | [1235/36] | 12.F.12. | 145-171 |
| Kilmoylan | 6 | 62 | 2794 | 11.B.12. | 612-619 |
| Kilmurry | 42 | 63 | 2717 | 1.G.10. | 33-36 |
| Kilpeacon | 103 | 66 | 2784, 2812, [1283/84] | 9.B.12., 10.C.4. | 678 |
| Kilquane | 127 | 67 | 2743 | 5.G.8. | 259-261 |
| Kilscannell | 23 | 62 | 2723, [1196a/97], [1204/05] | 3.A.2. | 77 |
| Kilteely | 69 | 64 | 2813, [1271/72] | 3.E.9., 4.A.12. | 178, 679 |
| Knockainy | 107 | 66 | 2814 ,[1285] [2994] | 9.E.9., 10.C.6. | 680-681 |
| Knocklong | 118 | 66 | 2744 | 5.G.12. | 262-264 |
| Knocknagaul | 36 | 63 | 2785 | 9.B.14. | |
| Limerick city | | | [2998-3035] | | 474-531 |
| Lismakeery | 15 | 62 | [1206/08] | 3.A.6. | |
| Loghill | 3 | 62 | 2795 | 11.C.12. | 620-626 |
| Ludden | 52 | 64 | | 2.A.2. | 37-38 |
| Mahoonagh | 76 | 65 | 2754. [1262/63] | 6.G.2. | 413-416 |
| Monagay | 75 | 65 | 2755, [1264/67] | 7.A.1. | 417-443 |
| Monasteranenagh | 39 | 63 | 2786, 2815, [1286/87] | 8.F.9., 9.C.4., 13.E.13. | 682-685, 554-560 |
| Morgans | 12 | 62 | 2724, [1209/11] | 3.A.9. | |
| Mungret | 32 | 63 | 2787 | 8.F.9., 9.C.10. | 561-577 |
| Nantinan | 16 | 62 | 2725, 2796, [1212/15] | 11.D.6., 3.A.11. | 78-80, 627-632 |
| Newcastle | 71 | 64 | 2756, [1266/69] | 11.D.7., 7.C.1. | 444-445 |
| Oola | 68 | 64 | [1240] | 3.E.9., 4.B.2. | 179 |
| Particles | 123 | 67 | 2745-46-47 | 6.A.6. | 265-267 |
| Rathjordan | 59 | 64 | | 2.A.6. | |
| Rathkeale | 21 | 62 | 2726, [1216/18, 3041/44] | 3.B.5. | 81-92 |
| Rathronan | 10 | 62 | 2797 | 11.D.8. | 633-659 |
| Robertstown | 5 | 62 | 2798 | 11.E.8. | |
| Rochestown | 54 | 64 | | 2.A.10. | |
| Shanagolden | 4 | 62 | 2799, [3045] | 11.D.6. | 660-662 |
| St John's | 1 | 62 | [3007] | 14.B.2., 14.C.3., 2.A.10. | |
| St Lawrence's | 44 | 63 | 2718, [3012] | 14.B.3., 14.E.7., 2.A.12. | |
| St Michael's | 33 | 63 | 2788, [3006] | 14.B.3., 14.F.10., 8.F.9., 9.D.10. | 493-499, 530-531, 578-580 |
| St Munchin's | 31 | 63 | 2789, [3014], [3034], [3035] | 14.B.5., 15.C.14., 13.G.8., 14.A.2. | 500-508, 581-582 |
| St Nicholas | 45 | 63 | 2719, [3015], [3032], [3035] | 15.D.5., 13.G.8., 14.A.6., 2.B.2. | 39 |
| St Patrick's | 41 | 63 | 2720, [4034], [3033] | 14.B.5., 15.D.10. | 40-41, 509-529 |
| St Peter's & St Paul's | 114 | 66 | | 7.D.6. | 469-473 |
| Stradbally | 40 | 63 | | 2.C.2. | 42-59 |
| Tankardstown | 99 | 66 | | 13.E.14. | |
| Templebredon | 70 | 64 | [1240/42] | 4.B.14. | 180-181 |
| Tomdeely | 13 | 62 | 2727, [1219/20] | 3.D.9. | |
| Tullabracky | 94 | 66 | 2816, [1251], [1288/89] | 13.F.2., | 314-316 |

| PARISH | TITHES 1823–38 TAB 17/ | FILM | VALUATION FIELD BOOKS 1830s OL4./ HOUSE BOOKS [OL5.] | TENEMENT VALUATION FICHE 1850/52 | 1841–1851 CENSUS SEARCH Cen /S/17 |
|---|---|---|---|---|---|
| Tuogh | 62 | 64 | 2774-2776 | 8.C.2., 8.E.6. | 539-541 |
| Tuoghcluggin or Cluggin | 67 | 64 | | 4.C.4. | |
| Uregare | 98 | 66 | 2817 [1290] | 13.F.5., 10.E.10. | 317, 686-687 |

| TOWNS | VALUATION HOUSE BOOK 1830s [OL5.] |
|---|---|
| Cappamore | [2986] |
| Castleconnel | [2985] |
| Glin | [2992] |
| Herbertstown | [2993] |
| Killeely | [3011, 3035] |
| Limerick No. 1 & 2 | [2998] |
| Limerick No. 3 | [2999] |
| Limerick No. 4 | [3000] |
| Limerick No. 5 | [3001] |
| Limerick No. 6 | [3002] |
| Limerick No. 7 | [3003] |
| Limerick No. 8 | [3004] |
| Limerick No. 9 | [3005] |
| Montpelier | [2985] |
| Moroe | [3036] |
| No. 1-14 | [3016/29] |
| Pallas Green | [3037] |
| Pallaskenry | [3038] |
| Patrickswell | [3039/40] |
| St John's 11 | [3007] |
| St John's 12 | [3008] |
| St John's 13 | [3009] |
| St John's 14 | [3010] |
| St Lawrence | [3012] |
| St Mary's | [3013] [4033] |
| St Mary's | [3030/31] |
| St Michael's 10 | [3006] |
| St Munchin's | [3014, 3034, 3035] |
| St Nicholas | [3015, 3032, 3035] |
| St Patrick's | [3033] |

| PARISH | TITHES 1823–38 TAB 18/ | FILM | VALUATION FIELD BOOKS 1830s OL4./ HOUSE BOOKS [OL5.] | TENEMENT VALUATION 1854 FICHE | 1841–1851 CENSUS SEARCH Cen /S/18 |
|---|---|---|---|---|---|
| Abbeylara | 7 | 68 | 1116-17, [1291] | 2.D.8. | 25-31 |
| Abbeyshrule | 23 | 69 | 1158-59, [1294] | 1.F.12. | 331-332 |
| Agharra | 24 | 69 | 1160-61 | 1.G.2. | |
| Ardagh | 9 | 68 | 1099, 1134-35, 2818 | 4.A.4., 3.E.4. | 1-3 |
| Ballymacormick | 14 | 69 | 1100-01, 1136-37 | 4.B.3., 3.E.7. | 292 |
| Cashel | 19 | 69 | 1147-48 | 1.A.14., 3.G.4. | 313-318 |
| Clonbroney | 5 | 68 | 1102-03, 1118-19, 2819, [1293] | 2.B.12., 2.E.4. | 32-65 |
| Clongesh | 3 | 68 | 1124-25 | 4.D.6. | 161-165 |
| Columbkille | 4 | 68 | 1120-21 | 2.F.7., 5.C.8. | 66-111 |
| Forgney | 25 | 69 | 1162-63, 1162-63 | 1.G.4. | 333-337 |
| Granard | 6 | 68 | 1104-05, 2819/20, [1292], [3062/65] | 2.B.12., 3.A.1. | 112-133 |
| Kilcommock | 20 | 69 | 1138, 1149-50, 1164 | 1.D.12., 1.C.4., 1.G.11. | 292-299, 319-322 |
| Kilglass | 16 | 69 | 1106-07, 1139-40, 1165 | 1.F.4., 4.B.9., 1.E.3., 1.G.12. | 300, 339-341 |
| Killashee | 13 | 69 | 1126-27, 1141-42 | 4.F.3., 1.E.7., 3.F.1. | 301-304 |
| Killoe | 1 | 68 | 1122-23, 1128-29 | 3.C.8., 5.C.8., 2.D.6., 4.F.7. | 134-160, 166-282 |
| Mohill | 2 | 68 | 1130-31 | 4.E.12. | 283-286 |
| Mostrim | 10 | 68 | 1108-09 | 2.B.13. | 4-14 |
| Moydow | 15 | 69 | 1143-44 | 1.E.7., 3.F.12. | 305-309 |
| Noughaval | 26 | 69 | 1151-52, 1166-67 | 1.C.12., 1.G.14. | |
| Rathcline | 18 | 69 | 1153-54 | 1.C.12., 3.G.4. | 323-329 |
| Rathreagh | 12 | 68 | 1110-11 | 1.F.6. | 15-16 |
| Shrule | 21 | 69 | 1155, 2821 | 1.C.12. | 330 |
| Street | 11 | 68 | 1112-13 | 2.D.1. | 17 |
| Taghsheenod | 17 | 69 | 1145-46, 1168-69 | 1.E.10., 2.A.5. | 310-312 |
| Taghshinny | 22 | 69 | 1156-57, 1170-71 | 1.D.10., 2.A.6. | 338, 342 |
| Templemichael | 8 | 68 | 1114-15, 1132-33 | 4.B.10., 5.B.11. | 18-24, 287-291 |

| TOWNS | VALUATION HOUSE BOOK 1830s [OL5.] |
|---|---|
| Ballymahon | [3056, 3057] |
| Drumlish | [3058/59] |
| Edgeworthstown | [3058, 3060/61] |
| Longford | [3058] |
| Newtownforbes | [3058, 3061] |
| Keenagh | [3066] |
| Lanesboro[ugh] | [3067] |
| Longford | [3068/69] |

| PARISH/TOWN | TITHES 1823–38 TAB 20/ | FILM | VALUATION FIELD BOOKS 1830s OL4./ HOUSE BOOKS [OL5.] | TENEMENT VALUATION 1854 FICHE | 1841–1851 CENSUS SEARCH Cen /S/20 |
|---|---|---|---|---|---|
| Ardee | 29 | 71 | 1172, 2822, [3071/2] | 1.A.14. | 1-9 |
| Ballybarrack | 14 | 70 | 1199, [4049-50] | 5.A.13. | 189 |
| Ballyboys | 3 | 70 | 1195, [4045] | 6.A.9. | 110-111 |
| Ballymakenny | 62 | 72 | 1193 & 3a, 1214, 2848, [4035-36] | 2.E.14., 2.D.12. | 280 |
| Ballymascanlan | 1 | 70 | 1196, 1200, 2843, 2844, [4046, 4051] | 6.A.12., 5.A.14. | 112-154, 190-92 |
| Barronstown | 10 | 70 | 1201 | 5.B.1. | 193 |
| Beaulieu | 61 | 72 | 1215, 2849, [1300] | 2.F.2. | 281 |
| Cappoge | 38 | 71 | 1173, 2823 | 1.C.10. | 10 |
| Carlingford | 2 | 70 | 1197, 2845, [4047] | 6.C.13. | 155-188 |
| Carrickbaggot | 51 | 71 | 1216, 2850 | 2.F.4. | |
| Castlebellingham (Gernonstown) | | | [3073] | | |
| Castletown | 11 | 70 | 1198, 1202 ,[4052-53, 1295] | 6.G.13., 5.B.5. | 194 |
| Charlestown | 27 | 71 | 1174, 2824 | 1.C.12. | 11-12 |
| Clogher | 57 | 72 | 1217, 2851, [3074] | 2.F.6. | |
| Clonkeehan | 21 | 71 | 1236, 2866, [4070] | 2.C.8. | 336 |
| Clonkeen | 26 | 71 | 1175, 1176, 2825 | 1.D.2. | 13-17 |
| Clonmore | 46 | 71 | 1218 | 2.F.13. | 282 |
| Collon | 48 | 71 | 1219, 2842, [3075] | 2.A.12. | 282-297 |
| Creggan | 6 | 70 | 1203, [4054] | 5.B.8. | 195-198 |
| Darver | 20 | 71 | 1237, 2867, [4071] | 4.F.2. | |
| Drogheda | | | [3076/90, 3100, 4037-4043] | | 79-109 |
| Dromin | 37 | 71 | 1177, 2826 | 1.D.9. | |
| Dromiskin | 19 | 71 | 1238, 2868, [4072] | 4.F.4. | 337-344 |
| Drumcar | 35 | 71 | 1178 | 1.D.13. | 18-21 |
| Drumshallon | 55 | 72 | 1220, 2853, [1296] | 2.G.2. | 298-301 |
| Dunany | 43 | 71 | 1221, 2854, 2855 | 2.B.9. | 302-303 |
| Dunbin | 13 | 70 | 1204, [4055-56] | 5.B.13. | 199-211 |
| Dundalk | 12 | 70 | 1205, 2846, [3101/9, 4044, 4057-58] | 5.C.4., 5.F.2. | 213-241 |
| Dunleer | 44 | 71 | 1222, 2856, [1297, 3110] | 2.B.12. | 304 |
| Dysart | 45 | 71 | 1223, 2857 | 2.G.8. | 305 |
| Faughart | 5 | 70 | 1206, 2847, [4059] | 5.D.5. | 242-257 |
| Gernonstown | 32 | 71 | 1179, 2828 | 1.E.6. | 22-25 |
| Haggardstown | 15 | 70 | 1207, 2847, [4060-61] | 5.D.13. | 258-265 |
| Haynestown | 16 | 70 | 1208, 2847, [4062-63] | 5.E.2. | |
| Inishkeen | 9 | 70 | 1209, 1239, 2847 | 5.D.2., 4.F.13. | 266-268 |
| Kane | 8 | 70 | 1210, 2847 | 5.E.3. | 269 |
| Kildemock | 40 | 71 | 1180, 2829 | 1.E.11. | 26-28 |
| Killanny | 23 | 71 | 1181, 2830 | 4.E.6. | 29-35 |
| Killincoole | 18 | 71 | 1240, 2869, [4073] | 4.F.13. | |
| Kilsaran | 31 | 71 | 1182, 2831 | 1.F.2. | 36-47 |
| Louth | 17 | 70 | 1183, 1211, 1241, 2832, 2870, [4065-66, 4074] | 5.E.5., 2.C.8., 4.G.2., 4.E .11. | 270-272 345-354 |
| Manfieldstown | 22 | 71 | 1242, [4075] | 2.C.10. | |
| Mapastown | 28 | 71 | 1184, 2833 | 1.F.7. | 48-49 |
| Marlestown | 50 | 71 | 1224, 2858 | 2.G.11. | 306 |
| Mayne | 56 | 72 | 1225, 2859 | 2.G.12. | |
| Monasterboice | 54 | 72 | 1226, 2860, [1298] | 2.G.14. | 307-309 |

| PARISH | TITHES 1823–38 TAB 20/ | FILM | VALUATION FIELD BOOKS 1830s OL4./ HOUSE BOOKS [OL5.] | TENEMENT VALUATION 1854 FICHE | 1841–1851 CENSUS SEARCH Cen /S/20 |
|---|---|---|---|---|---|
| Mosstown | 41 | 71 | 1185, 2834 | 1.F.9. | 50-51 |
| Mullary | 49 | 71 | 1227, 2861, [1299] | 3.A .5. | 310-315 |
| Parsonstown | 53 | 71 | 1228 | 3.A.10. | |
| Philipstown | 7 | 70 | 1212 | 5.E.9. | 52-56, 273 |
| Philipstown | 24 | 71 | 1186, 2835 [4067] | 1.G.1. | |
| Philipstown | 59 | 72 | 1229, 2862 [1301] | 3.A.10. | |
| Port | 47 | 71 | 1230 | 3.A.11. | |
| Rathdrumin | 52 | 71 | 1231, 2863 | 3.B.1. | 316 |
| Richardstown | 34 | 71 | 1187, 2836 | 1.G.8. | |
| Roche | 4 | 70 | 1213, 2847 [4068] | 5.E.10. | 274-279 |
| Salterstown | 42 | 71 | 1232 | 2.C.6. | |
| Shanlis | 36 | 71 | 1188, 2837 | 1.G.10. | |
| Smarmore | 39 | 71 | 1189, 2838 | 1.G.12. | |
| Stabannan | | | | | 58-62 |
| St Mary's (Drogheda) | 64 | 72 | [4040, 4069] | 3.E.10. | 66-70 |
| St Peter's | 63 | 72 | 1194, 1233, 2842 [4041] | 2.D.13., 3.G.2. | 71-78 |
| Stickillin | 33 | 71 | 1191, 2840 | 2.A.7. | |
| Tallanstown | 25 | 71 | 1192, 2841 | 2.A.8. | 63-65 |
| Termonfeckin | 60 | 72 | 1234, 2864 [3111] | 3.B.4. | 317-320 |
| Tullyallen | 58 | 72 | 1235, 2865 | 3.C.6. | 321-335 |

| PARISH | TITHES 1823–38 TAB 21/ | FILM | VALUATION FIELD BOOKS 1830s OL4./ HOUSE BOOKS [OL5.] | TENEMENT VALUATION FICHE 1855–57 | 1841–1851 CENSUS SEARCH Cen /S/21 |
|---|---|---|---|---|---|
| Achill | 19 | 74 | 1243, [4077] | 11.A.2. | 1-142 |
| Addergoole | 16 | 74 | 1298, [4167] | 1.A.14., 7.A.14. | 2586-2628 |
| Aghagower | 48 | 75 | 1244, 1294, 2904 | 14.C.12., 14.G.8. | 143-161, 2421-2446 |
| Aghamore | 70 | 76 | 1268, [4127] | 8.G.8., 12.A.12. | 640-817 |
| Aglish | 24 | 74 | 1249, 2872, [4089-90] | 5.D.14. | 313-337 |
| Annagh | 73 | 76 | 1269, [4128] | 8.G.12. | 818-930 |
| Ardagh | 14 | 74 | 1299, [4168] | 1.A.14. | 2629-2641 |
| Attymass | 36 | 75 | 1277, 2889 | 2.B.10. | 1655-1704 |
| Balla | 59 | 75 | 2884 | 6.F.14. | 469-475 |
| Ballinchalla | 52 | 75 | 1287, [4150] | 2.G.10. | 2255-2263 |
| Ballinrobe | 50 | 75 | 1288, [4151-52, 3119/23] | 3.A.4. | 2264-2288 |
| Ballintober | 30 | 74 | 1245, 1250, 2873, [4078, 4091-92] | 14.D.10., 2.E.10., 5.G.1. | 162, 338-345 |
| Ballynahaglish | 18 | 74 | 1300, [4169-71] | 1.B.7. | 2641-2669 |
| Ballyhean | 27 | 74 | 1251, 2875, [4093-94] | 6.A.1. | 346-356 |
| Ballyovey | 34 | 75 | 1252, 2874, [4096] | 2.E.11. | 357-380 |
| Ballysakeery | 12 | 73 | 1301, [4172] | 1.C.8. | 2670-2689 |
| Bekan | 72 | 76 | 1270, [4131] | 9.B.14. | 931-975 |
| Bohola | 43 | 75 | 1278, 2890 | 6.G.10., 13.A.4. | 1705-1766 |
| Breaghwy | 26 | 74 | 1253, 2876, [4099-4102] | 6.A.13. | 381-382 |
| Burriscarra | 31 | 74 | 1254, 2877, [4103] | 2.F.10., 6.B.6. | 383-387 |
| Burrishoole | 20 | 74 | 1246, [4079-80] | 11.C.12. | 163-240 |
| Castlemore | 69 | 76 | 1271, [4135] | 7.E.4. | 976-1009 |
| Cong | 55 | 75 | 1289, [4153-55, 3135] | 3.C.7. | 1441-1596, 2289, 2290-2310 |
| Crossboyne | 63 | 76 | 1262 | 8.A.12. | 476-511 |
| Crossmolina | 13 | 73 | 1302, [4175-76, 4191] | 1.D.6. | 2690-2737 |
| Doonfeeny | 3 | 73 | 1303, [4177] | 10.A.12. | 2738-2762 |
| Drum | 29 | 74 | 1255, 2878, [4106] | 6.B.8. | 388-390 |
| Inishbofin (Island) | 46 | 75 | 1295, 2902 | 9.G.4. | 2447-2454 |
| Islandeady | 23 | 74 | 1247, 1256, 2879 [4081, 4109] | 14.D.11. | 241-252, 391-409 |
| Kilbeagh | 66 | 76 | 1272, [4138] | 7.F.1., 12.C.10. | 1010-1117 |
| Kilbelfad | 17 | 74 | 1304, [4181] | 1.F.14. | 2763-2779 |
| Kilbride | 4 | 73 | 1305, [4179] | 10.B.14. | 2780-2794 |
| Kilcolman | 61 | 76 | 1263, 1273, [4141] | 8.C.7. 7.F.3. | 512-577, 1118-1176 |
| Kilcommon | 2 | 73 | 2885-2887 | 4.D.4., 11.F.12. | 1441-1596 2289, 2311-2361 |
| Kilcommon | 51 | 75 | 2898, [4156] | 3.D.14., 9.E.12. | |
| Kilconduff | 41 | 75 | 1279, 2891, [4146] | 13.B.2. | 1767-1862 |
| Kilcummin | 5 | 73 | 1306, [4180] | 10.C.6. | 2795-2824 |
| Kildacommoge | 42 | 75 | 1257, 1280, [4112, 4147] | 6.D.2., 6.G.10 | 410-418, 1863-1876 |
| Kilfian | 7 | 73 | 1307 | 1.G.11., 10.D.1. | 2825-2859 |
| Kilgarvan | 35 | 75 | 1281, 2892 | 2.C.9. | 1877-1966 |
| Kilgeever | 47 | 75 | 1296, 2903, 2905 | 15.D.6. | 2445-2501 |
| Killala | 10 | 73 | 1308, [4182, 3138/39] | 10.E.1. | 2860-2865 |

| PARISH | TITHES 1823–38 TAB 21/ | FILM | VALUATION FIELD BOOKS 1830s OL4./ HOUSE BOOKS [OL5.] | TENEMENT VALUATION FICHE 1855–57 | 1841–1851 CENSUS SEARCH Cen /S/21 |
|---|---|---|---|---|---|
| Killasser | 38 | 75 | 1282, 2893 | 13.D.4. | 1967-2028 |
| Killedan | 44 | 75 | 1283, 2894, [4148] | 13.E.14. | 2029-2160 |
| Kilmaclasser | 22 | 74 | 1248, [4082] | 14.E.7. | 253-270, 311-312 |
| Kilmainebeg | 56 | 75 | | | 2362-2369 |
| Kilmainemore | 54 | 75 | 1291, [4159] | 3.F.10. | 2370-2392 |
| Kilmeena | 21 | 74 | 2871, [4083] | 11.F.7., 14.E.14. | 271-310, 311-312 |
| Kilmolara | 53 | 75 | 2899 | 3.G.11. | 2393-2394 |
| Kilmore | 1 | 73 | 2888 | 4.G.13. | 1597-1654 |
| Kilmoremoy | 15 | 74 | 1309, [4185] | 2.A.1. | 2866-2902 |
| Kilmovee | 68 | 76 | 1274, [4143] | 12.F.5. | 1177-1371 |
| Kilturra | 65 | 76 | 1275, [4144] | 12.G.14. | 1372-1379 |
| Kilvine | 64 | 76 | 1264, [4085] | 8.E.7. | 578-609 |
| Knock | 71 | 76 | 1265, 1276, [4086, 4145] | 8.F.1., 9.D.13. | 610-627, 1380-1440 |
| Lackan | 6 | 73 | 1310 | 10.E.11. | 2903-2925 |
| Manulla | 28 | 74 | 1258, 2880 [4115] | 6.D.7. | 419-425 |
| Mayo | 60 | 76 | 1266, 1292 [4087, 4162] | 4.A.3., 2.G.8., 6.G.7., 8.F.3. | 628-631, 2395 |
| Meelick | 40 | 75 | 1284, 2895 | 13.G.11. | 2161-2198 |
| Moorgagagh | 57 | 75 | 2900 | 4.A.6. | |
| Moygawnagh | 11 | 73 | 1311, [4187] | 10.F.5. | 2926-2937 |
| Oughaval | 45 | 75 | 1297, 2906, [4166] | 15.A.8. | 2502-2585 |
| Rathreagh | 8 | 73 | 1312, [4188] | 10.F.12. | 2938-2941 |
| Robeen | 49 | 75 | 1293, [4163] | 4.A.7. | 2396-2409 |
| Rosslee | 32 | 75 | 1259, 2881, [4118] | 2.G.1., 6.E.1. | 426-427 |
| Shrule | 58 | 75 | 2901, [4164, 3144/45] | 4.B.5. | 2410-2420 |
| Tagheen | 62 | 76 | 1267, [4088] | 8.F.11. | 632-639 |
| Templemore | 39 | 75 | 1285, 2896 | 7.A.3. | 2199-2232 |
| Templemurry | 9 | 73 | 1313, [4190] | 10.G.2. | 2942-2954 |
| Toomore | 37 | 75 | 1286, 2897, [4149] | 14.A.11. | 2233-2254 |
| Touaghty | 33 | 75 | 1260, 2882, [4121] | 2.G.3. | 428-429 |
| Turlough | 25 | 74 | 1261, 2883, [4124] | 6.E.3. | 430-468 |

| TOWNS | VALUATION HOUSE BOOKS 1830s [OL5.] |
|---|---|
| Ballaghadereen | [3112,3113] |
| Ballyhaunis | [3113, 3124/35] |
| Ballina | [3114/17] |
| Ballindine | [3118] |
| Ballyharris | [3124/25] |
| Belmullet | [3126/27] |
| Castlebar | [3128/31] |
| Clare | [3132/33] |
| Claremorris | [3134] |
| Foxford | [3136/37] |
| Kiltamagh | [3140] |
| Louisburgh | [3141] |
| Newport | [3142/43] |
| Swineford | [3146] |
| Westport | [3147/49] |
| Westport Quay | [3150/51] |

| PARISH | TITHES 1823–38 TAB 22/ | FILM | VALUATION FIELD BOOKS 1830s OL4./ HOUSE BOOKS [OL5.] | TENEMENT VALUATION FICHE 1855–57 | 1841–1851 CENSUS SEARCH Cen /S/22 |
|---|---|---|---|---|---|
| Agher | 138 | 80 | 1314, 1323, 2907 | 9.A.4., 9.A.12. | 4 |
| Ardagh | 17 | 77 | 1386 (Part Missing), 2960, [4206] | 5.C.12., 5.C.6. | |
| Ardbraccan | 50 | 78 | 1404 | 7.E.10. | 197-202 |
| Ardcath | 102 | 79 | 1344, 2922 | 2.G.14. | 47-49 |
| Ardmulchan | 79 | 79 | 1434 | 7.C.6. | 263 |
| Ardsallagh | 57 | 78 | 1405 | 7.F.6. | 203-207 |
| Assey | 116 | 79 | 1315 | 7.D.14. | |
| Athboy | 70 | 78 | 1381, [3152] | 9.F.12. | 134-139 |
| Athlumney | 80 | 79 | 1435 | 7.C.9. | 264-271 |
| Balfeaghan | 141 | 80 | 2909, 2915 | 4.F.6. | |
| Ballyboggan | 110 | 79 | 1399 | 4.G.10. | |
| Ballygarth | 100 | 79 | 1345, 2923-24 | 3.A.7. | |
| Ballymagarvey | 68 | 78 | 1331, 2917 | 7.B.6. | 12 |
| Ballymaglassan | 135 | 80 | 1422 | 4.B.7. | |
| Balrathboyne | 36 | 77 | 1372, 1406, [4197] | 6.A.8., 6.A.2. | 107-109, 208 |
| Balsoon | 117 | 79 | 1316, [1302] | 7.E.1., 9.A.4. | |
| Bective | | 79 | 1415 | 7.E.2. | |
| Brownstown | 84 | 79 | 1436 | 7.C.14. | 272 |
| Burry | 35 | 77 | 1373, [4198] | 6.A.11. | |
| Castlejordan | 111 | 79 | 1400 | 4.G.14. | 187-189 |
| Castlerickard | 108 | 79 | 1382, 1401 | 10.A.1., 9.E.12. | |
| Castletown | 11 | 77 | 1387 | 5.C.14., 6.F.4. | 144-145 |
| Churchtown | 55 | 78 | 1407 | 7.F.7. | 209 |
| Clonalvy | 106 | 79 | 1346, 2925 | 3.A.8. | 18-19 |
| Clonard | 109 | 79 | 1402 | 5.A.8., 9.F.1. | 190-196 |
| Clongill | 15 | 77 | 1388 | 6.F.7. | |
| Clonmacduff | 73 | 79 | 1416 | 8.F.12. | |
| Collon | | 78 | 1460 | 2.E.12. | 294-297 |
| Colp | 61 | 78 | 1332, 2918 | 3.C.1. | 13-17 |
| Cookstown | 129 | 80 | 1423 | 4.B.9. | |
| Crickstown | 128 | 80 | 1424, 2956 | 4.B.10. | |
| Cruicetown | 5 | 77 | 1362 | 5.D.14. | 72-75 |
| Culmullin | 137 | 80 | 1324, 1425, 2908 | 4.B.11., 3.G.7. | 5-8 |
| Cushinstown | | 79 | 1437 | 4.D.11. | 273-274 |
| Danestown | 88 | 79 | 1333, 1438, 2919 | 7.B.7., 7.D.1. | |
| Derrypatrick | 123 | 80 | 1317 | 3.F.12. | 1-3 |
| Diamor | 29 | 77 | 1356 | 8.B.10. | |
| Donaghmore | 52 | 78 | 1408 | 4.B.11. | ? |
| Donaghmore | 133 | 80 | 1426 | 7.E.9. | 210-216 |
| Donaghpatrick | 38 | 78 | 1374, 1409, [4199] | 6.A.14., 7.E.6., 7.F.14. | 110-111 |
| Donore | | 78 | 1334, 2920 | 3.C.11. | 20-25 |
| Dowdstown | 85 | 79 | 1439 | 7.D.2. | 275 |
| Dowth | 48 | 78 | 1461 | 2.G.8. | 298-299 |
| Drakestown | 12 | 77 | 1389 | 6.F.8. | |
| Drumcondra | 18 | 77 | 1455, [4207] | 2.C.13., 5.C.11. | 282-287 |
| Drumlargan | 139 | 80 | 1325, 2910 | 9.A .13. | |
| Dulane | 33 | 77 | 1375, [4200] | 6.A 14. | 112 |
| Duleek | 64 | 78 | 1335, 1347, 2926-27 | 3.D.2., 3.A.11. | 26-41, 50-55 |
| Duleek Abbey | | 79 | 1348, 2928-29 | 3.B.3. | |
| Dunboyne | 145 | 80 | 1354, 2939, [4194-95, 3154] | 4.A.6. | |

| PARISH | TITHES 1823–38 TAB 22/ | FILM | VALUATION FIELD BOOKS 1830s OL4./ HOUSE BOOKS [OL5.] | TENEMENT VALUATION FICHE 1855–57 | 1841–1851 CENSUS SEARCH Cen /S/22 |
|---|---|---|---|---|---|
| Dunmoe | 53 | 78 | 1410 | 7.G.1. | |
| Dunsany | 95 | 79 | 1440 | 4.D.12. | |
| Dunshaughlin | 126 | 80 | 1427, 2948, 2949, [4212, 1307] | 4.B.13. | 257-260 |
| Emlagh | 7 | 77 | 1363 | 5.E.1. | 76 |
| Ennisken | 9 | 77 | 1364, 1390 | 5.E.1., 5.C.14. | |
| Fennor | 58 | 78 | 1336, 2921 | 7.B.7. | |
| Follistown | 82 | 79 | 1441 | 7.D.3. | 276 |
| Gallow | 140 | 80 | 1326, 2911 | 9.A.13. | |
| Galtrim | 121 | 79 | | 9.A.6. | |
| Gernonstown | 41 | 78 | 1462 | 6.G.8. | 300-302 |
| Girley | 39 | 78 | 1376, 2941 [4201] | 6.B.4. | 113-114 |
| Grangegeeth | | 78 | 1463 | 2.E.14. | 303-305 |
| Greenoge | 134 | 80 | 1428 | 4.C.7. | |
| Inishmot | 20 | 77 | 1456, [4208] | 2.D.8. | |
| Julianstown | 66 | 78 | 1337, 1349, 2930-31 [4192] | 3.E.4., 3.B.3. | |
| Kells | | 77 | 1377, [4213, 3155/57] | 6.B.7. | 115-117 |
| Kentstown | 67 | 78 | 1338 | 7.B.8 | |
| Kilbeg | 4 | 77 | 1365, [4196] | 5.E.5. | 77-84 |
| Kilberry | 16 | 77 | 1391 | 6.F.10. | 146-151 |
| Kilbrew | 125 | 80 | 1429, 2950 | 4.C.8. | 261 |
| Kilbride | 24 | 77 | 1357 | 4.B.4. | ? |
| Kilbride | | 80 | 1355 | 8.B.12. | 56-57 |
| Kilcarn | 81 | 79 | 1442 | 7.D.4. | 277 |
| Kilclone | 143 | 80 | 1327, 2911 | 3.G.10. | |
| Kilcooly | 78 | 79 | 1417 | 8.F.14. | 256 |
| Kildalkey | 71 | 79 | 1383 | 10.A.1. | 140 |
| Killaconnigan | 72 | 79 | 1384 | 10.A.11. | 141-142 |
| Killallon | 30 | 77 | 1358 | 8.B.13. | 58 |
| Killary | 23 | 77 | 1457, 2961, [4209] | 2.D.9. | 288-290 |
| Killeen | 94 | 79 | 1443 | 4.D.13. | |
| Killegland | 130 | 80 | 1430, [4205] | 4.C.10. | |
| Killeagh | 26 | 77 | 1359 | 8.C.6. | 59-61 |
| Killyon | 107 | 79 | 1403 | 5.B.6., 9.F.7. | |
| Kilmainham | 2 | 77 | 1366 | 5.E.11. | 85-93 |
| Kilmessan | 120 | 79 | 1318 | 3.F.13. | |
| Kilmoon | 98 | 79 | 1444 | 4.E.1. | |
| Kilmore | 136 | 80 | 1328, 2913 | 3.G.12. | 9-10 |
| Kilsharvan | 65 | 78 | 1339, 1350, 2932-33 | 3.E.7., 3.B.4. | |
| Kilshine | 14 | 77 | 1392 | 6.G.3. | |
| Kilskeer | 31 | 77 | 1378, [4202-03] | 6.C.12., 8.E.8. | 118-120 |
| Kiltale | 122 | 80 | 1319 | 3.G.2. | |
| Knock | 13 | 77 | 1393 | 6.G.5. | 152 |
| Knockcommon | 63 | 78 | 1340 | 7.B.10. | 42-43 |
| Knockmark | 124 | 80 | 1320 | 3.G.4. | |
| Laracor | 113 | 79 | 1395, 2942, [1303] | 9.B.4. | 157-160 |
| Liscartan | 51 | 78 | 1411 | 7.G.1. | |
| Lismullin | | 79 | 1145 | 7.D.6. | |
| Loughan (Castlekeeran) | 32 | 77 | 1379 | 6.D.8. | 121-129 |
| Loughbrackan | 19 | 77 | 2962 | 2.E.2. | 291 |
| Loughcrew | | 77 | 1360 | 8.C.12. | 62 |

| PARISH | TITHES 1823–38 TAB 22/ | FILM | VALUATION FIELD BOOKS 1830s OL4./ HOUSE BOOKS [OL5.] | TENEMENT VALUATION FICHE 1855–57 | 1841–1851 CENSUS SEARCH Cen /S/22 |
|---|---|---|---|---|---|
| Macetown | 97 | 79 | 1446 | 4.E.4. | |
| Martry | 49 | 78 | 1412 | 6.A.3. | 217-219 |
| Mitchelstown | 21 | 77 | 1458, 2962a, [4210] | 2.E.5. | 292 |
| Monknewtown | | 78 | 1464 | 2.G.10. | 306-312 |
| Monktown | | 79 | 1447 | 7.D.7. | 278-279 |
| Moorechurch | 101 | 79 | 1351, 2934-35 | 3.B.5. | |
| Moybolgue | 1 | 77 | 1367 | 5.F.2. | 94 |
| Moyglare | 144 | 80 | 1329, 2916 | 4.A.2., 4.F.7. | |
| Moylagh | 27 | 77 | 2940 | 8.D.2. | 63-68 |
| Moymet | 75 | 79 | 1418 | 8.G.1. | |
| Moynalty | 3 | 77 | 1368 | 5.F.8. | 95-103 |
| Navan | 54 | 78 | 1413, [4214, 3160] | 7.G.3. | 220-251 |
| Newtown | 6 | 77 | 1369 | 5.G.11. | |
| Newtownclonbun | 77 | 79 | 1419 | 8.G.4. | |
| Nobber | 10 | 77 | 1370, 1394 | 5.G.12., 5.D.5. | 153-156 |
| Oldcastle | 25 | 77 | 1361, [3161] | 8.D.9. | 69-71 |
| Painestown | 62 | 78 | 1341 | 7.B.14. | 46 |
| Piercetown | 105 | 79 | 1342, 1352, 2936 | 7.C.4., 4.A.3. | |
| Rataine | 56 | 78 | 1414 | 8.A.12. | 253-254 |
| Rathbeggan | 132 | 80 | 1431, 2951, 2957 | 4.C.11. | |
| Rathcore | 115 | 79 | 1330, 1396, 2914, 2943, [1304] | 9.B.14., 9.B.2. | 11, 161-171 |
| Rathfeigh | 92 | 79 | 1448 | 4.E.6. | |
| Rathkenny | 40 | 78 | 1465 | 6.G.11. | 313-341 |
| Rathmore | 69 | 78 | 1385 | 10.B.5. | 143 |
| Rathmolyon | 114 | 79 | 1397, 2944-47, [1305, 3162] | 9.C.11. | 172-182 |
| Rathregan | 131 | 80 | 1432, 2952 | 4.C.13. | |
| Ratoath | 127 | 80 | 1433, 2953-54, 2958-59 [3163] | 4.C.14. | 262 |
| Rodanstown | 142 | 80 | | 4.F.9. | |
| Scurlockstown | 119 | 79 | 1321 | 9.A.9. | |
| Siddan | 22 | 77 | 1459, [4211] | 2.E.6. | 293 |
| Skreen | 91 | 79 | 1449 | 4.E.7. | 280 |
| Slane | 44 | 78 | 1466 | 7.A.5. | 342-347 |
| St Marys | 60 | 78 | 1343 | 3.E.9. | 44-45 |
| Stackallan | 46 | 78 | 1467 | 7.B.1. | 348-349 |
| Staffordstown | 83 | 79 | 1450 | 7.D.9. | |
| Staholmog | 8 | 77 | 1371 | 5.G.13. | 104-106 |
| Stamullin | 104 | 79 | 1353, 2937-38 | 3.B..9 | |
| Tara | 89 | 79 | 1451 | 7.D.9. | |
| Teltown | 20/37 | 78 | 1380, [4204] | 6.D.14. | 130-133 |
| Templekeeran | 86 | 79 | 1452 | 7.D.11. | |
| Timoole | 93 | 79 | 1453 | 4.E.12. | |
| Trevet | 96 | 79 | 1454, 2955 | 4.E.12., 4.D.10. | 281 |
| Trim | 112 | 79 | 1398, 1420, [1306, 3167/70] | 8.G.5., 9.D.8. | 183-186, 255 |
| Trubley | 118 | 79 | 1322 | 9.A.11. | |
| Tullaghanoge | 74 | 79 | 1421 | 9.A.2. | |
| Tullyallen | 45 | 78 | 1468 | 2.G.13. | |

| TOWNS | VALUATION HOUSE BOOK 1830s [OL5.] |
|---|---|
| Clonee | [3153] |
| Dunboyne | [3154] |
| Kells | |
| Longwood | [3158] |
| Mornington | [3159] |
| Robinstown | [3164] |
| Summerhill | [3165/66] |

| PARISH/TOWN | TITHES 1823–38 TAB 23/ | FILM | VALUATION FIELD BOOKS 1830s OL4./ HOUSE BOOK [OL5.] | TENEMENT VALUATION c.1858–61 FICHE | 1841/1851 CENSUS SEARCH Cen /S/3 |
|---|---|---|---|---|---|
| Aghabog | 12 | 82 | 1481/2, 2967/8 | 4.D.10., 5.E.12., 8.G.12. | 241-291 |
| Aghnamullen | 18 | 82 | 1469/70, 2963/4 | 2.C.8., 3.E.2., 5.D.6. | 1-87 |
| Ballybay | 17 | 82 | 1471/2, 1502/3, [3171] | 4.A.4., 3.A.B. | 88-121 |
| Carrickmacross | | | [3173/74] | | |
| Castleblayney | | | [3175] | 2.G.11. | |
| Clones | 9 | 81 | 1483/4, 1504/5, 2969-76, [1309/10], [3172] | 4.D.14., 7.C.10., 9.A.2. | 292-323 647-663 |
| Clontibret | 15 | 82 | 1473/4, 2965, [1308] | 3.B.6., 8.E.12. | 122-213 |
| Currin | 13 | 82 | 1485/6, 2977-8 | 4.G.9., 5.F.12. | 324-345 |
| Donagh | 2 | 81 | 1518, 3012, [1313] | 6.C.8. | 797-812 |
| Donaghmoyne | 20 | 83 | 1492/3, 2990 | 1.A.14., 3.G.6. | 411-520 |
| Drummully | 11 | 82 | 1487 | 5.A.6. | 346-348 |
| Drumsnat | 5 | 81 | 1506-7, 3003 | 7.D.8. | 664-666 |
| Ematris | 14 | 82 | 1488-9, 2981 | 5.G.8. | 349-367 |
| Emyvale (Donagh) | | | [3177] | | |
| Errigal Trough | 1 | 81 | 1519, 4437 | 4.B.8., 6.F.5. | 813-866 |
| Glaslough (Donagh) | | | [3176] | | |
| Inishkeen | 21 | 83 | 1494, 3002 | 9.B.13. | 521-542 |
| Killanny | 23 | 83 | 1496/7, 2993/4 | 1.D.14. | 543-554 |
| Killeevan | 10 | 82 | 1490/1, 2982/5 | 5.A.13., 9.A.4. | 368-410 |
| Kilmore | 6 | 81 | 1508/9, 3004 | 7.E.8. | 667-677 |
| Magheracloone | 22 | 83 | 1498/9, 2994/6 | 2.A.8. | 555-569 |
| Magheross | 19 | 83 | 1500/1, 3001/2, [3173/4] | 1.E.11. | 570-646 |
| Monaghan | 7 | 81 | 1510/11, 3005/6, [1311], [3178/80], | 8.B.3. | 678-717 |
| Newbliss (Killeevan) | | | [3181] | | |
| Smithborough (Clones) | | | [3182/3] | | |
| Muckno | 16 | 82 | 1475/6, [3175] | 2.E.2. | 214-238 |
| Tedavnet | 3 | 81 | 1512/3, 3010 | 6.G.10. | 718-765 |
| Tehallan | 4 | 81 | 1514/5, 3011, [1312] | 8.A.2., 8.G.7. | 239-240, 766-770 |
| Tullycorbet | 8 | 81 | 1516/7 | 7.F.14., 8 .G.3. | 771-796 |

| PARISH | TITHES 1823–38 TAB 15/ | FILM | VALUATION FIELD BOOKS 1830s OL4./ HOUSE BOOKS [OL5.] | TENEMENT VALUATION 1854 FICHE | 1841–1851 CENSUS SEARCH Cen /S/15 |
|---|---|---|---|---|---|
| Aghancon | 38 | 58 | 1005, 3018, 3036 [1319, 1349] | 7.C.6., 6.D.1. | 12-15, 79-80 |
| Ardnurcher (Horseleap) | 3 | 56 | 1031, 3069, [1389] | 4.G.9. | |
| Ballyboy | 27 | 57 | 3014, [1314/16, 3184] | 2.B.7. | 1-7 |
| Ballyburly | 6 | 56 | 3084, [1394/95, 1409/10] | 1.E.7., 1.D.10. | 334-336, 352-354 |
| Ballycommon | 21 | 57 | 1036, 3075, [1396/97] | 4.C.14. | |
| Ballykean | 29 | 57 | 1040, 3068, [1384, 1403/05] | 6.A.2., 4.E.12. | 337-340 |
| Ballymacwilliam | 7 | 56 | 1044, 3085, [1411/12] | 1.E.11 | 355 |
| Ballynakill | 24 | 57 | 1018, 3032 | 1.A.12. | 127-130 |
| Birr | 34 | 58 | 0994, 3019, [1320/21] | 2.E.10., 3.A.1. | 16-36 |
| Borrisnafarney | 51 | 58 | 1006 [1350] | 6.D.12. | 81 |
| Castlejordan | 5 | 56 | 1019, 1045, 1046, [1362, 1413/14] | 1.F.1. | 131, 356-359 |
| Castletownely | 48 | 58 | 1007, 3038, [1351] | 6.D.14. | |
| Castropetie (Monasteroris) | 23 | 57 | | | |
| Clonyhurk | 30 | 57 | 1041, 3079, [1406] | 7.F.8. | 341 |
| Clonmacnoise | 8 | 56 | 1023, 3060, [1369] | 3.B.9. | 151-179 |
| Clonsast | 25 | 57 | 3034, [1363/64] | 1.B.3. | 132-137 |
| Corbally | 40 | 58 | 0995, 1008, 3039 [1322, 1352] | 7.C.12., 6.E.2. | |
| Croghan | 19 | 57 | 1037, [1398] | 1.D.13. | 341 |
| Cullenwaine | 50 | 58 | 3040, [1353] | 6.E.4. | 82-84 |
| Drumcullen | 32 | 57 | 1021, 3058, [1366/67] | 1.G.10. | 148-149 |
| Dunkerrin | 46 | 58 | 1010, 3041, [1354] | 6.E.12. | |
| Durrow | 15 | 56 | 1001, [1338/40] | 5.C.1. | 54-55 |
| Eglish | 31 | 57 | 1022, 3059, [1368] | 2.A.8. | 150 |
| Ettagh | 43 | 58 | 0996, 3021, [1323, 1355] | 7.C.14., 6.F 8. | 85-95 |
| Finglas | 49 | 58 | 1012, 3034, [1356] | 6.F.14. | |
| Gallen | 12 | 56 | 1024, 3061, [1370/71] | 3.A.3. | 180-199 |
| Geashill | 28 | 57 | 1030, 3080, 3081, [1385/87, 1407/08] | 7.G.10., 6.A.2., 1.E.4., 4.E.12. | 284-305, 343-346 |
| Kilbride | 4 | 56 | 1032, 1002, 3070, 3031, [1390/91] | 4.G.13. | 56-62, 306-326 |
| Kilbride (Tullamore) | 17 | 57 | [1341/42] | 5.C.9. | |
| Kilclonfert | 20 | 57 | 1038, 3077, [1399/400] | 4.D.5. | 347-348 |
| Kilcolman | 41 | 58 | 1013, 3023, 3044, 3055, [1324/25, 1356a] | 2.C.13., 6.G.2. | 37-40, 96-102 |
| Kilcomin | 45 | 58 | 3046, [1357] | 6.G.6. | |
| Kilcumreragh | 1 | 56 | 1033, 3072, [1392] | 5.B.2. | |
| Killaderry | 22 | 57 | 1039, 3078, [1401/02] | 4.D.13. | 349-351 |
| Killagally (Wheery) | 11 | 56 | [1381/83] | 4.A.6. | 274-283, 349-351 |
| Kilmurryely | 42 | 58 | 1014, [1358] | 6.C.12. | 104-107 |
| Killoughy | 26 | 57 | 3015-3016, [1317/18] | 4.F.5. | 8-11 |
| Kilmanaghan | 2 | 56 | 1034, 3073, [1393] | 5.B.6. | 327-333 |
| Kinnitty | 36 | 58 | 0997, 3024, [1326/27, 3198/99] | 2.D.2. | 41 |
| Lemanaghan | 9 | 56 | 1025, 3062-3063, [1372] | 3.F.5., 5.B.14. | 200-242 |
| Letterluna | 33 | 58 | 0998, 3025, [1328/29] | 2.D.10. | 42-46 |

| PARISH | TITHES 1823–38 TAB 15/ | FILM | VALUATION FIELD BOOKS 1830s OL4./ HOUSE BOOKS [OL5.] | TENEMENT VALUATION 1854 FICHE | 1841–1851 CENSUS SEARCH Cen /S/15 |
|---|---|---|---|---|---|
| Lusmagh | 14 | 56 | 3065, [1373/75] | 3.D.3. | 243-250 |
| Lynally | 18 | 57 | 1003, [1343/45] | 5.F.1. | 63-67 |
| Monasteroris (Edenderry) | 23 | 57 | 3035, [1365] | | 138-147 |
| Rahan | 16 | 56 | 1004, [1346/48] | 5.F.10. | 68-78 |
| Reynagh | 13 | 56 | 1026, 3066, [1376/78] | 3.E.1. | 251-267 |
| Roscomroe | 37 | 58 | 3028, [1330/32] | 2.E.2. | 47-48 |
| Roscrea | 39 | 58 | 1015, 3026, [1333/34, 1359] | 7.D.4., 7.A.4. | 49-50, 108-110 |
| Seirkieran | 35 | 58 | 1000, 3029, [1335/37] | 2.E.4., 7.D.8., | 51-53 |
| Shinrone | 44 | 58 | 1016, 3049, [1360, 3212/13] | 7.A.8. | 111-123 |
| Templeharry | 47 | 58 | 1017, 3050, [1361] | 7.B.4. | 124-126 |
| Tisaran | 10 | 56 | 1027, 3067, [1379/80] | 3.G.12. | 268-273 |
| Wheery/Killagally | | | | 4.A.6. | 274-283 |

| TOWNS | VALUATION HOUSE BOOK 1830s [OL5.] |
|---|---|
| Ballycumber | [3185] |
| Banagher | [3186/87] |
| Birr (See Parsonstown) | |
| Crinkell | [3188/89] |
| Clara | [3190/91] |
| Edenderry | [3192/94] |
| Frankford | [3195] |
| Ferbane | [3196/97] |
| Moneygall | [3200/01] |
| Parsonstown | [3202/06] |
| Philipstown | [3207/08] |
| Portarlington | [3209/10] |
| Shannon Bridge | [3211] |
| Tullamore | [3214/17] |

| PARISH | TITHES 1823–38 TAB 25/ | FILM | VALUATION FIELD BOOKS 1830s OL4./ HOUSE BOOKS [OL5.] | TENEMENT VALUATION 1857–8 FICHE | 1841–1851 CENSUS SEARCH Cen /S/25 |
|---|---|---|---|---|---|
| Ardcarn | 4 | 87 | 1617 | 2.G.6., 4.D.12. | 378-414 |
| Athleague | 44 | 89 | [3218] | 5.A.12. | 1-13 |
| Aughrim | 19 | 88 | 1636 | 4.G.4. | 888-892 |
| Ballintober | 18 | 88 | 1625 | 8.E.2. | 523-534 |
| Ballynakill | 35 | 88 | 1612 | 6.D.12. | 349 |
| Baslick | 16 | 88 | 1626 | 8.E.8. | 535-549 |
| Boyle | 2 | 87 | 1613, [3222/25] | 3.B.2. | 415-446 |
| Bumlin | 26 | 88 | 1637 | 7.C.4. | 893-921 |
| Cam | 51 | 89 | 1590 | 1.E.7. | 14-31 |
| Castlemore | 98 | 87 | 1630 | 9.D.12. | 638-647 |
| Clooncraff | 21 | 88 | 1638 | 4.G.14., 7.C.14. | 922-935 |
| Cloonfinlough | 28 | 88 | 1639 | 6.E 10., 7.D.8. | 936-942 |
| Cloontuskert | 40 | 89 | 1606-07 | 5.F.8. | 273-293 |
| Cloonygormican | 34 | 88 | 1613 | 6.D.13., 8.D.6. | 350-365 |
| Creagh | 57 | 90 | 1634 | 2.D.4. | 862-864 |
| Creeve | 13 | 87 | 1631, 1640 | 4.F.12., 7.E.5. | 648-653 |
| Drum | 56 | 90 | 1591 | 1.A.14. | 32-42 |
| Drumatemple | 33 | 88 | 1614 | 8.D.10. | 366-371 |
| Dunamon | 37 | 88 | 1615 | 6.E.1. | |
| Dysart | 53 | 89 | 1592 | 1.F.5. | 43-50 |
| Elphin | 22 | 88 | 1641, [3227] | 7.E.6. | 943-985 |
| Estersnow | 6 | 87 | 1619 | 3.D.10. | 447-461 |
| Fuerty | 43 | 89 | 1593 | 5.B.11. | 52-77 |
| Kilbride | 38 | 88 | 1608, 1642 | 7.F.11., 5.G.4. | 294-316, 956 |
| Kilbryan | 3 | 87 | 1620 | 3.E.4. | 462-463 |
| Kilcolagh | 11 | 87 | 1632 | 3.G.14., 3.G.4. | 654-668 |
| Kilcolman | 9a | 87 | 3088 | 9.E.1. | 669-677 |
| Kilcooley | 25 | 88 | 1643 | 7.F.12. | 987-989 |
| Kilcorkey | 14 | 88 | 1627 | 8.F.4. | 550-554, 697-698 |
| Kilgefin | 39 | 89 | 1609 | 6.A.5. | 317-332 |
| Kilglass | 31 | 88 | 1603, 1644 | 7.G.4., 6.F.12. | 185-217 |
| Kilkeevin | 15 | 88 | 1628 | 8.F.13. | 571-601 |
| Killinvoy | 46-? | 89 | 1594 | 2.A.1., 5.C.14. | 78-84 |
| Killukin | 7 | 87 | 1621 | 3.E.9., 4.E.1. | 464-468, 990-995 |
| Killukin | 27 | 88 | 1645 | 7.G.4. | |
| Killummod | 8 | 87 | 1623 | 3.E.11., 4.E.8. | 469-477 |
| Kilmacumsy | 12 | 87 | 1633 | 4.A.8. | 678-688 |
| Kilmeane | 45 | 89 | 1595 | 5.D.9. | 85-90 |
| Kilmore | 45 | 88 | 1604 | 4.C.10. | 218-226 |
| Kilnamanagh | 9 | 87 | | 4.B.1., 9.E.2. | 689-696 |
| Kilronan | 1 | 87 | 1623 | 3.E.12. | 478-501 |
| Kilteevan | 42 | 89 | 1610 | 6.B.3. | 333-337 |
| Kiltoom | 52 | 89 | 1596 | 1.F.12. | 91-100 |
| Kiltrustan | 23 | 88 | 1646 | 7.G.12. | 996-1001 |
| Kiltullagh | 17 | 88 | 1629 | 9.B.5. | 603-637 |
| Lissonuffy | 29 | 88 | 1647 | 8.A.9. | 1002-1034 |
| Moore | 58 | 90 | 1635 | 2.E.1. | 865-887 |
| Ogulla | 24 | 88 | 1648 | 8.B.8. | 1035-1047 |
| Oran | 36 | 88 | 1616 | 6.E.3. | 372-377 |
| Rahara | 48 | 89 | 1597 | 2.B.10. | 101-106 |
| Roscommon | 41 | 89 | 1611, 3087, [3231/33] | 6.C.1. | 338-347 |

| PARISH | TITHES 1823–38 TAB 25/ | FILM | VALUATION FIELD BOOKS 1830s OL4./ HOUSE BOOKS [OL5.] | TENEMENT VALUATION 1857–8 FICHE | 1841–1851 CENSUS SEARCH Cen /S/25 |
|---|---|---|---|---|---|
| Shankill | 20 | 88 | 3090 | 4.B.8., 8.B.13., 10.B.12. | 1048-1052 |
| St John's | 49 | 89 | 1598 | 2.A.12., 5.E.9. | 107-117 |
| St Peter's | 55 | 90 | 1599 | 1.C.11. | 118-139 |
| Taghboy | 50 | 89 | 1600 | 2.A.2., 5.E.9. | 140-153 |
| Taghmaconnell | 54 | 89 | 1601 | 1.C.2., 2.C.10. | 51, 154-171 |
| Termonbarry | 32 | 88 | 1605 | 7.A.8. | 227-264, 348 |
| Tibohine | 10 | 87 | 3089 | 9.E.6., 10.C.14. | 699-861 |
| Tisrara | 47 | 89 | 1602 | 5.E.9. | 172-184 |
| Tumna | 5 | 87 | 1624 | 3.G.10., 4.E.13. | 502-505, 522 |

| TOWNS | VALUATION HOUSE BOOK 1830s [OL5.] |
|---|---|
| Athlone (Part) | [3219] |
| Ballyfarnham | [3220] |
| Bellanagare | [3221] |
| Castlereagh | [3226] |
| Frenchpark | [3230] |
| Keadew | [3220] |
| Knockcroghery | [3228] |
| Lanesborough | [3229] |
| Loughglynn | [3230] |
| Roosky | [3231] |
| Strokestown | [3234] |

| PARISH/TOWN | TITHES 1823–38 TAB 26/ | FILM | VALUATION FIELD BOOKS 1830s OL4./ HOUSE BOOKS [OL5.] | TENEMENT VALUATION 1858 FICHE | 1841–1851 CENSUS SEARCH Cen /S/26 |
|---|---|---|---|---|---|
| Achonry | 19 | 93 | 1675 | 6.G.10. | 375-491 |
| Aghanagh | 38 | 94 | 1683 | 1.F.4. | 776-803 |
| Ahamlish | 1 | 91 | 1649, 1650 | 3.F.10. | 1-24 |
| Ballymote | | | 1667, [3238] | | |
| Ballynakill | 31 | 93 | 1684 | 6.A.10. | 804-828 |
| Ballysadare | 16 | 93 | 1676, 1685, [3239] | 5.E.4., 5.F.2., 6.G.8. | 492-498, 829-839 |
| Ballysumaghan | 30 | 93 | 1686 | 6.A.4. | 840-850 |
| Calry | 4 | 91 | 1651, 1652, 3091 | 4.E.2. | 25-34 |
| Castleconor | 14 | 92 | 3092 | 2.C.4., 3.A.1. | 580-593 |
| Cloonoghil | 23 | 93 | 1668 | 6.F.6. | 239-245 |
| Dromard | 13 | 92 | 1679 | 3.D.11. | 594-605 |
| Drumcliff | 3 | 91 | 1653-54 | 4.B.5. | 35-74 |
| Drumcolumb | 32 | 93 | 1687 | 1.G.3. | 851-858 |
| Drumrat | 27 | 93 | 1669 | 1.D.6. | 246-260 |
| Easky | 9 | 92 | 1680 | 2.E.10. | 606-642 |
| Emlaghfad | 21 | 93 | 1670 | 1.D.13., 6.D.1., 6.G.2. | 261-297 |
| Kilcolman | 40 | 94 | 1664 | 1.A.12. | 121-150 |
| Kilfree | 39 | 94 | 1665 | 1.B.5. | 151-214 |
| Kilglass | 8 | 92 | 1681 | 2.F.14. | 643-660 |
| Killadoon | 35 | 94 | 1688 | 1.G.3. | 859-870 |
| Killaraght | 41 | 94 | 1666 | 1.C.9. | 215-238 |
| Killaspugbrone | 5 | 91 | 1655-56 | 4.F.9. | 75-78 |
| Killerry | 28 | 93 | 1689 | 5.G.6. | 871-887 |
| Killoran | 17 | 93 | | 5.E.4., 7.D.8. | 499-525 |
| Kilmacallan | 34 | 93 | 1690 | 1.G.9., 6.B.6. | 888-899 |
| Kilmacowen | 7 | 91 | 1657-58 | 4.G.7. | 79-82 |
| Kilmacshalgan | 10 | 92 | 1682 | 3.A.13. | 661-691 |
| Kilmacteige | 20 | 93 | 1677 | 7.E.12. | 526-555 |
| Kilmactranny | 37 | 94 | 1691 | 1.G.11. | 900-935 |
| Kilmoremoy | 15 | 92 | 3093 | 2.C.6. | 692-732 |
| Kilmorgan | 22 | 93 | 1671 | 6.C.8. | 298-309 |
| Kilross | 29 | 93 | 1692 | 5.G.1. | 936-941 |
| Kilshalvy | 26 | 93 | 1672 | 1.E.1., 6.G.4. | 310-331 |
| Kilturra | 25 | 93 | 1673 | 6.G.4. | 332-339 |
| Kilvarnet | 18 | 93 | 1678 | 7.E.6. | 556-561 |
| Rossinver | 2 | 91 | 1659-60 | 4.A.12. | 83-91 |
| Shancough | 36 | 94 | 1693 | 2.A.12. | 942-949 |
| Skreen | 12 | 92 | 3094 | 3.C.10. | 733-747 |
| St John's | 6 | 91 | 1661-63 | 5.C.14., 5.A.14., 5.A.2., 5.B.4., 4.E.13. | 92-120 |
| Sligo Town | | | [3241/53] | | 562-579 |
| Tawnagh | 33 | 93 | 1694 | 6.C.4. | 950-954 |
| Templeboy | 11 | 92 | 3095 | 3.B.12. | 748-775 |
| Toomour | 24 | 93 | 1674 | 1.E.9., 6.E.2. | 340-374 |

| TOWNS | VALUATION HOUSE BOOK 1830s [OL5.] | TOWNS | VALUATION HOUSE BOOK 1830s [OL5.] |
|---|---|---|---|
| Aclare | [3235] | Collooney | [3239] |
| Ardnaree | [3236/37] | Riverstown | [3254] |
| Bellahy | [3240] | Tobercurry | [3254] |

| PARISH/TOWN | TITHES 1823–38 TAB | FILM | VALUATION FIELD BOOKS 1830s OL4./ HOUSE BOOKS [OL5.] | TENEMENT VALUATION 1848–51 FICHE | 1841–1851 CENSUS SEARCH Cen /S/27 |
|---|---|---|---|---|---|
| Abington | 27N/28 | 96 | | 17.F.8. | |
| Aghacrew | 27S/4 | 98 | 3208, 3218-20 | 7.F.14. | 134-136 |
| Aghnameadle | 27N38 | 96 | 3273, [1787/93 | 14.F.10. | 251-255, 257-260 |
| Aglishcloghane | 27N/4 | 95 | 3250, [1727/28] | 15.G.8. | 184-186 |
| Ardcrony | 27N/13 | 95 | 3251, [1729/30] | 16.A.2. | 187-191 |
| Ardfinnan | 27S/94 | 100 | 3170, [1555/56, 3259] | 5.A.4. | 91-93 |
| Ardmayle | 27S/37 | 99 | 3235, [1632/34] | 8.D.12. | 152-153 |
| Athnid | 27N/71 | 97 | 3137, [1496] | 12.A.14. | |
| Ballingarry | 27N/10 | 95 | 3252, [1731/36, 3260] | | 192-196 |
| Ballingarry | 27S/77 | 100 | 3293, [1854/61, 3260] | 16.A.8., 10.E.2. | 339-349 |
| Ballintemple | 27S/77 | 98 | 3209, 3228, [1607] | 7.F.4. | |
| Ballybacon | 27S/97 | 101 | 3171-72, [1557] | 5.A.8. | |
| Ballycahill | 27N/68 | 97 | 3230, [1468/69] | 6.E.12.,12.A.14. | |
| Ballyclerahan | 27S/101 | 101 | [1510, 3261] | 3.D.12. | 55 |
| Ballygibbon | 27N/29 | 96 | 3274, [1794/95] | 14.G.6. | 256, 261 |
| Ballygriffin | 27S/14 | 98 | [1415/16] | 1.A.14. | |
| Ballymackey | 27N/31 | 96 | [1796/99] | 14.G.11. | 262-263 |
| Ballymurreen | 27N/79 | 97 | 3138, [1470/71] | 12.B.4. | |
| Ballynaclogh | 27N/36 | 96 | [1800/03] | 15.A.8. | 264-265 |
| Ballysheehan | 27S/38 | 99 | 3237, [1635/37] | 8.E.6. | 154 |
| Baptistgrange | 27S/68 | 99 | 3238, [1638/39] | 8.F.2. | |
| Barnane-ely | 27N/51 | 97 | 3190, [1581] | 13.D.12. | |
| Barrettsgrange | 27S/60 | 99 | 3238, [1640/41 | 8.F.6. | |
| Borrisokane | 27N/8 | 95 | 3253, [1737/38, 4219, 3264/66] | 16.A.14. | 197-204 |
| Bourney | 27N/45 | 97 | 3192, 3204-05, [1584/87, 1599] | 13.E.2. | 121-122 |
| Boytonrath | 27S/56 | 99 | 3239, [1642] | 8.F.10. | 155 |
| Brickendown | 27S/43 | 99 | 3240, [1643, 1680] | 8.F.12. | 156 |
| Bruis | 27S/27 | 98 | 3097, [1417/18] | 1.B.6. | 1 |
| Buolick | 27S/72 | 99 | 3294, 3311, [1862/64] | 10.F.10. | 350-352 |
| Burgesbeg | 27N/22 | 96 | 3282-83, 3289, [1834] | 17.F.14. | |
| Borrisnafarney | 27N/47 | 97 | 3191, [1582/83] | 13.D.14. | |
| Caher | 27S/91 | 100 | 3147, [1558/59, 3270/73] | 5.B.6., 3.D.2. | 94-98 |
| Carrick | 27S/116 | 101 | 3148, [1514/16] | 3.D.4. | 56-59 |
| Cashel (See St John Baptist) | | | | | |
| Castletownarra | 27N/19 | 96 | 3284, [1835] | 17.G.12. | 301-304 |
| Cloghprior | 27N/12 | 95 | 3254 | 16.B.12. | 205 |
| Clonbeg | 27S/33 | 98 | 3098, 3123, 3124, [1418] | 1.B.10. | 2-4 |
| Clonbullogue | 27S/32 | 98 | 3099, 3125, [1421] | 1.C.12. | 5 |
| Cloneen | 27S/54 | 99 | 3241, 3295-96, [1644/45, 1688/90, 1865/67] | 8.F.14., 10.G.6. | |
| Clonmel St Mary's | 27S/114 | 101 | [1550/51, 3296/3309] | 4.D.2. | 75-88 |
| Clonoulty | 27S/3 | 98 | 3211, 3222, [1609] | 7.G.8., 1.D.4. | 137, 139-140 |
| Clonpet | 27S/28 | 98 | 3127, [1433] | 1.D.6. | |
| Clogher | 27S/1 | 98 | 3210, 3221, [1608] | | 138 |
| Colman | 27S/66 | 99 | 3238 ,[1646/48] | 8.G.6. | |
| Cooleagh | 27S/45 | 99 | [1649/51] | 8.G.8. | |
| Coolmundry | 27S/63 | 99 | 3241, [1652] | 8.G.12. | |
| Corbally | 27N/43 | 97 | 3192, 3206, [1588/91, 1599] | 13.F.4. | 123-124 |
| Cordangan | 27S/29 | 98 | 3100, 3124, 3128, 3136 [1422/24] | 1.D.10. | 6 |

| PARISH/TOWN | TITHES 1823–38 TAB | FILM | VALUATION FIELD BOOKS 1830s OL4./ HOUSE BOOKS [OL5.] | TENEMENT VALUATION 1848–51 FICHE | 1841–1851 CENSUS SEARCH Cen /S/27 |
|---|---|---|---|---|---|
| Corroge | 27S/25 | 98 | 3136, [1425/26] | 1.E.10. | |
| Crohane | 27S/78 | 100 | 3297, 3313, [1868/69] | 10.G.8. | 353 |
| Cullen | 27S/17 | 98 | 3101, [1427/29, 3295] | 1.E.14. | 7-11 |
| Cullenwaine | 27N/46 | 97 | 3193, [1592/93] | 13.G.2. | |
| Dangandargan | 27S/49 | 99 | [1430/31, 1653/54, 1663] | 1.F.6., 8.G.14. | |
| Derrygarth | 27S/92 | 100 | 3171-72, [1560/61] | 5.D.6. | |
| Dogstown | 27S/57 | 99 | [1655/58] | 9.A.2. | |
| Dolla | 27N/35 | 96 | [1804/05] | 15.A.12. | 265a-271 |
| Donaghmore | 27S/67 | 99 | 3149, 3238, [1659] | 9.A.4., 3.F.6. | |
| Donohill | 27S/2 | 98 | 3102, 3212-13, 3223-24, [1432, 1434, 1610/11] | 8.A.10., 1.F.8. | |
| Doon | 27N/57 | 97 | [1622/23] | 6.F.2. | 143 |
| Dorrha | 27N/2 | 95 | 3255, [1743/45] | 16.C.2. | 206-209 |
| Drangan | 27S/48 | 99 | [1660/62, 1664] | 9.A.6. | 157-159 |
| Drom | 27N/62 | 97 | [1472/73] | 12.B.6. | |
| Dromineer | 27N/15 | 96 | 3256, [1746/48] | 16.D.2. | |
| Emly | 27S/22 | 98 | 3103, [1435/36, 3310] | 1.G.2. | 12 |
| Erry | 27S/39 | 99 | [1665/67] | 9.A.14. | 160 |
| Fennor | 27S/71 | 99 | 3298, 3311, 3322, [1870/72] | 11.A.2. | 354 |
| Fertiana | 27N/74 | 97 | [1474/75] | 12.B.12. | |
| Fethard | 27S/62 | 99 | 3238, [1668/70, 3311/15] | 9.B.2. | 161-164 |
| Finnoe | 27N/7 | 95 | 3257, [1749/52] | 16.D.5. | 210 |
| Gaile | 27S/36 | 99 | 3242, [1671, 1672/73] | 9.C.6. | 165-166 |
| Galbooly | 27N/75 | 97 | [1476/77] | 12.C.1. | |
| Garrangibbon | 27S/106 | 101 | 3150, 3299, 3313, [1517/20, 1873/76] | 11.A.10., 3.F.8. | |
| Glenbane | 27S/23 | 98 | 3104, 3129, [1437] | 2.A.4. | |
| Glenkeen | 27N/54 | 97 | [1624/25] | 6.F.5. | 144-147 |
| Grangemockler | 27S/84 | 100 | 3300, 3313, [1877/80, 1924/25] | 11.A.14. | |
| Graystown | 27N/74 | 100 | 3237, 3301, 3312, 3313, [1881/82] | 9.C.8., 11.B.4. | 355 |
| Holycross | 27S/73 | 97 | 3139, [1478] | 9.C.10., 12.C.3. | 42 [166a] |
| Holycross | 27S/35 | 98 | 3242, [1672/73, 1674/75] | | |
| Horeabbey | 27S/41 | 99 | [1675a/77] | 9.C.12. | |
| Inch | 27N/66 | 97 | [1479/80] | 12.C.11. | |
| Inishlounaght | 27S/102 | 101 | 3151, [1521/23] | 3.F.10. | |
| Isertkieran | 27S/102 | 100 | 3302, 3313, [1883/85] | 11.B.12. | |
| Kilbarron | 27N/6 | 95 | [1753/56] | 16.D.12. | |
| Kilbragh | 27S/59 | 99 | [1678, 1679] | 9.C.14. | |
| Kilcash | 27S/107 | 101 | 3152, [1524/26] | 3.G.8. | 60-61 |
| Kilclonagh | 27N/67 | 97 | 3137, [1496] | 12.D.3. | |
| Kilcomenty | 27N/24 | 96 | 3285, [1836/37] | 18.B.10. | 305-306 |
| Kilconnell | 27S/51 | 99 | 3243, [1681/83, 1680] | 9.D.2. | |
| Kilcooly | 27N/77 | 97 | [1481/82] | 11.B.14., 12.D.3. | |
| Kilcooly | 27S/73 | 99 | 3303, 3312, 3313, 3314, [1886/91] | | 356-359 |
| Kilcornan | 27S/16 | 98 | 3106, [1433/40] | 2.A.6. | 13-15 |
| Kilfeakle | 27S/20 | 98 | 3107, [1441/42] | 2.A.10. | 16 |
| Kilfithmone | 27N/61 | 97 | [1483/84] | 12.D.4. | |
| Kilgrant | 27S/110 | 101 | 3153, [1527/29] | 3.G.12. | 62 |

| PARISH/TOWN | TITHES 1823–38 TAB | FILM | VALUATION FIELD BOOKS 1830s OL4./ HOUSE BOOKS [OL5.] | TENEMENT VALUATION 1848–51 FICHE | 1841–1851 CENSUS SEARCH Cen /S/27 |
|---|---|---|---|---|---|
| Kilkeary | 27N/37 | 96 | 3275, [1806/07, 1810] | 15.B.4. | |
| Killaloan | 27S/115 | 101 | [1530] | 4.A.4. | |
| Killardry | 27S/31 | 98 | 3105, 3125, 3130, [1443/44] | 2.B.2. | 17-19 |
| Killavinoge | 27N/49 | 97 | 3195, 3202, [1594] | 13.G.4. | 125 |
| Killea | 27N/48 | 97 | 3196, [1595] | 13.G.14. | 126 |
| Killeenasteena | 27S/55 | 99 | [1684, 1717] | 9.D.6. | 167 |
| Killenaule | 27S/75 | 100 | 3304, 3312, 3313, [1892/94, 3317/19] | 11.C.14. | 360 |
| Killodiernan | 27N/11 | 95 | 3258, [1757/60] | 16.E.8. | 223 |
| Killoscully | 27N/25 | 96 | 3286, [1838/39] | 18.C.9. | 307-312 |
| Killoskehan | 27N/50 | 97 | 3197, [1596] | 14.A.6. | |
| Kilmastulla | 27N/23 | 96 | 3287[1840] | 18.D.9. | 313 |
| Kilmore | 27N/34 | 96 | 3276, [1811/15] | | 272-283[A] |
| Kilmore (Oughterleague) | 27S/7 | 98 | 3214, 3226, [1612] | 8.B.10., 15.B.6. | 141-142 |
| Kilmucklin | 27S/12 | 98 | [1445, 1450] | 2.B.12. | |
| Kilmurry | 27S/112 | 101 | 3154, [1431/33] | 4.A.6. | 63 |
| Kilnaneave | 27N/39 | 96 | 3277, [1816/17] | 15.G.12. | 284-288 |
| Kilnarath | 27N/27 | 96 | 3288, [1841/43] | 18.E.6. | 314-319 |
| Kilpatrick | 27S/5 | 98 | 3215, 3227, [1613/15] | 8.B.14. | |
| Kilruane | 27N/30 | 96 | 3278, [1761/62, 1818/20] | 16.E.12., 15.D.5 | 289-291 |
| Kilshane | 27S/30 | 98 | 3108, 3136, [1446/47] | 2.B.14. | |
| Kilsheelan | 27S/111 | 101 | 3155, [1534/36] | 4.A.14. | 64-67 |
| Kiltegan | 27S/109 | 101 | 3156, [1437/39] | 4.B.6. | |
| Kiltinan | 27S/69 | 99 | 3238, [1685/87, 1688/90] | 9.D.8. | 168 |
| Kilvellane | 27N/26 | 96 | 3284, [1844/45] | 18.F.6. | 320-334 |
| Kilvemnon | 27S/83 | 100 | 3305, 3312, 3313, 3315-16, [1895/902] | 11.D.14. | 361-363 |
| Knigh | 27N/16 | 96 | 3260, [1763/65] | 16.E.14. | |
| Knockgraffon | 27S/64 | 99 | 3244, [1691/92] | 9.D.12. | 169-170 |
| Laginstown | 27S/117 | 101 | | | |
| Latteragh | 27N/40 | 96 | 3279, [1821/23] | 15.D.9. | 292 |
| Lattin | 27S/26 | 98 | 3109, [1417, 1448] | 2.C.7. | 20-24 |
| Lickfinn | 27S/76 | 100 | 3306, 3313, 3317, [1903/05] | 11.F.4. | |
| Lisbunny | 27N/32 | 96 | 3279, [1824/26] | 15.D.13. | |
| Lismalin | 27S/80 | 100 | 3307, 3318, [1906/11] | 11.F.6. | 364 |
| Lisronagh | 27S/104 | 101 | 3157, [1540] | 4.B.8. | 68 |
| Lorrha | 27N/1 | 95 | 3261, [1769/71] | 16.F.4. | 211-216 |
| Loughkeen | 27N/5 | 95 | 3262, [1766/68] | 16.G.4. | 217-221 |
| Loughmoe East | 27N/64 | 97 | 3140-42, [1485/86] | 12.D.5. | |
| Loughmoe West | 27N/63 | 97 | [1487/89] | 12.D.14. | 43 |
| Magorban | 27S/44 | 99 | 3245, [1693/95] | 9.E.8. | |
| Magowry | 27S/47 | 99 | [1696/99] | 9.E.12. | |
| Modeshil | 27S/81 | 100 | 3308, 3313, 3323, [1912/14] | 11.F.10. | |
| Modreeny | 27N/14 | 96 | 3263, [1772/74] | 17.A.2. | 222, 224-234 |
| Molough | 27S/99 | 101 | 3173-74, [1564] | 5.D.11. | 99-101 |
| Monsea | 27N/17 | 96 | 3264, 3289, [1775/77, 1846/47] | 17.B.7., 18.G.10. | |
| Mora | 27S/65 | 99 | 3246, [1700/02] | 9.F.2. | 171-172 |
| Mortlestown | 27S/86 | 100 | 3175, [1562/63] | 5.D.14. | |

| PARISH/TOWN | TITHES 1823–38 TAB | FILM | VALUATION FIELD BOOKS 1830s OL4./ HOUSE BOOKS [OL5.] | TENEMENT VALUATION 1848–51 FICHE | 1841–1851 CENSUS SEARCH Cen /S/27 |
|---|---|---|---|---|---|
| Mowney | 27S/79 | 100 | 3319, [1915/17] | 11.F.14. | 365 |
| Moyaliff | 27N/59 | 97 | [1626] | 7.A.8. | 148-150 |
| Moycarky | 27N/78 | 97 | [1490/91] | 12.E.6. | 44-45 |
| Moyne | 27N/65 | 97 | [1492] | 12.E.11. | 46 |
| Neddans | 27S/98 | 101 | 3176-77, 3186, [1565] | 5.E.2. | |
| Nenagh | 27N/18 | 96 | 3265, 3279, [1778/79, 1827/29, 3325/33] | 17.B.12., 15.E.3. | 235-248, 293 |
| Newcastle | 27S/100 | 101 | 3187, [1566/68] | 5.E.5. | 102-106 |
| Newchapel | 27S/102 | 101 | 3158, [1541/44] | 4.B.10. | 69-74 |
| Newtownlennan | 27S/113 | 101 | 3159, 3309, [1545/46, 1918] | 11.G.2., 4.C.4. | |
| Oughterleague | 27S/8 | 98 | 3110, 3131, 3216, 3228, [1431, 1449, 1616] | 8.C.6., 2.C.8. | |
| Outeragh | 27S/70 | 99 | 3246, [1703/05] | 9.F.6. | 173 |
| Peppardstown | 27S/53 | 99 | 3241, [1706/08] | 9.F.8. | |
| Rahelty | 27N/72 | 97 | [1493/94] | 12.F.4. | 47-49 |
| Railstown | 27S/50 | 99 | [1709, 1717] | 9.F.12. | |
| Rathcool | 27S/52 | 99 | 3241, [1710/11] | 9.F.14. | |
| Rathkennan | 27S/1a | 98 | 3217, 3229 | 8.C.12. | |
| Rathlynin | 27S/13 | 98 | 3111, [1450, 1451] | 2.C.10. | 25 |
| Rathnaveoge | 27N/44 | 97 | 3198, [1597/98, 1599] | 14.A.8. | 127 |
| Rathronan | 27S/108 | 101 | 3160, [1547/49] | 4.C.10. | |
| Redcity | 27S/61 | 99 | 3238, [1712] | 9.G.6. | |
| Relickmurry and Athassel | 27S/21 | 98 | 3132, 3096, 3236, [1452/56] | 2.C.14., 9.G.8. | 26-29 |
| Rochestown | 27S/93 | 100 | [3568, 1569/70] | 5.F.4. | |
| Roscrea | 27N/42 | 97 | 3207, [1600/03, 3334/44] | 14.A.14. | 128-132 |
| Shanrahan | 27S/88 | 100 | 3179, [1571/72] | 5.F.5. | 108-112 |
| Shronell | 27S/24 | 98 | 3112, 3133, [1417, 1457] | 2.E.7. | 30 |
| Shyane | 27N/70 | 97 | 3137, [1495, 1496] | 12.F.9. | |
| Solloghhodbeg | 27S/11 | 98 | 3113, [1458/59] | 2.E.10. | 31 |
| Solloghodmore | 27S/10 | 98 | 3114, 3134, [1460/61] | 2.E.14. | 32-35 |
| St John Baptist (Cashel) | 27S/42 | 99 | 3247, 3310, 3312, 3320, [1713/16, 1717, 1919/21] | 9.G.10., 11.G.4. | 174-182 |
| St Johnstown | 27S/46 | 99 | [1718/20] | 10.B.8. | |
| St Patricksrock | 27S/40 | 99 | 3248-49, [1721/22] | 10.B.12. | |
| Temple | 27S/34 | 98 | | | |
| Temple-etney | 27S/105 | 101 | 3162, [1552/54] | 4.F.14. | 89-90 |
| Templeachally | 27N/21 | 96 | 3290, [1848/51] | 18.C.11. | 335-337 |
| Templebeg | 27N/56 | 97 | [1627/28] | 7.B.8. | |
| Templebredon | 27S/15 | 98 | 3117, [1462/64] | 2.F.10. | |
| Templederry | 27N/41 | 96 | 3280, [1830/32] | 15.E.8. | 294-297 |
| Templedowney | 27N/33 | 96 | [1810, 1833] | 15.F.2. | 298-300 |
| Templenoe | 27S/19 | 98 | 3116, [1450, 1466] | 2.G.12. | |
| Templemichael | 27S/85 | 100 | 3311, 3321, [1922/23, 1924/25] | 11.G.6. | 366 |
| Templemore | 27N/60 | 97 | 3145, 3199, [1497/98, 1604, 3346/51] | 14.D.2., 12.F.10. | 50-51 |
| Templeneiry | | | | | 36-38 |
| Templeree | 27N/52 | 97 | 3200, [1605] | 14.D.6. | 133 |
| Templetenny | 27S/87 | 100 | 3179, 3188, [1573/75] | 5.G.11. | 113-118 |
| Templetoughy | 27N/53 | 97 | 3201, [1499, 1606] | 14.D.12., 12.G.13. | |

| PARISH/TOWN | TITHES 1823–38 TAB/ | FILM | VALUATION FIELD BOOKS 1830s OL4./ HOUSE BOOKS [OL5.] | TENEMENT VALUATION 1848–51 FICHE | 1841–1851 CENSUS SEARCH Cen /S/27 |
|---|---|---|---|---|---|
| Terryglass | 27N/3 | 95 | 3265a, [1780/83] | 17.D.10. | 248-250 |
| Thurles | 27N/69 | 97 | [1500/04, 3352/60] | 12.G.13. | 52-53 |
| Tipperary | 27S/18 | 98 | 3118, 3136, [4218, 3361/67] | 3.A.4. | 39-41 |
| Toem | 27N/58 | 97 | [1629] | | |
| Toem | 27S/9 | 98 | 3119, 3135, [1469] | 3.B.14., 7.B.14. | |
| Tubbrid | 27S/89 | 100 | [1576] | 6.B.9. | 119-120 |
| Tullaghmelan | 27S/95 | 100 | 3180-81, 3189, [1577] | 6.C.7. | 74 |
| Tullaghorton | 27S/96 | 100 | 3182-83, [1578] | 6.C.11. | |
| Tullamain | 27S/58 | 99 | 3246, [1679, 1723/26] | 10.C.14. | |
| Twomileborris | 27N/76 | 97 | [1505/09] | 13.C.3. | 54 |
| Upperchurch | 27N/55 | 97 | [1630/31] | 7.D.2. | 151 |
| Uskane | 27N/9 | 95 | 3266, [1784/86] | 17.E.7. | |
| Whitechurch | 27S/90 | 100 | 3184, [1579/80] | 6.D.3. | |
| Youghalarra | 27N/20 | 96 | 3291, [1852/53] | 19.B.12. | 338 |

| TOWNS | VALUATION HOUSE BOOK 1830s [OL5.] |
|---|---|
| Abbey | [3255/58] |
| Ballyporeen | [3262] |
| Bansha | [3263] |
| Borrisoleigh | [3267/69] |
| Cappagh White | [3274/75] |
| Carrick-on-Suir | [3276/82] |
| Cashel | [3283/90] |
| Clogheen | [3291] |
| Cloghjordan | [3292/94] |
| Cullen | [3295] |
| Golden | [3316] |
| Killenaule | [3317/19] |
| Marlfield | [3320/21] |
| Mullinahone | [3322/24a] |
| Silvermines | [3345] |
| Toberaheena | [3368/69] |
| Toomevarra | [3370/72] |

| PARISH/TOWN | TITHES 1823–38 TAB 29/ | FILM | VALUATION FIELD BOOKS 1830s OL4./ HOUSE BOOKS [OL5.] | TENEMENT VALUATION 1848–51 FICHE | 1841–1851 CENSUS SEARCH Cen /S/29 |
|---|---|---|---|---|---|
| Affane | 19 | 102 | 3365-66, [1944/46] | 4.A.4. | |
| Aglish | 68 | 104 | | 2.E.5., 2.E.12. | 62-65 |
| Ardmore | 69 | 104 | 3356, 3357-59 | 2.E.5., 2.F.14. | 66, 72 |
| Ballygunner | 58 | 103 | 3407, [1985/87] | 6.D.6. | 130 |
| Ballylaneen | 34 | 103 | 3367-72, [1947, 4220] | 4.B.2. | 73-76 |
| Ballymacart | 74 | 104 | | 2.E.5., 3.B.10. | 67 |
| Ballynakill | 51 | 103 | 3408. [1988/91] | 6.D.9. | |
| Clashmore | 71 | 104 | 3360, 3361 | 2.E.5., 3.B.14. | 68 |
| Clonagam | 11 | 102 | 3465, 3479, 3495, [2118/19] | 8.D.14. | 244-250 |
| Clonea | 32 | 103 | 3373-75, [1948/50] | 4.C.2. | |
| Colligan | 27 | 102 | 3376, [1951/52] | 3.G.8., 4.C.6. | 77-78 |
| Corbally | 66 | 104 | 3409, [1992/95] | 6.D.11. | 131 |
| Crooke | 60 | 104 | 3410, [1996/99] | 6.D.12. | 132-136 |
| Drumcannon | 47 | 103 | 3436-37, [2000/03, 2073/82] | 7.D.14., 6.E.2. | 186-220 |
| Dungarvan | 30 | 103 | 3377, [1953/54], [3383] | 3.G.8., 4.C.12. | 79-87 |
| Dunhill | 44 | 103 | 3438-39, [2083/86] | 7.F.8. | 221-226 |
| Dysert | 6 | 102 | 3466, 3480, 3489, 6496, [2120/21, 4227] | 8.E.13. | |
| Faithlegg | 53 | 103 | [2004/09] | 6.E.2. | 137-139 |
| Fenoagh | 8 | 102 | 3467, 3481, 3490, 3497, [2122/23] | 8.F.4. | |
| Fews | 25 | 102 | 3378, [1955, 4226] | 4.G.8. | 88 |
| Guilcagh | 12 | 102 | 3468, 3482, 3498, [2124/26, 4226] | 8.F.9. | 251 |
| Inishlounaght | 1 | 102 | 3426a-3428, [2067/68] | 7.A.14. | 178-179 |
| Islandikane | 48 | 103 | 3440-41, [2087/91] | 7.G.4. | 227-232 |
| Kilbarry | 54 | 103 | 3411, [2010/14] | 6.E.6. | |
| Kilbarrymeadan | 36 | 103 | 3379-80, [1956] | 4.G.12. | 89-91 |
| Kilbride | 46 | 103 | 3442-43, [2092, 2103] | 7.G.10. | 233-235 |
| Kilburne | 42 | 103 | 3444-45, [2093/95, 4223] | 7.G.14. | 236 |
| Kilcaragh | 57 | 103 | [2015/18] | 6.E.8. | |
| Kilcockan | 17 | 102 | 3331, [1926/28] | 1.A.14., 1.B.2. | 1-2 |
| Kilcop | 59 | 104 | 3412, [2019/22] | 6.E.9. | |
| Kilculliheen | 13 | 102 | 3435, [2023/24, [2072] | 7.C.14., 9.D.10., 9.D.14. | 280 |
| Kilgobnet | 23 | 102 | 3381-82 | 5.A.10. | 92-98 |
| Kill St Lawrence | 55 | 103 | 3419, [2025/28] | 6.F.4. | |
| Kill St Nicholas | 52 | 103 | 3414, [2029/31] | 6.F.5. | |
| Killaloan | 4 | 102 | 3469, 3483, 3499, [2127/28] | 8.F.11. | |
| Killea | 65 | 104 | 3413, [2032/36] | 6.E.10. | 140-154 |
| Killoteran | 38 | 103 | 3464, [2096/97] | 8.A.4. | |
| Killure | 56 | 103 | [2037/40] | 6.F.12. | 155 |
| Kilmacleague | 62 | 104 | 3415, [2041/44] | 6.F.12. | 156-162 |
| Kilmacomb | 63 | 104 | [2045/48] | 6.G.3. | 163 |
| Kilmeadan | 37 | 103 | 3449-50, 3470, 3484, 3491, 3500, [2098/100, 2129/30] | 8.F.13., 8.A.8. | 237-238 |
| Kilmolash | 28 | 103 | 3361, 3383-84, [1957/58] | 5.B.14., 3.C.14. | 69 |
| Kilmoleran | 7 | 102 | 3471, 3476, 3485, 3501, [2131/32] | 8.G.1. | 252 |
| Kilrossanty | 24 | 102 | 3385-86, [1959/60, 4221] | 3.G.9., 5.C.4. | 99-100 |

| PARISH/TOWN | TITHES 1823–38 TAB 29/ | FILM | VALUATION FIELD BOOKS OL4./ HOUSE BOOKS [OL5.] | TENEMENT VALUATION 1848—1 FICHE | 1841–1851 CENSUS SEARCH CEN S\|29\|1 |
|---|---|---|---|---|---|
| Kilronan | 2 | 102 | 3430-33, [2069/71] | 7.B.6. | 180-185 |
| Kilronan | 43 | 103 | 3451-52, [2101/02, 2103] | 8.B.4. | |
| Kilrush | 31 | 103 | 3387-88, [1961/62] | 5.D.8. | |
| Kilsheelan | 5 | 102 | 3472, 3486, 3502, [2133/34] | 8.G.12. | |
| Kilwatermoy | 28/16 | 102 | 3332, [1930] | 1.B.10. | 3-4 |
| Kinsalebeg | 72 | 104 | 3362-63 | 2.E.6., 3.D.4. | |
| Leitrim | 13a | 102 | 3333, [1931/32] | 1.C.6. | |
| Lickoran | 21 | 102 | 3390-91, [1963] | 5.E.2. | 101-103 |
| Lisgenan or Grange | 73 | 104 | | 3.E.4. | 70, 104 |
| Lismore and Mocollop | 14 | 102 | 3334-35, 3350-54, [1933/38], [3387] | 1.A.14., 1.C.8. | 5-51 |
| Lisnaskill | 41 | 103 | 3453, 3464, [2104/07] | 8.B.6. | 239 |
| Modelligo | 20 | 102 | 3392-93, [1964/67] | 3.G.9., 5.E.6. | 105 [105a] |
| Monamintra | 61 | 104 | [2049/51] | 6.G.6. | |
| Monksland | 35 | 103 | 3394-95, [1968/71] | 3.G.9., 5.F.4. | |
| Mothel | 10 | 102 | 3473-74, 3487, 3492-93, 3503, [2135/36, 4228] | 8.G.14. | 253 |
| Newcastle | 40 | 103 | 3396-97, 3454-55, 3464, [1972/74a, 2108/11] | 5.F.10., 8.B.10. | 240 |
| Newtownlennan | 75 | 104 | | | |
| Rathgormuck | 9 | 102 | 3475, 3488, 3494, 3504, [2137, 4224] | 9.A.11. | 254-264 |
| Rathmoylan | 67 | 104 | 3420, [2052/56] | 6.G.6. | 164-172 |
| Reisk | 45 | 103 | 3456-57, 3464, [2112/15] | 8.B.14. | 241 |
| Ringagonagh | 70 | 104 | 3364 | 2.E.6., 3.E.14. | 71 |
| Rossduff | 64 | 104 | 3421, [2057/60] | 6.G.10. | 173-174 |
| Rossmire | 26 | 102 | 3398-99, [1975/77, 2138/39] | 9.B.5., 3.G.9., 5.F.12. | 106-110 |
| Seskinan | 22 | 102 | 3400, [1978/79] | 3.G.9., 5.G.8. | 111-125 |
| St John's [without] | 50 | 103 | 3424, [2061/64, 3415/17] | 9.D.10., 9.E.14. | 278, 175-177, 273, 284 |
| St Mary's Clonmel | 3 | 102 | 3478, 3505-07, [2140, 4225] | 9.B.5. | 265-269 |
| Stradbally | 33 | 103 | 3389, 3401, [1980/82] | 3.G.10., 6.A.10. | 126-127 |
| Tallow | 15 | 102 | 3346, [1939/41, 3394] | 1.A.14., 2.B.10. | 52-56 |
| Templemichael | 18 | 102 | 3347, 3348, 3355, [1942/43] | 1.A.14., 2.C.14. | 57-61 |
| Trinity without | 39 | 103 | 3458-59, [2116/17, 3426/35] | 8.C.6., 9.D.11., 10.B.8. | 242-243 |
| Waterford City Parishes | 49 | 103 | (see below) | | 270-294 |
| Whitechurch | 29 | 103 | 3402-03, [1983/84] | 3.G.10., 6.B.10. | 128-129 |

| TOWNS | VALUATION HOUSE BOOK 1830s [OL5.] |
|---|---|
| No. 1 Kilculliheen | [3399] |
| No. 2 St John's Within | [3400] [3414] |
| No. 3 St John's Without | [3401] [3415/17] |
| No. 4 St Michael's | [3402] [3418] |
| No. 5 St Olave's | [3403] [3419] |
| No. 6 St Patrick's | [3404] [3420] |
| No. 7 St Peter's | [3405] |
| No 8 St Stephen's Within | [3406] [3421] |
| No. 9 St Stephen's Without | [3407] [3422/24] |
| No. 10 Trinity Within | [3408] [3425] |
| No. 11 Trinity Without | [3409] [3426/35] |
| No. 12 Trinity Without | [3410] |
| No. 13 Trinity Without | [3411] |
| No. 14 Trinity Without | [3412] |
| No. 12? Trinity Without | [3413] |
| Waterford (Town) | [3438] |
| Abbeyside | [3373] |
| Cappoquin | [3374/75] |
| Carrickbeg | [3376/78] |
| Carrick-on-Suir | [3379/81] |
| Clonmel | [3382] |
| Dunmore | [3384, 3389] |
| Kilmacthomas | [3385/86] |
| Passage | [3388/89] |
| Portlaw | [3390/93] |
| Tramore | [3395/98] |

| PARISH/TOWN | TITHES 1823–38 TAB 30/ | FILM | VALUATION FIELD BOOKS 1830s OL4./ HOUSE BOOKS [OL5.] | TENEMENT VALUATION 1854 FICHE | 1841–1851 CENSUS SEARCH Cen /S/30 |
|---|---|---|---|---|---|
| Ardnurcher (Horseleap) | 50 | 106 | 1747 | 5.D.10., 7.A.10. | 164-167 |
| Athlone | | | [3439/41] | | 1-12 |
| Ballyloughloe | 46 | 106 | 1695 | 1.E.3. | 18-19 |
| Ballymore | 36 | 106 | 1761 | 1.G.14., 2.F.2. | 214-218 |
| Ballymorin | 38 | 106 | 1762 | 4.G.8. | 219 |
| Bunown | 30 | 105 | 1740 | 1.B.8. | 123-127 |
| Carrick | 59 | 107 | 1722 | 5.G.2. | 83 |
| Castlelost | 63 | 107 | 1723 | 5.G.4. | 84-85 |
| Castletowndelvin | 27 | 105 | 3511-12, [3446/7] | 3.A.4. | 45-55 |
| Castletownkin-delan | 51 | 107 | 1748, [2144, 3448] | 5.E.2. | 168-183 |
| Churchtown | 40 | 106 | 1763 | 4.G.10. | 220-223 |
| Clonarney | 24 | 105 | 1710-11 | 3.B.9. | |
| Clonfad | 62 | 107 | 1724 | 5.G.11. | 86-88 |
| Conry | 39 | 106 | 1764, 3524 | 4.G.14. | |
| Delvin | | | | | 56-68 |
| Drumraney | 32 | 105 | 1741, [2143] | 1.D.4., 2.D.10. | 128-136 |
| Durrow | 54 | 107 | 1749, 3522 | 7.A.13. | 184-185 |
| Dysart | 43 | 106 | 1744, 1750-51, [4232] | 5.A.2., 6.D.12., 5.F.5. | 147, 186 |
| Enniscoffey | 58 | 107 | 1725 | 6.A.2. | |
| Faughalstown | 7 | 105 | 1732 | 3.D.3., 4.A.2. | 96-101 |
| Foyran | 1 | 105 | 1733, 3515 | 4.A.3. | 102-106 |
| Kilbeggan | 52 | 107 | 1752-53, [2145, 3449] | 7.C.6. | 187-188 |
| Kilbixy | 13 | 105 | 3523, [3455] | 4.E.6. | 199-201 |
| Kilbride | 60 | 107 | 1726, 3516 | 6.A.5. | 89-91 |
| Kilcleagh | 47 | 106 | 1696-97 | 1.F.5. | 20-28 |
| Kilcumny | 23 | 105 | 1712-13, [2141] | 3.B.12. | |
| Kilcumreragh | 49 | 106 | 1698-99, 1754, [2146] | 1.D.8., 1.A.14. | 189-192 |
| Kilkenny West | 31 | 105 | 1742 [4230] | 1.C.1., 2.E.5. | 137-141 |
| Killagh | 28 | 105 | 1714-15 | 3.C.2. | |
| Killare | 37 | 106 | 1765, 3525, [3444] | 2.F.8. | 224-225 |
| Killua | 25 | 105 | 1716-17 | 3.C.4. | |
| Killucan | 44 | 106 | 1718-19, 3513, [4229] | 3.C.12., 6.B.8., 3.F.11. | 74-82 |
| Killulagh | 26 | 105 | 1720-21, [2142] | 3.C.12. | 69-73 |
| Kilmacnevan | 12 | 105 | [3455] | 4.F.2. | 202-203 |
| Kilmanaghan | | | | | 29-30 |
| Kilpatrick | 8 | 105 | 1734 | 3.D.7. | |
| Lackan | 15 | 105 | 1702 | 5.B.8. | 31-33 |
| Leny | 17 | 105 | 1703 | 5.B.11. | 34 |
| Lickbla | 2 | 105 | 1735, 3517 | 3.D.9., 4.A.10. | 107-109 |
| Lynn | 56 | 107 | 1727 | 6.A.8. | |
| Mayne | 3 | 105 | 1736 | 4.B.2. | 110-112 |
| Moylisker | 57 | 107 | 1728 | 6.A.12. | 92-93 |
| Mullingar | 42 | 106 | 1729, 1745, 3520, [3451/54, 4231] | 6.E.13., 6.A.14. | 148-158 |
| Multyfarnham | 16 | 105 | 1704, 3509, [3443] | 5.C.3. | 35 |
| Newtown | 53 | 107 | 1730, 1755-56 | 5.F.5., 6.B.1. | 94-95, 193-198 |
| Noughaval | 29 | 105 | 1743 | 1.D.2., 2.E.6. | 142-146 |
| Pass of Kilbride | 61 | 107 | 1731 | 6.B.4. | |

| PARISH/TOWN | TITHES 1823–38 TAB 30/ | FILM | VALUATION FIELD BOOKS 1830s OL4./ HOUSE BOOKS [OL5.] | TENEMENT VALUATION 1854 FICHE | 1841–1851 CENSUS SEARCH Cen /S/30 |
|---|---|---|---|---|---|
| Piercetown | 33 | 106 | 3526 | 2.F.13., 5.A.10. | 226-228 |
| Portloman | 22 | 105 | 1705 | 5.C.8. | |
| Portnashangan | 19 | 105 | 1706 | 5.C.12. | 36 |
| Rahugh | 55 | 107 | 1757, [2147] | 5.F.14., 7.C.1. | |
| Rathaspick | 11 | 105 | 1758, [3455] | 4.B.12., 4.F.9. | 204-210 |
| Rathconnell | 41 | 106 | 1746 | 6.E.1. | 159-163 |
| Rathconrath | 34 | 106 | 1766, 3521 | 2.G.2., 5.A.11. | 229-231 |
| Rathgarve | 4 | 105 | 1737, 3518 | 3.D.9., 4.B.10. | 113-116 |
| Russagh | 10 | 105 | | 4.C.2. | 211-212 |
| St Feighin's | 5 | 105 | 1738 | 3.E.8. | 117-120 |
| St Mary's (Athlone) | 6 | 105 | 1739, 3519 | 2.A.4. | 1-17, 121-122 |
| St Mary's | 45 | 106 | 3508 | 3.F.6. | |
| Stonehall | 18 | 105 | 1707 | 5.C.14. | 37-38 |
| Street | 9 | 105 | 1759 | 4.C.5., 4.G.1. | |
| Taghmon | 21 | 105 | 1708 | 5.D.3. | 39-43 |
| Templeoran | | | | | 213 |
| Moygoish | 14 | 105 | | | |
| Templepatrick | 35 | 106 | | 2.G.3. | |
| Tyfarnham | 20 | 105 | 1709, 3510 | 5.D.7. | 44 |

| TOWNS | VALUATION HOUSE BOOK 1830s [OL5.] |
|---|---|
| Ballinagore | [3442] |
| Ballinalack | [3443] |
| Ballymore | [3444] |
| Ballynacarrigy | [3445] |
| Castlepollard | [3443] |
| Clonmellan | [3447] |
| Collenstown | [3443] |
| Finnea | [3443] |
| Killucan | [3443] |
| Moate | [3450] |
| Rathowen | [3445] |
| Rochfordbridge | [3456] |
| Tyrrellspass | [3457/58] |

| PARISH/TOWN | TITHES 1823–38 TAB 31/ | FILM | VALUATION FIELD BOOKS 1830s OL4./ HOUSE BOOKS [OL5.] | TENEMENT VALUATION 1853 FICHE | 1841–1851 CENSUS SEARCH Cen /S/31 |
|---|---|---|---|---|---|
| Adamstown | 50 | 109 | 1792-93, 3542, [2169] | 6.G.4. | 44-47 |
| Ambrosetown | 102 | 111 | 1828, 3555, [2191] | 10.C.11. | 174-178 |
| Ardamine | 30 | 109 | 1767, [2148] | 5.C.2. | 1-3 |
| Ardcandrisk | 71 | 110 | 1918, [2282] | 8.C.4. | |
| Ardcavan | 85 | 110 | 1910, 3646, [2273a] | 8.F.2. | 449-453 |
| Ardcolm | 86 | 110 | 1911, 3647, [2274] | 8.F.6. | 454 |
| Artramon | 84 | 110 | 1912, 3648, [2275] | 8.F.11. | 455-458 |
| Ballingly | 80 | 110 | 1919, [2283] | 8.C.6. | 475 |
| Ballyanne | 46 | 109 | 1794, [2170] | 6.G.11. | 48-56 |
| Ballybrazil | 89 | 110 | 1897, 3620, [2261] | 5.G.12. | 402 |
| Ballybrennan | 136 | 111 | 1841, [2204] | 9.A.4. | 210-216 |
| Ballycanew | 24 | 109 | 1867, 3583, [2228/29] | 4.A.14. | 263-268 |
| Ballycarney | 6 | 108 | 3604, [2247] | 1.E.3. | 299-302 |
| Ballyconnick | 103 | 108 | 1829, 3556, [2192] | 10.C.14. | |
| Ballyhoge | 53 | 109 | 1795-96, 1920, 3543, [2171, 2284] | 2.D.6., 1.B.4. | |
| Ballyhuskard* | 58 | 110 | 1768, 3527, [2149] | 3.D.8. | 4, 21-25 |
| Ballylannan | 79 | 110 | 1921, [2285] | 7.F.8. | 476-479 |
| Ballymitty | 81 | 110 | 1922, [2286] | 8.C.7. | 480 |
| Ballymore | 129 | 111 | 1842, [2205] | 9.A.6. | 217-218 |
| Ballynaslaney | 64 | 110 | 1769, 1913, 3649 [2150, 2276] | 3.C.13., 1.B.9. | |
| Ballyvaldon | 62 | 110 | 1771, [2151] | 3.C.4. | 26 |
| Ballyvaloo | 68 | 110 | 1770, 3528 | 3.B.6. | |
| Bannow | 105 | 111 | 1830, 3557, [2193] | 10.D.2. | 179-180 |
| Carn | 138 | 111 | 1843, [2206] | 9.A.10. | 219 |
| Carnagh | 54 | 109 | 1797-98, 3544, [2172] | 7.A.4. | 57-63 |
| Carnew | 3 | 108 | 1868, 1184, 3584, 3605 [2230, 2248] | 5.A.13., 3.B.6., 4.B.7 | 303-310 |
| Carrick | 78 | 110 | 1923, [2287] | 8.C.9. | 481 |
| Castle-Ellis | 60 | 110 | 1772, 3529, [2152] | 3.B.9. | 27 |
| Chapel | 44 | 109 | 1799, [2173] | 2.D.9. | 64-66 |
| Clone | 11 | 108 | 1885, 3606, [2249] | 1.E.10. | 311-314 |
| Clongeen | 72 | 110 | 1924, [2288] | 7.F.12. | |
| Clonleigh | 42 | 109 | 1800, 3545, [2174] | 7.A.6. | 67-71 |
| Clonmines | 97 | 111 | 1898, 3621, [2262] | 6.A.1. | |
| Clonmore | 45 | 109 | 1801-02, 1925, [2175, 4234] | 2.D.14., 1.B.6 | 72-73 |
| Coolstuff | 76 | 110 | 1926, [2289] | 8.D.1. | |
| Crosspatrick | 13 | 108 | 3585-75, [2231] | 4.B.5. | |
| Donaghmore | 31 | 109 | 1773, 1869, 3530, 3587 [2153/54, 2232] | 4.B.7., 5.C.10. | 5-7 |
| Doonooney | 51 | 109 | 1803, [2176] | 11.A.13. | |
| Drinagh | 120 | 111 | 1844, [2207] | 9.B.12. | |
| Duncormick | 106 | 111 | 1831, 3558, [2194] | 10.C.12. | 181-182 |
| Edermine | 63 | 110 | 1774 | 3.F.10. | 28 |
| Ferns | 7 | 108 | 1870, 1886, 3588, 3607 [2233, 2250] | 1.D.3., 5.B.5., 1.B.12. | 315-316 |
| Fethard | 99 | 111 | 1899, 3623, [2263] | 6.A.2. | 403-418 |
| Hook | 100 | 111 | 1900, 3624, [2264] | 6.B.1. | |
| Horetown | 74 | 110 | 1927, [2290] | 7.G.5. | 482-483 |
| Inch | 16 | 108 | 1871, 3589, [2234] | 7.G.11. | |

| PARISH/TOWN | TITHES 1823–38 TAB 31/ | FILM | VALUATION FIELD BOOKS 1830s OL4./ HOUSE BOOKS [OL5.] | TENEMENT VALUATION 1853 FICHE | 1841–1851 CENSUS SEARCH Cen /S/31 |
|---|---|---|---|---|---|
| Inch | 73 | 110 | [1928, 2291] | 4.B.7. | 269, 484 |
| Ishartmon | 133 | 111 | 1845, [2208] | 9.B.5. | |
| Kerloge | 117 | 111 | 1846, [2209] | 9.B.7. | |
| Kilbride | 8 | 108 | 1887, 3608, [2251] | 5.B.5., 1.D.1. | 317-319 |
| Kilbrideglynn | 77 | 110 | 1929, [2292] | 8.D.4. | 485-486 |
| Kilcavan | 19 | 108 | 1872, 3590, [2235] | 4.E.3., 5.D.5. | |
| Kilcavan | 101 | 111 | 1775, 1832, 3531, 3559 [2155, 2195] | 8.A.10., 10.E.8. | 183-184, 270-271 |
| Kilcomb | 4 | 108 | 1888, 3609, [2252] | 5.B.6. | 320-322 |
| Kilcormick | 25 | 109 | 1776, 1873, 3532, 3591 [2156, 2236] | 1.B.12., 3.A.5., 5.E.8. | 8-9, 272-273 |
| Kilcowan | 107 | 111 | 1833, 3560, [2196] | 10.E.11. | 185-186 |
| Kilcowanmore | 52 | 109 | 1804-05, [2177] | 2.E.7. | |
| Kildavin | 118 | 111 | 1847, [2210] | 9.B.8. | 220-221 |
| Kilgarvan | 69 | 110 | 1930, [2293] | | 487-490 |
| Kilgorman | 17 | 108 | 1874, 3592, [2237] | 4.F.10. | |
| Killag | 109 | 111 | 1834, 3561, [2197] | 10.F.1. | |
| Killann | 36 | 109 | 1806-07, 3546, [2178] | 2.E.1. | 74-88 |
| Killenagh | 29 | 109 | 3534, 3548 | 5.D.6. | |
| Killesk | 93 | 111 | 1901, [2265] | 6.B.5. | 419 |
| Killiane | 122 | 111 | 1848, [2211] | 9.C.1. | |
| Killegney | 43 | 109 | 1808-09, 3547, [2179] | 2.F.10. | 89-104 |
| Killila | 61 | 110 | 1777, 3533 | 3.G.3. | 29 |
| Killincooly | 33 | 109 | 1778, 3535, [2157] | 3.A.11. | 10 |
| Killinick | 125 | 111 | 1849, [2212] | 9.C.3. | |
| Killisk | 59 | 110 | 1779, 3536, [2158] | 3.E.7. | 30-32, 419 |
| Kilmacree | 123 | 111 | 1850, [2213] | 9.C.7. | 222 |
| Kilmakilloge | 21 | 108 | 1780, 1875, 3593, [2159, 2238] | 4.G.2., 5.E.5. | 33-34, 274-277 |
| Kilmallock | 65 | 110 | 1781, 3537, [2160] | 3.D.2. | 35-38 |
| Kilmannan | 104 | 111 | 1835, 3562, [2198] | 10.F.4. | |
| Kilmokea | | | 1902 | | 420 |
| Kilmore | 110 | 111 | 1836, 3563, [2199] | 10.F.11. | 187-189 |
| Kilmuckridge | 34 | 109 | 1782, 3538, [2161] | 3.A.14., 5.E.9. | |
| Kilnahue | 18 | 108 | 1876, 3594, [2239] | 4.D.2. | 278-281 |
| Kilnamanagh | 32 | 109 | 1783, [2162] | 5.D.12. | 11-14 |
| Kilnenor | 15 | 108 | 1877, 3595, [2240] | 5.A.3. | 282 |
| Kilpatrick | 83 | 110 | 1914, 3650, [2278] | 1.B.10., 8.G.1. | 459-462 |
| Kilpipe | 14 | 108 | 1878, 3597, [2241] | 4.A.10. | 283 |
| Kilrane | 131 | 111 | 1851, [2214] | 9.C.9. | 223-224 |
| Kilrush | 2 | 108 | 1889, 3610, [2253] | 1.C.3. | 323-335 |
| Kilscanlan | 55 | 109 | 1810, 3549, [2180] | 9.A.9. | 105-109 |
| Kilscoran | 130 | 111 | 1852, [2215] | 9.C.12. | 225-234 |
| Kiltennell | 28 | 109 | 1784, [2163] | 5.D.14. | 15 |
| Kiltrisk | 27 | 109 | 1785, 1879, 3539, 3598 [2242] | 4.C.12., 5.D.14. | 284 |
| Kilturk | 111 | 111 | 1837, 3564, [2200] | 10.G.8. | |
| Lady's Island | 136 | 111 | 1853, [2216] | 9.D.3. | |
| Liskinfere | 23 | 108 | 3599-3600, [2243] | 4.C.1. | 285 |
| Maudlintown | 116 | 111 | 1854 ,[2217, 3518/21] | | 235 |
| Meelnagh | 35 | 109 | 1786, [2164] | 3.A.14., 5.E.14. | 16-18 |

| PARISH/TOWN | TITHES 1823–38 TAB 31/ | FILM | VALUATION FIELD BOOKS 1830s OL4./ HOUSE BOOKS [OL5.] | TENEMENT VALUATION 1853 FICHE | 1841–1851 CENSUS SEARCH Cen /S/31 |
|---|---|---|---|---|---|
| Monamolin | 26 | 109 | 1787, 1880, 3601, [2165, 2244] | 4.F.1., 5.F.1. | 19-20, 286-288 |
| Monart | 10 | 108 | 1890, 3611, [2254] | 2.C.5. | 336-350 |
| Moyacomb | 1 | 108 | 1891, 3612, [2255] | 1.D.3, 3.B.9. | 351-356 |
| Maglass | 124 | 111 | 1855, [2218] | 9.D.5. | 236 |
| Mulrankin | 108 | 111 | 1838, 3565, [2201] | 10.G.12. | 190-201 |
| Newbawn | 49 | 109 | 1811-12, 1932, [2181, 2294] | 7.A.11., 8.A.5. | 110-113, 491-494 |
| Oldross | 48 | 109 | 1813, 3550, [2182] | 7.A.14. | 114-126 |
| Owenduff | 91 | 111 | 1903, 3627, [2267] | 6.B.14. | 421-424 |
| Rathaspick | 119 | 111 | 1856, [2219] | 9.D.12. | |
| Rathmacknee | 121 | 111 | 1857, [2220] | 9.E.3. | 237 |
| Rathroe | 95 | 111 | 1904, 3628, [2268] | 6.C.10. | 425-428 |
| Rossdroit | 38 | 109 | 1814-15, [2183] | 2.G.3. | 127-130 |
| Rosslare | 128 | 111 | 1858, [2221] | 9.E.7. | 238-246 |
| Rossminoge | 20 | 108 | 1881, 3602, [2245] | 4.C.6. | 289-293 |
| Skreen | 67 | 110 | 1790, 1916, 3540, 3651, [2280, 3509] | 11.B.10., 8.G.10. | 39-40, 463-466 |
| St Helen's | 132 | 111 | 1859, [2222] | 9.F.5. | 247 |
| St Bridget's | | | [3522/23] | 10.C.9. | |
| St. Doologes | | | [3524/26] | 10.C.7. | |
| St Iberius | | | | 10.B.9. | |
| St Iberius | 135 | 111 | 1860, 3572-73, [2223, 3527/30] | 9.F.6. | 248-249 |
| St James & Dunbrody | 94 | 111 | 1905, [2269] | 6.C.13. | 429-440 |
| St John's | 40 | 109 | 1816-17, 3551, [2184, 3531/36] | | |
| St John's | 113 | 111 | 1861 | 9.G.2. | |
| St Margaret's | 137 | 111 | 1862, [2166, 2224] | 9.F.10., 8.G.6. | |
| St Margaret's | 87 | 110 | 1788, 1915, 3652, [2279] | 11.B.10. | 250, 467-468 |
| St Mary's | 47 | 109 | 1818, 3574-75, [2185, 3537/39] | 10.C.4. | 131-145, 251, 357-364 |
| St Mary's (Enniscorthy) | 12 | 108 | 1892, 3613, [2256] | | |
| St Mary's (N Barry) | 5 | 108 | 1893, 3614, [2257] | | 357-364 |
| St Michael's | 127 | 111 | 1789, 1863-64, 3576, [2225, 3540/43, 3544] | 9.F.11. | |
| St Michael's of Feagh | | | [3540/44] | 10.A.7. | |
| St Mullin's | 41 | 109 | 1819-20, [2186] | 7.E.6. | |
| St Nicholas | 66 | 110 | [2167] | 3.C.3. | 41 |
| St Patrick's | | | [3545/48] | | |
| St Peter's | 115 | 111 | 1865, 3579, [2226, 3544, 3549/52] | 9.G.14. | |
| St Selskar's | | | [3553/55] | 10.B.2. | |
| Tacumshin | 134 | 111 | 1866, [2227] | 9.E.13. | |
| Taghmon | 75 | 110 | 1839, 1933, 3566, [2202, 4236] [3510/11] | 8.A.9., 8.D.12 | 202-204, 495-502 |
| Tellarought | 90 | 110 | 1906, 3629, [2270] | | 441-442 |
| Templescoby | 39 | 109 | 1823-24, [2188] | 3.A.2. | 171 |
| Templeshanbo | 9 | 108 | 1894, [2258] | 2.B.10. | 365-395 |

| PARISH/TOWN | TITHES 1823–38 TAB 31/ | FILM | VALUATION FIELD BOOKS 1830s OL4./ HOUSE BOOKS [OL5.] | TENEMENT VALUATION 1853 FICHE | 1841–1851 CENSUS SEARCH Cen /S/31 |
|---|---|---|---|---|---|
| Templeshannon | 57 | 109 | 1791, 1895, 3541, 3615-16, [2168, 2259] | 1.E.2., 3.E.13. | 41-43 |
| Templetown | 98 | 111 | 1907, 3630, [2271] | 6.E.3. | 443 |
| Templeludigan | 37 | 109 | 1821-22, 3552, [2187] | 7.E.12. | 146-170 |
| Tikillin | 82 | 110 | 1917, 3653, [2281] | 8.G.11. | 469-474 |
| Tintern | 96 | 111 | 1908, 3631, [2272] | 6.E.13. | 444-446 |
| Tomhaggard | 112 | 111 | 1840, 3567, [2203] | 11.A.6. | 205-209 |
| Toome | 22 | 108 | 1882, 1896, 3603, 3617, [2246, 2260]396-401 | 5.B.11., 4.F.7. | 294-298, 396-401 |
| Wexford Town | 114 | 111 | | | 251-262 |
| Whitechurch | 88 | 110 | 1825, 1909, 3553, 3632, [2189, 2273] [3460] | 7.F.7., 6.F.11. | 447-448 |
| Whitechurchglynn | 56 | 109 | 1826-27, 1934, 3554, [2190] | 11.A.14. | 172-173 |

* Enniscorthy workhouse included.

| TOWNS | VALUATION HOUSE BOOK 1830s [OL5.] |
|---|---|
| Arthurstown | [3459, 3460, 3464] |
| Ballaghkeen | [3461] |
| Ballycanew | [3490] |
| Ballygarret | [3463] |
| Ballyhack | [3464] |
| Blackwater | [3462] |
| Camolin | [3465/66] |
| Castlebridge | [3467] |
| Clohamon | [3468/69] |
| Clonroche | [3470] |
| Coolgreany | [3471, 3490] |
| Courtown | [3472] |
| Duncannon | [3460, 3464] |
| Duncannon | [3473] |
| Enniscorthy | [3474/84] |
| Ferns | [3485] |
| Ford | [3487] |
| Fethard | [3460, 3486] |
| Gorey | [3463, 3488/89, 3490] |
| Monamolin | [3491] |
| New Ross | [3492/506] |
| Newtownbarry | [3512/16] |
| Oilgate | [3507] |
| Riverchapel | [3508] |
| Saltmills | [3486] |
| Screen | [3509] |
| Watch House | [3517] |

| PARISH/TOWN | TITHES 1823–38 TAB 32/ | FILM | VALUATION FIELD BOOKS 1830s OL4./ HOUSE BOOKS [OL5.] | TENEMENT VALUATION 1852–4 FICHE | 1841–1851 CENSUS SEARCH Cen /S/32 |
|---|---|---|---|---|---|
| Aghowle | 55 | 114 | 1969, 3736-39, [2338] | 6.B.6. | 72-75 |
| Ardoyne | | 114 | 1970, 3740-42, [2339] | 6.B.14. | 76 |
| Arklow | 50 | 114 | 1935, 3653a-3654, [2295, 3556/58] | 4.A.8. | 1-12 |
| Ballinacarrig | | | 1994 | | |
| Ballinacor | 34 | 113 | 3691-93, [4237] | 5.A.7. | 38 |
| Ballintemple | 47 | 114 | 1936, 3655-56, [2297] | 4.C.5. | |
| Ballymacsimon (Glenealy) | | | 3715 | | 39 |
| Ballynure | 15 | 112 | 1984, 3782-84, [2346] | 5.A.13. | |
| Ballykine | | | 3694-98, [4238] | 5.A.13. | |
| Baltinglass | 20 | 112 | 1986, 3785-87, [2347] | 1.E.2., 1.D.10. | 113-119 |
| Blessington | 2 | 112 | 1977, 3765-66, 3564/65, 4246] | 2.C.6. | 89-91 |
| Boystown | 4 | 112 | 1978, 3767-68, [4247] | 1.B.5., 2.D.2. | 92-98 |
| Bray | 12 | 112 | 3731, [2330/31, 3566/68] | 2.F.2. | 64 |
| Burgage | 3 | 112 | 1979, 3769, [4248] | 2.D.11. | 99 |
| Calary | 23 | 123 | 1948, 1959, 1965, 3677-79, 3716, [2310, 2314/16, 2332/33] | 2.G.4., 5.B.12., 3.C.14. | 24-25, 47, 65 |
| Carnew | 59 | 114 | 1971, 3743-46, [2340, 3569/71] | 6.D.3. | 77-83 |
| Castlemacadam | 44 | 114 | 1937, 3657-58, [2296] | 4.C.10. | 13-14 |
| Crecrin | 53 | 114 | 1972, 3747-48, [2341] | 6.C.2. | |
| Crehelp | 6 | 112 | 1980, 3770, [4249] | 1.B.9. | |
| Crosspatrick | 57 | 114 | 1951, 1973, 3749-51, [2342] | 5.F.10., 6.C.2. | 84-87 |
| Delgany | 13 | 112 | 1966, 3732-33, [2334/35] | 2.G.8. | 66 |
| Derrylossary | 24 | 113 | 1960, 3680-83, 3717, [2311, 2317/18] | 5.C.2. | 27-34 |
| Donaghmore | 19 | 112 | 1986, 3788-91, 3806, [2348] | 1.G.5. | 120-126 |
| Donard | 9 | 112 | 1981, 3771-72, [3565, 3572, 4250] | 1.B.11. | 100 |
| Drumkay | 41 | 113 | 1938, 1961, 3659-60, [2298] | 4.D.13. | 15 |
| Dunganstown | 43 | 113 | 1939, 3661-62, [2299/300] | 4.E.2. | 16-17 |
| Dunlavin | 8 | 112 | 1982, 1987, 3773-74, 3792, [2349, 3565, 4251] | 1.C.3., 1.F.1. | 101-103 |
| Ennereilly | 46 | 114 | 1940, 3663-64, [2301] | 4.F.2. | 18-19 |
| Freynestown | 16 | 112 | 1988, 3793-94, [2350] | 1.F.1. | |
| Glenealy | 33 | 113 | 1941, 1962, 3665-66, 3718-19, [2302, 2319] | 3.D.7. 4.F.4. | |
| Hacketstown | 35 | 113 | 1952, 3699-3700, [4239] | 1.A.14. | 40-41 |
| Hollywood | 7 | 112 | 1983, 3775-77, [4252] | | 104-110 |
| Inch | 51 | 114 | 1942, 3667, [2303] | 4.F.5. | |
| Kilbride | 1, 48 | 112, 114 | 1943, 3668-69, 3778-80, [2304/05, 4253] | 2.D.13. 4.F.6. | 111-2 |
| Kilcommon | 32, 38 | 113 | 1944, 1953, 3670, 3701-03, 3720, [2306, 2320/21, 4240] | 3.D.11., 4.F.13., 5.G.2. | 42-43, |
| Kilcoole | 27 | 113 | 3721-22, [2322] | 3.D.13. | 50-54 |
| Killahurler | 49 | 114 | 1945, 3671-72, [2307] | 4.G.1. | 20 |
| Killiskey | 30 | 113 | 3723-24, [2323/24] | 3.E.8. | 55 |

| PARISH/TOWN | TITHES 1823–38 TAB 32/ | FILM | VALUATION FIELD BOOKS 1830s OL4./ HOUSE BOOKS [OL5.] | TENEMENT VALUATION 1852–4 FICHE | 1841–1851 CENSUS SEARCH Cen /S/32 |
|---|---|---|---|---|---|
| Kilmacanoge | 11 | 112 | 1967, 3734, [2336] | 3.A.4. | 67-68 |
| Kilpoole | 42 | 113 | 1946, 3673-74, [2308] | 4.G.4. | 21 |
| Kilpipe | 40 | 113 | 1954, 3704-07, [4241] | 5.B.8., 6.A.3. | |
| Kilranelagh | 21 | 112 | 1989, 3795-97, [2351/52] | 1.F.3. | 127 |
| Kiltegan | 22 | 112 | 1955, 1990, 3798-99, 3806, [2353/54, 4242] | 2.A.6., 1.B.1. | 44-45, 128-130 |
| Knockrath | 25 | 113 | 1949, 1956, 3684-86, 3708, [2312] | 5.D.3., 5.B.7. | 35-36 |
| Liscolman | 52 | 114 | 1974, 3752-3756, [2343] | 6.C.6. | |
| Moyacomb | 58 | 114 | 1975, 3757-3761, [2344] | 6.C.7. | 88 |
| Moyne | | | 1957, 3709-11, [4243] | 6.A.10. | 46 |
| Mullinacuff | 56 | 114 | 1976, 3762-64, [2345] | 6.C.11. | |
| Newcastle Lower & Upper | 29 | 113 | 1963, 3725/26, [2325/27] | 3.F.3., 3.F.7. | 56-60 |
| Powerscourt | 10 | 112 | 1968, 3735, [2337, 4245] | 3.A.14. | 69-71 |
| Preban | 39 | 113 | 1958, 3712-13, [4244] | 6.B.1. | |
| Rathbran | | 112 | 1991, 3800-02, [2356] | 1.F.8. | 131-134 |
| Rathdrum | 26 | 113 | 1950, 3687-90, [2313, 3575/77] | 5.D.12. | 37 |
| Rathnew | 31 | 113 | 1964, 3727-30, [2328/29, 3578] | 3.G.3. | 61-62 |
| Rathsallagh | 14 | 112 | 1992, 3803-04, [2357] | 1.G.2. | |
| Rathtoole | 17 | 112 | 1993, 3805, [2357a] | 1.G.3. | |
| Redcross | 45 | 114 | 1947, 3675-76, [2309, 3579/80] | 5.A.1. | 22-23 |
| Tober | 5 | 112 | 3781, [4254] | 1.D.8. | |
| Wicklow Town | | | [3587/89] | | 63 |

| TOWNS | VALUATION HOUSE BOOK 1830s [OL5.] |
|---|---|
| Ballinlea | [3559] |
| Baltinglass | [3560/63] |
| Enniskerry | [3568, 3573] |
| Newtownmountkennedy | [3574] |
| Stratford | [3581/83] |
| Tinahely | [3584/86] |

# GLOSSARY

ACT OF UNION
In 1800, legislation in Dublin and Westminster created the United Kingdom of Great Britain and Ireland, dissolved the Irish parliament in Dublin, and brought Ireland into one parliament at Westminster, effective 1 January 1801. The 1798 rebellion was the immediate impetus for this legislation. The Act of Union was controversial from the outset, and efforts in Ireland were launched almost immediately to repeal it. The momentum for Home Rule intensified towards the end of the 19th century, and led eventually to the **Partition** of Ireland in 1922. The term 'Unionist' designates those who support continued political union of Northern Ireland with Great Britain.

*Alumni Dublinensis*
This provides a list of registered students of Trinity College Dublin from 1593 to 1860, giving place of birth, father's name and profession, teacher or school attended, and degrees taken (G.D. Burtchaell and T.U. Sadleir (eds), 2 vols, 1935).

BARONY
A unit used in Ireland between the 16th and 19th centuries for administrative (census, taxation, and legal) purposes. Drawn on pre-existing Gaelic divisions – the *triocha ced* – the baronies consisted of large groupings of **townlands** within a county. They were superseded as an administrative unit by the creation of county councils in 1898. The 1891 census is the last to use the barony as an administrative unit.

BOARDS OF GUARDIANS *See* Poor Law Union.

CATHOLIC CHURCH
The largest of the Churches in Ireland and Northern Ireland. More than 90% of the population in the Republic identifies itself as Catholic, as does 45% of the population of Northern Ireland. The Catholic Archbishop of Armagh and Primate of All Ireland is based in Armagh City. *See* **Catholic emancipation**

CATHOLIC EMANCIPATION
From the 1690s through the 1720s, a series of anti-Catholic laws – popularly called 'the penal laws' – were passed by the Irish parliament that severely restricted or denied most civil and religious rights to Catholics and Protestant dissenters, including the right to practise their religion freely, buy land or inherit land from Protestants, hold public office, travel abroad for education, operate schools,

practise law, serve on **Grand Juries** or in the military, and to vote. While these laws may have been applied only regionally and intermittently, their overall effect was to copperfasten 'Protestant Ascendancy' and to create the highly unusual situation of religious discrimination against a majority population. Political resistance to these restrictions gradually escalated in the late 18th century, and various Catholic Relief Acts were passed towards the end of the century. In the 1820s, under the flamboyant and effective leadership of Daniel O'Connell, the Catholic Association successfully forced the British Government to pass the final Catholic Relief Act in April 1829 conceding the right of Catholics to sit in parliament.

CENSUS RETURNS

The earliest census taken, for which partial records are extant, is the so-called 'Census of 1659', edited by Seamus Pender in 1939 (*see* Bibliography). It is a poll tax list, not a true census, but is of historical significance for recording proportions of settler and native families, the names of principal landowners and tabulations of the most numerous Irish families for each barony. In 1749 Bishop Edward Synge initiated an impressively detailed census for his Church of Ireland Diocese of **Elphin**. There are partial returns of individuals of different denominations in the '1766 census'. The first modern census in Ireland began in 1821 and has been held every ten years subsequently, though with Independence, Ireland conducted a census in 1926, 1936, 1946 and thereafter at five-year intervals. Northern Ireland took a census in 1926, 1937, 1951, 1961, 1966, 1971 and every ten years thereafter. The decennial census remains the most important, however. The individual returns up to 1901 were largely destroyed, partially in the First World War, when they were pulped as part of the war effort, and partially in the Irish Civil War in 1922. However, abstracts were published and those since 1841 provide important information by individual parish on population, religion, housing, occupation, literacy, etc. The first full census for which the individual returns survive is 1901: its records, with those from 1911, are publicly available for all 32 counties. Arranged by county, district, electoral division and townland, it provides the occupant's name, age, religion, occupation, ability to read or write, marital status, relationship to householder, county of birth or country if not born in Ireland, and ability to speak English and/or Irish. Details of houses are also provided, including the number of rooms occupied by each family, type of roof, and number of windows. Many of the institutions listed in this Guide hold copies of the returns on microfilm for both 1901 and 1911, in whole or in part.

CHURCH OF IRELAND

The Church of Ireland, affiliated with the Anglican/Episcopalian tradition, was the Established Church in Ireland from the Reformation in the 16th century to its formal disestablishment in 1869, effective in 1870. Members of other religious denominations, notably Catholics and Dissenters, were forced to pay tithes to maintain the Church of Ireland. It is the largest Protestant denomination in the Republic of Ireland and on the island of Ireland, but second in numbers to the Presbyterian Church in Northern Ireland. The Church's leader, the Archbishop of Armagh and Primate of All Ireland, is based in Armagh.

CIVIL SURVEY (1654)
This mid-17th century survey records the principal property-holders in each county.

COUNTY
The county system as a form of territorial division was introduced into Ireland shortly after the Norman Conquest in the late 12th century. The creation of counties or shires was gradual, however. The sheriff was the chief administrative officer in the county and was vested with considerable powers, including public safety and administration. In 1898 the primary administrative duties were assigned to county councils, which remain the principal administrative body in the Republic but were abolished in Northern Ireland in 1972 with the introduction of Direct Rule by the British Government. Counties remain a powerful focus of local allegiance, symbolized by the use of the unit as the basis for the organization of the **GAA** games of hurling and Gaelic football.

DÁIL ÉIREANN
The Irish parliament, first convened in January 1919 to declare Ireland's Independence. The Dáil's 166 members, **TDs**, are elected by proportional representation. Each Dáil sits for a term of up to five years.

ELPHIN CENSUS
In 1749 the Church of Ireland bishop Edward Synge (1691–1762) organized a census of the people in his diocese, which at that time covered Co. Roscommon and a large part of Counties Sligo and Galway. This census encompasses all inhabitants, regardless of religious affiliation.

ENCUMBERED ESTATES RECORDS
In 1849, parliament passed legislation setting up Encumbered Estate Courts to settle claims against the growing number of estates bankrupted by the Famine. The courts freed up complicated land titles, and placed thousands of estates on the open market. Their printed sales brochures frequently contain detailed lists of townlands, tenants, and leases. These brochures can be found at various locations in Ireland, including the **NATIONAL ARCHIVES OF IRELAND**, the **NATIONAL LIBRARY OF IRELAND**, and the **PUBLIC RECORD OFFICE OF NORTHERN IRELAND**.

FLIGHT OF THE EARLS
On 4 September 1607, Hugh O'Neill, Earl of Tyrone, and Rory O'Donnell, Earl of Tyrconnell, together with a contingent of their followers, sailed from the port of Rathmullen in Co. Donegal for Spain, but were diverted to France and eventually to Italy. 'The Great O'Neill' (*c.*1550–1616) spent the last years of his life in Rome, where he is buried. The departure of Ireland's greatest chieftains symbolized the end of overt Gaelic resistance and paved the way to the **Ulster Plantation**.

GAA

The Gaelic Athletic Association was founded in 1884 to promote distinctive Irish sports. It is now probably the world's largest community sporting organization. There is huge grassroots involvement, especially in rural communities, where clubs represent **parishes**. The GAA principally runs Gaelic football, hurling and handball. Today Gaelic football remains the most popular spectator sport in Ireland, and hurling (the fastest field sport in the world) also attracts huge crowds to GAA headquarters, the impressively rebuilt 80,000-capacity state-of-the-art Croke Park stadium in Dublin. Gaelic football has enough similarity with Australian Rules football for internationals to be played, in which the amateur Irish hold their own against the professional Australians. From its inception, the GAA has been an explicitly nationalist body. Until 1971 members were forbidden to play or watch 'foreign' sports such as soccer ('the Ban'), and until 2001 the security forces in Northern Ireland were barred from membership.

GRAND JURIES

Established in the 13th century, Grand Juries were appointed by the High Sheriff in each county and their membership was drawn largely from local landowners. Responsibilities included the maintenance of roads and bridges and the upkeep of courthouses, hospitals, and lunatic asylums. The Juries, which kept minute books and presentment books, had their administrative functions transferred to County Councils in 1898.

GRIFFITH'S VALUATION (1847–64)

Compiled by Sir Richard Griffith, the purpose of this undertaking was to value house and land holdings to determine the payment of rates, i.e. property taxes. Tax receipts were administered by the Poor Law Guardians, who oversaw the administration of Workhouses and certain public projects, such as road maintenance. The meticulously detailed Griffith's Valuation, more formally known as 'The Primary Valuation', is arranged by **townland** or street within civil parishes grouped by **barony** and **Poor Law Union** within each county. This survey – of the utmost genealogical significance – is available on microfiche and in hard copy and covers the 32 counties. Most institutions listed in this Guide hold at least a copy of the summary printed version of Griffith's Valuation for their region.

HEARTH MONEY ROLLS

In 1662 the Irish parliament enacted legislation levying a tax of two shillings on every hearth, firing place and stove in Ireland, with exemptions, mostly for the indigent, including widows. Tax evasion was common. The Rolls record the names of householders arranged by **parish** or **townland**. Few original Rolls survived the destruction of the Public Record Office in 1922, but many copies had been transcribed and these are still available for about half of the counties of Ireland, mainly in the provinces of Ulster and Leinster.

INCUMBERED ESTATES RECORDS *See* **Encumbered Estates Records**

INDEXES TO WILLS

Published indexes to wills, compiled before the destruction of the Public Record Office, provide important information on wills that are no longer extant.

INDOOR WORKHOUSE REGISTERS

Registers often included the following information: date of admission; first name and last name; sex and age; marital status; occupation; religion; name of spouse and number of children; electoral division or townland of residence; date the person left the Workhouse or died; and the date of birth if born in the work house.

IRISH FOLKLORE COMMISSION SCHOOLS SCHEME PROJECT

Over a period of 18 months between 1937 and 1938, the Irish Folklore Commission, founded in 1935, organized a project that involved Irish schoolchildren in collecting and documenting a wide range of Irish folk material, including folk tales and folk legends, riddles and proverbs, songs, customs and beliefs, games and pastimes, and traditional work practices and crafts. The stories and information collected have been preserved on microfilm and offer a good deal of useful historical and genealogical information.

KING'S INNS ADMISSION PAPERS

A summary catalogue and index to these admission papers was published by the Stationery Office, Dublin on behalf of the Irish Manuscripts Commission in 1982. This printed volume lists legal students who were admitted to the King's Inns from 1607 to 1867, giving name of father and maiden name of mother, place of birth, and qualifications gained.

METHODIST CHURCH

The Methodist Church is the third-largest Protestant denomination in Ireland, with a total membership of about 60,000, most of whom reside in Northern Ireland. A chairman is elected annually.

ORDNANCE SURVEY

Though inaugurated in England in the early 1790s for military purposes, the mapping of Ireland commenced in 1825 for civil purposes, in anticipation of **Griffith's Valuation**. More than 2,000 workers carried out the survey, county by county, completing their work in 1841. In all, some 1,900 maps were drawn, the most detailed mapping of an entire country ever carried out up to that time, and an invaluable record of the state of the Irish landscape on the eve of the Great Famine. From 1825 until 1841, all of Ireland was mapped at the intimate scale of six inches to the mile. At this scale field fences and houses are marked. These are particularly useful for family research, as they help locate holdings listed in **Griffith's Valuation**.

ORDNANCE SURVEY LETTERS AND MEMOIRS

As the country was being mapped, John O'Donovan and other members of the **Ordnance Survey** teams sent erudite and entertaining letters back to headquarters describing the countryside, monuments, placenames, big houses, etc. These letters were never published, but were made available in typescript form *c.*1930. Recently the Royal Irish Academy (where the Ordnance Survey letters and parish memoirs are housed) has published full editions of the Ordnance Survey letters for some counties by Michael Herity. The Ordnance Survey Letters already published are for Counties Donegal, Down, Dublin, Kildare and Meath. For much of Ulster and some of the counties that border it, detailed memoirs were also compiled for each parish, and these have now been published in a 40-volume series by the Institute of Irish Studies, Queen's University Belfast (series editors Angélique Day and Patrick McWilliams). See www.qub.ac.uk/iis/publications.html.

PALMER'S INDEX TO *THE TIMES* 1790–1905 ON CD-ROM
This index provides a wealth of information about Irish affairs in the 19th century. It is especially useful for genealogists wishing to glean information about people, places and social events.

PARISH
This territorial division refers to both civil and ecclesiastical boundaries. Civil parishes largely follow the pattern that was established in medieval times, drawn largely along ecclesiastical lines. Ecclesiastical parishes do not always coincide with civil parish boundaries, however. Following the Reformation in the 16th century, the Church of Ireland maintained the pre-Reformation arrangement, but low populations forced it to expand its parishes into large groupings of civil parishes. When the Catholic Church began its institutional re-emergence in the late 18th and 19th century, it had to construct an entirely new network of Catholic parishes. The Irish system of parishes is therefore very complex indeed.

PARISH REGISTERS. *See* Appendix 1, Karel Kiely's 'Tracing Your Co. Kildare Ancestors'.

PARTITION
The Government of Ireland Act, passed by the British parliament in 1920, created two separate Home Rule parliaments, one based in Dublin for the 26 counties in the south and north-west, the other based in Belfast for the six north-eastern counties that were to become Northern Ireland in 1921. The latter area is often referred to as Ulster, but in fact includes only six of the nine counties in the province of Ulster, namely Antrim, Armagh, Derry or Londonderry, Down, Fermanagh and Tyrone. The three Ulster counties that came under Dublin's jurisdiction are Cavan, Donegal and Monaghan. The South rejected Home Rule, and in 1922 became the Irish Free State, with Dominion status.

PENAL LAWS
Starting in 1695, the Irish parliament passed a series of draconian measures that were intended to limit not only the civil and religious rights of Catholics, but also the rights of all dissenters, i.e. those who did not belong to the Established Church of Ireland. Catholics, however, suffered the most severe restrictions. *See* **Catholic Emancipation**.

PENDER'S CENSUS (1659) *See* **Census Returns** and Bibliography.

PLANTATION *See* **Ulster Plantation.**

POOR LAW UNION
Under the Poor Law Act of 1838 Ireland was divided initially into 130 Poor Law Unions, each administered by an area Board of Guardians, responsible in turn to the Poor Law Commission. The boards were chiefly responsible for supervising the running of the Workhouses and administering poor relief in their unions. Later health services were added to their responsibilities. In 1898 the Local Government Act removed health matters from the boards and assigned these to Rural District Councils. The Boards of Guardians and the Rural District Councils were abolished in the Republic of Ireland in 1930. The Boards of Guardians survived in Northern Ireland until the Hospitals Authority Act of 1948 which included a clause designating Workhouse records as public records.

PRESBYTERIAN CHURCH
The second largest Protestant denomination in Ireland, its membership is largely concentrated in the northern counties of the Republic and in Northern Ireland, where it slightly outnumbers the **Church of Ireland**. Its leader is the Moderator, elected annually by the General Assembly of the Church.

PROVINCES
There are four provinces in Ireland: Ulster in the north, Leinster in the east, Munster in the south, and Connacht or Connaught in the west.

REPUBLIC OF IRELAND
Formally established in 1949 as the successor to the Irish Free State of 1922, it consists of 26 counties in the south and north-west. The Irish Constitution of 1937, Articles 2 and 3, laid territorial claim to all 32 counties, but this claim was revoked by referendum as part of the Good Friday Agreement of 10 April 1998.

RIC
Royal Irish Constabulary. Founded originally in 1836 as the Irish Constabulary, the RIC was a national, armed force that took on a distinct military character for much of the 19th century. It was disbanded in 1922 and replaced in the Republic by the Gárda Siochána and in Northern Ireland by the Royal Ulster Constabulary (**RUC**). The latter was disbanded in 2001 and replaced by the Police Service of Northern Ireland.

ROMAN CATHOLIC CHURCH *See* **Catholic Church.**

RUC
Founded in 1922 with the establishment of Northern Ireland, the Royal Ulster Constabulary was controversial from the outset. Overwhelmingly Protestant and Unionist in composition, it was widely distrusted by the Catholic community. The

Good Friday Agreement of 10 April 1998 specifically called for its reform. The subsequent Patten Commission recommended sweeping changes, and the Police Service of Northern Ireland replaced it in 2001.

RURAL DISTRICT COUNCILS *See* **Poor Law Union.**

TAOISEACH
Prime Minister of Ireland.

TD
Teachta Dála, i.e. member of the Irish parliament or Dáil.

TITHE APPLOTMENT BOOKS (1823–37)
The Tithe Books were compiled for each civil parish to assess payment of tithes to the **Church of Ireland**, the Established Church in Ireland until 1869. All occupiers of land, regardless of their religious affiliation, were required to pay these tithes. Recorded is the name of the occupier, the acreage and quality of his holding, and the amount of tithe payable. The landlord's name is also listed. These records, with variable degrees of detail, are held on microfilm and cover the 32 counties.

TOWNLAND
This is the smallest administrative territorial unit in Ireland, varying in size from a single acre to over 7,000 acres. Originating in the older Gaelic dispensation, townlands were used as the basis of leases in the estate system, and subsequently to assess valuations and tithes in the 18th and 19th centuries. They survive as important markers of identity and as postal addresses.

ULSTER PLANTATION
Following the **Flight of the Earls**, lands formerly owned by Gaelic chieftains were confiscated by the British Crown and granted out for the most part to English and Scottish landlords in 1610. The counties included in the official plantation scheme were Armagh, Cavan, Donegal, Fermanagh, Londonderry and Tyrone. In addition there were private plantations in counties Antrim and Down. Over the course of the next thirty years thousands of settlers from England and in particular Scotland, nearly all of them Protestant, migrated to Ulster, contributing to the distinctive identity of the province.

WORKHOUSES *See* **Poor Law Union** and **Indoor Workhouse Registers.**

For more detailed information on these and other terms, please consult the Bibliography. Especially helpful are: Connolly's *The Oxford Companion to Irish History*, Nolan's *Tracing the Past*, and Begley's *Handbook on Irish Genealogy*.

# BIBLIOGRAPHY

A select list of general books and monographs only is included here. Monographs primarily of a local interest or serial-type publications, such as Parnham's *1911 Census Ireland References*, or memorial inscriptions of cemeteries, are not included because of space considerations. For articles and CD-ROMs, as well as monographs dealing with local history, consult bibliographies in works listed above, especially James Ryan's works, as well as the catalogues and websites of major distributors of genealogical publications, such as the Ulster Historical Foundation (www.ancestryireland.com), the New England Historic and Genealogical Society (www.newenglandancestors.org), Kennys Bookshop and Art Galleries (www.kennys.ie), and the Genealogical Publishing Company (www.genealogical.com).

ALLEN, F.H.A., KEVIN WHELAN, and MATTHEW STOUT. *Atlas of the Irish Rural Landscape.* Cork: Cork University Press, 1997.

ANDREWS, J.H. *A Paper Landscape: the Ordnance Survey in Nineteenth Century Ireland.* Oxford: Oxford University Press, 1975; reprint Dublin: Four Courts Press, 2001.

BARDEN, JUDITH, ed. *Directory of British and Irish Law Libraries.* 4th edn. Hebden Bridge: Published for the British and Irish Association of Law Librarians by Legal Information Resources Limited, *c.*1992.

BARDON, JONATHAN. *A History of Ulster.* Belfast: Blackstaff Press, 1992; new edition, 2001.

BAXTER, ANGUS. *In Search of Your British & Irish Roots: A Complete Guide to Tracing Your English, Welsh, Scottish, & Irish Ancestors.* 4th edn. Baltimore, MD: Genealogical Publishing Company, 2000.

BEGLEY, DONAL F. *Handbook on Irish Genealogy.* 6th edn. Dublin: Heraldic Artists, 1984.

*Irish Genealogy: a Record Finder.* Dublin: Heraldic Artists, 1981.

BLESSING, PATRICK J. *The Irish in America: A Guide to the Literature and the Manuscript Collections.* Washington, DC: Catholic University of America Press, 1992.

BOYLAN, HENRY, ed. *A Dictionary of Irish Biography.* 3rd edn. Dublin: Gill & Macmillan, 1998.

BRIGGS, ELIZABETH. *Access to Ancestry: A Genealogical Resource Manual for Canadians Tracing Their Heritage.* Winnipeg: Westgarth, 1995.

*Calendar of Fiants of the Tudor Sovereigns 1521–1603, with Index of Personal and Placenames.* 4 vols. Dublin: E. Burke, 1994.

*Calendar of State Papers Relating to Ireland.* 24 vols. London: 1860–1912.

CARROLL, FRIEDA, comp. *Ireland School Registers, 1861–1872; 1891–1939.* Irish Genealogical Source No. 6. Dún Laoghaire: Dún Laoghaire Genealogical Society, 1998.

*Church of Ireland Parish Register Series.* Dublin: Representative Church Body Library, 1994–2001.

CONNOLLY, S.J. *The Oxford Companion to Irish History.* 2nd edn. Oxford: Oxford University Press, 2002.

DAY, ANGELIQUE, and PATRICK MCWILLIAMS, eds. *The Ordnance Survey Parish Memoirs of Ireland.* 40 vols. Belfast: Institute of Irish Studies, Queen's University, in association with the Royal Irish Academy, 1990–1998.

DE BRÚN, PÁDRAIG, and MÁIRE HERBERT. *Catalogue of Irish Manuscripts in Cambridge Libraries.* Cambridge (UK), New York: Cambridge University Press, 1986.

DELANEY, ENDA. *Demography, State and Society. Irish Migration to Britain, 1921–1971.* Liverpool: Liverpool University Press, 2000.

DONOVAN, BRIAN C., and DAVID EDWARDS. *British Sources for Irish History, 1485–1641: A Guide to Manuscripts in Local, Regional and Specialised Repositories in England, Scotland and Wales.* Dublin: Irish Manuscripts Commission, 1997.

DOOLEY, TERENCE. *Sources for the History of Landed Estates in Ireland.* Dublin: Irish Academic Press, 2000.

ELLIOTT, MARIANNE. *The Catholics of Ulster: A History.* London: Allen Lane, 2000.

FANNING, CHARLES, ed. *New Perspectives on the Irish Diaspora.* Carbondale, IL: Southern Illinois University Press, 2000.

FOSTER, JANET, and JULIA SHEPPARD. *British Archives: A Guide to Archive Resources in the United Kingdom.* 3rd edn. London: Macmillan, 1995 (reprinted 1996); New York: Stockton Press, 1995.

FOSTER, R.F. *Modern Ireland, 1600–1972.* London: Penguin, 1988.

FOWLER, SIMON. *Tracing Irish Ancestors.* Richmond, UK: Public Record Office, 2001.

The Genealogical Office, Dublin. *A Guide.* Dublin: Irish Manuscripts Commission, 1998.

GIBBEN, ARTHUR, and RUTH-ANN HARRIS, eds. *The Great Famine and the Irish Diaspora in America.* Amherst: University of Massachusetts Press, 1999.

GLAZIER, MICHAEL. *The Encyclopedia of the Irish in America.* Notre Dame, IN: University of Notre Dame Press, 1999.

GRENHAM, JOHN. *Tracing Your Irish Ancestors: The Complete Guide.* 2nd edn. Dublin: Gill & Macmillan, 1999.

GRIFFIN, WILLIAM D. *The Book of Irish Americans.* New York: Random House, 1990.

HANDRAN, GEORGE B. *Townlands in Poor Law Unions: A Reprint of Poor Law Union Pamphlets of the General Registrar's Office with an Introduction, and Six*

*Appendices Relating to Irish Genealogical Research*. Salem, MA: Higginson Book Company, 1997.

HARTY, PATRICIA, ed. *Greatest Irish Americans of the 20th Century*. Dublin: Oak Tree Press, 2001.

HAYES, R.J. *Manuscript Sources for the Study of Irish Civilisation*. 11 vols, plus supplement (3 vols). Boston: G.K. Hall, 1965–79.

HELFERTY, SEAMUS, and RAYMOND REFASUSSÉ, eds. *Directory of Irish Archives*. 3rd edn. Dublin: Four Courts Press, 1999.

HERITY, MICHAEL. *Ordnance Survey Letters* [of John O'Donovan, 1830s], Counties Donegal, Down, Dublin, Kildare, Meath. Dublin: Royal Irish Academy, *c.*1999–

HOUSTON, CECIL J., and WILLIAM J. SMYTH. *Irish Emigration and Canadian Settlement: Patterns, Links, and Letters*. Toronto: University of Toronto Press, 1990.

JACKSON, ALVIN. *Ireland, 1798–1998*. Oxford: Blackwell, 1999.

KEANE E., E. ELLIS, and P.B. EUSTACE. *Registry of Deeds, Dublin, Abstracts of Wills*, vols. I–III (1708–1832). Dublin: Stationery Office, 1954–1984.

KEANE, E., P.B. PHAIR, and T.U. SADLIER. *King's Inn's Admission Papers, 1607–1867*. Dublin: Stationery Office, 1982.

KENNY, KEVIN. *The American Irish: A History*. Harlow, UK; New York: Longman, 2000.

KILLEN, JOHN. *A History of the Linen Hall Library, 1788–1988*. Belfast: Linen Hall Library, 1990.

MCCAFFREY, LAWRENCE J. *The Irish Catholic Diaspora in America*. Washington, DC: Catholic University of America Press, 1997.

MCCARTHY, TONY and TIM CADOGAN. *A Guide to Tracing Your Cork Ancestors*. Glenageary, Co. Dublin: Flyleaf Press, 1998.

MAC CONGHAIL, MÁIRE, and PAUL GORRY. *Tracing Irish Ancestors: A Practical Guide to Irish Genealogy*. London: Harper Collins, 1997.

MCKAY, PATRICK. *A Dictionary of Ulster Placenames*. Belfast: Institute of Irish Studies, Queen's University, 1999.

MACLYSAGHT, EDWARD. *The Surnames of Ireland*. 6th edn. Dublin: Irish Academic Press, 1985. (Originally published in 1957 as *Irish Families*, followed in 1960 by *More Irish Families*, and in 1964 by a *Supplement to Irish Families*.)

MCREDMOND, LOUIS, gen. ed. *Modern Irish Lives: Dictionary of 20th-century Irish Biography*. Dublin: Gill & Macmillan, 1996.

MCTERNAN, JOHN C., ed. *Sligo: Sources of Local History: A Catalogue of the Local History Collection, with an Introduction and Guide to Sources*. New edn. Sligo: Sligo County Library, 1994.

MCWILLIAMS, PATRICK, ed. *The Ordnance Survey Memoirs of Ireland. Index of People & Places*. Belfast: Institute of Irish Studies, Queen's University Belfast, in Association with the Royal Irish Academy, 2002.

MASTERSON, JOSEPHINE. *Ireland: 1841/1851 Census Abstracts* (Northern Ireland). Baltimore: Genealogical Publishing Company, 1999.

MASTERSON, JOSEPHINE. *Ireland: 1841/1851 Census Abstracts* (Republic of Ireland). Baltimore: Genealogical Publishing Company, 1999.

MAXWELL, IAN. *Tracing Your Ancestors in Northern Ireland.* Edinburgh: Stationery Office, 1997.

MAXWELL, IAN. *Researching Armagh Ancestors: A Practical Guide for the Family and Local Historian.* Belfast: Ulster Historical Foundation, 2000.

MITCHELL, BRIAN. *A Guide to Irish Parish Registers.* Baltimore: Genealogical Publishing Company, 1997.

MITCHELL, BRIAN. *A New Genealogical Atlas of Ireland.* Baltimore: Genealogical Publishing Company, 2001

MOODY, T.W., F.X. MARTIN, and F.J. BYRNE, eds. *A New History of Ireland.* Vol. III. *Early Modern Ireland, 1534–1691.* Oxford: Oxford University Press, 1976.

MOODY, T.W. and W.E. VAUGHAN, eds. *A New History of Ireland.* Vol. IV. *Eighteenth-century Ireland, 1691–1800.* Oxford: Oxford University Press, 1986.

MOODY, T.W., F.X. MARTIN, and F.J. BYRNE, eds. *A New History of Ireland.* Vol. IX. *Maps, Genealogies, Lists.* Oxford: Oxford University Press, 1976.

MORRIN, JAMES, ed. *Calendar of the Patent and Close Rolls of Chancery in Ireland, Henry VIII–Elizabeth.* 2 vols. Dublin, 1861–2.

MOSCINSKI, SHARON. *Tracing Our Irish Roots.* Santa Fe, NM: J. Muir Publications, 1993.

NOLAN, WILLIAM. *Tracing the Past.* Dublin: Geography Publications, 1982.

Ó CÉIRÍN, KIT, and CYRIL Ó CÉIRÍN. *Women of Ireland: A Biographic Dictionary.* Newtownlynch, Kinvara, Co. Galway: Tír Eolas, 1996.

O'CONNOR, JOHN. *From The Workhouses of Ireland: The Fate of Ireland's Poor.* Dublin: Anvil Books, 1995.

O'CONNOR, THOMAS, MARIE DALY, and EDWARD L. GALVIN. *The Irish in New England.* Boston: New England Historic Genealogical Society, 1985.

O'FARRELL, PADRAIC. *Irish Surnames.* Dublin: Gill & Macmillan, 2002.

O'FARRELL, PATRICK. *The Irish in Australia, 1788 to the Present.* Cork: Cork University Press, 2001.

O'NEILL, ROBERT K. *A Visitors' Guide: Ulster Libraries, Archives, Museums & Ancestral Heritage Centres.* Belfast: Ulster Historical Foundation, 1997.

PENDER, SEAMUS, ed. *A Census of Ireland, circa 1659. With Supplemental Material from the Poll Money Ordinances (1660–1661).* 1939, reprinted 1997 by Clearfield Publishing Company, Baltimore, MD.

PHILLIMORE, W.P.W., and GERTRUDE THRIFT, eds. *Indexes to Irish Wills.* London: Phillimore & Co., 1909–20, reprinted 1997.

QUINN, SEAN E. *Tracing Your Irish Ancestors.* Bray: Magh Itha Teoranta, *c.*1989.

RADFORD, DWIGHT A., and KYLE J. BETIT, *A Genealogist's Guide to Discovering Your Irish Ancestors: How to Find and Record Your Unique Heritage.* Cincinnati: Butterway Books, 2001.

REFASUSSÉ, RAYMOND. *Church of Ireland Records*. Dublin: Irish Academic Press, 2000.

RYAN, JAMES G. *A Guide to Tracing Your Dublin Ancestors*. 2nd edn. Glenageary, Co. Dublin: Flyleaf Press, 1998.

RYAN, JAMES G., ed. *Irish Church Records: Their History, Availability and Use in Family and Local History Research*. Glenageary, Co. Dublin: Flyleaf Press, 2001.

RYAN, JAMES G., ed. *Irish Records: Sources for Family and Local History*. Rev. edn. Salt Lake City, UT: Ancestry, *c*.1997.

RYAN, JAMES G., comp. *Sources for Irish Family History: A Listing of Books and Articles on the History of Irish Families*. Glenageary, Co. Dublin: Flyleaf Press, 2001.

VAUGHAN, W.E., ed. *A New History of Ireland.* Vol. V. *Ireland under the Union I: 1801–1870*. Oxford: Oxford University Press, 1989.

VAUGHAN, W.E., ed. *A New History of Ireland.* Vol. VI. *Ireland under the Union II: 1870–1921*. Oxford: Oxford University Press, 1996.

VICARS, SIR ARTHUR. *Index to Prerogative Wills of Ireland: 1536–1810*. 1897, reprinted 1997.

# INDEX